Student Guide

and

Workbook

for use with

macroeconomics

fifth edition

N. Gregory Mankiw

Roger T. Kaufman

Smith College

WORTH PUBLISHERS

Student Guide and Workbook
by Roger T. Kaufman
for use with
Mankiw: Macroeconomics, Fifth Edition

Printed in the United States of America

ISBN: 0-7167-5397-9 (EAN: 9780716753971)

Sixth printing

Worth Publishers
41 Madison Ave.
New York, NY 10010
www.worthpublishers.com

Contents

Preface

To the Student

Gregory Mankiw's *Macroeconomics* is an exciting textbook in which you will learn how to apply a variety of economic models to some fascinating macroeconomic questions. Although these models are not complicated, it is easy, initially, to become confused about the relationships they represent, and consequently not to fully appreciate their power and usefulness. I have found that students understand the underlying concepts much better if they actively take part in constructing economic models and applying them. This Student Guide provides a variety of ways to engage you in this type of active learning. Each chapter of the Student Guide is divided into five or six sections:

The **Fill-in Questions** give you the opportunity to review and check your knowledge of the key terms and concepts presented in the chapter. Note that some of the terms are used more than once.

The **Multiple-Choice Questions** allow you to test yourself on the chapter material. There are 12 to 25 multiple-choice questions for each chapter, ranging from easy to difficult.

The bulk of the Student Guide consists of a series of **Exercises** for each chapter. These exercises contain step-by-step presentations and applications of the models discussed in the textbook. You will be asked to complete tables of data, plot graphs, and illustrate shifts in curves. The exercises can be answered entirely in the Student Guide. When you are given a choice of two or more underlined alternatives, circle the correct one. After you complete each exercise, I strongly encourage you to spend two minutes reviewing it to reinforce the concepts. I also suggest that you try to work through some of the exercises *before* the lecture material is discussed. The only mathematics required in this section is simple algebra and an understanding of the slopes of lines. A mathematical review of these concepts is contained in the Exercises for Chapter 1.

The **Problems** ask you to apply the models on your own. I have made a concerted effort to include problems on policy-oriented questions from both the United States and abroad. These problems are similar to the questions you might expect to be asked on an examination. You should complete them on a separate sheet of paper. Several of these problems require the use of calculus, and these are marked **C** (see the Key to Symbols table on page xiii). Some problems that are more challenging are marked with a **CH**. The symbol **A** is used to designate a question, exercise, or problem discussed in the appendix to the textbook chapter. Although the answers to most of the problems appear at the back of the Student Guide, the problems marked **▪** have been suggested to your instructor as prime candidates for homework assignments and exams; their answers are not given here.

Most chapters include one or two **Data Questions**, in which you are required to find actual economic data to answer the question. Because I am aware of your busy schedules, the data for all of these questions are available from one source—the latest edition of the *Economic Report of the President*. This very useful book, published every January, is undoubtedly in your college library and is also available at www.access.gpo.gov/eop on the Internet. Because the data are frequently revised, I have not provided answers to the data questions.

Questions to Think About often go beyond the material presented in the textbook and ask you to think critically about the model itself or some application of the model. This material will probably not be covered in class and it will almost never appear on an examination, but your professor would be thrilled if you told him or her that you were interested in discussing it (and he or she believed you!). I should warn you, however, that good economists disagree about the correct answers to some of these questions. Consequently, no answers are provided. However, developing your ability to think critically will enhance your education in macroeconomics, so I encourage you to tackle some of these questions.

The answers to all but the specially marked Problems, the Data Questions, and the Questions to Think About are printed at the back of the Student Guide.

Although you may want to complete all the questions for each chapter, you may be limited by time constraints. The Exercises have been especially helpful for most of my students, but you should decide which of the sections of questions and problems are most helpful for you. I can assure you, however, that your understanding of macroeconomics will be substantially deeper and longer-lasting if you complete most of the Student Guide. If you have any specific comments, please send them to me at Smith College, Northampton, MA 01063 or e-mail me at rkaufman@smith.edu..

To the Instructor

This Student Guide is designed to involve students in active learning. I have found that students who have reconstructed the economic models themselves and applied them independently have a much deeper and longer-lasting understanding of the material.

The difficulty many students have with the models taught in intermediate macroeconomics precludes their appreciation of the usefulness of these models in answering important macroeconomic questions. This situation leads some instructors to spend more time than they would like on the formal models and less time on important applications. Others respond by glossing over the models. It is my hope that Greg Mankiw's innovative textbook and this Student Guide will allow you to teach a course in which students understand both the relevant macroeconomic models and their applications.

The Student Guide is printed on perforated pages. With the exception of the **Problems,** the answers to all of the questions can be written directly into the Student Guide. Consequently, instructors may wish to make parts of the Student Guide required assignments. (You should be aware, however, that the answers to all but the specially marked Problems, the Data Questions, and the Questions to Think About are printed at the back of this Student Guide.)

Each chapter of the Student Guide includes five or six sections:

The **Fill-in Questions** review the Key Concepts listed at the end of each chapter of the textbook. I have made these questions a bit more challenging by using some of the concepts more than once.

The 12 to 25 **Multiple-Choice Questions** for each chapter range in difficulty from easy to difficult. Several of these questions are suitable for examinations.

The bulk of the Student Guide consists of a series of **Exercises** for each chapter. In this section, students are guided step-by-step through the models presented in the chapter. I have found that students benefit greatly from solving simple algebraic models, plotting data on grids, and illustrating the comparative statics results themselves. Because the Exercises for some chapters are quite long, you may wish to give your students guidance about which exercises you consider most important. I urge students to spend an extra two minutes reviewing each exercise after they complete it to reinforce the concept. I have also experimented successfully with assigning exercises *before* the material is covered in class. This forces the student to read the assignment and engage the material, albeit at an elementary level. Each exercise begins with a brief description. The only mathematics required in this section is simple algebra and an understanding of the slopes of lines. A mathematical review of these concepts is contained in the Exercises for Chapter 1.

The questions in the **Problems** section are similar to those in the Problems and Applications section of the textbook. In these problems, students are asked to apply the models on their own. Many of the problems concern policy applications involving the United States or specific foreign countries. Several of these problems require the use of calculus, and these are marked **C** (see the Key to Symbols table on page xiii). Others are more challenging and noted by a **CH**. The symbol **A** is used to designate a question, exercise, or problem containing material presented in the appendix to the textbook chapter. Although the answers to most of the problems appear at the back of the Student Guide, the answers to those problems marked with a ■ are printed only in your *Solutions Manual*. Consequently, they can be used for homework assignments and exams.

Most chapters include one or two **Data Questions**, in which students are required to obtain actual economic data to answer the question. I believe students should be able to make reasonable estimates of the current inflation rate, unemployment rate, and gross domestic product. The data for all of these questions are contained in the *Economic Report of the President*, which is available at *www.access.gpo.gov/eop*. Although many students will have access to computerized databases, I will be satisfied if my students know how to use this valuable reference by the end of the course. Because the data are frequently revised in subsequent editions of the *Economic Report of the President,* answers to the data questions are not included in the Student Guide to avoid confusion. Instead, answers using the *2002 Economic Report of the President* are included in the *Solutions Manual.*

In the last section, several **Questions to Think About** go beyond the material presented in the textbook. By including this section, I hope to motivate the talented and industrious students to think more deeply about the models themselves and their applications. Although I rarely have enough time to cover this material in class, I have a number of special lunches each term and invite any students who wish to discuss these questions. You may want to cover some of them if time permits.

I hope you and your students find the Student Guide to be useful in developing their knowledge and skills. If you have any specific comments, please send them to me at Smith College, Northampton, MA 01063 or email me at rkaufman@smith.edu.

Roger Kaufman
June 2002

Economics Data on the Internet

During the past decade there has been an explosion of economics data that are available on the Internet. Insofar as the sites and addresses change literally every day, any compilation becomes obsolete very quickly. In this section I list 14 sites that I have found to be especially useful in obtaining economics data. I divide them into three groups. The first group consists of four sites that provide excellent gateways to the Internet. They include links to all sorts of national and international economics data, and they are easy to use. The second group lists the addresses of seven sites specializing in U.S. data, and the third group concentrates on international data.

Gateways to the Web

1. *www.rfe.org* This is the oldest, most well known, and probably most comprehensive site (even the Table of Contents is 26 pages long) for economics data and economics information in general. It is maintained and updated regularly by Bill Goffe, sponsored by the American Economic Association, and is easy to use.

2. *www.helsinki.fi/WebEc/WebEc* Originating in Finland and entitled WebEc, this site is another excellent source of economics data and information.

3. *www.economy.com/freelunch* Once you register (for free) you will gain access to 1.68 million data series, each of which you can easily export as an Excel file

4. *www.lib.umich.edu/govdocs/stats* This site is maintained by the University of Michigan and lists an impressive array of statistical data sites.

Sources of U.S. Data

5. *www.access.gpo.gov/eop* This site contains the most recent *Economic Report of the President*. All of the data questions in this Study Guide can be answered using this source. The entire report can be browsed or parts of it can be down-

loaded. Make sure to check the table of contents for the statistical section, which is located about two-thirds of the way through the report.

6. **www.fedstats.gov**   This site includes data for over 100 federal agencies and can be searched by topic or by agency.

7. **www.stat-usa.gov**   Maintained by the U.S. Department of Commerce, this is another good starting point for locating U.S. government data.

8. **www.whitehouse.gov/fsbr/esbr**   Called the White House Briefing room, this is one of the best sources for locating the most recent monthly and quarterly U.S. data.

9. **www.census.gov/statab/www**   This is the online edition of the latest *Statistical Abstract of the United States*, the traditional workhorse for many reference librarians.

10. **www.federalreserve.gov**   The homepage of the Federal Reserve Board of Governors contains extensive data and information on monetary issues.

11. **www.stls.frb.org/fred**   Another good source of monetary data, this site is maintained by the Federal Reserve Bank of St. Louis. It has a program that automatically calculates the growth rates for its data series.

Sources of International Data

12. **www.un.org/Depts/unsd**   This homepage of the Statistical Division of the United Nations Department of Economic and Social Affairs contains a wealth of economic and socioeconomic data for hundreds of countries.

13. **www.imf.org**   The gateway to the International Monetary Fund is another excellent source of international data and reports.

14. **www.odci.gov/cia/publications/factbook**   Called the *CIA World Factbook*, this site has useful information about many countries, although it isn't as lurid as you might imagine.

Acknowledgments

I would like to thank Greg Mankiw for writing such an excellent and enjoyable textbook and for thoroughly reviewing this Student Guide. I also thank Geoffrey Woglom for stimulating my interest in macroeconomics and for his numerous suggestions and support. Yan Zhang, Tanya Luthra, Robin Drouin, Nayantara Mukerji, Alka Srivastava, Eileen King, Ling Zhang, Dorothy Cratty, Muneeba Kayani, Kanta Murali, and Katrina Cokeng provided assistance in writing, editing, and proofreading the manuscript; I could not have completed it without their help. In preparing this edition of the Student Guide, I wish to thank Eve Moeller, Alan McClare, and Stacey Alexander of Worth Publishers for their helpful editorial and production assistance and guidance. Finally, I want to thank my children, Rebecca and Joshua, for being themselves.

Key to Symbols

C   This problem requires the use of calculus.

CH   This problem is especially challenging.

A   This question, exercise, or problem includes a topic discussed in the appendix to the textbook chapter.

■   This problem does not have its answer printed in the Student Guide.

The Science of Macroeconomics

Fill-in Questions

Use the key terms below to fill in the blanks in the following statements. Each term may be used more than once.

endogenous   microeconomics

exogenous   models

macroeconomics   price flexibility

market-clearing   price stickiness

1. _Macroeconomics_ is the study of the economy as a whole. It focuses on issues such as economic growth, inflation, and unemployment. _Microeconomics_ is the study of the economy in the small. It focuses on the individual firm, industry, or consumer.

2. Economists construct _models_ to assist them in understanding the real world.

3. One of the purposes of an economic model is to show how the _exogenous_ variables affect the _endogenous_ variables, where the former come from outside the model and the latter are determined within the model.

4. With regard to prices, most macroeconomists believe that _price flexibility_ is a reasonable assumption for studying long-run issues but that _price stickiness_ is a better assumption for studying short-run issues.

5. Models that exhibit price flexibility are examples of _market-clearing_ models.

Multiple-Choice Questions

1. Macroeconomists study all of the following issues EXCEPT the:
   a. determinants of inflation.
   b. relative market shares of General Motors and Ford.
   c. growth of total production in the United States.
   d. amount of imports and exports between the United States and Japan.

2. An example of a controlled experiment is:

   a. astronomers formulating the "big bang" theory of the origin of the universe by making observations through the Hubble telescope.

   b. economists analyzing the effects of an increase in the money supply by examining output, interest rates, and inflation following a large increase in the money supply.

   c. biologists modifying Darwin's original theory of evolution after examining newly found fossils.

   d. physicians testing the effects of aspirin on the incidence of heart disease by following two groups of men who differ only in their intake of aspirin.

3. The variable that is likely to be exogenous in a model that explains production in a small firm within a large industry is the:

   a. amount of output produced by the firm.

   b. price of the firm's inputs. *affected by factors beyond firm's control*

   c. number of workers hired by the firm.

   d. amount of machinery employed by the firm.

4. All of the following are reasons why wages and/or prices may be sticky in the short run EXCEPT:

   a. long-term labor contracts often set wages in advance for up to three years.

   b. many firms leave their product prices unchanged for long periods of time in order to prevent current customers from "shopping around."

   c. it is costly for firms to print new price lists and advertise frequently changing prices.

   d. firms are already charging the highest prices people will pay, so there is no reason to change them.

5. The market in which the assumption of continuous market clearing seems to be LEAST applicable is the:

   a. stock market.

   b. market for wheat.

   c. labor market.

   d. market for U.S. Treasury bonds.

Exercises: Review of Basic Math

In this first set of exercises, we review some basic mathematical concepts that are an essential part of this course. If you have any difficulty with these concepts, you should discuss your math background with your instructor as soon as possible.

1. **Percentage Change** *In this exercise we review the calculation of percentage change.*

   The percentage change in a variable Q that changes in value from Q_0 to Q_1 may be calculated by using the equation

$$\text{Percentage Change in } Q = 100 \times \frac{Q_1 - Q_0}{Q_0} \qquad \textbf{(1-1)}$$

Use the equation to calculate the percentage changes in the following examples.

a. $Q_0 = 100$; $Q_1 = 120$

$$100 \times \frac{120-100}{100} = 100 \times \frac{20}{100} = 100 \times \frac{20}{100} = 20\%$$

b. $Q_0 = 20$; $Q_1 = 85$

$$100 \times \frac{85-20}{20} = 100 \times \frac{65}{20} = 100 \times \frac{65}{20} = 5 \times 65 = 325\%$$

c. $Q_0 = 50$; $Q_1 = 40$

$$100 \times \frac{40-50}{50} = 100 \times \frac{-10}{50} = 100 \times \frac{-10}{5} = -200\%$$

$$-20\%$$

2. **Graphs, Slopes, and Simultaneous Equations** *In this exercise, we review how to plot pairs of points on a graph, calculate slopes and intercepts of lines, and solve two linear equations simultaneously.*

a. Consider the equation

$$Y = \tfrac{1}{2}X + 3. \tag{1-2}$$

In Table 1-1, list the values of Y according to Equation 1-2 for each of the stated values of X.

Table 1-1

(1) X	(2) Y
0	$Y = (1/2)(0) + 3 = 3$
1	$Y = (1/2)(1) + 3 = .5 + 3 = 3.5$
2	$Y = (1/2)2 + 3 = 1 + 3 = 4$
3	$Y = (1/2)3 + 3 = 1.5 + 3 = 4.5$

b. Plot these four pairs of points on Graph 1-1 and connect them.

Graph 1-1

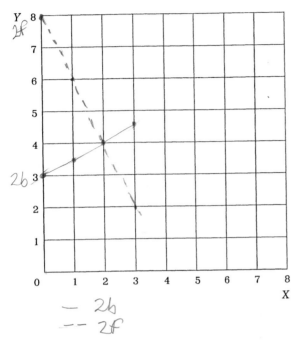

— 2b
-- 2f

c. Recall that the *slope* of a curve indicates the amount by which the variable measured on the vertical axis increases when the variable measured on the horizontal axis increases by one unit. The slope may be measured by "rise over run" or $\Delta Y/\Delta X$, that is, the change in Y divided by the change in X. What is the numerical value of the slope of this curve? Explain how you derived this result.

$\Delta = \Delta Y = \frac{1}{2} / \Delta X = 1.$ $\frac{1/2}{1} = \frac{1}{2}$

explanation:
every time the value of X increases by one unit, the value of Y increases by $1/2$

d. The *Y intercept* of a curve is equal to the value of the variable measured on the vertical axis when the curve intersects that axis. Alternatively, it is the value of Y when $X = 0$. What is the numerical value of the Y intercept of this curve? How did you derive this answer?

$Y = 3$ when $X = 0$ or

Y intercept $= 3$, ie., when $X = 0$, $Y = 3$

e. Now consider the equation

$$Y = -2X + 8 \tag{1-3}$$

In Table 1-2, list the values of Y according to Equation 1-3 for each of the stated values of X.

Table 1-2

(1) X	(2) Y
0	$Y = (-2)(0) + 8 = 8$
1	$Y = -2(1) + 8 = -2 + 8 = 6$
2	$Y = -2(2) + 8 = -4 + 8 = 4$
3	$Y = -2(3) + 8 = -6 + 8 = 2$

f. Plot the preceding four pairs of points on Graph 1-1 and connect them.

g. Calculate the slope and Y intercept of the equation in Part e.

slope = rise/run = $\Delta Y / \Delta X$

= -2 / 1

= 2

-2, 8

· by def where
x = 0

y intercept = what is y when x = 0 = (4)

h. Determine algebraically the values of X and Y that satisfy both equations by setting Equations 1-2 and 1-3 equal to each other. Check your answer by determining visually where the two curves intersect.   = x = 2, y = 4

1-2   1-3

$y = \frac{1}{2}x + 3$ $y = 2x + 8$

$\frac{2y = 2\frac{1}{2}x + 11}{2}$ → $y = \frac{1}{2}x + 11$

i. Explain why setting these two equations equal to each other yields the coordinates at the intersection.

By definition, the point of intersection must lie on both lines. This means that the values of X and Y at this point must satisfy both equations, that is $Y = \frac{1}{2}x + 3$ and $Y = -2x + 8$ consequently at the intersection

$\frac{1}{2}x + 3 = -2x + 8$

3.   **Exponents** *In this exercise, we review the use of positive and negative exponents, which are used occasionally in the text.*

a.   When n is a whole number that is greater than or equal to 1, the expression y^n is equal to the product of n y's multiplied by each other. Thus, $y^1 = y$, and $y^3 = y \times y \times y$. By convention, $y^0 = 1$.

Calculate each of the following:

$2^3 = \underline{2 \times 2 \times 2 = 8}$.

$3^2 = \underline{3 \times 3 = 9}$.

$5^1 = \underline{5 \times 1 = 5}$.

b.   The expression y^{-n} is equal to $1/y^n$. Therefore, $y^{-2} = 1/y^2$ and $y^{-3} = 1/y^3$.

Calculate each of the following:

$2^{-3} = \underline{1/2^3 = 1/2 \times 1/2 \times 1/2 = 1/8}$

$3^{-1} = \underline{-1/3}$.

$10^{-3} = \underline{1/10^3 = 1/10 \times 1/10 \times 1/8 = 1/1000}$

c.   Finally, recall that the expression $y^n \times y^p = y^{n+p}$, that is, we add exponents when we multiply. Thus, $2^2 \times 2^3 = 2^5$. This can easily be confirmed by noting that $2^2 \times 2^3 = 4 \times 8 = 32 = 2^5$. (Remember, however, that $y^n \times z^p$ *does not equal* $(yz)^{n+p}$.)

Compute each of the following using the multiplication rule for exponents and confirm your answers by calculating the product directly:

$5^2 \times 5^3 = \underline{5^{(2+3)} = 5^5}$ $5 \times 5 = 25$. $5 \times 5 \times 5 = 125$ $125 \times 25 = 3125$ $5 \times 5 \times 5 \times 5 \times 5 = 3125$

$6^3 \times 6^{-1} = \underline{6^{(3+1)} = 6^2 = 6 \times 6 = 36}$. $6 \times 6 \times 6 = 216$ $6^{-1} = 1/6$ $216/6 = 36$

$4^{1/2} \times 4^{1/2} = \underline{\sqrt{4} \times \sqrt{4} = 4}$. $4^{1/2} \times 4^{1/2} = 4^{1/2 + 1/2} = 4^1 = 4 = 2 \times 2$

(Recall that $y^{1/2}$ is equal to the square root of y.)

Problems

Answer the following problems on a separate sheet of paper.

1.   According to the textbook, natural scientists often conduct research via controlled experiments, whereas macroeconomists typically rely on natural experiments.

a.   What is a controlled experiment, and how does it differ from a natural experiment?

b.   Why are controlled experiments usually considered to be preferable for scientific research?

c.   Why can't macroeconomists typically perform controlled experiments?

2. Consider the market for coal.

   a. Draw hypothetical market supply and demand curves for coal, label them S_1 and D_1, and illustrate the initial equilibrium price and quantity.

   b. Suppose that the price of oil, which is an alternative fuel, triples. Draw the new supply and demand curves for coal on your preceding graph and label them S_2 and D_2. (*Hint:* one of the curves does not shift from its original position.) What happens to the equilibrium price and quantity of coal?

   c. Now return to the initial equilibrium price and quantity for coal. Suppose that the government imposes restrictions on strip mining that significantly increase the cost of producing coal. Draw the resulting supply and demand curves for coal on your graph and label them S_3 and D_3. What happens to the equilibrium price and quantity of coal?

Questions to Think About

1. The textbook discusses how economists build models—simplified representations of reality—to explain how the world works. How important do you think each of the following criteria should be in evaluating whether a model is good? (There is no single correct answer to this question.)

   a. Accuracy in prediction.

   b. Reasonableness of the assumptions.

   c. Simplicity of the model.

   d. Consistency with other models.

If the price for a market alternative increases, the demand for coal will escalate. Increased demand will create deminished supply. The demand curve will shift left while the supply curve remains where it is

CHAPTER 2 TWO

The Data of Macroeconomics

Fill-in Questions

Use the key terms below to fill in the blanks in the following statements. Each term may be used more than once.

consumer price index
depreciation
disposable personal income
flow
GDP deflator
labor-force participation rate
Laspeyres

nominal gross domestic product
nominal gross national product
Okun's law
Paasche
real gross domestic product
recession
stock
unemployment rate

1. _nominal gross nat'l product_ (domestic) measures the current dollar value of the final goods and services produced in a given time period within a country's borders. _real gross domestic_ measures the value of final goods and services measured at constant prices.

2. The _unemployment_ is the percentage of the labor force that does not have a job.

3. _Okun's law_ depicts a negative relationship between the percentage change in GDP and the change in the unemployment rate.

4. The _CPI_ traces the price of a fixed market basket of goods over time. Because the basket remains fixed as we move forward in time, this measurement is an example of a(n) _Laspeyres_ index.

5. The _GDP deflator_ compares the price of the current mix of output in GDP with what the current mix of output would have cost in a particular base year. It is calculated as _nominal GDP_ divided by _real GDP_. Because the mix of output changes as we move forward in time, this measure is an example of a(n) _Paasche_ index.

6. One of the more important distinctions in macroeconomics is the one between stocks and flows. Your personal wealth is an example of a(n) _stock_ whereas your income is an example of a(n) _flow_.

7. _Depreciation_ measures the reduction in value of the economy's stock of plants, equipment, and residential structures as these wear out.

8. The _labor-force participation rate_ measures the percentage of the economy's adult, noninstitutional population that is in the labor force.

9. The amount of income consumers have available to spend or save after paying taxes and receiving government transfer payments is called _disposable personal income_.

10. In a(n) _recession_, the _unemployment rate_ rises and real gross domestic product falls.

11. There are two measures of income for an open economy. _Nominal GDP_ is the nominal income earned by domestic citizens both here and abroad. _nominal GNP_ is the nominal income earned domestically by both domestic citizens and foreigners.

Multiple-Choice Questions

1. All of the following are flow variables EXCEPT:
   a. disposable personal income.
   b. consumption expenditures.
   c. personal wealth.
   d. gross domestic product.

2. During periods of inflation:
   a. nominal GDP rises at the same rate as real GDP.
   b. nominal GDP rises at a faster rate than real GDP.
   c. nominal GDP rises at a slower rate than real GDP.
   d. one cannot infer anything about the relative rates of growth of nominal and real GDP.

3. Suppose that in 2000 General Motors experienced a large increase in its inventories of unsold cars. Then in 2000:
   a. total income exceeded the total expenditure on goods and services. _firm has already "bought"_
   b. total income was less than the total expenditure on goods and services.
   c. total income was still equal to the total expenditure on goods and services, because increases in inventories were counted both as part of expenditure and as part of income.
   d. General Motors' investment was negative.

4. Suppose U.S. Steel sells steel to Chrysler for $5,000, and then this steel is used in a Voyager van that is sold to a new car dealer for $17,000. The car dealer then sells the van to a family for $20,000. In this scenario GDP has risen by: _final goods & svcs_
   a. $42,000.
   b. $37,000.
   c. $20,000.
   d. $17,000.

5. The value-added of a particular company is equal to:
   a. its sales.
   b. its profits.
   c. its sales minus its cost of intermediate goods.
   d. zero in the long run.

6. Suppose you purchase a new home for $150,000 and move in. In the national income accounts, consumption expenditures:

    a. rise by $150,000.

    b. rise by $150,000 divided by the number of years you expect to live in the house.

    c. rise by the imputed rent on the house, which is equal to what the market rent would be if it were rented.

    d. are unchanged.

7. The GDP deflator is defined as:

    a. nominal GDP/real GDP.   c. nominal GDP − real GDP.

    b. nominal GDP × real GDP.   d. nominal GDP + real GDP.

8. On occasion the GDP deflator can rise while real GDP falls (the last time this happened was in 1982). When this phenomenon occurs, nominal GDP:

    a. must also rise.

    b. must also fall.

    c. remains constant.

    d. can rise, fall, or remain constant.

9. In the national income accounts, investment is divided into three subcategories that include all of the following EXCEPT the:

    a. purchase of new plants and equipment by firms.

    b. purchase of stocks on the New York Stock Exchange.

    c. purchase of new housing by households and landlords. *consumption*

    d. increase in firms' inventories of goods.

10. All of the following would be counted as a government purchase of a good or a service EXCEPT:

    a. the purchase of a new stealth bomber.

    b. your grandmother's receipt of her monthly Social Security benefit.

    c. the construction of a new dam by the U.S. Army Corps of Engineers.

    d. the hiring of a new police officer by New York City.

11. The largest component of GDP in the United States is typically:

    a. consumption.   c. government purchases.

    b. investment.   d. net exports.

12. If OPEC were to collapse and the price of imported oil were to fall dramatically, then:

    a. the GDP deflator and the consumer price index (CPI) would fall at the same rate.

    b. the GDP deflator would probably fall at a faster rate than the CPI.

    c. the CPI would probably fall at a faster rate than the GDP deflator.

    d. nothing would happen to either the CPI or the GDP deflator.

13. All of the following could reduce the unemployment rate EXCEPT a(n):

    a. reduction in the number of people who are unemployed.

    b. increase in the number of people who are employed.

    c. decrease in the labor force unaccompanied by any change in the number of people who are unemployed.

    d. increase in the number of people who have given up looking for work.

14. Okun's law depicts a relationship between the:
    a. percentage change in real GDP and the change in the unemployment rate.
    b. percentage change in nominal GDP and the change in the labor force.
    c. absolute change in real GDP and the percentage change in the unemployment rate.
    d. absolute change in real GDP and the percentage change in the GDP deflator.

15. Suppose the unemployment rate at the beginning of the year is equal to 5 percent. According to Okun's law, the following statement is FALSE:
    a. if the unemployment rate is unchanged during the year, real GDP tends to rise by 3 percent.
    b. if the average unemployment rate for the year rises to 7 percent, real GDP tends to fall by 1 percent in that year.
    c. if the average unemployment rate for the year falls to 3 percent, real GDP tends to rise by 7 percent in that year.
    d. if the average unemployment rate for the year stays at 5 percent, real GDP remains constant.

16. If a U.S. citizen is employed by a U.S. company in Brazil, the income that she earns is:
    a. part of U.S. GDP and Brazil's GNP.   c. part of U.S. GNP and Brazil's GNP.
    b. part of U.S. GDP and Brazil's GDP.   d. part of U.S. GNP and Brazil's GDP.

17. If the GDP deflator grows by 4 percent from one year to the next and real GDP grows by 3 percent, then nominal GDP will:
    a. rise by approximately 1 percent.
    b. fall by approximately 1 percent.
    c. rise by approximately 7 percent.
    d. rise, but by somewhere between 1 percent and 7 percent, depending on the initial level of GDP.

18. If labor productivity Y/L falls from one year to the next, then:
    a. output Y must have fallen.
    b. labor input L must have risen.
    c. the percentage change in L must have been less than the percentage change in Y.
    d. the percentage change in L must have been greater than the percentage change in Y.

19. If the U.S. government wants to increase Social Security benefits to the elderly each year by an amount that allows the elderly to maintain the same standard of living, the percentage change in benefits should be:
    a. equal to the percentage change in the CPI.
    b. somewhat smaller than the percentage change in the CPI.
    c. somewhat greater than the percentage change in the CPI.
    d. equal to the percentage change in the GDP deflator.

20. Percentage changes in the CPI tend to overstate inflation because:

    a. people substitute away from goods whose relative price has risen.

    b. the continual introduction of new goods makes consumers better off even if prices do not fall.

    c. improvements in product quality tend to be underestimated by government agencies.

    d. all of the above.

Exercises

1. **Intermediate and Final Goods, Value-Added, and GDP** *In this exercise, we review the distinction between intermediate and final goods and illustrate how GDP can be calculated by totaling the production of final goods and services or by totaling firms' value-added.*

    a. Suppose that an economy consists of only four firms: Intel, Princeton Graphic Systems, IBM, and Anheuser Busch. Suppose that this year Intel manufactures 1 million computer chips, which it then sells to IBM for $200 each for IBM to use in the manufacture of its computer systems. Similarly, Princeton Graphic Systems produces 1 million computer monitors, which it sells for $300 each to IBM, again to use in its computer systems. IBM uses these components and its own to manufacture and sell 1 million computer systems at a price of $1,200 each. Anheuser Busch, on the other hand, produces 200 million six-packs of Busch beer, which it sells for $1.50 per six-pack. Assume, furthermore, that Anheuser Busch does not buy any new computer systems during the year. The GDP for this simple economy is the dollar value of the final goods produced during the year. Identify each of the following as a final or an intermediate good. (Circle the correct answer.)

    - Intel computer chip: final/intermediate good.
    - Princeton Graphic Systems computer monitor: final/intermediate good.
    - IBM computer system: final/intermediate good.
    - Anheuser Busch beer: final/intermediate good.

    b. GDP is calculated by multiplying the unit price of each final good by the number of units produced. Calculate the GDP for this simple economy.

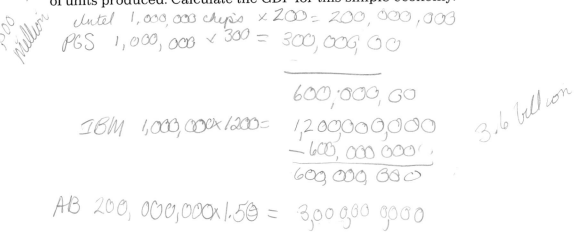

$1500 million

Intel 1,000,000 chips × 200 = 200,000,000
PGS 1,000,000 × 300 = 300,000,00

600,000,00

IBM 1,000,000 × 1200 = 1,200,000,000   3.6 billion
                       − 600,000,000
                        600,000,000

AB 200,000,000 × 1.50 = 300,000,000

c. Recall that the value-added for each firm is equal to its sales minus the cost of its intermediate products. Calculate the value-added for each of the four firms in Table 2-1 and confirm that the total is equal to GDP. (Use the space provided after the table for your work.)

Table 2-1

	(1) Value-Added per Unit	(2) Number of Units	(3) Company Value-Added
Intel	_____	_____	_____
Princeton Graphics	_____	_____	_____
IBM	_____	_____	_____
Anheuser Busch	_____	_____	_____
Total			_____

2. **Nominal and Real GDP** *In this exercise, we calculate nominal and real GDP for a simple economy. We then calculate real GDP growth using two base years and discuss the differences.*

a. Suppose that an economy consists of only two types of products: computers and automobiles. Sales and price data for these two products for two different years are as follows:

Table 2-2

(1) Year	(2) No. of Computers Sold	(3) Price per Computer	(4) No. of Automobiles Sold	(5) Price per Automobile
1990	500,000	$6,000	1,000,000	$12,000
2000	5,000,000	$2,000	1,500,000	$20,000

Nominal GDP in any year is calculated by multiplying the quantity of each final product sold by its price and summing over all final goods and services. Algebraically, this can be written as $\sum_{i} P_i Q_i$, where P_i and Q_i represent the price and quantity sold of the ith final good or service. Assuming that all computers and automobiles are final goods, calculate nominal GDP in 1990 and in 2000.

b. Real GDP in any year is calculated by multiplying that year's quantities of goods and services by their prices in some base year. Therefore, using 1990 as the base year, real GDP in 1990 is equal to nominal GDP in 1990. From Part a, this equals

_____ .

c. Calculate real GDP in 2000 using 1990 as the base year.

d. Calculate the percentage change in real GDP between 1990 and 2000 using 1990 as the base year.

e. Calculate real GDP in 1990 and 2000 using 2000 as the base year.

f. Calculate the percentage change in real GDP between 1990 and 2000 using 2000 as the base year.

g. Explain why your answers to Parts d and f are different.

3. **Using the New Chain-type Measures to Calculate Changes in Real GDP** *In this exercise we use the data from Table 2-2 in Exercise 2 to illustrate the new method of calculating real GDP using chain-type weighted measures. This method is described but not presented formally in the textbook.*

Partially in response to criticism about substitution biases and other problems, the U.S. Bureau of Economic Analysis has begun using a more sophisticated measure of changes in real GDP. This method uses a (geometric) average of two ratios. The first is the ratio of real GDP in the current year to real GDP in the preceding year, using current year prices. The second is the ratio of real GDP in the current year to real GDP in the preceding year using last year's prices. To illustrate this method we shall use the data from Table 2-2, but assume that they now refer to two adjacent years, 1999 and 2000:

Table 2-3

(1) Year	(2) No. of Computers Sold	(3) Price per Computer	(4) No. of Automobiles Sold	(5) Price per Automobile
1999	500,000	$6,000	1,000,000	$12,000
2000	5,000,000	$2,000	1,500,000	$20,000

Of course, it is unlikely that relative prices and quantities would change so dramatically from one year to the next.

a. As we saw in Exercise 2, real GDP in 2000 using (in this case) 1999 as the base year is calculated by multiplying the year 2000 quantities by the year 1999 prices for each good and summing. Calculate this amount and compare it with your answer for Exercise 2, Part c.

b. Now calculate real GDP in 1999 using 1999 as the base year, which is merely equal to nominal GDP in 1999, and compare your answer with Exercise 2, Part a.

c. Using the answers to Parts a and b, the percentage change in real GDP between 1999 and 2000 using year 1999 prices is _____. The first ratio we need is the ratio of real GDP in 2000 to real GDP in 1999, using 1999 as a base year. Using the answers to Parts a and b, this ratio is _____. Note that this ratio is equal to 1.0 plus the precentage change in real GDP (expressed as a decimal.)

d. Now use 2000 as the base year to calculate the percentage change in real GDP from 1999 to 2000. The former is calculated by multiplying the year 1999 quantities by the year 2000 prices for each good and summing. The latter is merely equal to nominal GDP in 2000. (Compare your answers with those from Exercise 2, Part e.)

e. The second ratio we need is that of real GDP in 2000 to real GDP in 1999, using 2000 as a base year. Using the numbers in Part d, this ratio is _____. Note that this ratio is equal to 1.0 plus the percentage change in real GDP (expressed as a decimal) you calculated in Part d.

f. The new chain-type measure uses a geometric mean of the ratios calculated in Parts c and e. It has many desirable, but rather complicated properties. The geometric mean of two numbers is the square root of the product of the two numbers. The square root of the product of these two ratios is _____. This ratio is 1.0 plus the percentage change in the chain-type measure of the percentage change in real GDP between 1999 and 2000 (expressed as a decimal). The percentage change in real GDP using this measure is therefore _____, which lies in between the estimates in Parts c and d.

4. **The GDP Deflator and the Consumer Price Index** *In this exercise, we calculate the consumer price index and GDP deflator using the data in Table 2-2 from Exercise 2. We then illustrate how and why the percentage changes in these two price indices can differ.*

a. The CPI in a given year is equal to the cost of a fixed market basket of consumer purchases in that year divided by the cost of that same market basket in a base year. Although the cost of the basket changes, its composition remains the same as in the base year. For ease in reporting, the official CPI is equal to this ratio multiplied by 100. Note that the ratio of these costs in the base year necessarily equals 1. Thus, if 1990 is the base year, the reported CPI for 1990 would equal $1 \times 100 = 100$. If the fixed market basket is the total amounts of computers and automobiles purchased in 1990, use the data in Table 2-2 to calculate the CPI in 2000, using 1990 as the base year (which is often denoted as "1990 = 100").

b. The GDP deflator for any year is equal to nominal GDP in that year divided by real GDP. Again, it is common practice to multiply this ratio by 100. Calculate the GDP deflator in 2000, using 1990 as the base year (1990 = 100).

c. The GDP deflator is often used to "deflate" nominal GDP in order to calculate real GDP. This is obvious from your calculations in Part b. If we did not know real GDP but did know both nominal GDP and the GDP deflator, we could calculate it by dividing nominal GDP by the GDP deflator (divided by 100). Using the numbers from Part b, this gives us _____/_____ = _____. Economists often use price indices, like the GDP deflator or the CPI, to calculate real values.

d. Calculate the percentage changes in CPI and the GDP deflator between 1990 and 2000.

e. Explain why your answers in Part d are so different from each other, and relate your explanation to the difference between Laspeyres and Paasche indices.

5. Working with Percentage Changes *In this exercise, we illustrate how to approximate the percentage changes in products and quotients.*

a. Economists often find it useful to examine percentage changes in variables. The percentage change in real GDP from one year to the next, for example, represents economic growth during the year. The percentage change in the CPI or GDP deflator represents the rate of inflation during the year. The percentage change of the product of two variables is approximately equal to the sum of the percentage changes in each variable. (This approximation is valid only for relatively small percentage changes.)

b. Recall that nominal GDP = $P \times Y$, where P is equal to the GDP deflator and Y equals real GDP. Consequently, the percentage change in nominal GDP is approximately equal to the percentage change in P *plus* the percentage change in Y. Consider the data in Table 2-4:

Table 2-4

(1) Period	(2) Nominal GDP (PY)	(3) % Change in PY	(4) P	(5) % Change in P	(6) Y	(7) % Change in Y
1	100		1.00		100	
2		___	1.02	___	103	___

Calculate the percentage changes in Y and P between Periods 1 and 2 in Table 2-4 and complete Columns 5 and 7.

c. Recall that % Change in PY (nominal GDP) is approximately equal to % Change in P + % Change in Y. Using your answers in Columns 5 and 7,
% Change in PY = _____ % + _____ % = _____ %.
Place this number in Column 3 in Table 2-4.

d. Now compute Nominal GDP in Period 2 exactly by calculating PY in Period 2 = _____ × _____ = _____ . Consequently, the actual % Change in nominal GDP is equal to 100 × (_____ – 100)/100 = _____ %.

Note the accuracy of our approximation.

e. If % Change in PY = % Change in P + % Change in Y, one can subtract % Change in Y from both sides to obtain:

$$\% \text{ Change in } PY - \% \text{ Change in } Y = \% \text{ Change in } P.$$

This is another application of percentage changes. Recall that the GDP deflator = (Nominal GDP)/(Real GDP), or $P = PY/Y$. The percentage change in a quotient is approximately equal to the % Change in the numerator *minus* the % Change in the denominator. Suppose you did not know the level of P in Table 2-4, but you knew the percentage changes in PY and Y in Columns 3 and 7. You could then calculate

$$\% \text{ Change in } P = \% \text{ Change in } PY - \% \text{ Change in } Y = \underline{\hspace{2cm}} \%.$$

f. As another example, consider labor productivity Y/L, which represents output per worker. Its percentage change from one year to the next is approximately equal to % Change in Y <u>plus/minus</u> % Change in L. Consequently, if Y grew by 5 percent in a year and L grew by 2 percent, then labor productivity would grow by approximately _____ percent.

6. **The Differences between GDP and GNP** *In this exercise, we discuss the differences between GDP and GNP by examining a series of transactions.*

a. In an open economy, there are two different measures of total income: gross domestic product (GDP) and gross national product (GNP). GDP defines output according to geographical boundaries. It includes the output produced (and the income received) by everyone within the borders of the country. GNP, on the other hand, includes the output produced (and the income received) by every citizen of that country, regardless of whether he or she is currently living in the country. With these differences in mind, complete Table 2-5.

Table 2-5

(1) Event	(2) Included in U.S. GNP	(3) Included in U.S. GDP
1. Michael Jackson performs a rock concert in New York	Yes	Yes
2. Michael Jackson performs a rock concert in London	_____	_____
3. The Rolling Stones perform a rock concert in New York	_____	_____
4. The Rolling Stones perform a rock concert in London	_____	_____
5. Toyota earns profits from its car factory in California	_____	_____
6. Ford earns profits from its car factory in England	_____	_____

7. **Semilogarithmic Graphs** *In this exercise, we graph the growth of real GDP on a semi-logarithmic graph and illustrate how straight lines on a semilog graph represent constant percentage (rather than absolute) changes over time.*

   a. Economists often use semilogarithmic graphs to make some interesting comparisons. In this exercise we shall see how these graphs work. Consider the following hypothetical economy:

Table 2-6

Plot and graph these five points on Graph 2-1.

(1) Year	(2) Real GDP ($ in billions)
1960	100
1970	150
1980	200
1990	280
2000	420

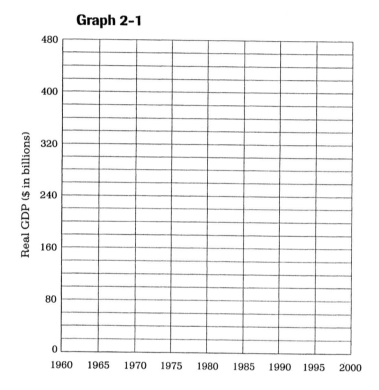

Graph 2-1

   Note that the slope of the line connecting the points is greatest between 1990 and 2000, the decade in which real GDP rose by $140 billion. Similarly, the slope is smallest between 1960 and 1980, when real GDP rose by only $50 billion in each decade. The point to be remembered is that on a conventional graph, segments having equal slopes reflect equal *absolute* changes in the variable that appears on the vertical axis.

   b. In economics we frequently want to compare *percentage changes* rather than absolute changes. For this purpose, semilogarithmic graphs can be very helpful. In conventional graphs the numbers on the vertical axis are spaced proportionately. Consequently, 150 lies above 100 by the same distance that 200 lies above 150. In semilogarithmic graphs, however, the numbers on the vertical axis are spaced proportionately according to their *logarithms*. You don't need a calculator to calculate logarithms. As you can see from Graph 2-2 below, the numbers are already marked on the vertical axis. Plot and connect the data from Table 2-6 on this graph.

Graph 2-2

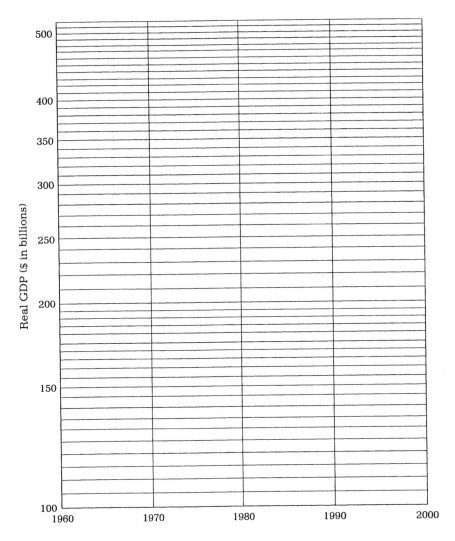

Note that the slope of the line now reaches a maximum on two segments: 1960–1970 and 1990–2000. This is true because the slope of a line segment in a semilogarithmic graph is directly related to percentage changes. The percentage change in real GDP is 50 percent in each of these two decades; hence, the slopes of the segments are equal. The percentage changes in real GDP in the other decades were smaller (33 percent in the 1970s and 40 percent in the 1980s). Consequently, the slopes of their line segments on a semilogarithmic graph are smaller, even though the absolute change of $80 billion during the 1980s was the second highest.

One obvious question you may have is, which graph is better? This depends upon the particular question you are addressing. If you are interested in comparing absolute changes, use a conventional graph. If you are interested in comparing percentage changes, use a semilogarithmic graph.

Problems

Answer the following problems on a separate piece of paper.

1. Consider the following data from 2000:

	($ in billions)
Gross National Product	$9,860.8
Consumption of Fixed Capital	1,241.3
Indirect Business Taxes and Related Items	638.6
Corporate Profits and Related Items	876.4
Social Insurance Contributions	701.5
Net Interest	532.7
Dividends and Related Items	412.3
Government Transfers to Individuals, etc.	1,036.0
Personal Interest Income	1,000.6
Personal Tax and Nontax Payments	1,288.2

   a. Calculate net national product.

   b. Calculate national income.

   c. Calculate personal income.

   d. Calculate disposable personal income.

2. When computing gross domestic product, economists multiply the price of individual goods by the quantity in order to compare apples and oranges. Why do you think they use prices rather than another common measure, such as the weight of each unit of the good?

3. In the national income accounts, expenditures on one's education (for example, college tuition) are treated as consumption. Some economists believe these should be treated as investment. Why?

4. In 1999, both GDP and GNP per capita in the United States were about $34,000 per person. In the same year, GNP per person was $291 in Bangladesh, $159 in Tajikstan, and $101 in Ethiopia. Does this mean that the standard of living in the United States was 117 times as great as that in Bangladesh, 214 times that in Tajikstan, and 337 times that in Ethiopia? Why or why not?

5. For *each* of the following transactions, indicate whether it represents an increase in the U.S. gross domestic product, and, if so, state whether it represents U.S. consumption, investment, government purchases of goods or services, or net exports.

   a. You buy a new Ford Taurus automobile.

   b. You buy a used computer from a friend.

   c. You buy 100 shares of General Motors stock.

   d. IBM builds a new factory in Massachusetts.

   e. General Motors' inventories of steel rise by 50,000 tons.

   f. The government sends your grandmother her monthly Social Security check.

   g. The government buys a new submarine for $1 billion.

6. Suppose a family purchases a new home for $150,000 and borrows the entire amount from the bank. The family pays $15,000 in interest on their new mortgage during the first year. The house would rent for $500 per month, or $6,000 per year. How are these transactions included in the national income accounts?

7. Some Americans are concerned about Japanese investment in the United States, especially when Japanese firms buy existing U.S. firms. Suppose that a Japanese firm buys an existing U.S. firm and sends some of its Japanese managers to run the firm with U.S. workers. If the firm's output is unchanged and the former U.S. managers remain unemployed, what happens to:

   a. U.S. GNP?

   b. U.S. GDP?

8. Suppose the entire economy consists of only two types of products: computers and automobiles. Sales and price data for these two products for two different years are shown below.

Year	Quantity of Computers Sold	Price per Computer	Quantity of Automobiles Sold	Price per Automobile
1990	2	$10,000	10	$5,000
2000	15	$ 4,000	20	$8,000

   a. Assuming that all computers and automobiles are final goods, calculate nominal GDP in 2000.

   b. Calculate *real* GDP in 2000 in 1990 dollars.

   c. Use the relationship between nominal and real GDP to calculate the GDP deflator in 2000 using 1990 prices (i.e., using 1990 as the base year).

Data Questions

The questions in these data sections require you to obtain actual macroeconomic data. All of the data should be included in the latest issue of the Economic Report of the President, *which can be obtained at www.access.gpo.gov/eop/ on the Internet. Other Internet sources appear in the Preface.*

1. a. Obtain the appropriate data to complete the following table for the latest calendar year. For each series state your statistical source and table number.

Table 2-7

(1)	(2) ($ in billions)
Gross Domestic Product	_____
EQUALS	
Consumption	_____
+ Investment	_____
+ Government Purchases of Goods and Services	_____
+ Exports	_____
– Imports	_____

  b. Confirm that GDP $= C + I + G + NX$.

2. a. Collect the relevant data for the consumer price index and the GDP deflator for the years 1972–1974, and complete the following table.

Table 2-8

(1) Year	(2) CPI	(3) % Change in CPI from Preceding Year	(4) GDP Deflator	(5) % Change in GDP Deflator from Preceding Year
1972	_____		_____	
		_____		_____
1973	_____		_____	
		_____		_____
1974	_____		_____	

b. In late 1973, OPEC tripled the price of oil. How does this help to explain the relative differences in the percentage changes in the two indices?

3.   a. Complete the following table.

Table 2-9

(1) Year	(2) Real GDP ($ in billions)	(3) Total U.S. Population (in millions)	(4) Real GDP per Capita	(5) % Change in Real GDP per Capita from Preceding Decade
1970	_____	_____	_____	
				_____
1980	_____	_____	_____	
				_____
1990	_____	_____	_____	
				_____
2000	_____	_____	_____	

b. In which decade did real GDP per capita grow the fastest in the United States? In which decade did it grow the slowest?

4. **a.** Complete Columns 2–5 in the following table.

Table 2-10

(1) Year	(2) GDP Deflator (P)	(3) % Change in P	(4) Real GDP (Y)	(5) % Change in Y	(6) Nominal GDP (PY)	(7) % Change in PY
1999	_____		_____		_____	
		_____		_____		_____
2000	_____		_____		_____	

b. According to the text,

% Change in nominal GDP (PY) = % Change in P + % Change in Y.

Using this approximation, the % Change in nominal GDP between 1999 and 2000 was approximately equal to _____ percent.

c. Now use the exact data for nominal GDP to complete Column 6. Calculate the exact percentage change in Column 7 and verify your approximation in Part b.

Questions to Think About

1. When the unemployment rate falls by one percentage point, total employment rises by about 1 percent. Okun's law, however, indicates that output rises by an extra 3 percent above its average rate of growth. Why do you think this is so?

2. If you had to choose only one measure to represent the level of economic well-being in a country, which of the following would you choose? Why?

   real gross domestic product per capita
   real gross domestic product per working hour
   the literacy rate
   the infant mortality rate
   life expectancy
   the degree of income inequality
   the unemployment rate
   the average level of education

National Income: Where It Comes From and Where It Goes

Fill-in Questions

Use the key terms below to fill in the blanks in the following statements. Each term may be used more than once.

accounting profit	marginal product of capital
Cobb-Douglas production function	marginal product of labor
competition	marginal propensity to consume
constant returns to scale	national saving
consumption function	nominal interest rate
crowding out	private saving
diminishing marginal productivity	production function
economic profit	public saving
Euler's theorem	real interest rate
factors of production	real rental price of capital
factor prices	real wage

1. _____ are the inputs used to produce goods and services.

2. _____ are the amounts paid (per unit) to the factors of production.

3. If a firm hires an additional unit of labor while keeping other inputs constant, its production increases by the _____; if it hires an additional unit of capital while keeping other inputs constant, its production increases by the _____.

4. The _____ expresses mathematically how the factors of production determine the amount of output produced.

5. If we double the amounts of labor and capital, and output also doubles, the production function is said to have _____.

6. Under perfect _____, profit-maximizing firms hire labor until the _____ equals the real wage. They hire capital until the marginal product of capital equals the _____.

7. The _____ is what a worker is paid (per hour) measured in units of output rather than in dollars.

8. _____ includes both economic profit and the return to capital.

9. According to _____, if a production function has constant returns to scale and each factor of production is paid its marginal product, then the sum of these factor payments equals total output. Consequently, _____ equals zero.

10. **A** One special production function that exhibits a constant ratio of labor income to capital income is $Y = F(K, L) = AK^{\alpha}L^{1-\alpha}$. This is called the _____.

11. Most production functions exhibit _____, whereby each additional unit of input increases total output by smaller and smaller increments, all other things being equal.

12. The _____ depicts the relationship between consumption and disposable income. Its slope, called the _____, represents the fraction of each additional dollar of disposable income that people spend on consumption.

13. The _____ is the rate investors pay to borrow money. It is equal to the _____ plus the rate of inflation.

14. According to the national income accounts identity, _____ equals investment.

15. Disposable income minus consumption equals _____.

16. An increase in government purchases decreases _____. If private saving remains unchanged, the interest rate increases and investment decreases. Consequently, an increase in government purchases results in the _____ of investment.

Multiple-Choice Questions

1. The production function is a mathematical law that:
   a. relates factor prices to the amounts of inputs demanded.
   b. relates marginal products of factors of production to factor prices.
   c. relates factors of production to the amount of output produced.
   d. always has constant returns to scale.

2. The variable that is held constant for a given production function is the:
   a. amount of labor input.   c. amount of capital input.
   b. amount of output.   d. production technology.

3. An economy's aggregate income equals:
   a. the total number of dollars earned by workers.
   b. aggregate output.
   c. the number of dollars received by producers as profits.
   d. the total rent collected by the owners of capital.

4. A competitive firm takes:
   a. the prices of its outputs as given, but not the prices of its inputs.
   b. the prices of its inputs as given, but not the prices of its outputs.
   c. the prices of both its inputs and its outputs as given.
   d. neither the prices of its inputs nor the prices of its outputs as given.

5. Profit is:
   a. total revenue minus total cost.
   b. the price of output minus the price of input.
   c. the amount of money paid by a company to its stockholders as dividends each year.
   d. the amount of money earned by firm managers.

6. Constant returns to scale occurs when:
   a. output doubles when the amounts of all factor inputs double.
   b. output remains constant over time.
   c. the marginal productivity of labor equals the marginal productivity of capital.
   d. the marginal products of capital and labor do not change.

7. The production function that illustrates diminishing marginal product of labor is:

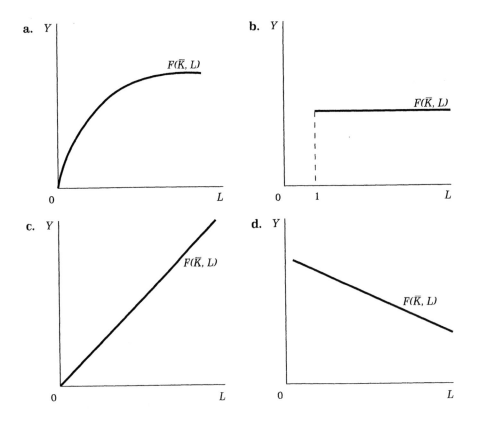

8. A profit-maximizing firm will hire labor up to the point where:

    a. the marginal product of labor equals the marginal product of capital.

    b. the marginal product of labor equals the real wage.

    c. marginal revenue equals zero.

    d. the real wage equals the real rental price of capital.

9. The FALSE statement below is:

    a. the extra revenue a firm gets from an extra unit of capital equals the marginal product of capital times the price of output.

    b. the extra revenue a firm gets from an extra unit of labor equals the marginal product of labor times the wage.

    c. a perfectly competitive firm's labor demand curve is the *MPL* schedule.

    d. constant returns to scale and profit maximization together imply that economic profit is zero.

10. According to Euler's theorem, the sum of all factor payments will equal total output if each factor of production is paid its marginal product and if:

    a. the production function has constant returns to scale.

    b. the production function displays diminishing marginal productivity.

    c. the amounts of capital and labor employed are equal.

    d. firms maximize profits.

11. Which of the following transactions is viewed as investment in the national income accounts?

    a. You buy 100 shares of stock in Apple Computer Corporation.

    b. You buy an Apple Macintosh computer to help your children do their homework.

    c. Apple Computer Corporation builds a new factory to manufacture computers.

    d. You eat an apple.

12. Which of the following transactions is viewed as investment in the national income accounts?

    a. You buy $1,000 of U.S. Treasury bonds.

    b. Richard, a carpenter, builds himself a log cabin.

    c. The Museum of Modern Art buys a painting by Picasso for $20 million.

    d. Your family buys a newly constructed home.

13. The interest rate on a loan depends on:

    a. the term of the loan.

    b. the riskiness of the loan.

    c. the tax treatment of the loan.

    d. all of the above.

14. The FALSE statement about national saving is:

    a. national saving is the total amount of savings deposits in banks.

    b. national saving is the sum of private saving plus public saving.

    c. national saving reflects the output that remains after the demand of consumers and the government has been satisfied.

    d. national saving equals investment at the equilibrium interest rate.

15. With total output fixed and national saving unrelated to the interest rate, an increase in government purchases increases:

    a. national saving.   c. the equilibrium interest rate.

    b. public saving.   d. private saving.

16. With total output fixed and national saving unrelated to the interest rate, an increase in taxes will:

    a. shift the vertical saving schedule to the left.

    b. decrease investment.

    c. increase consumption.

    d. decrease the equilibrium interest rate and increase investment.

17. If national saving is positively related to the interest rate, a technological advance that increases investment demand will:

    a. have no effect on the amount of national saving.

    b. shift the investment demand curve to the left.

    c. increase both investment and the equilibrium interest rate.

    d. have no effect on consumption.

18. Public saving is equal to:

    a. taxes plus government transfers minus government purchases.

    b. taxes minus government transfers minus government purchases.

    c. taxes plus government transfers plus government purchases.

    d. the government budget deficit.

19. If the nominal interest rate is 8 percent and prices are rising at 5 percent per year, the real interest rate is:

    a. 8 percent.   c. 13 percent.

    b. 3 percent.   d. –3 percent.

20. If consumption $C = 100 + 0.8(Y - T)$, disposable income equals 1,000, and $Y = 2,000$, then the marginal propensity to consume is:

    a. 0.5.   c. 0.8.

    b. 900.   d. 0.9.

21. All the following are characteristic of the Cobb-Douglas production function
A EXCEPT:

    a. constant returns to scale.

    b. diminishing marginal productivity of labor.

    c. constant marginal productivity of capital.

    d. a constant ratio of labor income to capital income.

Exercises

1. **Labor Demand and the Nominal Wage** *In this exercise, we derive the demand curve for labor in terms of the nominal wage by equating the nominal wage to the marginal product of labor multiplied by the price of output.*

   Continuing the example introduced in the textbook, consider the data in Columns 1 and 2 for a fictitious bakery—we'll call it the Bread and Butter Bakery.

Table 3-1

(1) No. of Workers (L)	(2) No. of Loaves Baked per Hour	(3) Marginal Product of Labor (MPL)	(4) Price per Loaf	(5) Price per Loaf $\times MPL$	(6) Nominal Wage Rate (W)	(7) Real Wage Rate (W/P)
0	0				$8	8
		20	$1	$20		
1	20				___	___
		___	___	___		
2	36				___	___
		___	___	___		
3	48				___	___
		___	___	___		
4	56				___	___
		___	___	___		
5	60				___	___
		___	___	___		
6	62				___	___

This company has a fixed amount of capital equipment. As it hires additional workers, total bread production increases, but by smaller and smaller increments.

a. Using the data from the first two columns of Table 3-1, graph the production function for the Bread and Butter Bakery on Graph 3-1.

Graph 3-1

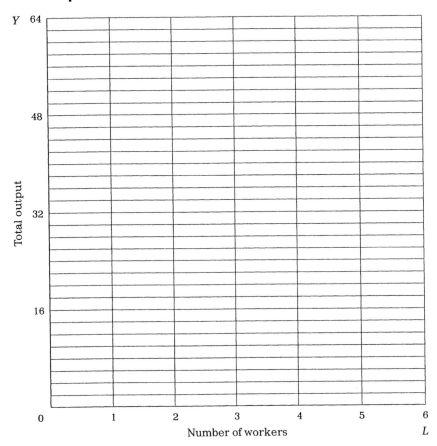

This curve has a positive slope. What does this tell us about the production function of this firm?

The slope decreases as the firm hires additional workers. What does this tell us?

The phenomenon just described is called the property of *diminishing marginal productivity*. As more inputs (here, labor) are added to a fixed amount of other inputs (here, capital), output will rise by smaller and smaller increments. (At some point the bakery could become so crowded that total output might even fall.)

b. Recall from the text that the *marginal product of labor (MPL)* is defined as the extra amount of output the firm gets from hiring an additional unit of labor. When the Bread and Butter Bakery hires its first worker, bread production rises from 0 to 20 loaves per hour. Consequently, the marginal product of labor of the first worker is 20. These data are shown in Column 3 of Table 3-1. Using the definition of *MPL*, complete the remainder of Column 3.

c. Now use the data from Columns 1 and 3 of Table 3-1 to complete Graph 3-2. The point for $L = 1$ is already shown on this graph. Note that this curve has a negative slope, illustrating that the marginal product of labor declines as more workers are hired. This is another example of the law of diminishing marginal productivity.

Graph 3-2

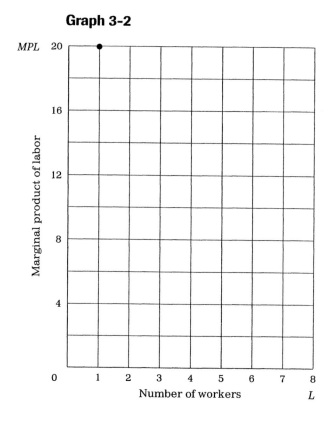

d. The number of workers that the Bread and Butter Bakery will hire depends on the production function and on two additional items: the wage rate the bakery must pay and the price it receives for each loaf of bread. As in the textbook, we assume that the firm operates in perfectly competitive input and output markets. Consequently, the baker will not drive up the wage of bakers if it hires additional employees or drive down the price of bread if it sells more bread. Assume initially that the market price for a loaf of bread is $1. Thus, as the firm hires additional workers, its revenues from sales will rise by $1 multiplied by *MPL*. For the first worker this will equal $1 × 20 = $20. Use this information to complete Columns 4 and 5 of Table 3-1.

e. Now assume that the market wage for each baker is $8 per hour. Complete Column 6 of Table 3-1 appropriately.

The Bread and Butter Bakery will hire an additional baker only when the extra sales revenue she generates exceeds or equals her wage of $8 per hour. (Although the bakery's profits will also be the same if it hires one fewer baker, we shall assume throughout this exercise and the next that more laborers will be hired as long as profits either increase or do not decrease.) Consequently, how many bakers will the bakery hire?

f. Note that when the fourth baker was hired, bread production rose by eight loaves, which were sold for an additional $8. This increase exactly offsets the baker's wage of $8, so she was hired. Algebraically, at this equilibrium

$$W = P \times MPL. \tag{3-1}$$

A fifth baker was not hired because his wage of $8 would have exceeded the $4 in extra revenue he would have generated. Indeed, he would be hired only if the nominal wage rate fell to $4. Similarly, a sixth baker would be hired only if the nominal wage rate fell to $2. Using all of this information, we can now draw the Bread and Butter Bakery's demand curve for labor on Graph 3-3. For each of the wage rates depicted on the vertical axis, plot the number of bakers who will be hired by using the rule $W = P \times MPL$ and connect the points.

Graph 3-3

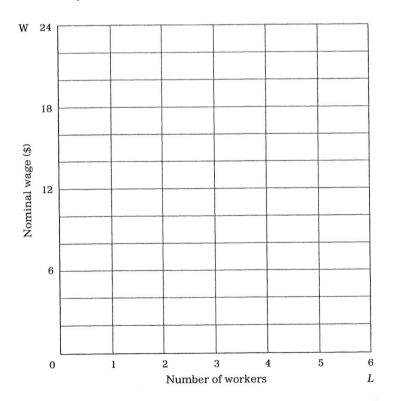

2. Labor Demand and the Real Wage *In this exercise, we derive the labor demand curve in terms of the real wage.*

a. As the textbook describes, one can divide $W = P \times MPL$ by P to rewrite the profit-maximizing rule as

$$\frac{W}{P} = MPL, \tag{3-2}$$

where W/P is defined as the real wage. Whereas the nominal wage represents a worker's remuneration in dollars, the real wage represents her remuneration in terms of the amount of goods and services (in this case, loaves of bread) she can purchase. To illustrate this, complete Column 7 of Table 3-1 in Exercise 1. Since $P = \$1$, $W/P = W/\$1$; therefore, the numbers in Column 7 of the table are the same as those in Column 6, although the units are now loaves of bread. Similarly, since $P = \$1$, we could also write W/P instead of W on the vertical axis on Graph 3-3.

b. Now suppose that the price of bread rises to $2 per loaf and the nominal wage rate doubles to $16 per hour. Assuming that the amount of bread produced by each worker remains the same, complete Table 3-2.

Table 3-2

(1) No. of Workers (L)	(2) No. of Loaves Baked per Hour	(3) Marginal Product of Labor (MPL)	(4) Price per Loaf	(5) Price per Loaf × MPL	(6) Nominal Wage Rate (W)	(7) Real Wage Rate (W/P)
0	0				$16	8
		20	$2	$40		
1	20				___	___
		___	___	___		
2	36				___	___
		___	___	___		
3	48				___	___
		___	___	___		
4	56				___	___
		___	___	___		
5	60				___	___
		___	___	___		
6	62				___	___

c. How many workers would the Bread and Butter Bakery now hire?

d. We can illustrate this new labor demand curve graphically in two ways. One way is to find the number of bakers the firm would hire at each nominal wage (just as we did in Exercise 1a). For example, the bakery would hire the first baker only if the wage rate fell to $40, because this is the amount by which revenues rise when the first baker is hired. Similarly, the second baker would be hired only if the nominal wage fell to $_____. Use this type of analysis to draw the Bread and Butter Bakery's demand curve for labor on Graph 3-4. Assume that the price of bread equals $2 per loaf and remember that bakers will be hired according to the rule $W = P \times MPL$. Note that this curve lies to the right/left of the demand curve in Exercise 1f.

Graph 3-4

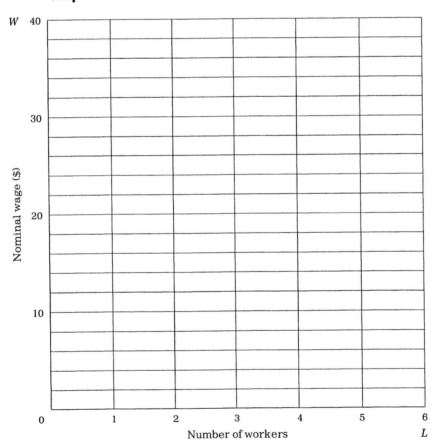

e. A second way to illustrate the labor demand curve graphically is to use the real wage W/P as the variable on the vertical axis and to draw the labor demand curve as a function of the real wage. Use the data from Column 3 of Table 3-2 to complete Table 3-3 and find the number of bakers hired at varying real wages.

Table 3-3

(1) Nominal Wage (W)	(2) Price of Bread (P)	(3) Real Wage (W/P)	(4) Number of Bakers Hired
$20	$1	_____	_____
40	2	_____	_____
16	1	_____	_____
32	2	_____	_____
12	1	_____	_____
24	2	_____	_____
8	1	8	4
16	2	8	4
4	1	_____	_____
8	2	_____	_____

From the data in this table, draw the labor demand curve in terms of the real wage on Graph 3-5. Note that this curve will not shift when inflation increases W and P by the same proportion.

Graph 3-5

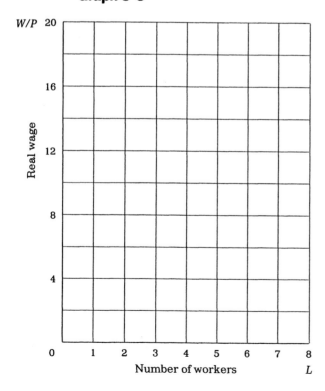

f. In Exercises 1 and 2, we derived the labor demand curve in terms of its nominal and real factor prices, that is, the nominal and real wages. Other factor inputs can be treated in an analogous fashion. For example, we could just as easily draw a table depicting the increase in bread production when the bakery adds more ovens (capital) while holding the number of bakers (labor) constant. This table would allow us to compute the marginal product of capital (*MPK*). We would then equate the *MPK* to the real factor price of capital, *R/P*—called the *real rental price of capital*—in order to determine how many ovens the Bread and Butter Bakery would need to maximize its profits. The curve representing the demand for capital would then be a downward-sloping function of the real rental price of capital.

3.   **The Cobb-Douglas Production Function**   *This exercise utilizes a simple Cobb-Douglas*
A   *production function to illustrate some of the concepts discussed in the textbook—constant returns to scale, diminishing returns, and Euler's theorem. Students who know calculus may choose to do Problem 3 instead of, or in addition to, this exercise.*

a. Consider the following Cobb-Douglas production function:

$$Y = K^{1/2}L^{1/2} = \sqrt{KL}.$$ (3-3)

Compute the value of Y for $K = 100$ and $L = 25$.

b. Define the term *constant returns to scale*.

Now show that the production function depicted by Equation 3-3 has constant returns to scale by completing Table 3-4. (You will need a calculator.)

Table 3-4

(1)	(2)	(3)
K	L	$Y = K^{1/2}L^{1/2}$
100	25	_____
200	50	_____
2,500	625	_____

When you doubled the amounts of capital and labor to 200 and 50, respectively, total output doubled/remained constant/fell by half. When you increased the amounts of capital and labor 25-fold to 2,500 and 625 (from 100 and 25), respectively, total output increased 25-fold/doubled/remained constant/fell. This phenomenon, called *constant returns to scale*, is characteristic of all Cobb-Douglas production functions. Mathematically, this occurs because the exponents on the inputs in the Cobb-Douglas production function sum to 1.0. You may wish to prove this.

c. Using the original values, where $K = 100$ and $L = 25$, compute the marginal product of labor at $L = 25$ by calculating how much output would rise if an additional worker were employed. This can be done by substituting $L = 26$ and $K = 100$ in the production function and noting the increase in Y. Note that in this exercise, as in the textbook, the *MPL* is calculated as the change in output when 1 unit of labor is *added*. This is different from Exercises 1 and 2 where the *MPL* is calculated as the change in output when 1 unit of labor is *subtracted*. (You will need a calculator to solve for $26^{1/2}$. Round off your answer to the nearest hundredth.)

Recall that, in equilibrium, firms will hire workers until the *MPL* equals the real wage *W/P*. Given your answer to the first part of Part c, if firms in the economy had decided to employ 25 workers, what would the equilibrium real wage have to be?

d. Start again at the original values of $K = 100$ and $L = 25$, and compute the marginal product of capital at $K = 100$ by calculating how much output would rise if an additional unit of capital were employed. This can be done by substituting $K = 101$ and $L = 25$ in the production function and noting the increase in Y. (You will again need a calculator. Round off your answer to the nearest hundredth.)

Recall that, in equilibrium, firms will hire capital until the *MPK* equals the real rental price of capital *R/P*. Given your answer to the first part of Part d, if firms in the economy had decided to employ 100 units of capital, what would the equilibrium real rental price of capital have to be?

e. Now we will compute the constant factor shares in this Cobb-Douglas production function.

Step 1   From Part a you found that when $K = 100$ and $L = 25$, $Y =$ _____.

Step 2   From Part c you discovered that the marginal product of labor and the equilibrium real wage at $L = 25$ were both equal to _____. Consequently, total real labor payments, $(W/P) \times L$, are equal to _____.

Step 3   Labor's share of total output is equal to total labor payments divided by total output, or $[(W/P) \times L]/Y =$ _____.

Step 4   From Part d you found that the marginal product of capital and the equilibrium real rental cost of capital at $K = 100$ were both equal to _____. Consequently, total real payments to capital, $(R/P) \times K$, are equal to _____.

Step 5   Capital's share of total output is equal to total payments to capital divided by total output, or $[(R/P) \times K]/Y =$ _____.

Step 6   Note that in a Cobb-Douglas production function, labor's share is always equal to the exponent on the labor input variable in the production function, and capital's share is equal to the exponent on the capital input variable.

Step 7   To see how Cobb-Douglas production functions yield constant factor
CH   shares even as inputs vary, verify that the relative shares would remain constant if K remains equal to 100 but L equals 625. To see this, it is necessary to recompute Y, *MPL*, *W/P*, *MPK*, *R/P*, and total factor payments for both capital and labor when $L = 625$. If you know calculus, it is easier to see this by answering Problem 3g.

f. Finally, add up the total factor payments from Part e, Steps 2 and 4, and compare the sum with your answer to Part a to illustrate Euler's theorem. This theorem states that if a production function has constant returns to scale and each factor of production is paid its marginal product, then the sum of these factor payments equals total output.

4. **The Consumption Function** *In this exercise, we introduce the marginal propensity to consume and the simple consumption function.*

a. As described in the textbook, consumption expenditures may be specified as a function of disposable income, where the latter is equal to GDP minus taxes, $Y - T$. Even if disposable income equals zero, people still need to eat, so they will consume out of their wealth, and consumption will still be positive. For each $1 increase in disposable income, consumption rises by $*MPC*, where *MPC* represents the *marginal propensity to consume,* defined as the fraction of each additional dollar of disposable income that is spent on consumption. Consider the following *consumption function:*

$$C = 125 + 0.75(Y - T). \qquad \textbf{(3-4)}$$

Use Equation 3-4 to complete Table 3-5.

Table 3-5

(1) Disposable Income $(Y - T)$	(2) Consumption
$ 0	_____
100	_____
200	_____
500	_____
800	_____
1,000	_____

b. Plot the points from Table 3-5 on Graph 3-6 and connect them.

Graph 3-6

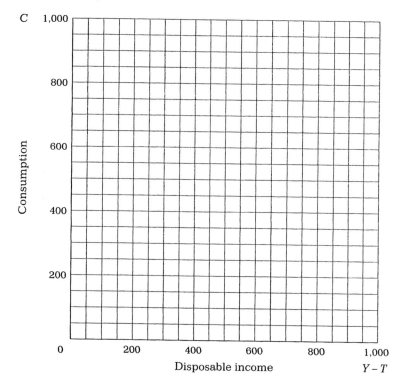

c. What is the value of the *y* intercept of this curve?

d. The slope of this curve is _____. Explain why the numerical value of the slope is also equal to the marginal propensity to consume.

5. **Taxes, Transfers, Budget Surpluses, and Budget Deficits** *In this exercise, we illustrate how the government budget surplus (or deficit) is related to government purchases, taxes, and transfers.*

   a. As the textbook suggests, in most economic models *T* is equal to total taxes minus government transfer payments. Some economists call these *net taxes,* which are equal to what households pay to the government in total taxes minus what they receive from the government in the form of transfer payments.

   According to this definition:

   If total taxes = 100 and government transfers = 0, net taxes *T* = _____.

   If total taxes = 100 and government transfers = 50, net taxes *T* = _____.

   If total taxes = 100 and government transfers = 150, net taxes *T* = _____.

   b. The *government budget surplus* is equal to total government tax revenues minus total government outlays, where the latter consist of both transfer payments and government purchases of goods and services. Since net taxes *T* already equals total taxes minus transfers, then the

   $$\text{Budget Surplus} = T - G. \qquad \text{(3-5)}$$

   The *budget deficit* is equal to the negative of the budget surplus:

   $$\text{Budget Deficit} = -(T - G) = G - T \qquad \text{(3-6)}$$

   Use Equations 3-5 and 3-6 to complete Table 3-6.

Table 3-6

(1) Net Taxes (*T*)	(2) Government Purchases	(3) Budget Surplus	(4) Budget Deficit
200	100	_____	_____
200	200	_____	_____
100	200	_____	_____
−100	100	_____	_____

6. The Saving-Investment Identity *In this exercise, we assume, as in the textbook, that the total output of the economy is fixed and that the factors of production are fully utilized. We then show that national saving is equal to investment.*

Assume that there are two factors of production, K and L, and that they are both fully employed at $K = \overline{K}$ and $L = \overline{L}$. Furthermore, assume that the economy is described by the following set of equations:

$$Y = \overline{Y} = F(\overline{K}, \overline{L}) = 1{,}200, \tag{3-7}$$

$$Y = C + I + G, \tag{3-8}$$

$$C = 125 + 0.75(Y - T), \tag{3-9}$$

$$I = I(r) = 200 - 10r, \tag{3-10}$$

$$G = \overline{G} = 150 \text{ and} \tag{3-11}$$

$$T = \overline{T} = 100. \tag{3-12}$$

These equations show the following:

Equation 3-7 represents the production function and the fact that the economy is operating at full employment when $Y = 1{,}200$.

Equation 3-8 is the national income accounts identity.

Equation 3-9 is the consumption function, whereby consumption is a function of disposable income, $(Y - T)$.

Equation 3-10 is an investment equation in which investment falls by 10 whenever the interest rate rises by 1 percentage point.

Equations 3-11 and 3-12 imply that government purchases and taxes are set exogenously at 150 and 100, respectively.

a. Substituting these values for Y and T in the consumption function, solve for the level of consumption.

$$C = 125 + 0.75\,(Y - T) = \underline{\hspace{5cm}}.$$

b. Rearranging Equations 3-7 and 3-8, we obtain

$$\overline{Y} - C - G = I. \tag{3-13}$$

As the textbook describes, the left-hand side of Equation 3-13 is equal to national saving S:

$$S = \overline{Y} - C - G. \tag{3-14}$$

This is the amount of saving that remains after the demands of consumers and the government have been satisfied. As Equations 3-13 and 3-14 illustrate, national saving must equal investment I:

$$S = I. \tag{3-15}$$

Substitute the values for Y, C, and G in Equation 3-14 and solve for the initial equilibrium values of both S and I.

$$S = I = \overline{Y} - C - G = \underline{\hspace{5cm}}.$$

Finally, substitute this value of I in the investment equation and solve for the real interest rate.

$$I = 200 - 10r = \underline{\hspace{4cm}}, \; r = \underline{\hspace{4cm}}.$$

c. In the model we developed in Parts a and b, national saving is assumed to be a fixed amount that is unrelated to the interest rate. Consequently, it is depicted as a vertical line on Graph 3-7. Complete the graph by drawing the curve representing the investment equation. (This is most easily done by solving the investment equation for r—that is, by isolating r on the left-hand side of the equation.) Indicate the slope of the investment curve, the initial equilibrium interest rate, and the initial levels of saving and investment.

Graph 3-7

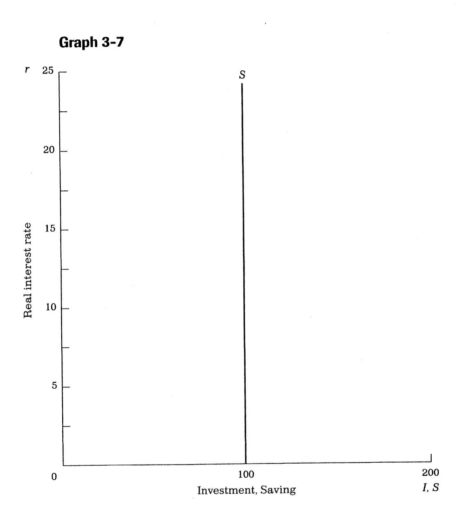

d. Economists often divide national saving into two parts in order to separate the saving of households from that of government. This is done by subtracting from and adding taxes T to the right-hand side of Equation 3-14. Therefore,

$$S = I = (Y - T - C) + (T - G). \qquad (3\text{-}16)$$

The term in the first set of parentheses is equal to disposable income minus consumption. This is called *private saving*. Recall that the term in the second set of parentheses is the government budget surplus, which is equal to *public saving*. Given your answers in Part b, calculate the initial levels of public and private saving and verify that they sum to the level of national saving.

7. **Shifts in the Saving and Investment Curves** *In this exercise, we use the saving-investment identity to analyze the effects of changes in government purchases, taxes, and technology on the level of investment and the equilibrium interest rate.*

Assume the same model as in Exercise 6.

$$Y = \overline{Y} = F(\overline{K}, \overline{L}) = 1,200$$
$$Y = C + I + G$$
$$C = 125 + 0.75(Y - T)$$
$$I = I(r) = 200 - 10r$$
$$G = \overline{G} = 150$$
$$T = \overline{T} = 100.$$

Using the same initial equilibrium values, let us now see what happens when there is a change in fiscal policy or in the investment equation.

a. Graph 3-8 depicts the same initial equilibrium as in Exercise 6. Suppose that government purchases increase by 50 to 200. If $\overline{Y}$ and T remain fixed at 1,200 and 100, respectively, consumption would remain constant at $C = 950$. Consequently, saving S would have to <u>rise/fall</u> by _____ to have

$$S = Y - C - G = \text{\underline{\hspace{3cm}}}$$

Graph 3-8

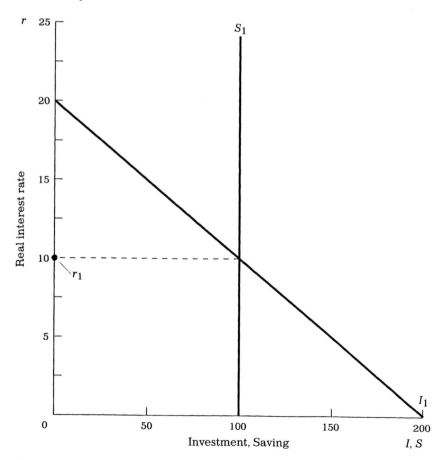

This would shift the vertical saving line to the left/right by _____.
Illustrate this shift on Graph 3-8 and label the new line S_2.

b. For the supply of output to remain equal to the demand for output,
investment would also have to rise/fall by _____ to
_____. This would be accomplished by a shift in/move-
ment along the investment curve. Consequently, the interest rate would rise/fall.
Solve for the new level of the interest rate by substituting this new value for
investment into the investment equation; illustrate the new equilibrium interest
rate on Graph 3-8 and label this point r_2.

c. In Parts a and b you found that if GDP is fixed at full employment $\overline{Y}$, an increase
in government purchases would increase/decrease national saving. This would
increase/decrease the real interest rate and thereby increase/decrease investment. Thus, an increase in government purchases is said to crowd out investment.

d. Now suppose that we start again at $G = 150$ and taxes are reduced by 20 to 80.
Given a value of $\overline{Y} = 1,200$, this would increase/decrease the level of consumption
to

$$C = 125 + 0.75(1,200 - 80) = \underline{\hspace{4cm}}.$$

Consequently, national saving would increase/decrease to

$$S = Y - C - G = \underline{\hspace{4cm}}.$$

This would shift the vertical saving line to the left/right by _____.
For output to remain in equilibrium, investment would also have to
rise/fall by _____ to _____. This would be accomplished
by a shift in/movement along the investment curve. Consequently, the interest
rate would rise/fall. Thus, a decrease in taxes also crowds out investment.

e. Finally, suppose that a technological breakthrough increases investment demand such that investment rises by 100 at each interest rate. Consequently, on Graph 3-9, the investment curve shifts to the right/left by 100. Draw the new curve and label it I_2.

Graph 3-9

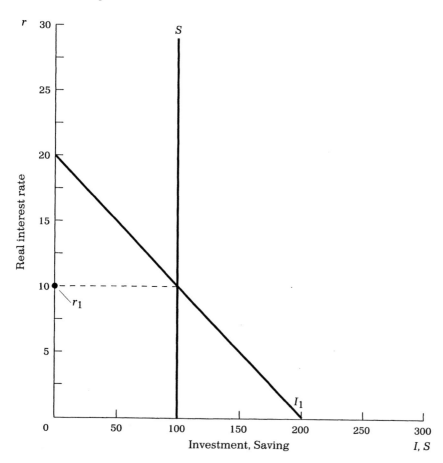

If $\overline{Y}$ initially remains unchanged, national saving will increase/remain consstant/decrease and the vertical saving line will shift right/not shift/shift left. As a result, the interest rate would rise/fall, and we would move along the new investment demand curve until investment equaled _____.

f. The result in Part e would be different if saving were positively related to the interest rate. A higher interest rate might reduce consumption and increase saving. If this were true, the saving schedule would have a positive/negative slope, as on Graph 3-10.

Graph 3-10

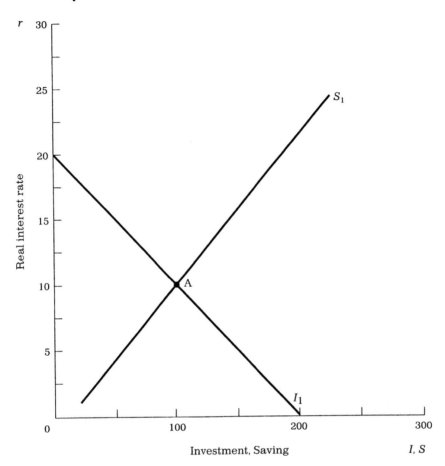

Now suppose that a technological breakthrough increases investment demand at each interest rate by shifting the investment demand curve to the right/left by 100, as in Part e. Draw the new investment curve on Graph 3-10, label it I_2, and label the new equilibrium Point B. The technological breakthrough would now tend to increase/decrease both the interest rate and the level of investment.

8. **The Identification Problem** *In this exercise, we illustrate the identification problem.*

CH Consider the situation depicted below, in which the saving schedule is positively sloped, as in Exercise 7f, rather than vertical.

Graph 3-11

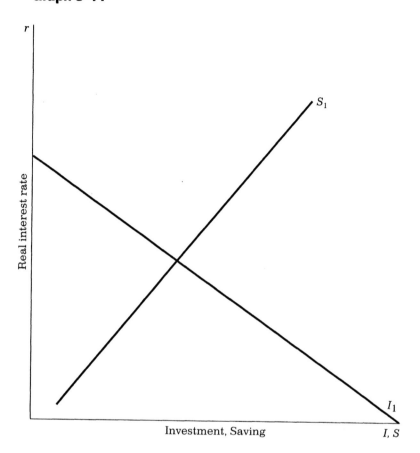

a. In Exercises 7b and 7d we saw that an increase in government purchases or a reduction in taxes would increase/have no effect/decrease national saving. Starting from the initial position S_1 on Graph 3-11, these policy changes would shift the saving schedule to the right/left. Draw the new saving schedule and label it S_2. The investment demand curve would not shift, but we would move along it to the new equilibrium. Consequently, the interest rate would rise/remain constant/fall, investment would rise/remain constant/fall, and we would observe a positive/negative relationship between the interest rate and investment.

b. Similarly, a reduction in government purchases or an increase in taxes would increase/decrease national saving. Starting again from S_1 on Graph 3-11, this set of policy changes would shift the saving schedule to the right/left. Draw the new saving schedule on Graph 3-11 and label it S_3. The investment demand curve would not shift, but we would move along it to the new equilibrium. Consequently, the interest rate would rise/fall, investment would rise/fall, and we would again observe a positive/negative relationship between the interest rate and investment.

c. Reviewing Exercise 7f, however, we see that a technological breakthrough that increases investment demand would shift the investment curve to the right/left and increase/decrease both the interest rate and investment. Similarly, a reduction in investment demand would shift the investment curve to the right/left and increase/decrease both the interest rate and investment. This would result in a positive/negative relationship between the interest rate and investment.

d. After putting the results from Parts a through c together, we see that one cannot predict whether the relationship between the interest rate and investment will be positive or negative. If the economy experiences shifts primarily in its saving schedule, the relationship will be positive/negative, but if it experiences shifts primarily in its investment demand curve, the relationship will be positive/negative.

Problems

Answer the following problems on a separate sheet of paper. Complete tables in the spaces provided.

1. How would Graphs 3-1 and 3-2 in Exercise 1 look if each additional worker added the same amount to total output, that is, if there were constant rather than diminishing returns?

2. Oranges grown in California and Florida are sold at the same price. Farm workers in both states work in a perfectly competitive labor market and receive identical wages. Suppose, however, that economists have discovered that the *average* product of labor in California orange groves is 50 percent greater than in Florida. The average product of labor is defined as total output divided by the number of workers (or worker-hours).

    a. Explain why the following statement could easily be false: Since the average product of labor is different in these two states, California and Florida orange groves obviously follow different economic rules in hiring workers; the firms in Florida must not be maximizing profits.

    b. Suppose that all groves in the two states are currently maximizing profits and evaluate the following statement: Because the average product of labor is higher in California, U.S. orange production would increase if farm workers moved from Florida to California orange groves.

3. This problem uses calculus to derive the same results as Exercise 3 concerning the
C A Cobb-Douglas production function.

Consider the following Cobb-Douglas production function:

$$Y = 60K^{1/3}L^{2/3}.$$

a. Complete Table 3-7. (You will need a calculator.)

Table 3-7

(1)	(2)	(3)
K	L	$Y = 60K^{1/3}L^{2/3}$
64	8	_____
128	16	_____
192	24	_____

Explain how these results illustrate the property of constant returns to scale.

b. Derive the algebraic expression for the marginal product of labor by differentiating the right-hand side of the production function with respect to L.

c. Evaluate the expression you just derived—that is, find the numerical value of *MPL*—when $K = 64$ and $L = 8$.

   Recall that, in equilibrium, firms will hire workers until their *MPL* equals the real wage W/P. Given your answer to the first part of Part c, if firms in the economy had decided to employ eight workers, what would the equilibrium real wage have to be?

d. Derive the algebraic expression for the marginal product of capital by differentiating the right-hand side of the production function with respect to K.

e. Evaluate the expression you just derived—that is, find the numerical value of *MPK*—when $K = 64$ and $L = 8$.

   Recall that, in equilibrium, firms will hire capital until the *MPK* equals the real rental price of capital R/P. Given your answer to the first part of Part e, if firms in the economy had decided to employ 64 units of capital, what would the equilibrium real rental price of capital have to be?

f. Illustrate how Cobb-Douglas production functions result in constant factor shares that are equal to the exponents on the respective factors of production. To show this, calculate total real labor payments, total real payments to capital, and labor's and capital's shares of total output when $K = 64$ and $L = 8$.

g. Use the algebraic expressions you derived for the marginal products of capital and labor (your answers to Parts b and d) to prove your result from Part f algebraically.

h. Finally, show that this production function satisfies Euler's theorem.

4.   Soon after his election in 1992, President Clinton proposed to reduce government spending and increase taxes.

    a.   What effect would this have on the government budget deficit?

    b.   State and explain what the long-run effects of this policy would be on private saving, public saving, and national saving.

    c.   Use the *I,S* diagram to state and illustrate what the long-run impact of this program would be on national saving, investment, and the real interest rate.

5.   Many Congressional Republicans have suggested cutting both government purchases and taxes.

    a.   If both taxes and government purchases were cut by equal amounts (which was not true in their proposal), state and explain what the long-run effects of this policy would be on private saving, public saving, and national saving.

    b.   Use the *I,S* diagram to state and illustrate what the long-run impact of this program would be on national saving, investment, and the real interest rate.

    c.   Explain how the magnitude of the changes you depicted in Part b depends on the size of the marginal propensity to consume.

6.   In his State of the Union Address in January, 2002, President Bush announced that he would ask Congress to approve substantial increases in defense spending to counter terrorism and significant reductions in taxes. If these policy changes are enacted:

    a.   What would happen to the government budget surplus?

    b.   State and explain what the *exact* long-run effects would be on private saving, public saving, and national saving.

    c.   Use the *I,S* diagram to state and illustrate the long-run impacts on national saving, investment, and the real interest rate.

The Open Economy

Fill-in Questions

Use the key terms below to fill in the blanks in the following statements. Each term may be used more than once.

balanced trade   small open economy
net exports   trade balance
net capital outflow   trade deficit
nominal exchange rate   trade surplus
purchasing-power parity   world interest rate
real exchange rate

1. The total expenditure on domestic output is the sum of consumption, investment, government purchases, and _____.

2. _____ indicates the amount domestic residents are lending abroad minus the amount foreigners are lending to us. It is equal to domestic saving minus domestic investment.

3. National income accounting tells us that $S - I$, or _____ must equal _____, where the latter is called the _____.

4. A(n) _____ is a small part of the world market and thus, by itself, can have only a negligible effect on the world interest rate.

5. If there is free access to world financial markets, investment in all small open economies will depend on the _____.

6. The _____ is the relative price of the currency of two countries, such as 1.5 euros per U.S. dollar.

7. The _____ is the rate at which one can trade the goods of one country for the goods of another. More specifically, it measures the number of foreign goods one can exchange for one comparable domestic good. It incorporates the relative price levels of the two countries as well as the _____.

8. According to the tenet of _____, a dollar (or any other currency) must have the same purchasing power in every country.

9. If a country's exports exceed its imports, it will have a(n) _____. If its imports exceed its exports, it will have a(n) _____. Finally, if its exports and imports are equal, it will have _____.

Multiple-Choice Questions

1. According to the national income accounts identity, total expenditure on domestic output is the sum of:

    a. consumption of domestic goods and services, investment of domestic goods and services, government purchases of domestic goods and services, and exports of domestic goods and services.

    b. consumption, investment, government purchases, and net exports.

    c. both a and b.

    d. domestic spending on foreign goods and expenditures on imports.

2. If national output $Y = 1,000$ and domestic spending on all domestic and foreign goods and services equals 900, net exports NX will equal:

    a. 100.

    b. −100.

    c. 1,900.

    d. 0.

3. The FALSE statement below is:

    a. net capital outflow is the excess of domestic saving over domestic investment.

    b. the trade surplus and net capital outflow must both equal zero.

    c. according to the national income accounts identity, net capital outflow must equal net exports.

    d. according to the national income accounts identity, net capital outflow must equal the trade surplus (or the trade balance).

4. If domestic investment exceeds domestic savings, one would observe:

    a. negative net capital outflow.

    b. a government budget deficit.

    c. a trade deficit.

    d. both a and c.

5. With a constant world interest rate, full employment, and an initial trade surplus of zero, a tax cut in a small open economy will result in:

    a. a trade deficit.

    b. a reduction in national saving.

    c. negative net capital outflow.

    d. all of the above.

6. Suppose that several large foreign countries decrease government spending, leading to a decrease in the world interest rate. In a small open economy, which of the following is most likely to happen?

    a. a decrease in saving

    b. a decrease in investment

    c. an increase in the trade deficit (or a reduction in the trade surplus)

    d. an increase in net capital outflow

7. If a computer costs $5,000 in the United States, how much will it cost in Germany if the nominal exchange rate is 2 euros per U.S. dollar?

    a. 5,000 euros

    b. 2,500 euros

    c. 10,000 euros

    d. 5,002 euros

8. Suppose that a comparable computer (or any other commodity) costs $5,000 in the United States and 20,000 euros in Germany. If the nominal exchange rate is 2 euros per U.S. dollar, then the real exchange rate of the U.S. dollar (that is, the number of German computers that can be traded for one U.S. computer) is equal to:

    a. 8.   **c.** 2.
    b. 4.   **d.** 0.5.

9. As the real exchange rate of the U.S. dollar increases:

    a. foreign goods become cheaper to U.S. citizens.
    b. U.S. net exports fall.
    c. the U.S. trade surplus decreases.
    d. all of the above occur.

10. The correct relationship among net exports *NX*, the excess of saving over investment *S − I*, and the real exchange rate ε occurs in graph:

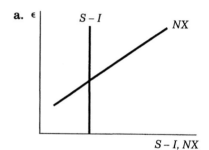

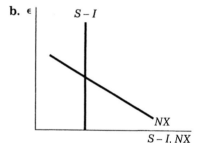

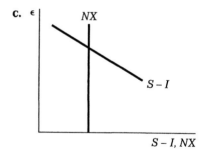

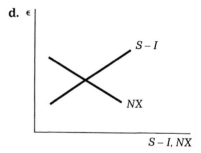

11. If the government of a small open economy increases personal income taxes, that country's:

    a. net exports increase.
    b. investment increases.
    c. equilibrium real exchange rate rises.
    d. consumption rises.

12. If the governments of several large foreign countries raise taxes:

    a. the world interest rate will rise.

    b. the U.S. trade surplus will rise.

    c. the real exchange rate of the dollar will rise.

    d. U.S. net exports will increase.

13. If investment demand decreases in a small open economy:

    a. the equilibrium real exchange rate rises.

    b. net exports increase.

    c. national saving increases.

    d. net capital outflow decreases.

14. In the long run, if the German government places high tariffs on all imports:

    a. Germany's net exports rise.

    b. Germany's real foreign exchange rate increases.

    c. net capital outflow in Germany decreases.

    d. all of the above.

15. Slower growth in the Japanese money supply will lead to:

    a. an increase in inflation in Japan.

    b. a decrease in inflation in the United States.

    c. a depreciation of the dollar relative to the Japanese yen.

    d. all of the above.

16. According to purchasing-power parity, if a television set sells for $500 in the United States and 2,000 yuan in China, the nominal exchange rate, expressed in yuan per dollar, is:

    a. 2.5.

    b. 10.

    c. 4.

    d. 1.

17. In a large open economy, an increase in government purchases or a reduction in
    [A] taxes causes:

    a. an increase in the real interest rate.

    b. a reduction in net capital outflow.

    c. an increase in the real exchange rate.

    d. all of the above.

18. In a large open economy, an increase in the investment tax credit, which increases
    [A] investment demand, will:

    a. increase the real interest rate.

    b. reduce net capital outflow.

    c. decrease net exports.

    d. do all of the above.

Exercises

1. **National Income Accounting in an Open Economy** *In this exercise, we incorporate international trade into the national income accounting identities in two alternative ways.*

    a. Total purchases by U.S. households, businesses, and governments are equal to purchases of goods and services produced in the United States plus purchases of goods and services produced in other countries. Using this knowledge, complete Table 5-1.

    Table 5-1

(1) Group	(2) Purchases of Goods and Services Produced in the U.S. ($ in billions)	(3) Purchases of Goods and Services Produced Elsewhere ($ in billions)	(4) Total Purchases ($ in billions)
U.S. households	$C^d = \$3,100$	$C^f = \$400$	$C = \$$_____
U.S. businesses	$I^d = \$\ 600$	$I^f = \$$_____	$I = \$\ 800$
U.S. governments	$G^d = \$$_____	$G^f = \$100$	$G = \$1,000$
Total	$\$$_____	$\$$_____	$\$$_____

    b. Now examine the total of Column 2 of Table 5-1. $C^d + I^d + G^d$ is total domestic spending on domestic goods and services. It represents total purchases by U.S. households, businesses, and governments of goods and services that are produced in the United States. In this example, total domestic spending on domestic goods is equal to $\$$_____ billion.

    c. The total of $C^f + I^f + G^f$ (Column 3 of Table 5-1) represents total purchases by U.S. households, businesses, and governments of goods and services that are produced in foreign countries. It is more commonly called total _____. In this example, this total is equal to $\$$_____ billion.

    d. The total of $C + I + G$ (Column 4 of Table 5-1) represents total purchases by U.S. households, businesses, and governments of all goods and services, both foreign and domestic. This is sometimes called total domestic spending. In this example, it is equal to $\$$_____ billion.

    e. Recall from Chapter 2 of the textbook that Y is equal to total national output (that is, the value of the goods and services produced in the economy). In the closed economy with no foreign trade, $Y = C + I + G$. In an open economy, however, national output is not merely equal to $C + I + G$ because they do not include foreign purchases of goods and services that are produced in the United States. These must be included in total U.S. output since they certainly represent U.S. production. On the other hand, $C + I + G$ includes purchases by U.S. households, businesses, and governments of foreign production, which should not be included in U.S. output and, therefore, must be subtracted. In Table 5-1, total imports into the United States equaled $_____ billion. If total exports equal $900 billion, U.S. output can be calculated as

C	$_____
+ I	$_____
+ G	$_____
+ Exports	$_____
– Imports	$_____
=	
Y	$_____ billion.

f. In the national income accounts, exports minus imports is often called net exports NX. In this example, NX = $_____ billion.

g. There is another way to calculate Y. Total U.S. production will equal total domestic spending on domestic goods and services plus U.S. exports:

C^d	$_____
+ I^d	$_____
+ G^d	$_____
+ Exports	$_____
=	
Y	$_____ billion.

2. **Net Capital Outflow and the Trade Balance** *In this exercise, we introduce net capital outflow and the trade balance, and we emphasize how they must equal each other.*

a. According to the national income accounts, net capital outflow, or $S - I$, must equal the trade balance NX. Thus, $S - I = NX$. Recall that S represents national saving, which is the sum of private saving $Y - T - C$ and public saving $T - G$. Japan's huge exports have led to a large Japanese trade surplus/deficit. Hence, in Japan, NX is positive/negative. Consequently, in Japan, $S - I$ is positive/negative. Therefore, the Japanese will borrow/lend the difference abroad, and we say that in Japan net capital outflow will be positive/negative. Note that net capital outflow is merely domestic purchases of foreign assets minus foreign purchases of domestic assets. Thus, Japanese purchases of foreign assets are greater/less than foreign purchases of Japanese assets.

b. For the past several years, the United States has had a trade deficit, implying that NX has been positive/negative. Consequently, in the United States, net capital outflow has been positive/negative. Thus, the United States is borrowing/lending abroad. This also indicates that U.S. purchases of foreign assets have been greater/less than foreign purchases of U.S. assets.

c. Now complete Table 5-2:

Table 5-2

					($ in billions)				
(1)	(2)	(3)	(4)	(5)	(6)	(7)	(8)	(9)	(10)
Case	Y	C	I	G	NX	T	Private Saving	Public Saving	National Saving
1.	5,000	3,000	700	1,000	_____	900	_____	_____	_____
2.	5,000	3,200	900	1,000	_____	900	_____	_____	_____
3.	5,000	3,200	900	900	_____	1,000	_____	_____	_____

d. For each of the three preceding cases, calculate the trade balance and net capital outflow:

Case 1: Trade surplus = $_____ billion.

Net Capital Outflow = $S - I$ = $ _____ billion.

Case 2: Trade surplus = $_____ billion.

Net Capital Outflow = $S - I$ = $ _____ billion.

Case 3: Trade surplus = $_____ billion.

Net Capital Outflow = $S - I$ = $ _____ billion.

e. Note in Case 2 above that a trade surplus of $_____ billion can also be expressed as a trade deficit of $_____ billion.

3. **National Saving and Investment in a Small Open Economy** *In this exercise, we discuss the effects of changes in national saving and investment in a small open economy if output is fixed at full employment.*

a. Suppose that the economy is described by the following set of equations. These equations are identical to those in Exercise 6 of Chapter 3, except for the inclusion of international trade:

$$Y = \bar{Y} = F(\bar{K}, \bar{L}) = 1,200$$
$$Y = C + I + G + NX$$
$$C = 125 + 0.75(Y - T)$$
$$I = I(r) = 200 - 10r$$
$$G = \bar{G} = 150$$
$$T = \bar{T} = 100.$$

If the real interest rate were equal to 10 percent, then $r = 10$ and:

$C = $ _____

$I = $ _____

$G = $ _____

and, thus,

$NX =$ _____ .

Consequently, the trade surplus would equal _____ .

b. Conversely,

disposable income = _____

private saving = _____

public saving = _____

national saving $S =$ _____

$S - I =$ _____

and, thus, net capital outflow would equal _____ .

c. Draw the investment and saving curves on Graph 5-1, label them I_1 and S_1, and label the initial equilibrium Point A.

Graph 5-1

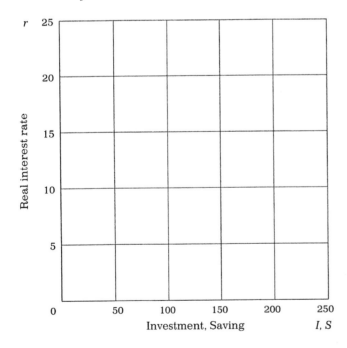

d. Now suppose that government purchases rose by 100 to 250. If Y remained equal to 1,200, this would shift the national saving curve to the <u>left/right</u> by _____ . The investment curve would <u>shift left/not shift/shift right</u>. Draw the new curve(s) on Graph 5-1 and label them I_2 and S_2.

e. If this economy were a closed economy, investment would always have to equal saving. Thus, when saving fell to ＿＿＿＿＿＿＿＿＿＿ in Part d, investment would also fall to ＿＿＿＿＿＿＿＿＿＿. This would be accomplished by an increase in r to ＿＿＿＿＿＿＿＿＿＿ percent. Label the new equilibrium for this closed economy Point B.

f. Now, however, suppose this is a small open economy and the world real interest rate r^* remains equal to 10 percent both before and after the increase of 100 in government purchases. Thus, investment remains equal to ＿＿＿＿＿＿＿＿＿＿. Following the increase in domestic government purchases, net capital outflow $S - I$ changes to ＿＿＿＿＿＿＿＿＿＿. Consequently, the trade surplus NX will change to ＿＿＿＿＿＿＿＿＿＿. The change in net capital outflow indicates that domestic purchases of foreign assets minus foreign purchases of domestic assets will <u>rise/fall</u> by ＿＿＿＿＿＿＿＿＿＿.

g. In the closed economy described in Chapter 3 of the textbook, a reduction in national saving leads to a(n) <u>increase/decrease</u> in the real interest rate and a(n) <u>increase/decrease</u> in investment. In a small open economy, however, a reduction in national saving <u>raises/does not change/lowers</u> the real interest rate. Consequently, investment <u>increases/does not change/decreases</u>. Instead, policies that decrease saving push net capital outflow <u>up/down</u> and the trade account toward <u>surplus/deficit</u>.

h. Now suppose that we start again at $G = 150$, $I = I_1$, $S = S_1$, and the world real interest rate $r^* = 10$ percent. If domestic investment in this small open economy rose by 50 at every level of the real interest rate, the investment curve would shift to the <u>right/left</u> by 50, while the national saving curve would <u>shift to the right/not shift/shift to the left</u>. Draw the new curve(s) on Graph 5-2 and label them I_3 and S_3.

Graph 5-2

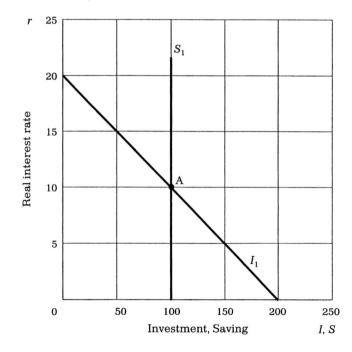

As a result of the autonomous increase in domestic investment, net capital out-flow would now equal _____, while the trade surplus would now equal _____.

i. Finally, suppose we start again at Point A and the world real interest rate rises to 15 percent. This may have occurred as a result of a decline in world saving, which, in turn, may have resulted from changes in the fiscal policies of one or more large foreign countries. These changes in foreign fiscal policy that raise the world interest rate could include a(n) increase/decrease in foreign government purchases or a(n) increase/decrease in foreign government taxes. According to Equations 5-1 to 5-6, investment I would now equal _____. (Note that this represents a movement along I_1 rather than a shift in the curve.) National saving S would increase/not change/decrease. Consequently, net capital outflow $S - I$ would now equal _____, while the trade surplus NX would equal _____. Illustrate the extent of the new level of net capital outflow on Graph 5-2 and label it $CF(r^* = 15)$.

4. **The Nominal Exchange Rate** *In this exercise, we introduce the nominal exchange rate. We show why net exports fall as the nominal exchange rate increases when we hold the domestic and foreign price levels constant.*

Consider the trade of two mainframe computers between the United States and Germany. The IBM computer made in the United States sells for $10,000. A comparable computer made by Siemens in Germany sells for 15,000 euros. Although it is important to understand that net exports depend on the real exchange rate, in this exercise we assume that the price levels in both the United States and Germany remain constant. In this case, changes in the real exchange rate are reflected by changes in the nominal exchange rate.

a. Complete Table 5-3.

Table 5-3

(1) Nominal Foreign Exchange Rate (euros per dollar)	(2) Price of IBM Computer in the U.S.	(3) Price of IBM Computer in Germany	(4) Price of Siemens Computer in Germany	(5) Price of Siemens Computer in the U.S.
1.0	$10,000	_____	15,000 euros	_____
1.5	$10,000	_____	15,000 euros	_____
2.0	$10,000	_____	15,000 euros	_____

b. Examining the numbers in Table 5-3, note that, as the nominal foreign exchange rate increases, the price of the IBM computer in Germany increases/decreases, while the price of the Siemens computer in Germany remains constant. Consequently, as the U.S. foreign exchange rate increases, U.S. exports of IBM computers will increase/decrease, assuming the price levels in both countries remain constant.

c. Similarly, as the nominal foreign exchange rate increases, the price of the IBM computer in the United States increases/remains constant/decreases, while the price of the Siemens computer in the United States increases/remains constant/decreases. Consequently, as the U.S. foreign exchange rate increases, U.S. imports of Siemens computers will increase/decrease.

d. Recall that net exports are calculated as exports/imports minus exports/imports. From Parts a–c we see that as the U.S. nominal foreign exchange rate increases, U.S. net exports increase/decrease, assuming the price levels in both countries remain constant.

e. As the nominal exchange rate of the dollar increases, it is said that the dollar has appreciated relative to the euro. Consequently, as the dollar appreciates, U.S. net exports increase/decrease.

5. **The Real Exchange Rate** *In this exercise, we allow the price levels in different countries to grow at different rates. We then show how these changes, along with changes in the nominal foreign exchange rate, are incorporated into the real exchange rate, and we illustrate its effects on net exports.*

a. Suppose that the United States now experiences 20 percent inflation while Germany's price level remains constant. As a result, the price of IBM computers in the United States rises to $12,000 while the price of Siemens computers remains equal to 15,000 euros. Complete Table 5-4.

Table 5-4

(1) Nominal Foreign Exchange Rate (euros per dollar)	(2) Price of IBM Computer in the U.S.	(3) Price of IBM Computer in Germany	(4) Price of Siemens Computer in Germany	(5) Price of Siemens Computer in the U.S.
1.5	$10,000	_____	15,000 euros	_____
1.5	$12,000	_____	15,000 euros	_____

b. Before U.S. inflation, at an initial nominal foreign exchange rate of 1.5 euros per dollar, the price of the IBM computer was greater than/equal to/less than than the price of the Siemens computer in both Germany and the United States. After the U.S. price level rises by 20 percent, however, the price of the IBM computer becomes greater than/equal to/less than the price of the Siemens computer in both countries. Consequently, U.S. net exports would increase/not change/decrease.

c. Now suppose that at the same time the nominal exchange rate falls to 1.25 euros per dollar. Complete Table 5-5.

Table 5-5

(1) Nominal Foreign Exchange Rate (euros per dollar)	(2) Price of IBM Computer in the U.S.	(3) Price of IBM Computer in Germany	(4) Price of Siemens Computer in Germany	(5) Price of Siemens Computer in the U.S.
1.50	$10,000	_____	15,000 euros	_____
1.25	$12,000	_____	15,000 euros	_____

Note that the percentage change from 1.25 euros to 1.50 euros is _____ percent, while the percentage change from $10,000 to $12,000 is _____ percent. Therefore, if the nominal foreign exchange rate decreases by the same proportion as the domestic price level increases (holding the foreign price level constant), the price of the IBM computer will increase above/remain equal to/decrease below the price of the Siemens computer in both countries. Hence, net exports would increase/not change/decrease.

d. Whereas the nominal exchange rate indicates the amount of foreign currency a domestic resident gets (or a foreigner gives up) for one unit of domestic currency, the real exchange rate indicates the amount of foreign goods and services a domestic resident gets (or a foreigner gives up) for one equivalent domestic good or service. If you sell one American good, you get P, where P is the domestic (American) price level. To buy German goods you must trade these P into euros at the nominal foreign exchange rate of e, for example, 1.5 euros/$1. These $1.5 \times P$ euros will then buy $1.5P/P^*$ foreign (German) goods, where P^* equals the foreign (German) price level. The real exchange rate ε is the number of foreign goods one can buy with one domestic good. Thus,

$$\varepsilon = 1.5P/P^* = e \times (P/P^*).$$ \hfill (5-7)

Use this formula to complete Table 5-6.

Table 5-6

(1) Nominal Foreign Exchange Rate (euros per dollar)	(2) U.S. Price Level	(3) German Price Level	(4) Real Foreign Exchange Rate
1.0	$10,000	15,000 euros	_____
1.5	$10,000	15,000 euros	_____
1.25	$12,000	15,000 euros	_____
1.5	$12,000	15,000 euros	_____
2.0	$10,000	15,000 euros	_____

e. Reexamining Parts a–d, we can see how net exports depend on the real foreign exchange rate. As the real foreign exchange rate rises, U.S. exports will increase/decrease, U.S. imports will increase/decrease, and U.S. net exports will increase/decrease. Remember that the real foreign exchange rate increases whenever the nominal exchange rate increases/decreases, the domestic price level increases/decreases, or the foreign price level increases/decreases.

6. **Determinants of the Real Exchange Rate in a Small Open Economy** *In this exercise, we discuss how the real exchange rate in a small open economy adjusts to equate net capital outflow and the trade surplus.*

a. The real exchange rate adjusts so that the trade surplus is equal to net capital outflow, $S - I$. Net capital outflow does not depend on the real exchange rate if the world real interest rate is constant and output remains equal to its full employment level. We have already seen, however, that the trade surplus NX increases/decreases as the real exchange rate increases.

b. Suppose that $S - I = 150$ and $NX = 250 - 100\varepsilon$. Draw these two curves on Graph 5-3 and label them $(S - I)_1$ and NX_1.

Graph 5-3

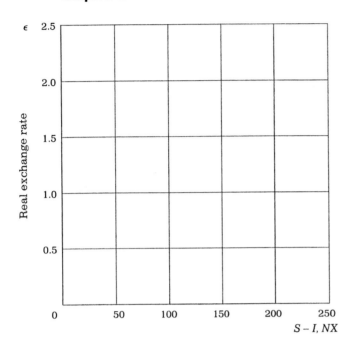

c. On Graph 5-3, net capital outflow equals _____. Consequently, the trade surplus must equal _____, which will occur when ε equals _____. Label this initial equilibrium Point A on Graph 5-3.

d. Now suppose that the domestic government increases government purchases by 50. This will increase/decrease national saving by _____, while investment increases/remains the same/decreases, since the interest rate remains equal to the world real interest rate. Consequently, net capital outflow $S - I$ will increase/decrease by _____ to _____. This will shift the $S - I$ curve to the left/right by _____. Draw the new curve on Graph 5-3, label it $(S - I)_2$, and label the new equilibrium Point B. This implies that domestic purchases of foreign assets minus foreign purchases of domestic assets will increase/decrease as the domestic country increases its borrowing/lending abroad. Given the change in net capital outflow, the trade surplus must also increase/decrease by _____ to _____. This occurs at a new equilibrium real exchange rate of _____. Consequently, domestic fiscal expansion, via an increase in government purchases or a reduction in taxes, leads to a(n) increase/decrease in the equilibrium real exchange rate.

e. Let's start again at the initial equilibrium. Redraw NX_1, $(S - I)_1$, and Point A on Graph 5-4.

Graph 5-4

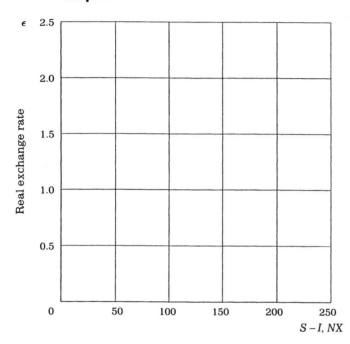

Some large foreign country now raises its taxes. This leads to a(n) increase/decrease in world saving and a(n) increase/decrease in the world real interest rate. Consequently, domestic investment would increase/decrease, $(S - I)$ would increase/decrease, and the $(S - I)$ curve would shift to the left/right. Draw the directional shift on Graph 5-4, label your new curve $(S - I)_3$, and label the new equilibrium Point B. This change would indicate a(n) increase/decrease in net capital outflow and a(n) increase/decrease in the trade surplus. To obtain this change in the trade surplus, the real exchange rate would have to rise/fall.

7. **The Nominal Foreign Exchange Rate and Purchasing-Power Parity** *In this exercise, we discuss the determinants of the nominal foreign exchange rate and purchasing-power parity.*

a. Recall that the equation for the real exchange rate is

$$\varepsilon = e \times (P/P^*). \tag{5-8}$$

If we multiply both sides of Equation 5-8 by P^*, we obtain

$$P^* \times \varepsilon = e \times P. \tag{5-9}$$

Using the percentage change rule from Chapter 2 of the textbook, we obtain

$$\% \text{ Change in } P^* + \% \text{ Change in } \varepsilon = \% \text{ Change in } e + \% \text{ Change in } P, \qquad \textbf{(5-10)}$$

or, by rearranging,

$$\% \text{ Change in } e = \% \text{ Change in } \varepsilon + \% \text{ Change in } P^* - \% \text{ Change in } P. \qquad \textbf{(5-11)}$$

Recall that the percentage change in the domestic price level is merely equal to the domestic rate of inflation π, while the percentage change in the foreign price level P^* is equal to the foreign rate of inflation π^*. Making these substitutions in Equation 5-11, complete the following equation:

$$\% \text{ Change in } e = \underline{\hspace{6cm}}. \qquad \textbf{(5-12)}$$

Assuming that changes in the real exchange rate are relatively small, this equation implies that when the domestic rate of inflation exceeds the foreign rate of inflation, the nominal exchange rate will increase/decrease and the U.S. dollar will appreciate/depreciate. Conversely, when inflation is higher abroad, the nominal exchange rate tends to increase/decrease and the U.S. dollar appreciate/depreciate.

b. Suppose that two countries, Poland and the United States, produce only one commodity, high-quality vodka. Suppose that the Polish vodka sells in Poland for 100 zlotys per liter while the U.S. vodka sells in the United States for $20 per liter. If both countries trade on the world market and the vodkas are comparable, then their world prices must be comparable. In the United States, for example, Polish vodka must sell for $\underline{\hspace{4cm}}$ per liter, while U.S. vodka must sell for $\underline{\hspace{4cm}}$ zlotys per liter in Poland. Consequently, for each country to continue producing vodka in the long run, the exchange rate must equal $\underline{\hspace{4cm}}$ zlotys per dollar. This illustrates the concept of purchasing-power parity, which states that a dollar (or any other currency) must have the same purchasing power in every country. In this example, purchasing power is defined in terms of buying a liter of vodka. Many economists believe that purchasing-power parity is a reasonable approximation of the real-world movements in exchange rates, especially in the long run.

c. Now suppose that the U.S. money supply doubles, leading to a doubling of the U.S. price level. Consequently, a liter of vodka will now sell for $\underline{\hspace{4cm}}$ in the United States. In Poland, on the other hand, the price level remains constant so that the price of vodka remains equal to $\underline{\hspace{4cm}}$ zlotys. For trade to persist in the long run between the two countries, the foreign exchange rate must rise/fall to $\underline{\hspace{4cm}}$ zlotys per dollar.

d. Let's start over and now assume that the Polish price level doubles while U.S. prices remain constant. Consequently, a liter of vodka will sell for $20 per liter in the United States and _____ zlotys per liter in Poland. For trade to persist in the long run between the two countries, the foreign exchange rate must increase/decrease to _____ zlotys per dollar.

e. Use the data from Parts b–d to complete Table 5-7.

Table 5-7

(1) Long-Run Nominal Foreign Exchange Rate (zlotys per dollar)	(2) U.S. Price Level	(3) Polish Price Level	(4) Long-Run Real Foreign Exchange Rate
_____	20	100	_____
_____	40	100	_____
_____	20	200	_____

Note that purchasing-power parity implies that the real foreign exchange rate is _____. For this to be true, the net export curve must be vertical/horizontal.

f. In the case of purchasing-power parity, ε always equals _____, so the percentage change in ε equals _____, and, from Part a, the % Change in e = _____. Thus, in this special case, all/some/none of the changes in the nominal exchange rate will reflect international differences in inflation rates.

8. Net Capital Outflow in a Large Open Economy *In this exercise, we examine the determinants of net capital outflow in a large open economy using the model presented in the appendix to Chapter 5 of the textbook.*

Ⓐ

a. In a large open economy like the United States, the world real interest rate will change in response to that country's domestic policies. This occurs because the large country is borrowing more than just a tiny portion of world saving, so changes in U.S. saving will have a significant effect on the international capital market. In addition, foreigners may not be willing to lend to us in unlimited amounts because of capital immobility, and the U.S. interest rate may differ from interest rates abroad. As the U.S. real interest rate rises (relative to interest rates abroad), U.S. investors will want to lend more/less domestically and more/less abroad. Similarly, foreigners will want to lend more/less to the United States and more/less to borrowers in their own countries. Recall that net capital outflow $S - I$ represents the amount U.S. investors lend abroad minus the amount foreigners lend to us. Consequently, as the U.S. interest rate rises, net capital outflow will rise/fall.

b. Alternatively, U.S. net capital outflow also reflects U.S. purchases of foreign assets, including bonds, minus foreign purchases of U.S. assets. As the U.S. interest rate rises, U.S. residents will want to purchase more/fewer foreign bonds and foreigners will want to purchase more/fewer U.S. bonds. Consequently, as U.S. interest rates rise, net capital outflow will rise/fall.

9. **Equilibrium in a Large Open Economy** *In this exercise, we illustrate the equilibrium*
A *conditions for a large open economy.*

Suppose that the economy is initially described by the following equations:

$$I_1 = 200 - 10r \qquad \textbf{(5-13)}$$
$$S_1 = 150 \qquad \textbf{(5-14)}$$
$$CF_1 = 100 - 5r. \qquad \textbf{(5-15)}$$

a. Equation 5-15 represents the fact that as the domestic real interest rate in a large open economy rises, net capital outflow will rise/fall. To draw this curve, it is helpful to rewrite Equation 5-15 with r on the left-hand side:

$$r = \underline{\hspace{1.5cm}} - \underline{\hspace{1.5cm}} \, CF_1.$$

Now draw this net capital outflow curve on Graph 5-5 and label it *CF*.

Graph 5-5

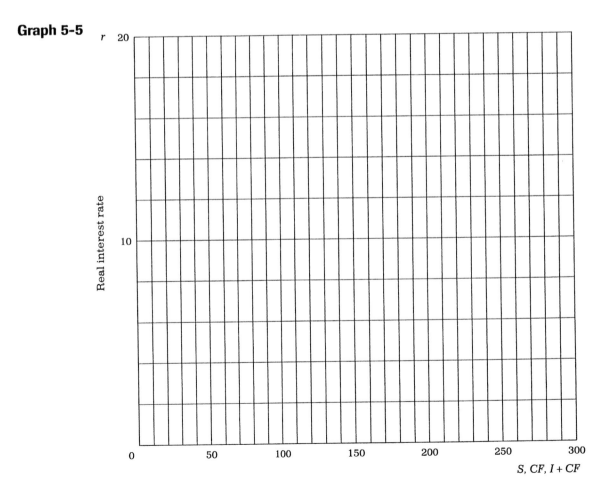

r

Real interest rate

20

10

0   50   100   150   200   250   300

S, CF, I + CF

b. Recall that net capital outflow $CF = S - I$. Adding I to both sides of this equation and rearranging yields

$$S = I + CF. \tag{5-16}$$

We write Equation 5-16 this way because both I and CF respond to changes in r, whereas S does not. Draw the S curve on Graph 5-5 and label it S. Since saving is independent of the real interest rate, the S curve is vertical/negatively sloped.

c. Now add Equations 5-13 and 5-15 together to derive the equation for $I + CF$:

$$I + CF = \underline{\hspace{1.5cm}} - \underline{\hspace{1.5cm}} r. \tag{5-17}$$

Rewriting Equation 5-17 with r on the left-hand side yields

$$r = \underline{\hspace{1.5cm}} - \underline{\hspace{1.5cm}} (I + CF).$$

Draw this curve on Graph 5-5 and label it $I + CF$. Note that the $I + CF$ curve is flatter/steeper than either the I or CF curve because as the interest rate rises both I and CF will fall. Locate the initial equilibrium point at which $S = I + CF$ and label it Point A.

d. At Point A, $S = \underline{\hspace{1.5cm}}$ and $I + CF = \underline{\hspace{1.5cm}}$. Substitute this value into Equation 5-17 and solve for the equilibrium real interest rate:

$$r = \underline{\hspace{4cm}}.$$ Now substitute this value of r into Equations 5-13 and 5-15 to obtain the equilibrium levels of I and CF:

$$I = \underline{\hspace{1.5cm}} \text{ and } CF = \underline{\hspace{1.5cm}}.$$

e. Since we also know that net capital outflow $S - I$ must equal the trade surplus NX, net exports must equal $\underline{\hspace{4cm}}$.

10. **Policy Changes in a Large Open Economy** *In this exercise, we use the model pre-sented in the preceding question to examine the effects of policy changes in a large open economy.*

A

a. Let us now use the model presented in Exercise 9 to examine the effects of various policy changes. The three equations in that model are

$$I_1 = 200 - 10r \qquad \text{(5-18)}$$
$$S_1 = 150 \qquad \text{(5-19)}$$
$$CF_1 = 100 - 5r. \qquad \text{(5-20)}$$

Following the presentation in the textbook, draw the vertical S curve in Panel A of Graph 5-6 and label it S_1. Now draw the CF curve in Panel B of Graph 5-6 and label it CF. Finally, add Equations 5-18 and 5-20, derive the equation for the $I + CF$ curve, draw it in Panel A of Graph 5-6, and label it $I + CF$.

Graph 5-6

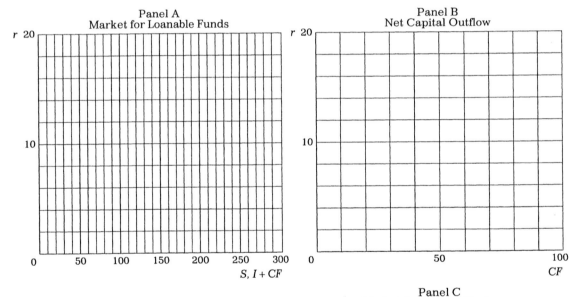

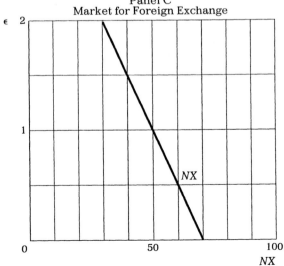

b. At the initial equilibrium, $S =$ _____, $I + CF =$ _____, $r =$ _____, and $CF =$ _____.

c. Recall that net capital outflow is assumed to be independent of the real exchange rate, whereas the trade surplus (net exports) will fall as the real exchange rate rises, as depicted in Panel C of Graph 5-6. Draw the equilibrium level of net capital outflow as a vertical line in Panel C and label it CF ($r = r_1$). Since net capital outflow must equal the trade surplus, locate the original equilibrium in Panel C and label it Point A. From the graph, note that the original equilibrium value of the real exchange rate is _____.

d. Suppose domestic government purchases rise by 30. As in earlier exercises, national saving <u>rises/falls</u> by _____ to _____, which shifts the S curve to the <u>left/right</u> by _____. Draw the new S_2 curve in Panel A of Graph 5-6 and label the new equilibrium at which $S_2 = I + CF$ Point B.

e. Since $S_2 = I + CF$, use the equations for $I + CF$, I, and CF to solve for the new levels of the equilibrium interest rate, investment, and net capital outflow:

$r =$ _____; $I =$ _____; $CF =$ _____. Locate the new value of CF in Panel B of Graph 5-6 and also label it Point B.

f. Now draw the final level of net capital outflow as a vertical line in Panel C and label it CF ($r = r_2$). Label the new equilibrium Point B. As a result of the increase in government purchases, the real exchange rate <u>rises/falls</u> to

_____.

g. In this exercise, we found that an increase in government purchases by a large open economy will <u>increase/decrease</u> national saving, <u>increase/decrease</u> the domestic real interest rate, <u>increase/decrease</u> investment, and <u>increase/decrease</u> net capital outflow. Consequently, the trade surplus NX must <u>increase/decrease</u>. For this to happen, the real exchange rate ε must <u>increase/decrease</u>.

h. If, on the other hand, an investment tax credit were enacted that increased investment at any real interest rate, the $I + CF$ curve would <u>shift right/shift left/not shift</u>, whereas the S curve would <u>shift right/shift left/not shift</u>. Consequently, the domestic real interest rate would <u>rise/fall</u>. This would <u>increase/decrease</u> net capital outflow and the trade surplus, and, consequently, the real exchange rate would <u>rise/fall</u>.

Problems

Answer the following problems on a separate sheet of paper.

1. **a.** The saving rate in the United States is low compared with many of the countries with which the United States trades. If the United States were a closed economy, how would this affect U.S. investment relative to investment in our trading partners? Explain why.

   b. The United States, of course, is not a closed economy. Consequently, our low saving rate has resulted in national saving being substantially less than investment. What effects has this had on net capital outflow and the U.S. trade balance?

2. **a.** During the 1980s, the United States cut tax rates and increased defense spending, resulting in record budget deficits. State and explain what the effects were on:

   i. the levels of investment in Europe and Japan.

   ii. European and Japanese net capital outflow.

   iii. the European and Japanese trade balances.

   iv. the European and Japanese real exchange rates.

   b. During the same period, Belgium also experienced very high budget deficits. What were the effects of the Belgian deficits on:

   i. the levels of investment elsewhere in Europe and Japan?

   ii. net capital outflow elsewhere in Europe and Japan?

   iii. the trade balances elsewhere in Europe and Japan?

   iv. the real exchange rates elsewhere in Europe and Japan?

   c. Explain why your answers to Parts a and b are different.

3. What does purchasing-power parity imply about:

   a. the nominal exchange rate between any two countries?

   b. the real exchange rate between any two countries?

   c. Explain your answers to both Parts a and b.

4. In Problem 9 of Chapter 4 in this workbook, you analyzed Senator Connie Mack's proposal, which involves a reduction in the growth rate of the U.S. money supply. If this proposal were enacted and money growth in the United States fell substantially relative to money growth rates abroad, what would the *long-run* effect be on the:

   a. real U.S. foreign exchange rate? Use the appropriate theory to explain your answer.

   b. nominal U.S. foreign exchange rate? Use the appropriate equations and theories to illustrate and explain your answer.

5. Imagine that you are the chairman of the Federal Reserve. Assume, further, that the money supply has been growing at 3 percent per year. You have been called before Congress to testify about the long-run effects of increasing the growth of the money supply to 10 percent per year. State and then *explain* the long-run effects of this change on each of the following (give numerical estimates when possible):

   a. the annual rate of inflation

   b. the real interest rate

   c. the nominal interest rate

   d. the real exchange rate

   e. the nominal exchange rate

   f. investment (ignore both taxes and uncertainty)

   g. real GDP

6. Suppose the price of a Big Mac hamburger is $2.42 in the United States and 9.90 yuan in China. Furthermore, suppose the nominal foreign exchange rate is 8.28 yuan per dollar.

   a. Calculate the real exchange rate.

   b. If the nominal prices of Big Macs remain unchanged in both countries, what would the purchasing-power parity theory predict would eventually be:

      i. the real exchange rate. Explain.

      ii. the nominal exchange rate.

7. a. Many people think that the reunification of Germany created substantial investment opportunities in what was formerly East Germany. If this is true, what would the effects be on German net capital outflow, the German trade balance, and the German foreign exchange rate?

   b. At the same time, Germany had to increase its government spending dramatically to pay for the costs of reunification. How did this development affect your answers to Part a?

8. At the beginning of his presidency in 1993, President Clinton proposed tax increases and cuts in government spending in order to reduce the budget deficit. Throughout this problem assume (incorrectly) that the tax increases were equal to the cuts in government spending.

   a. Explain the long-run impact of this program on private saving, public saving, and national saving.

   b. Suppose the United States were a closed economy. Use the I, S diagram to illustrate what the long-run impact of this program would be on national saving, investment, and the real interest rate.

   c. Obviously, the United States is not a closed economy. Furthermore, the United States has a trade deficit (and negative net capital outflow). In 1993, the world real interest rate was about 4 percent. Illustrate this initial situation graphically using the I, S diagram.

   d. Treating the United States as a small open economy, use your graph from Part b to illustrate the long-run impact of these tax increases and (equal) cuts in government spending on national saving, investment, the real interest rate, and the trade deficit.

   e. On the appropriate graph, illustrate the effect of this program on the U.S. real exchange rate and net exports if the United States were a small open economy.

9. What does economic theory suggest is the long-run relationship between changes in a country's level of saving and its level of investment? Explain how your answer depends upon whether the country is a closed economy, a small open economy, or a large open economy.

10. Early in the 1996 Presidential campaign, Bob Dole promised to cut both taxes and government spending if elected. Furthermore, he promised to cut government spending by more than his proposed cut in taxes in order to eliminate the federal budget deficit.

    a. What would the long-run effect of Dole's plan be on public saving, private saving, and national saving?

    b. Assume the United States is a closed economy. Use a graph to compare the effects of Dole's plan on investment and the real interest rate.

    c. Obviously, the United States is not a closed economy. Furthermore, the United States has a trade deficit (and negative net capital outflow). In 1996, the world real interest rate was about 3.5 percent. Illustrate this initial situation graphically using the I, S diagram.

    d. Treating the United States as a small open economy, redraw your graph from Part c and illustrate the long-run impact of Dole's plan on national saving, investment, and the real interest rate. Consequently, what happens to $S - I$?

    e. On the appropriate graph, illustrate the effect of this program on the U.S. real exchange rate and net exports if the United States were a small open economy.

11. In 1995, both the Republicans and Democrats in Congress proposed budget changes
    that would balance the federal budget (i.e., *eliminate the existing budget deficit
    entirely*) within 10 years. There were, however, important differences between the
    two plans. The Republicans proposed cutting personal (income) taxes and dramati-
    cally reducing government expenditures (by much more than the cut in taxes).
    Democrats initially proposed smaller cuts in government expenditures and practi-
    cally no tax cuts. For the purposes of this problem, assume that both plans would
    eliminate the deficit by the same amount (i.e., entirely) at the same time.

    a. In the absence of these plans, budget deficits were projected to rise sub-
       stantially. Relative to these projections, compare the long-run effect of *each*
       of the two plans on public saving, private saving, and national saving.
       Distinguish between (and explain) the effects of each plan when they differ,
       even if the difference is in size rather than direction.

    b. Assume the United States is a closed economy. Use a graph to compare the
       effects of each of the two plans on investment and the real interest rate. Label
       the 1995 curves with the subscript C, the Democratic curves with the subscript D,
       and the Republican curves with the subscript R.

    c. Obviously, the United States is not a closed economy. Furthermore, the United
       States had a trade deficit (and negative net capital outflow). In 1995, the world
       real interest rate was about 3.5 percent. Illustrate this initial situation graphical-
       ly using the *I,S* diagram.

    d. Treating the United States as a small open economy, redraw your graph from
       Part c and illustrate the long-run impact of *both* the Democratic and Republican
       plans on national saving, investment, and the real interest rate. (As before, label
       the 1995 curves C, the Democratic curves D, and the Republican curves R.)

    e. On the appropriate graph, illustrate the effect of these two programs on the
       U.S. real exchange rate and net exports if the United States were a small open
       economy.

12. Consider the *small open economy* of Chile. Assume Chile has a trade surplus and
    the real world interest rate is 3 percent.

    a. Indicate this initial situation on an appropriately labled *I,S* graph and then on an
       appropriately labeled *(S-I), NX* graph.

    Now suppose foreigners develop a craving for Chilean wines. Consequently, the
    demand for Chilean exports increases.

    b. On the same graph you drew for Part a, illustrate the effect of this change in
       tastes on Chile's *NX* curve and its real exchange rate. As a result, what happens
       to Chile's trade surplus?

    c. In order to assist its other industries, the Chilean government wants to adjust
       taxes in order to maintain the real exchange rate at its initial level.

       i. In which direction should it change taxes? (First read Part (ii) below.)

       ii. Use a second set of graphs for a small open economy to illustrate *and state*
           the effects on the amounts of saving, investment, net exports, and the real
           interest rate if foreigners develop a craving for Chilean wine and the
           Chilean government responds as you indicated in Part (i) to keep the real
           exchange rate unchanged.

13. In his State of the Union Address in January, 2002, President Bush proposed *increasing* government spending for the war on terrorism and additional *decreases* in taxes. The amount of the spending increase was *not* equal to the amount of the tax decrease.

    a. Explain or show (don't just state) what the *exact* long-run impact of this program would be on:

        i. real GDP

        ii. public saving

        iii. private saving

        iv. national saving

    b. Treating the United States as a small open economy with an initial trade deficit, illustrate *and state* the long-run impact of these tax cuts and increases in government spending on national saving, investment, and the real interest rate.

    c. On the appropriate graph, illustrate *and state* the effects of this program on the United States real exchange rate and net exports if the United States were a small open economy.

    d. Obviously, the United States is a large open economy. Use the appropriate
    🅰 graphs to illustrate *and state* how President Bush's proposals to increase government spending and reduce taxes would affect national saving, investment, the domestic real interest rate, net capital outflow, net exports, and the real exchange rate.

14. Assume the United States is a large open economy. Use the appropriate graphs to
🅰 show how President Clinton's 1993 proposals to increase taxes and reduce government spending would have affected national saving, investment, the real interest rate, net capital outflow, net exports, and the real exchange rate. Assume (again, incorrectly) that the tax increases were equal to the cuts in government spending.

15. Assume the United States is a large open economy. Show how Bob Dole's 1996
🅰 promise to reduce taxes and government spending and eliminate the budget deficit
🅾 would affect national saving, investment, the real interest rate, net capital outflow, net exports, and the real exchange rate.

16. Some economists believe that United States businesses will discover that the marginal product of capital that uses the latest technologies is lower than they had hoped. As a result, investment demand may decline. The United States is a large open economy with a trade deficit. Use the appropriate graphs for a large open economy to illustrate *and state* the effects of a decline in investment demand on each of the following: the domestic real interest rate, national saving, the amount of investment, net capital outflow, the real exchange rate, and net exports.

Data Questions

Locate the necessary economic data and apply them to answer the following data questions. All of the relevant data may be found in the Economic Report of the President.

1. **a.** Obtain the appropriate data for the United States and complete Table 5-8.

Table 5-8

(1) Year	(2) Nominal GDP ($ in billions)	(3) Exports of Goods and Services ($ in billions)	(4) Exports as a % of Nominal GDP	(5) Imports of Goods and Services ($ in billions)	(6) Imports as a % of Nominal GDP
1970	————	————	————	————	————
1985	————	————	————	————	————
2000	————	————	————	————	————

  b. From Table 5-8, it is clear that U.S. foreign trade has increased/decreased relative to GDP during the past 30 years. Consequently, the U.S. economy has become a more/less open economy during this period.

  c. Use the data from Table 5-8 to complete Table 5-9.

Table 5-9

(1) Year	(2) Net Exports of Goods and Services ($ in billions)	(3) Net Exports as a % of Nominal GDP
1970	————	————
1985	————	————
2000	————	————

  d. In 1970, the United States had a trade surplus of $_____ billion. Ignoring official reserve transactions, which measure the purchase and sale of foreign currency by the central bank, this implies that net capital outflow in 1970 was $_____ billion.

  e. In 2000, the United States had a trade surplus of $_____ billion. Ignoring official reserve transactions, this implies that net capital outflow in 2000 was $_____ billion.

2.   **a.** Foreign exchange rate data and consumer price data for several foreign countries appear at the back of the *Economic Report of the President*. Use these data to complete Table 5-10.

Table 5-10

(1) Year	(2) U.S. CPI (1982–1984 = 100)	(3) Italian CPI (1982–1984 = 100)	(4) Italian Lire per U.S. Dollar
1986	——	——	——
1995	——	——	——

   b. Between 1986 and 1995, the number of Italian lire per U.S. dollar <u>increased/ decreased</u>. This implies that the nominal foreign exchange rate of the dollar <u>rose/fell</u> and the dollar <u>appreciated/depreciated</u> relative to the lire.

   c. Now assume that the real foreign exchange rate of the dollar was 1.0 in 1986. Since the nominal exchange rate was _____ lire per dollar, this implies that a typical item that cost \$1 in the United States cost _____ lire in Italy. Since $\epsilon = e(P/P^*) = 1$, this implies that the relative price ratio P/P^* was equal to _____ in 1986.

   d. According to the CPI data for each country in Table 5-10, an item that cost \$1 in the United States in 1986 cost \$_____ in 1995, and an item that cost 1,491.16 lire in Italy in 1986 cost _____ lire in 1995.

   e. Use the data from Table 5-10 and Parts a–d to calculate the real foreign exchange rate of the dollar relative to the lire in 1995.

   f. Consequently, the real foreign exchange rate of the dollar relative to the lire <u>rose/fell</u> between 1986 and 1995. Note how one cannot infer anything about changes in the real exchange rate over time merely by examining changes in the nominal exchange rate.

Unemployment

Fill-in Questions

Use the key terms below to fill in the blanks in the following statements. Each term may be used more than once.

discouraged workers

efficiency wage

frictional unemployment

insiders

labor force

natural rate of unemployment

outsiders

sectoral shift

steady state

structural unemployment

unemployment insurance

unemployment rate

wage rigidity

1. The unemployment rate is calculated as the percentage of the
    _____ that is unemployed.

2. The labor market reaches a(n) _____ when the
    _____ is constant and the flows into and out of unemployment
    are equal. This average rate of unemployment around which the economy fluctu-
    ates is called the _____.

3. One of the causes of _____ is the change in the composition of
    demand among firms, industries, or regions, which economists call a(n)
    _____. One policy that increases _____
    is _____, a government program in which unemployed work-
    ers can collect a fraction of their former wages for a certain period of time after los-
    ing their jobs.

4. _____ occurs when the real wage fails to adjust until labor
    supply equals labor demand. The resulting unemployment is called

    _____.

5. The unemployment caused by unions and by the threat of unionization is an in-
    stance of conflict between two different groups of workers—_____,
    such as senior union members, and _____, such as unemployed work-
    ers who would like a job in the unionized industry.

6. _____ theories, another cause of _____,
suggest that high wages make workers more productive.

7. The official number of unemployed may underestimate the number of people
who would like to work because it does not include those individuals, called
_____, who may want a job but who, after an unsuccessful
search, have given up looking.

Multiple-Choice Questions

1. Zero percent unemployment is an unrealistic and perhaps undesirable policy goal
for all of the following reasons EXCEPT:
   a. it takes time to match jobs and workers.
   b. it would be inhumane to force the elderly to work.
   c. minimum wage laws restrict employment opportunities.
   d. some of the unemployed are unwilling to work at jobs that are available to them.

2. The main determinant of the natural rate of unemployment is the:
   a. rate of job separation and job finding.
   b. average period of unemployment.
   c. size of the labor force.
   d. quit rate.

3. Let L equal the size of the labor force, E the number of employed workers, and U the
number of unemployed workers. The unemployment rate is equal to:
   a. $(L - E)/L$.
   c. $1 - (E/L)$.
   b. U/L.
   d. all of the above.

4. Let s denote the rate of job separation and f the rate of job finding. If the labor market is in a steady state, the natural rate of unemployment is equal to:
   a. $1/s$.
   c. $s/(s + f)$.
   b. $1/(s + f)$.
   d. $f/(s + f)$.

5. A government policy that will increase frictional unemployment is a(n):
   a. extension of job training programs.
   b. increase in unemployment insurance benefits.
   c. reduction in the minimum wage.
   d. dissemination of information about job vacancies.

6. Frictional unemployment occurs in each of the following cases EXCEPT when:
   a. there is a sectoral shift in the economy.
   b. certain firms go bankrupt.
   c. workers quit their current jobs to look for new ones in a different occupation.
   d. workers quit their current jobs and stop looking for work altogether.

7. Structural unemployment occurs when:

   a. wages are perfectly flexible.

   b. jobs are rationed.

   c. labor demand exceeds labor supply at the going wage.

   d. the labor market is perfectly competitive.

8. Economists believe that wage rigidity can be caused by:

   a. unions.

   b. minimum wage laws.

   c. efficiency wages.

   d. all of the above.

9. According to various efficiency wage theories, higher wages make workers more productive for all of the following reasons EXCEPT higher wages:

   a. allow workers to afford more nutritious diets.

   b. attract higher-quality workers.

   c. may improve worker effort by increasing the cost of losing one's job.

   d. move people into higher tax brackets, so they have to work harder to have the same after-tax income.

10. The FALSE statement about unemployment is:

   a. most people who become unemployed are unemployed for fewer than six weeks.

   b. most of the total *weeks* of unemployment are experienced by people who will be unemployed for more than two months.

   c. teenagers and black adults tend to have higher unemployment rates than white adults.

   d. adult women today have significantly higher unemployment rates than adult men.

Exercises

1. **Labor-Force Movements and the Natural Rate of Unemployment** *In this exercise, we examine labor-force movements when the economy has reached its natural rate of unemployment.*

   a. The natural rate of unemployment is also the steady-state unemployment rate, the unemployment rate toward which the economy moves. Once the economy reaches this steady state, the unemployment rate tends to remain the same. Now consider the following example: Suppose that there are 2,300 employed people in the economy and 200 unemployed people. Suppose, further, that 23 percent, or 0.23, of the unemployed find jobs each month and that 2 percent, or 0.02, of the employed lose their jobs each month.

      i. During the next month, 23 percent of the 200 currently unemployed people, or $0.23 \times 200 =$ _____ people, will find a job.

      ii. During the next month, 2 percent of the 2,300 people now employed, or $0.02 \times 2,300 =$ _____ people, will lose their jobs and become unemployed.

iii. Consequently, at the beginning of the next month, the total number of unemployed people U will equal 200 − _____ + _____ = _____, and the total number of employed people E will equal 2,300 + _____ − _____ = _____.

iv. Why is this situation an example of a steady-state unemployment rate?

b. Calculate the unemployment rate u in Part a. (Remember that the unemployment rate u expressed as a percent is equal to 100 multiplied by the number of unemployed people U divided by the labor force L or $100 \times U/L$.)

c. The number of people moving out of unemployment, fU, mus t equal the number of people moving into unemployment, sE, at the steady state. Since employment $E = L - U$:

$$fU = sE = s(L - U) \text{ or} \tag{6-1}$$

$$fU = sL - sU. \tag{6-2}$$

Bringing all terms involving U to the left-hand side of Equation 5-2 yields:

$$(s + f)U = sL. \tag{6-3}$$

Dividing both sides of Equation 6-3 by $(s + f)L$ yields the formula for the steady-state unemployment rate:

$$\frac{U}{L} = \frac{s}{(s + f)}. \tag{6-4}$$

Perform the necessary calculations to show that the steady-state unemployment rate derived using this formula (which is the same equation used in the textbook) is identical to the unemployment rate you calculated in Part a.

2. **The Transition to a New Natural Rate of Unemployment** *In this exercise, we examine the transition to a new natural rate of unemployment when the rates of job finding and job separation change.*

a. We use the same numbers as in Exercise 1: there are 2,300 employed people and 200 unemployed people. Suppose that the government now increases the amount of unemployment benefits paid to unemployment insurance recipients. As the textbook suggests, an increase in unemployment insurance tends to decrease the probability of the unemployed finding a job and to increase the probability of job separation. Suppose that the rate of job finding falls to 20 percent per month, while the rate of job separation rises to 3 percent per month.

i. Use calculations similar to the ones you performed in Exercise 1a to calculate how many of the 200 currently unemployed people will find a job during the first month following the change in unemployment benefits.

ii. How many of the 2,300 people now employed will lose their jobs and become unemployed during the month?

iii. Consequently, at the beginning of the next month, the total number of unemployed U will equal _____, and the total number of employed E will equal _____.

iv. The unemployment rate at the beginning of the next month will equal $u = (U/L) \times 100 = $ _____ percent.

b. Suppose that the rates of job finding and job separation remain equal to 20 percent and 3 percent, respectively.

i. During the second month following the change in unemployment benefits, how many unemployed people will find a job? (Use your answer from Exercise 2a(iii) as the initial number of unemployed and round off your answer to the nearest whole person.)

ii. How many employed people will lose their jobs and become unemployed during the second month? (Again, use your answer from Exercise 2a(iii) as the initial number of employed and round off to the nearest whole person.)

iii. Consequently, at the beginning of the third month, the total number of un-employed people U will equal _____ – _____ + _____ = _____, and the total number of employed people E will equal _____ + _____ – _____ = _____.

iv. The unemployment rate at the beginning of the third month will equal $u =$ $(U/L) \times 100 =$ _____ percent.

c. Use the formula $u = U/L = s/(s + f)$ to calculate the new steady-state natural rate of unemployment.

3. **Demographics and the Natural Rate of Unemployment** *In this exercise, we explore how a change in demographics can affect the natural rate of unemployment.*

It appears that the natural rate of unemployment rose from about 4 percent in the 1950s to 5–6 percent in the 1970s. Many economists cited the influx of women and teenagers into the labor force as one reason for this increase. In this exercise, we see how a change in the demographic composition of the labor force can affect the aggregate unemployment rate even if the unemployment rates for each demographic group remain constant.

a. The data in Table 6-1 depict a hypothetical economy that resembles in some important ways the experience of the United States between the 1950s and the 1970s. In Column 1, we see that the total labor force in the 1950s was 90 million, of which one-third, or 30 million, were female and two-thirds, or 60 million, were male. In the 1950s, 3 million women and 1.5 million men were unemployed, for a total number of unemployed of 4.5 million. Recalling that the unemployment rate u is equal to the number of unemployed U divided by the labor force L, the unemployment rate among women in the 1950s was 3/30 = 10 percent. Use a similar calculation to complete the second and third lines of Column 3.

Table 6-1

	(1) Labor Force (in millions)	(2) Number of Unemployed (in millions)	(3) Unemployment Rate ($u = U/L$)
1950s			
Female	30	3.0	$u = U/L = 3/30 = 10\%$
Male	60	1.5	$u =$ _____
Total	90	4.5	$u =$ _____
1970s			
Female	40	4.0	$u =$ _____
Male	60	1.5	$u =$ _____
Total	100	5.5	$u =$ _____

b. Note from the data in Table 6-1 that the unemployment rate for women was much higher than the unemployment rate for men. List several possible reasons for this situation.

c. By the 1970s, the total labor force in this economy had grown to 100 million because of a sharp increase in the number of women who wanted to work. At the same time, the number of unemployed had also increased, again solely among women. Now complete the remainder of Column 3 in Table 6-1.

d. What happened to the unemployment rates for females and males between the 1950s and the 1970s?

e. What happened to the total unemployment rate between the 1950s and the 1970s?

f. Explain how the total unemployment rate can change even while the unemployment rate for each group remains constant.

g. The U.S. economy is similar to our hypothetical economy in that the unemployment rate rose between the 1950s and the 1970s along with female labor-force participation. In addition, the unemployment rate for females was generally higher than the unemployment rate for males throughout most of this period. However, the difference between male and female unemployment rates largely disappeared in the 1980s. Some economists cite an increasing attachment to the labor force on the part of women, which would decrease the female unemployment rate. Others point to a decline in stable, high-paying, blue-collar manufacturing jobs that were typically held by men, which would increase the male unemployment rate. Consequently, the sharp rise in unemployment during the early 1980s <u>can/cannot</u> be attributed to the continuing increase in female labor-force participation.

h. In the 1990s, a similar phenomenon contributed to a significant reduction in the unemployment rate. Middle-age workers have lower unemployment rates than younger workers, in part because they are more committed to their jobs. As the baby-boom generation moved into their middle ages during the 1990s, middle-age workers became a greater portion of the labor force, just as women did after 1950. If we substitute "middle-age workers" and "younger workers" for "male" and "female" workers in Table 6-1, we find that the increase in the share of middle-age workers in the 1990s would increase/decrease the overall unemployment rate even if the unemployment rates of middle-age and younger workers, respectively, remained constant.

Problems

Answer the following problems on a separate sheet of paper.

1. a. In which two ways does unemployment insurance affect the natural rate of unemployment? Explain how each way changes the rate of unemployment.

   b. Despite its impact on the unemployment rate, the unemployment insurance program does have some beneficial effects.

      i. In which ways is the program perceived to increase overall equity (fairness)?

      ii. In which ways might the program increase overall efficiency (that is, increase real GDP)?

2. a. Explain how the elasticity of demand for low-wage workers determines the change in total wage income accruing to those workers following an increase in the minimum wage.

   b. Would policymakers be more or less likely to support higher minimum wages if economists found that the demand for low-wage workers was very inelastic? Explain.

   c. In 1991, Congress passed a subminimum wage proposal whereby young workers could be paid less than the adult minimum wage for a limited period of time. **CH** Give reasons why minimum wage laws are thought to be more onerous and less essential for teenagers than for adults.

   d. Several economists and politicians have argued that subminimum wage laws for teenagers might reduce total adult employment.

      i. Explain why these economists take this position.

      ii. Why would the effect of subminimum wage laws for teenagers and adult unemployment depend on whether adults and teenagers are substitutes or complements in production?

3. During the 1950s and 1960s, most of the countries in Western Europe maintained very low rates of unemployment. In comparing the labor markets of North America and Western Europe, several economists discovered that there was considerably less mobility from employment to unemployment in Western Europe. This situation was partially the result of numerous laws in Western Europe that restricted companies' ability to lay off workers quickly.

   a. In Chapter 6 of the textbook, it was stated that the probability of job finding each month was 0.20, or 20 percent, and the probability of job separation was 0.01, or 1 percent. Suppose that these probabilities in Western Europe during the 1960s were 23.4 percent and 0.6 percent, respectively. Calculate the Western European natural rate of unemployment in the 1960s and compare it to the U.S. natural rate calculated in the textbook.

   b. Starting in the 1970s, several changes in Western Europe altered the rates of job finding and job separation considerably, and critics claimed that these countries suffered from a "disease" they called "Eurosclerosis." Calculate the new natural rate of unemployment in Europe if the probability of job finding decreases to 9.2 percent while the probability of job separation rises to 0.8 percent. (Note that the latter is still less than that in the United States.)

4. a. Differentiate the equation for the natural rate of unemployment with respect to f. Then show how an increase in f will affect that rate. Explain your answer.

   b. Now differentiate the equation for the natural rate of unemployment with respect to s. Then show how an increase in s will affect that rate. Explain your answer.

5. While it is very difficult to measure the natural rate of unemployment, the U.S. government publishes exact data every month on the overall rate of unemployment. Why do we care about the natural rate of unemployment if we have a much more precise estimate of the overall rate of unemployment?

6. As Chapter 6 of the textbook illustrates, the average unemployment rate in the United States increased from the 1950s through the mid-1980s. At the same time, however, the *employment/population ratio* continued to grow and reached an all-time high of 64.5 percent in 2000. The employment/population ratio is defined as the ratio of total employment to total population, expressed as a percentage, or $(E/P) \times 100$.

   a. Show the algebraic relationship among the employment/population ratio, the labor-force participation rate L/P, and the employment rate. The employment rate is equal to E/L, or 1 minus the unemployment rate u.

   b. Some economists believe that the employment/population ratio is a better measure of the economy's health than the unemployment rate. Give some reasons for supporting this position.

   c. On the other hand, many economists still believe that the unemployment rate is a better measure of the economy's health than the employment/population ratio. Give some reasons for supporting this position.

7. The strength of organized labor (unions) in the United States is declining. The percentage of the labor force that is unionized has fallen below 20 percent. Since wages for a large majority of workers are determined in competitive, nonunion markets, how can it still be said that unions increase the natural rate of unemployment?

Data Questions

Locate the necessary economic data and apply them to answer the following data questions. All of the relevant data may be found in the Economic Report of the President.

1. **a.** Using the appropriate data, complete Table 6-2.

Table 6-2

| (1) | Labor-Force Participation Rates (in percent) | | |
| | (2) | (3) | (4) |
Year	Male and Female Civilians	Civilian Males	Civilian Females
1970	———	———	———
1980	———	———	———
1990	———	———	———
2000	———	———	———

b. How can the changes in Columns 3 and 4 during the past 30 years be explained?

c. As more women enter the labor force, the amount of household production formerly performed by housewives falls slightly. Recalling from Chapter 2 the way in which household production is treated in the national income accounts, what does this fall in household production suggest about the relationship between real GDP growth from 1970 to 2000 and the actual increase in total production? Explain your answer.

7. A(n) _____ exists when capital accumulation by one firm results in technological advances that other firms can freely use to benefit themselves and society.

8. According to _____, the rate of technological progress is not exogenous. Many of its adherents believe that the economy can exhibit constant returns to capital, as long as capital is broadly defined to include knowledge.

Multiple-Choice Questions

1. The Solow growth model predicts that countries with higher population growth rates will have:
   a. lower steady-state levels of output per worker.
   b. lower steady-state growth rates of output per worker.
   c. both a and b.
   d. higher steady-state growth rates of output per worker.

2. In the Solow growth model with population growth n and labor-augmenting technological progress g, the change in capital per effective worker is equal to:
   a. $sf(k) + (\delta + n + g)k$.
   b. $sf(k) + (\delta - n - g)k$.
   c. $sf(k) - (\delta + n + g)k$.
   d. $sf(k) - (\delta - n - g)k$.

3. In the Solow growth model with population growth and technological progress, the steady-state growth rate in output per *effective* worker is equal to:
   a. zero.
   b. the rate of technological progress g.
   c. the growth rate of population n plus the rate of technological progress g.
   d. the saving rate s.

4. In the Solow growth model with population growth and technological progress, the steady-state growth rate in output per worker is equal to:
   a. zero.
   b. the rate of technological progress g.
   c. the growth rate of population n plus the rate of technological progress g.
   d. the saving rate s.

5. In the Solow growth model, persistent increases in standards of living are due to:

    a. technological progress, which leads to sustained growth in output per worker.
    b. a high saving rate, which leads to sustained high rates of growth.
    c. a high rate of population growth, which leads to a larger labor force.
    d. all of the above.

6. The capital stock in the U.S. economy is well below the Golden Rule level because the net marginal product of capital, $MPK - \delta$, is:

    a. greater than the long-run growth rate of real GNP.
    b. greater than the sum of the long-run rates of population growth and technological progress.
    c. both a and b.
    d. none of the above.

7. If the capital stock in a country is initially below the Golden Rule level of capital, the country can move toward the Golden Rule steady state by:

    a. increasing the rate of saving.
    b. reducing government expenditures on noninvestment items.
    c. providing tax incentives that reward new investment.
    d. all of the above.

8. Technological progress is encouraged by:

    a. the patent system.
    b. tax incentives for research and development.
    c. government subsidies for research.
    d. all of the above.

9. The worldwide slowdown in economic growth from the years 1972 to 1995 may be explained by:

    a. the entrance of the "baby boomers" into the workforce, which has lowered the average level of experience.
    b. the depletion of the planet's natural resources.
    c. the decline in oil prices in the 1990s.
    d. all of the above.

10. Since 1995, economic growth rates in most industrialized countries except Germany and Japan:

    a. continued their downward spiral that began in 1972.
    b. have been greater than at any other time since World War II.
    c. rebounded from the slowdown that occurred between 1972 and 1995.
    d. have been close to zero.

11. Evidence concerning convergence among different countries' standards of living indicates that:

    a. unadjusted incomes per capita are not converging.

    b. incomes per capita among countries with similar cultures and policies are converging.

    c. countries with different saving rates, population growth rates, and education levels appear to be converging to different steady states.

    d. all of the above.

12. When the steady state has been reached:

    a. real wages grow at the rate of technological progress.

    b. the real rental cost of capital grows at the rate of technological progress.

    c. the number of effective workers grows at the rate of technological progress.

    d. all of the above.

13. Which of the following reasons would theoretically justify a government technology policy that encouraged investment in certain areas:

    a. a decline in the rate of investment.

    b. the identification and measurement of technological externalities in capital accumulation.

    c. a decline in the real interest rate.

    d. all of the above.

14. In the Solow growth model, the rate of technological progress is:

    a. exogenous.

    b. endogenous.

    c. 3 percent.

    d. 0 percent.

15. Acceptance of endogenous growth theory implies:

    a. additional saving and investment can lead to persistent growth.

    b. capital may not be subject to diminishing returns if knowledge is viewed as a type of capital.

    c. the rate of technical change is endogenous.

    d. all of the above.

16. Empirical research indicates that the social rate of return to investment in research is:

    a. less than the private rate of return to investment in physical capital.

    b. about equal to the private rate of return to investment in physical capital.

    c. greater than the private rate of return to investment in physical capital.

    d. less than the private rate of return to investment in human capital.

17. The Solow residual is:

A a. the change in total factor productivity.

    b. the change in output that cannot be explained by changes in inputs.

    c. an often-used measure of technological progress.

    d. all of the above.

18. Empirical studies indicate that the unusually high growth rates in Hong Kong,

A Singapore, South Korea, and Taiwan from 1966–1990 were due to unusually large increases in all of the following EXCEPT:

    a. labor force participation.   c. total factor productivity.

    b. the capital stock.   d. educational attainment.

Exercises

1. **Technological Progress** *In this exercise, we incorporate technological progress into the Solow growth model.*

    a. Now assume that each worker becomes more productive over time. To do this, we now measure the number of effective workers $L \times E$, where E grows at some constant rate g. Thus,

$$Y = F(K, L \times E) \tag{8-1}$$

    E measures the productive abilities of labor, which depend upon health, experience, and knowledge. Recall from Exercise 5 in Chapter 2 that the percentage change of a product of two variables is approximately equal to the sum of the percentage changes in each of the variables. Thus, if the percentage change (i.e., the growth rate) in L is n and the percentage change (i.e., the growth rate) in E is g, then the percentage change in $L \times E$ (and hence the growth in the number of effective workers) is approximately equal to _____ + _____.

    b. We now analyze the economy in terms of quantities per effective worker. Let $k = K/(L \times E)$ stand for capital per effective worker, and $y = Y/(L \times E)$ represent output per effective worker. Thus, we can again write $y = f(k)$. Note that we can also write k as $k = (K/L)/E$. Suppose the amount of capital per worker K/L (as opposed to capital per effective worker) remains constant over time and the efficiency of labor grows by 1 percent per year. According to the percentage change approximation for a ratio, the percentage change in $k = (K/L)/E$ will then equal

_____ − _____ = _____ . Thus, the amount of capital per effective worker k will fall by about _____ percent per year because the same amount of capital per worker must now be spread over an increasing number of effective workers. If investment per effective worker i is added and it is assumed, as before, that the rate of depreciation $\delta = 0.05$ and the rate of population growth $n = 0.02$, the change in the capital stock per effective worker will now be:

$$\Delta k = i - \delta k - nk - gk = i - 0.05k - 0.02k - 0.01k. \qquad \text{(8-2)}$$

Note in Equation 8-2 that if i, δ, and n all equal 0, k falls by _____ percent per year.

c. Investment per effective worker is assumed to be a constant fraction s of output per worker. Assume that $s = 0.2$. Substituting s into Equation 8-2 yields:

$$\Delta k = sf(k) - \delta k - nk - gk = sf(k) - (\delta + n + g)k = 0.2f(k) - 0.08k. \qquad \text{(8-3)}$$

Assume that $f(k) = (k)^{1/2}$. Use these values for s, δ, and n to complete Table 8-1.

Table 8-1

(1) Capital per Effective Worker k	(2) Output per Effective Worker $f(k) = k^{1/2}$	(3) Investment per Effective Worker $sf(k)$	(4) Break-even Investment per Effective Worker $(\delta + n + g)k$	(5) Change in Capital per Effective Worker $sf(k) - (\delta + n + g)k$
0	_____	_____	_____	_____
4	_____	_____	_____	_____
6	_____	_____	_____	_____
8	_____	_____	_____	_____
16	_____	_____	_____	_____
36	_____	_____	_____	_____

d. Plot and graph Columns 1, 2, and 3 of Table 8-1 on Graph 8-1 and label the curves *f(k)*, *sf(k)*, and (δ + *n* + *g*)*k*, respectively.

Graph 8-1

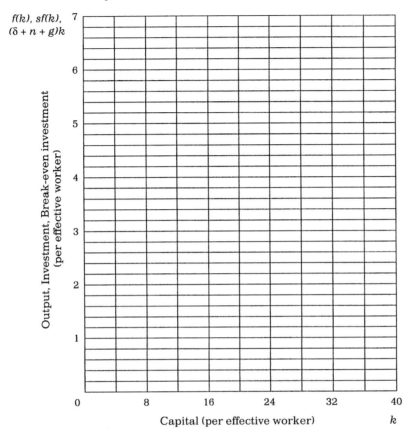

e. In the steady state, the change in the capital stock per effective worker equals
_____. Consequently, rearranging Equation 8-3, in the steady state, *sf(k)*
= _____. Locate the steady-state level of *k** in Graph 8-1, and label it Point
A. Use the preceding values of *s*, δ, *n*, and *g* to calculate *k** to within two decimal
places.

$$k^* = \underline{\hspace{2cm}}.$$

f. In the steady state, capital per effective worker is constant — that is, Δ*k* = 0, and
sf(k) = (δ + *n* + *g*)*k*. Similarly, output per effective worker is constant. Since the
number of effective workers per worker is growing at rate *g*, however, output
per worker will grow at rate _____. Thus, in the Solow growth model,
steady-state growth in output per worker depends solely on the rate of
saving/depreciation/technological change.

g. Since the number of workers is growing at rate n, total output will grow at the rate of _____ + _____ .

h. Technological change also affects the Golden Rule level of capital. In a world with technological progress, population growth, and capital depreciation, the Golden Rule level of capital is defined as the steady-state level of capital per effective worker that maximizes consumption per effective worker. Recall that consumption per effective worker can be computed as:

$$c = y - i \qquad\qquad \text{(8-4)}$$

Output per effective worker is equal to $f(k)$, and, in the steady state $\Delta k = 0$, so $i = sf(k) = (\delta + n + g)k$. Substituting $f(k)$ and $(\delta + n + g)k$ into Equation 8-4 yields:

$$c = f(k) - (\delta + n + g)k \qquad\qquad \text{(8-5)}$$

As in Chapter 7, consumption per effective worker is maximized when the slope of the $f(k)$ curve, which is equal to MPK, is equal to the slope of the $(\delta + n + g)k$ curve, which is equal to _____. Consequently, the Golden Rule level of k^*_{gold} is the level of k at which the following occurs:

$$MPK = \underline{\qquad} + \underline{\qquad} + \underline{\qquad} \qquad\qquad \text{(8-6)}$$

2. Endogenous Growth *In this exercise, we examine a simple one-sector model to illustrate the idea of endogenous growth.*

a. Consider the simple production function:

$$Y = AK \qquad\qquad \text{(8-7)}$$

where Y is total output, K is the total capital stock, and A is a constant. Dividing both sides of Equation 8-7 by K indicates that A is equal to _____, or the amount of output produced for each unit of capital.

b. Recall that the percentage change in the product of two variables is approximately equal to the sum of the percentage changes in each of the variables. Applying this rule to Equation 8-7 yields:

$$\% \text{ Change in } Y = \% \text{ Change in } A + \% \text{ Change in } K. \qquad\qquad \text{(8-8)}$$

Since A is a constant,

$$\% \text{ Change in } Y = \underline{\qquad} . \qquad\qquad \text{(8-9)}$$

Insofar as the percentage change in any variable X is calculated as $\Delta X/X$, we can rewrite Equation 8-9 as:

$$\underline{\qquad} = \underline{\qquad} . \qquad\qquad \text{(8-10)}$$

c. As before, let *s* be the fraction of total income that is saved and invested and let δ be the rate at which capital depreciates. Consequently, the change in the capital stock

$$\Delta K = sY - \delta K \qquad \text{(8-11)}$$

Making this substitution for the numerator of the right-hand side of Equation 8-10 yields:

$$\Delta Y/Y = (sY - \delta K)/K = \underline{\hspace{2cm}} - \underline{\hspace{2cm}}. \qquad \text{(8-12)}$$

d. Recall from rearranging Equation 8-7 that $Y/K = \underline{\hspace{2cm}}$. Making this substitution in Equation 8-12 yields:

$$\Delta Y/Y = sA - \delta. \qquad \text{(8-13)}$$

e. Equation 8-13 can be used to illustrate the idea behind endogenous growth theory. Note that the growth rate of output $\Delta Y/Y$ will be positive, and output will grow indefinitely, as long as $\underline{\hspace{2cm}}$ is greater than $\underline{\hspace{2cm}}$. This occurs because the production function in Equation 8-7 exhibits constant, rather than diminishing, returns to capital. Advocates of endogenous growth theory believe that this assumption is reasonable if the capital stock is interpreted more broadly to include knowledge as a type of capital because knowledge may not be subject to diminishing returns. Consequently, economies that are more successful in producing knowledge may be able to sustain higher rates of economic growth, even in the long run.

3. **Growth Accounting** *In this exercise, we use a Cobb-Douglas production function and*
A *an extension of the percentage change rule that is discussed in Chapter 2 of the text-book to derive the formula for the growth in total factor productivity.*

a. Consider the following Cobb-Douglas production function:

$$Y = AK^{\alpha} L^{1-\alpha} = AK^{0.3} L^{0.7}. \qquad \text{(8-14)}$$

An extension of the percentage change rule presented in Chapter 2 of the text-book can be used to derive an equation for the approximate percentage change in *Y*:

$$\% \text{ Change in } Y = \% \text{ Change in } A + \alpha \times (\% \text{ Change in } K) +$$
$$(1 - \alpha) \times (\% \text{ Change in } L) =$$
$$\% \text{ Change in } A + \underline{\hspace{1.5cm}} \times (\% \text{ Change in } K) + \qquad \text{(8-15)}$$
$$\underline{\hspace{1.5cm}} \times (\% \text{ Change in } L).$$

The first term on the right-hand side of Equation 8-15, % Change in *A*, is commonly called the *percentage change in total factor productivity*. It measures increases in *Y* that occur over time even if the amounts of capital and labor remain constant. Equation 8-15 states that the percentage change in output over time is equal to the percentage change in total factor productivity plus 0.3 times the percentage change in capital plus 0.7 times the percentage change in labor. The coefficients on the changes in capital and labor are precisely equal to their exponents in the Cobb-Douglas production function.

b. Invert Equation 8-15 to solve for total factor productivity growth if $\alpha = 0.3$:

% Change in *A* = _____.

c. Now use these results along with the data from Table 8-3 of the textbook to confirm the estimate of annual total factor productivity growth for the United States between 1950 and 1999. In this period, the annual growth rates of GNP, capital, and labor were 3.6, 4.0, and 1.9 percent, respectively. Consequently, the estimated annual growth rate of total factor productivity during this period was
% Change in *A* = _____ – _____ – _____ = _____ percent.

Problems

Answer the following problems on a separate sheet of paper.

1. Suppose that the production function is $Y = 10(K)^{1/4}(EL)^{3/4}$ and capital lasts an average of 10 years, so that 10 percent of capital wears out every year. Assume that the rate of growth of population is 4 percent, the rate of technological growth is 2 percent and the saving rate $s = 0.128$.

   a. Derive the equation for output per effective worker $y = Y/EL = f(k)$, where k equals the amount of capital per effective worker.

   b. Calculate the steady-state levels for each of the following: capital per effective worker, output per effective worker, consumption per effective worker, saving and investment per effective worker, and depreciation per effective worker.

   c. Now calculate the steady-state growth rates of capital per worker, output per worker, saving and investment per worker, and consumption per worker.

   d. Finally, calculate the steady-state growth rates of capital, output, saving and investment, and consumption.

2. Consider an economy in a steady state with population growth rate n, a rate of capital depreciation δ, and a rate of labor-augmenting technological progress g.

    a. At the steady state $\Delta k = 0$, where k equals capital per effective worker. What condition must be met for this to hold? Describe the condition in words as well as symbols.

    b. Describe in words what is maximized at the Golden Rule level of k.

    c. What other condition must be met at the Golden Rule level of k?

3. Suppose the production function is $Y = 10(K)^{1/4}(EL)^{3/4}$ and capital lasts an average of 10 years. Assume that the rate of growth of population is 4 percent and the rate of technological growth is 2 percent. The marginal product of capital can be expressed as $MPK = 2.5\,(k)^{-3/4}$ where k is the level of capital per effective worker.

    a. Derive the equation for output per effective worker $y = Y/EL = f(k)$, where k equals the amount of capital per effective worker.

    b. Calculate the Golden Rule level of capital per effective worker and the saving rate associated with this steady state.

    c. Calculate all of the following at their Golden Rule levels: output per effective worker, saving and investment per effective worker, and consumption per effective worker.

4. In Chapter 3 of the textbook the marginal product of capital was defined as the amount by which total output changes when capital rises by 1 unit, or $MPK = dY/dK$. In Chapter 8 of the text MPK is equal to amount by which output per effective worker rises when capital per effective worker rises by 1 unit, or $MPK = df(k)/dk = f'(k)$, where $k = K/EL$. Use calculus and the chain rule to show that the two definitions are the same.

5. As in Problems 1 and 3, suppose the production function is $Y = 10(K)^{1/4}(EL)^{3/4}$ and capital lasts an average of 10 years. Assume once more that the rate of growth of population is 4 percent and the rate of technological growth is 2 percent.

    a. Derive the equation for output per effective worker $y = Y/EL = f(k)$, where k equals the amount of capital per effective worker.

    b. Use calculus to derive the marginal product of capital $MPK = f'(k)$.

    c. In the steady state consumption per effective worker

    $$c = f(k) - (\delta + n + g)k.$$

    Use calculus to derive the condition for the Golden Rule level of k and solve.

6. Totally differentiate the ratio of capital to effective labor $k = K/(E \times L)$ to prove that the change in the ratio dk is equal to $i - \delta k - nk - gk$, where i, δ, n, and g represent investment per effective worker, the rate of depreciation, the population growth rate, and the rate of technological progress, respectively.

7. Consider an economy in a steady state with population growth rate n, a rate of capital depreciation δ, and a rate of labor-augmenting technological progress g.

    a. Use the appropriate graphs to illustrate and explain how an increase in the saving rate would affect the steady-state capital stock per effective worker

    b. Draw three graphs with time on the horizontal axis (like the one below) to illustrate the time paths of capital per effective worker k, output per effective worker y, and output per worker in the initial steady state (to the left of line A), after the saving rate is increased but before the new steady state is reached (between lines A and B), and after the final steady state is reached (to the right of line B).

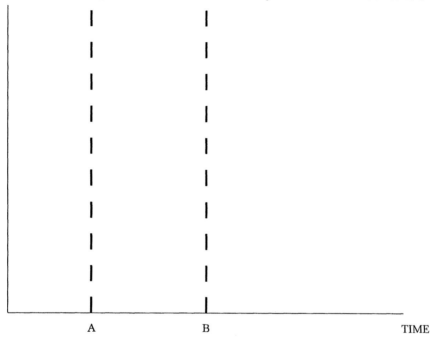

8. Suppose that a country is initially operating at a steady-state level of capital per worker and is able to double its rate of labor-augmenting technological progress.

    a. What will happen to its steady-state level of capital per effective worker?

    b. Consequently, what can one say about the growth rates of capital per effective worker and output per effective worker on the path to the new steady state?

    c. At the new steady state, what can we say about the growth rates of capital per effective worker, consumption per effective worker, and output per effective worker?

    d. Comparing the initial and final steady states, what happens to the growth rates of capital, output, and consumption *per worker*?

9. In each of the following cases determine whether the level of the capital stock per effective worker is above, below, or at the Golden Rule steady state:

   a. The country of Fertilia has a population growth rate of 4 percent and a rate of technological progress of 3 percent. Capital income is 30 percent of GDP, the depreciation of capital is 12 percent of GDP, and the capital stock is 3 times one year's GDP.

   b. The country of Begonia has a steady-state growth rate of real GDP of 4 percent per year. Capital typically lasts for 20 years, and the marginal product of capital is 9 percent of the value of each unit of capital.

10. Suppose that the production function is $Y = AK^{0.3}L^{0.7}$.

   A a. If total factor productivity grows at 2 percent per year and both the capital stock and the number of workers grow at 1 percent per year each, calculate the growth rate of output.

   b. If the rate of capital accumulation doubles to 2 percent per year, calculate the new growth rate of output.

Questions to Think About

1. Can countries differ in their rates of technological progress over long periods of time? Why can't lagging countries simply adopt the more advanced technologies?

2. In the Solow growth model with technological progress, the Golden Rule criterion maximizes the level of consumption per efficiency unit. Is this the ethically correct criterion for policymakers? If the capital stock is now below the Golden Rule steady state, reaching the Golden Rule requires a sacrifice by current generations for the benefit of future generations. Technological progress, however, will automatically make future generations richer because each person will be born with more efficiency units. Should policymakers ask current generations to sacrifice some of their consumption to benefit their richer descendants?

3. Considering the effects of the proposed solutions to the Social Security crisis on the budget deficit, economic growth, and income distribution, which proposal do you prefer?

4. How would one measure the "stepping on toes" and "standing on shoulders" effects?

Aggregate Demand I

Fill-in Questions

Use the key terms below to fill in the blanks in the following statements. Each term may be used more than once.

actual expenditure   *LM* curve
IS curve   multiplier
Keynesian cross   planned expenditure
liquidity preference theory

1. _____ is the amount households, firms, and the government spend on goods and services. _____ is the amount households, firms, and the government would like to spend on goods and services. In equilibrium, the two are equal.

2. In the _____ model, the equilibrium level of income is determined by the intersection of the planned expenditure curve and the actual expenditure curve.

3. In the _____ model, every $1 increase in government purchases increases equilibrium income by $1 times the government-purchases _____.

4. The _____ shows the relationship between the interest rate and the level of income at which planned expenditure is equal to actual expenditure.

5. The _____ illustrates the combinations of income and interest rates at which real money supply is equal to real money demand.

6. A change in fiscal policy will shift the _____; a change in monetary policy will shift the _____.

7. According to the _____, people wish to hold a smaller quantity of real money balances when the interest rate increases.

Multiple-Choice Questions

1. If investment, taxes, and government purchases are held constant, the planned expenditure curve:
   a. slopes upward and its slope is equal to the *MPC*.
   b. slopes downward and its slope is equal to the *MPC*.
   c. is a 45-degree line.
   d. is a vertical line.

2. In the Keynesian cross model, the 45-degree line indicates that:
   a. GDP rises whenever consumption rises.
   b. actual expenditure is always equal to income.
   c. the equilibrium level of income increases whenever actual income increases.
   d. all of the above.

3. At the equilibrium level of income:
   a. unintended inventory accumulation is equal to zero.
   b. planned expenditure is equal to actual expenditure.
   c. there is no tendency for GDP to change.
   d. all of the above.

4. If income exceeds planned expenditure, firms will cut back production because unplanned inventory accumulation will be:
   a. positive.
   b. negative.
   c. zero.
   d. indeterminate.

5. If the consumption function is $C = 100 + 0.8(Y - T)$, the government-purchases multiplier is:
   a. 0.8.
   b. 1.25.
   c. 4.
   d. 5.

6. If the consumption function is $C = 100 + 0.8(Y - T)$ and taxes decrease by $1, the equilibrium level of income will:
   a. decrease by $5.
   b. decrease by $4.
   c. increase by $5.
   d. increase by $4.

7. If the consumption function is $C = 100 + 0.8(Y - T)$ and both taxes and government purchases increase by $1, the equilibrium level of income will:
   a. remain constant.
   b. increase by $3.
   c. increase by $1.
   d. decrease by $4.

8. The FALSE statement below is:

   a. a decrease in the interest rate increases planned investment.

   b. a decrease in the interest rate shifts the planned expenditure curve upward.

   c. a decrease in the interest rate shifts the *IS* curve to the right.

   d. as the interest rate falls, planned expenditure is equal to actual expenditure at a higher level of income.

9. An increase of $1 in government purchases will:

   a. shift the planned expenditure curve upward by $1.

   b. shift the *IS* curve to the right by $1/(1 − *MPC*).

   c. not shift the *LM* curve.

   d. all of the above.

10. According to the loanable funds interpretation of the *IS* curve:

    a. firms want to invest more as their income rises.

    b. banks want to lend more as the interest rate rises.

    c. an increase in income raises saving and lowers the interest rate that equilibrates the supply of and demand for loanable funds.

    d. all of the above.

11. A decrease in taxes will shift the planned expenditure curve _____ and the *IS* curve to the _____ .

    a. upward; left

    b. upward; right

    c. downward; left

    d. downward; right

12. The following statement about the *LM* curve is TRUE:

    a. the *LM* curve slopes upward and it is drawn for a given level of income.

    b. the *LM* curve slopes downward and an increase in price shifts it upward.

    c. the *LM* curve slopes upward and it is drawn for a given supply of real money balances.

    d. along the *LM* curve, actual expenditure is equal to planned expenditure.

13. An increase in the money supply shifts the:

    a. *LM* curve upward (to the left).

    b. *LM* curve downward (to the right).

    c. *IS* curve to the right.

    d. *IS* curve to the left.

14. According to the quantity equation $MV = PY$. If velocity is constant, the:

    a. *LM* curve will slope upward.

    b. *LM* curve will slope downward.

    c. *LM* curve will be horizontal.

    d. *LM* curve will be vertical.

15. A normal *LM* curve can be derived from the quantity equation if it is assumed that:

    a. a higher interest rate reduces money demand and raises velocity.

    b. a higher interest rate reduces both money demand and velocity.

    c. velocity is constant.

    d. the price level is constant.

16. At the intersection of the *IS* and *LM* curves:

    a. actual expenditure is equal to planned expenditure.

    b. real money supply is equal to real money demand.

    c. the levels of *Y* and *r* satisfy both the goods market equilibrium condition and the money market equilibrium condition.

    d. all of the above.

Exercises

1. **The Keynesian Cross** *In this exercise, we illustrate the Keynesian cross using a simple model of a closed economy.*

   a. Consider the following model of the economy (in billions of dollars):

$$Y = C + I + G \qquad\qquad \text{(10-1)}$$
$$C = C(Y - T) = 125 + 0.75(Y - T) \qquad\qquad \text{(10-2)}$$
$$I = \bar{I} = 100 \qquad\qquad \text{(10-3)}$$
$$G = \overline{G} = 150 \qquad\qquad \text{(10-4)}$$
$$T = \bar{T} = 100. \qquad\qquad \text{(10-5)}$$

   The *MPC* is defined as _____.

   The value of the *MPC* in this model = _____. If consumption were graphed as a function of disposable income $(Y - T)$, as is done in Chapter 3 of the textbook, the *y* intercept, which is the value of the variable depicted on the vertical axis when the value of the variable depicted on the horizontal axis is 0, would equal _____. The slope of the curve would equal _____.

b. Now, however, consumption will be graphed as a function of Y, rather than of $(Y - T)$. Substituting $T = 100$ into the equation, we obtain

$$C = 125 + 0.75 \, (Y - 100), \text{ or}$$

$$C = \underline{\hspace{2cm}} + \underline{\hspace{2cm}} Y.$$

Use this information to plot and draw the consumption expenditure curve on Graph 10-1 and label it C.

Graph 10-1

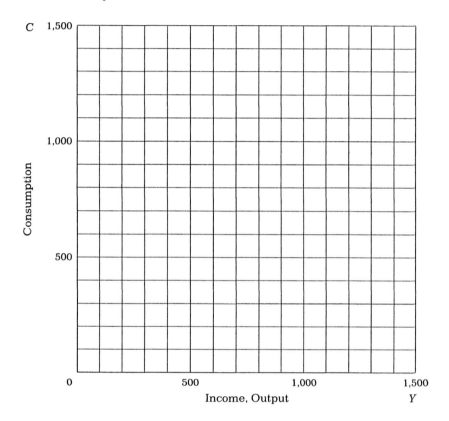

The y intercept of this consumption expenditure curve, which is the value of consumption when income $Y = 0$, is _____, and the slope is _____. When we draw consumption as a function of income Y, note that the y intercept differs from when we draw consumption as a function of disposable income $Y - T$, as you can see by comparing your answers to those in Parts a and b. When $Y = 0$ and $T = 100$, $(Y - T) = $ _____, which is greater than/less than/equal to.

c. In this simple model, both planned investment and government purchases are constant and independent of the level of Y, that is, they are exogenous. Use the information from Part a to draw the relationship between planned investment and Y on Graph 10-2, and label it I. Draw the relationship between government purchases and Y on Graph 10-3 and label it G.

Graph 10-2

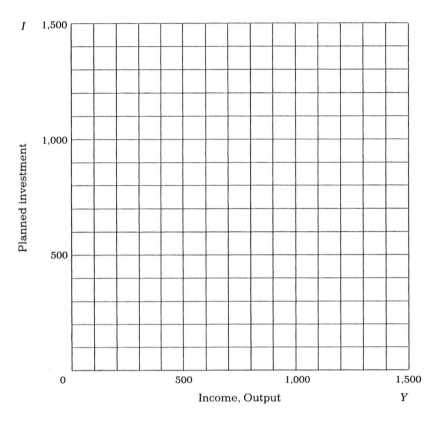

Graph 10-3

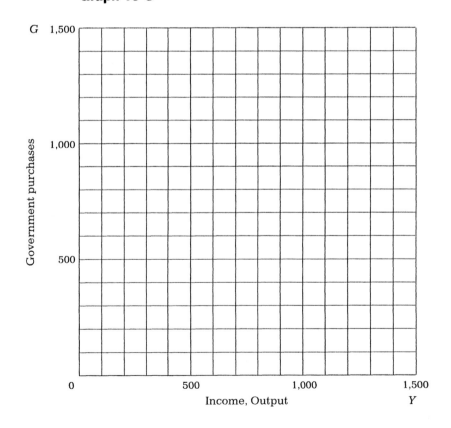

d. Recall that total planned expenditure E is equal to $C + I + G$. Use the information from Graphs 10-1, 10-2, and 10-3 to draw the planned expenditure curve on Graph 10-4. Label your curve E.

Graph 10-4

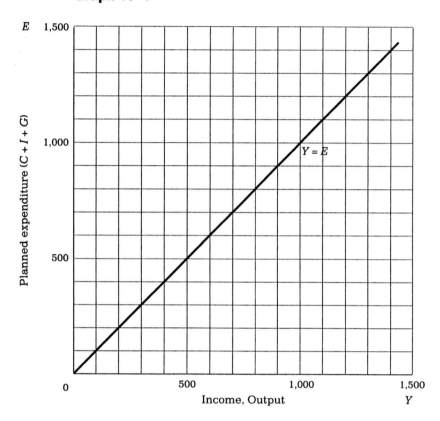

e. The value of the y intercept on Graph 10-4 is equal to the level of planned expenditure when $Y = 0$. This value is equal to the level of consumption when $Y = 0$, plus the level of planned investment when $Y = 0$, plus the level of government purchases when $Y = 0$. This value is equal to _____ + _____ + _____ = _____. Similarly, the numerical value of the slope of the planned expenditure curve on Graph 10-4 is equal to the slope of the consumption function curve, plus the slope of the planned investment curve, plus the slope of the government-purchases curve, or _____ + _____ + _____ = _____.

f.   Since $E = C + I + G$, the equation for the planned expenditure curve can be derived by adding together the equations for C, I, and G. Thus,

$$E = 125 + 0.75(Y - T) + I + G. \tag{10-6}$$

Substituting the exogenous values of T, I, and G into this equation, we get

$$E = 125 + 0.75(Y - 100) + 100 + 150.$$

This equation can be simplified to

$$E = \underline{\hspace{1.5cm}} + \underline{\hspace{1.5cm}} Y. \tag{10-7}$$

g.   Equation 10-7 will yield values of planned expenditure E for any value of Y. The equilibrium, however, occurs only along the 45-degree line labeled $Y = E$ on Graph 10-4. Only along this curve will income (or output) equal planned expenditure. The slope of this 45-degree line is \underline{\hspace{5cm}}. Solve for the equilibrium level of income in this model by setting $Y = E = 300 + 0.75Y$ and solving for Y.

$Y = \underline{\hspace{5cm}}$.

On Graph 10-4, label this initial equilibrium Y_1.

h.   If income (output) exceeds planned expenditure, there will be unplanned investment in the form of unplanned inventory accumulation. For example, if $Y = 1,600$, planned expenditure E will equal $300 + 0.75(1,600) = \underline{\hspace{5cm}}$.
Consequently, the level of unplanned inventory accumulation will equal $Y - E = $
$1,600 - \underline{\hspace{5cm}} = \underline{\hspace{5cm}}$. As inventories
increase, firms will <u>hire/lay off</u> workers and <u>increase/decrease</u> production. As a result, Y will <u>rise/fall</u> until equilibrium is reached at $Y = \underline{\hspace{5cm}}$.
When this equilibrium is reached, unplanned inventory investment will equal

\underline{\hspace{5cm}}.

i. Conversely, when Y is less than planned expenditure, inventories will fall. For example, if $Y = 1,000$, planned expenditure E will equal $300 + 0.75(1,000) =$ _____. Consequently, the level of unplanned inventory accumulation will equal $Y - E = 1,000 -$ _____ = _____. As inventories decrease, firms will hire more/lay off workers and increase/decrease production. As a result, Y will rise/fall until an equilibrium is reached at $Y =$ _____. When this equilibrium is reached, unplanned inventory investment will equal _____.

2. The Government-Purchases Multiplier *In this exercise, we derive and graphically illustrate the government-purchases multiplier.*

Assume the same information as in Exercise 1 (again, in billions of dollars):

$$Y = C + I + G \qquad\qquad (10\text{-}8)$$
$$C = C(Y - T) = 125 + 0.75(Y - T) \qquad\qquad (10\text{-}9)$$
$$I = \bar{I} = 100 \qquad\qquad (10\text{-}10)$$
$$G = \overline{G} = 150 \qquad\qquad (10\text{-}11)$$
$$T = \overline{T} = 100. \qquad\qquad (10\text{-}12)$$

The initial equilibrium is depicted on Graph 10-5.

Graph 10-5

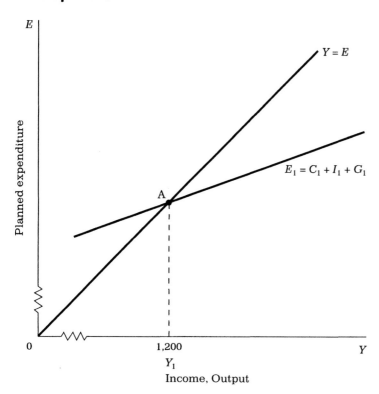

a. The initial level of government purchases is _____. This is illustrated by the curve G_1 on Graph 10-6.

Graph 10-6

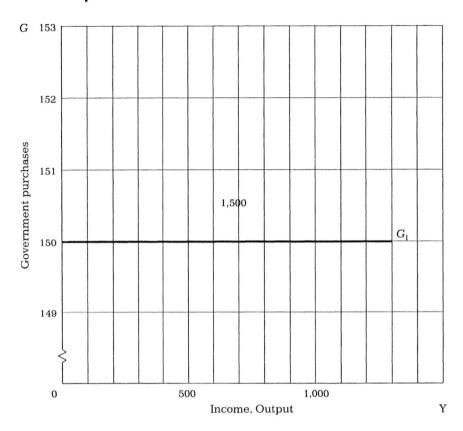

Suppose that the government decides to purchase two additional B-2 stealth bombers at a total cost of $1 billion. Consequently, government purchases G will rise at all levels of Y to _____. This will shift the whole government purchases curve on Graph 10-6 upward by _____.
Plot and draw this new curve on Graph 10-6 and label it G_2.

b. Since taxes T and planned investment I have not changed, the consumption and investment functions on Graphs 10-1 and 10-2 in Exercise 1 will not shift. Consequently, the planned expenditure curve $E = C + I + G$ will shift upward by _____. Plot and draw the new planned expenditure curve on Graph 10-5 and label it E_2.

c. As in Exercise 1f, the equation for the new planned expenditure curve E_2 can be derived by adding together the equations for C, I, and G. Thus,

$$E_2 = 125 + 0.75(Y - T) + I + G_2.$$

Substituting the same values of T and I but the new value of G into this equation, we get

$$E_2 = 125 + 0.75(Y - 100) + 100 + 151.$$

This can be simplified to

$E_2 = $ _____ $+$ _____ Y.

d. It is tempting to say that the \$1 billion increase in government purchases will increase the equilibrium level of income by \$1 billion, but this would be incorrect. As government purchases increase, Y increases. This, in turn, increases disposable income and the level of consumption. Consequently, Y will increase by more than \$1 billion. Recall that in equilibrium, expenditure is equal to income (that is, $E = Y$). Calculate the new equilibrium level of income by setting the equation for E_2 in Part c equal to Y and solving for Y.

$E_2 = $ _____ $+$ _____ $Y = Y$.

$Y = $ _____.

On Graph 10-5, label the equilibrium Point B and label the new equilibrium level of output Y_2.

e. From Part d we see that an increase in government purchases of $1 billion leads to a $_____ billion increase in national income and output. This value is equal to the increase in government purchases multiplied by the government-purchases multiplier, where the latter is defined as $\Delta Y/\Delta G$. In this model, the multiplier equals $1/(1 - MPC)$.

f. The theory behind the government-purchases multiplier can be seen by completing Table 10-1 (sometimes called the *round-by-round story*).

Table 10-1

	Change in $Y = C + I + G$
Round 1 G rises by $1 billion as the government purchases two new stealth bombers. Y rises immediately by . . .	+ $1 billion
Round 2 The total disposable income of workers, suppliers, and owners at Northrop Corporation (a major producer of the stealth bomber) rises by $1 billion. Consequently, their total consumption rises by $MPC \times$ ($1 billion). As new goods (Chevrolet automobiles, for example) are produced to meet this increase in consumption demand, Y rises by . . .	+ $MPC billion
Round 3 The total disposable income of workers, suppliers, and owners at General Motors Corporation rises by $MPC billion. Thus, their total consumption rises by $MPC(MPC \times$ $1 billion) = $_____ billion. As new goods (for example, Levi's jeans) are produced, Y rises by . . .	+ $_____ billion
Round 4 The total disposable income of workers, suppliers, and owners at Levi Strauss & Co. rises by $MPC^2 billion. Consequently, their total consumption rises by $MPC($MPC^2 \times$ $1 billion) = $_____ billion. As new goods are produced, Y rises by . . .	+ $_____ billion

The total change in Y is equal to the sum of all the changes resulting from each round. Since $MPC < 1$, the increase in Y from each successive round becomes smaller and smaller and eventually approaches zero. The sum of all of these increments is equal to $1 + MPC + MPC^2 + MPC^3 + MPC^4 + MPC^5 + . . . = 1/(1 - MPC)$. Since the MPC in our model = _____, the government-purchases multiplier = $1/(1 - $ _____$) = $ _____.

3. **The Tax Multiplier** *In this exercise, we derive and graphically illustrate the tax multiplier and, in Part g, the balanced-budget multiplier.*

Assume the same information as in Exercise 2 (again in billions of dollars):

$$Y = C + I + G \tag{10-13}$$

$$C = C(Y - T) = 125 + 0.75(Y - T) \tag{10-14}$$

$$I = \bar{I} = 100 \tag{10-15}$$

$$G = \overline{G} = 150 \tag{10-16}$$

$$T = \overline{T} = 100. \tag{10-17}$$

The initial equilibrium is illustrated on Graph 10-7.

Graph 10-7

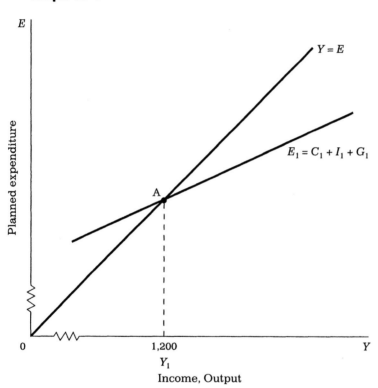

a. Suppose that the government decides to decrease taxes by $1 billion by decreasing tax revenues or by increasing transfer payments. Since disposable income equals $Y - T$, this tax decrease will increase the level of disposable income at every level of Y by $1 billion. Consequently, consumption will increase by $MPC \times$ $1 billion at each level of Y. (Reread the last two sentences carefully.) As a result, the consumption expenditure curve on Graph 10-8 will shift upward from C_1 to C_3 by $$MPC$ billion.

Graph 10-8

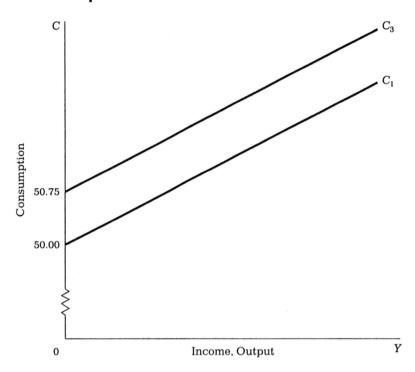

Neither government purchases nor planned investment has changed, so the I and G curves will be the same as in Graphs 10-2 and 10-3. Since $E = C + I + G$ and $MPC = 0.75$, the \$1 billion tax reduction will shift the planned expenditure curve upward by \$ _____ billion. Plot and draw the new planned expenditure curve on Graph 10-7 and label it E_3.

b. Once again, the equation for the new planned expenditure curve E_3 can be derived by adding together the equations for C, I, and G. Thus,

$$E_3 = 125 + 0.75(Y - T) + I + G.$$

Substituting the same values of I and G but the new value of T into this equation, we get

$$E_3 = 125 + 0.75(Y - 99) + 100 + 150.$$

This can be simplified to

$$E_3 = \text{\underline{\hspace{4cm}}} + \text{\underline{\hspace{4cm}}}Y.$$

c. Calculate the new equilibrium level of income by setting the equation for E_3 in Part b equal to Y and then solving for Y.

$E_3 = $ _____ + _____ $Y = Y$.

$Y = $ _____. On Graph 10-7, label the new equilibrium Point C and label the new equilibrium level of output Y_3.

d. From Part c, we see that a $1 billion reduction in taxes leads to a

$_____ billion increase in national income and output. This is equal to the decrease in taxes ($1 billion) multiplied by the tax multiplier, where the latter is equal to $MPC/(1 - MPC)$.

e. Complete Table 10-2 to see the rationale behind the tax multiplier.

Table 10-2

	Change in $Y = C + I + G$
Round 1	
T falls by $1 billion. Disposable income rises by $1 billion and consumption rises by $MPC \times $1 billion. As new goods (Chevrolet automobiles) are produced, Y rises by . . .	+ $$MPC$ billion
Round 2	
The total disposable income of workers, suppliers, and owners at General Motors Corporation rises by $$MPC$ billion. Thus, their total consumption rises by $MPC(MPC \times 1 billion) = $$_____ billion. As new goods (Levi's jeans) are produced, Y rises by . . .	+ $$_____ billion
Round 3	
The total disposable income of workers, suppliers, and owners at Levi Strauss & Co. rises by $$MPC^2$ billion. Consequently, their total consumption rises by $MPC($MPC^2$ billion) = $$_____ . As new goods are produced, Y rises by . . .	+ $$_____ billion

The total change in Y is equal to the sum of all the changes resulting from each round. As Chapter 10 of the textbook illustrates, the sum of all these increments is equal to $MPC + MPC^2 + MPC^3 + MPC^4 + MPC^5 + . . . = MPC/(1 - MPC)$. Since the MPC in our model = _____, $MPC/(1 - MPC) = $

_____/(1 − _____) =

_____.

f. Compare the algebraic expression for the tax multiplier in Part e with the algebraic expression for the government-purchases multiplier in Exercise 2f. Note that the tax multiplier is equal to the government-purchases multiplier minus 1, which equals

$$[1/(1 - MPC)] - 1 = [1 - (1 - MPC)]/(1 - MPC) = \underline{\hspace{4cm}}.$$

Examine the two round-by-round stories in Tables 10-1 and 10-2. Note that the only difference between the effects of an increase in government purchases and the effects of an equal decrease in taxes on Y is that the (direct) Round 1 effect of the increase in government purchases does not occur when taxes are reduced.

g. Now suppose that both government purchases and taxes were simultaneously increased by $1 billion. Since the government budget surplus would remain unchanged, this policy is sometimes called a *balanced-budget change* in G and T. The $1 billion increase in G would shift the planned expenditure curve upward/downward by $\underline{\hspace{4cm}}$ billion, while the $1 billion increase in T would shift the planned expenditure upward/downward by $\underline{\hspace{4cm}}$ billion. Consequently, the combined policy changes would shift the planned expenditure curve upward/downward by $\underline{\hspace{4cm}}$ billion, and the equilibrium level of Y would rise/fall/remain constant. This occurs because an increase in G has a larger/smaller effect on Y than an equal reduction in taxes, just as Tables 10-1 and 10-2 indicated. In Exercise 2, an increase in government expenditures of $1 billion increased the equilibrium level of Y by $\underline{\hspace{4cm}}$ billion. In Exercise 3, a reduction in taxes of $1 billion increased the equilibrium level of Y by $\underline{\hspace{4cm}}$ billion. Reversing this second result, a $1 billion increase in taxes would increase/decrease the equilibrium level of Y by $\underline{\hspace{4cm}}$ billion. Thus, a simultaneous increase in both G and T by $1 billion will increase/decrease the equilibrium level of Y by $\underline{\hspace{4cm}}$ billion.

4. **The *IS* Curve** *In this exercise, we use a simple model of the economy to derive the* IS *curve and we discuss the parameters that affect its slope.*

Consider the following model of the economy (in billions of dollars):

$$Y = C + I + G \qquad \text{(10-18)}$$
$$C = C(Y - T) = 125 + 0.75(Y - T) \qquad \text{(10-19)}$$
$$I = 200 - 10r \qquad \text{(10-20)}$$
$$G = \overline{G} = 150 \qquad \text{(10-21)}$$
$$T = \overline{T} = 100. \qquad \text{(10-22)}$$

a. Note that this model is identical to the one used in Exercises 1–3, except that planned investment now depends on the interest rate. For each percentage point increase in the real interest rate r, planned investment falls by

_____. Now use the new investment equation to complete Column 2 in Table 10-3. Plot the data from Columns 1 and 2 on Graph 10-9, draw this investment curve, and label it I.

Table 10-3

(1) Interest Rate (%)	(2) Planned Investment	(3) Equilibrium Level of Income
0	_____	_____
5	_____	_____
10	100	1,200
15	_____	_____
20	_____	_____

Graph 10-9

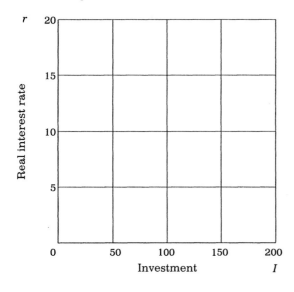

b. From Table 10-3, note that when $r = 10$, $I = 100$, and the equilibrium level of Y is the same as in Exercise 1. The equilibrium level of Y can be computed for other values of the interest rate in two ways. First, recall that total planned expenditure E is equal to $C + I + G$. Now use the new equation for investment, along with the initial levels of T and G (which have not changed), and solve for E in terms of Y and r:

$E = 125 + 0.75(Y - 100) + (200 - 10r) + 150$.

$E = $ _____ + _____ $Y -$ _____ r.

c. Next, recall that the equilibrium level of Y is defined as the level of Y at which income Y is equal to total planned expenditure E. Calculate the new equilibrium level of income by setting the equation for E in Part b equal to Y and solving for Y. Note that the equilibrium Y will be a function of r:

$E = $ _____ + _____ $Y -$ _____ $r = Y$.

$Y = $ _____ $-$ _____ r.

Use this equation to complete Column 3 of Table 10-3.

d. Alternatively, the remaining equilibrium values of Y can be computed using the multiplier analysis derived in Exercise 2. The initial equilibrium is illustrated on Graph 10-10. When $r = 10$ percent, $I =$ _____, the planned expenditure curve is E_1, and $Y =$ _____.

Graph 10-10

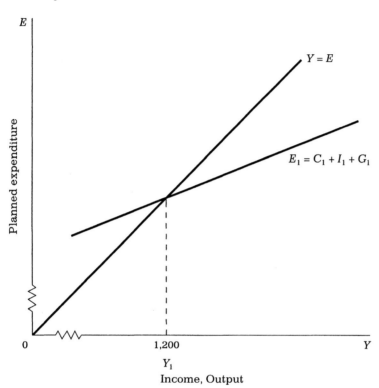

e. If r falls by 5 percentage points to 5 percent, I increases by $5(10) =$ _____. As a result, the planned expenditure curve E would shift upward by _____. Draw the new planned expenditure curve on Graph 10-10 and label it E_2. Since this shift is the same as one that would follow an increase in government purchases of _____, the multiplier effects on consumption will be the same, and the government-purchases multiplier can be used to calculate the change in Y. Thus, the change in Y will equal the increase in investment multiplied by the government-purchases multiplier, or

Change in $Y =$ _____ $\times 1/(1 - MPC)$.

Since $MPC =$ _____, the numerical value for the

Change in $Y =$ _____ $\times 1/(1 -$ _____$) =$ _____.

This should be the same as the change indicated in Table 10-3.

f. The *IS* curve depicts the relationship between the interest rate *r* and the equilibrium value of income from the investment function and the Keynesian cross. (This is sometimes called the equilibrium in the goods market.) Reexamine Table 10-3 and note that as the interest rate falls, the level of planned investment <u>falls/rises/remains the same</u>. This shifts the planned expenditure curve <u>upward/downward</u> by the same amount as the increase in planned investment. Finally, the equilibrium level of income *Y* rises by the increase in planned investment multiplied by the government-purchases multiplier. This shift occurs because *Y* rises by the initial increase in investment plus the multiplier effects on consumption.

g. Use the data in Columns 1 and 3 of Table 10-3 to plot and draw the *IS* curve on Graph 10-11 (label the curve *IS*). Reread Part f to make sure that you understand how the *IS* curve is derived.

Graph 10-11

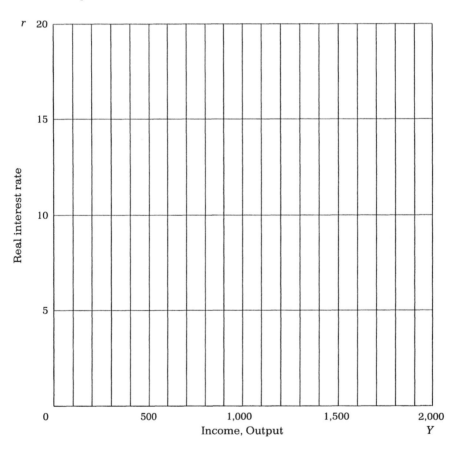

5. Fiscal Policy and the *IS* Curve *In this exercise, we show how changes in fiscal policy shift the* IS *curve.*

a. Consider the same model of the economy as in Exercise 4 (in billions of dollars), in which planned investment depends on the interest rate:

$$Y = C + I + G \tag{10-23}$$
$$C = C(Y - T) = 125 + 0.75(Y - T) \tag{10-24}$$
$$I = 200 - 10r \tag{10-25}$$
$$G = \overline{G} = 150 \tag{10-26}$$
$$T = \overline{T} = 100. \tag{10-27}$$

As we saw in Exercise 4, when $r = 10$, $I = $ _____ and $Y = $ _____. This original equilibrium is illustrated on Graphs 10-12 and 10-13.

Suppose that government purchases now increase by $1 billion to $151 billion, as in Exercise 2. If the interest rate remains equal to 10 percent, then investment is unchanged, the planned expenditure curve shifts upward by $1 billion, and the equilibrium level of Y rises by $1 billion multiplied by the government-purchases multiplier, which equals $1 billion × $1/(1 - MPC)$.

Thus, if the interest rate remains equal to 10 percent and $MPC = 0.75$, the equilibrium level of Y rises by $1 billion × $1/(1 - $ _____ $) = $ $ _____ billion. The new equilibrium level of Y = _____.

b. Draw the new planned expenditure curve on Graph 10-12, label it $E_2(r = 10)$, and illustrate the change in Y if r remains constant. Note that the scales of the x and y axes have been broken so that a small shift in the expenditure curve and a small change in Y will be noticeable.

c. This change can also be depicted on Graph 10-13 by a shift in the *IS* curve to the right/left. The amount of the horizontal shift measures the change in Y if r remains constant. Given the answer to Part b, the horizontal shift in the *IS* curve must equal $1 billion × $1/(1 - MPC) = $ $ _____ billion. Draw the new *IS* curve on Graph 10-13, and label it IS_2.

d. Thus, an increase in government purchases will shift the *IS* curve to the right/left by the change in government purchases multiplied by the government-purchases multiplier. Conversely, a decrease in government purchases will shift the *IS* curve to the right/left by the change in government purchases multiplied by the _____.

Graph 10-12

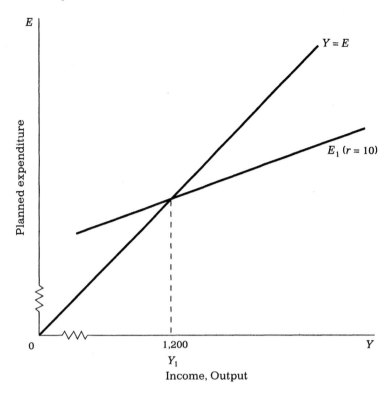

Graph 10-13

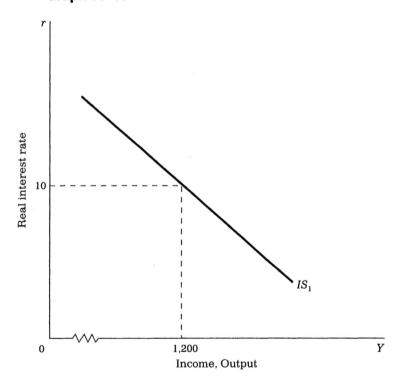

e. The government-purchases multiplier equals $1/(1 - MPC)$. As the MPC gets larger, the denominator gets <u>larger/smaller</u> and the value of the multiplier gets <u>larger/smaller</u>. Consequently, as the MPC gets larger, the horizontal shift in the IS curve following a change in government purchases gets <u>larger/smaller</u>. Therefore, as the MPC gets larger, the round-by-round multiplier effects depicted in Table 10-1 become <u>larger/smaller</u>, and the change in the equilibrium level of Y becomes <u>larger/smaller</u>.

f. Now assume that $G = 150$ and that taxes fall by \$1 billion. In Exercises 3a and d, it was shown that the planned expenditure curve would shift upward by \$$MPC$ billion, and Y would increase by the reduction in taxes (\$1 billion) multiplied by the tax multiplier $MPC/(1 - MPC)$, or by \$$MPC/(1 - MPC)$ billion. Thus, if the interest rate remains equal to 10 percent and $MPC = 0.75$, the equilibrium level of Y rises by \$_____ billion × _____/(1 − _____) = \$_____ billion. The new equilibrium level of $Y = $ _____.

Draw the new expenditure curve on Graph 10-14, label it E_3 $(r = 10)$, and indicate the change in Y if r remains constant.

g. This change can be depicted on Graph 10-15 by a shift in the IS curve to the <u>right/left</u>. The amount of the horizontal shift measures the change in Y if r remains constant. Given your answer to Part f, the horizontal shift in the IS curve must equal \$1 billion × $MPC/(1 - MPC)$. If $MPC = 0.75$, this is equal to \$_____ billion. Draw the new IS curve on Graph 10-15 and label it IS_3.

h. Thus, a decrease in taxes (resulting from either a reduction in taxes or an increase in government transfers) will shift the IS curve to the <u>right/left</u> by the decrease in taxes multiplied by the tax multiplier. Conversely, an increase in taxes will shift the IS curve to the <u>right/left</u> by the change in taxes multiplied by the _____.

i. The tax multiplier equals $MPC/(1 - MPC)$. As the MPC gets larger, the numerator gets <u>larger/smaller</u> and the denominator gets <u>larger/smaller</u>. Consequently, the tax multiplier gets <u>larger/smaller</u>. Thus, as the MPC gets larger, the horizontal shift in the IS curve following a change in taxes would get <u>larger/smaller</u>. As the MPC gets larger, the round-by-round multiplier effects depicted in Table 10-2 become <u>larger/smaller</u>, and the change in the equilibrium level of Y becomes <u>larger/smaller</u>. Consequently, a larger MPC implies a <u>flatter/steeper</u> IS curve.

Graph 10-14

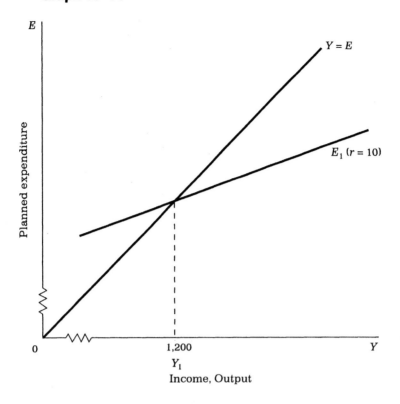

Graph 10-15

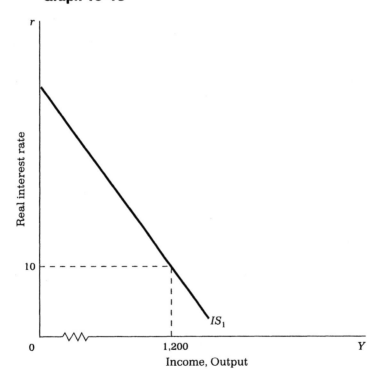

6.   The *LM* Curve *In this exercise, we use the money supply/money demand diagram to derive the* LM *curve.*

a.   Suppose that the following equation (in billions of dollars) describes the supply of real money balances:

$$(M^s/P) = \overline{M} / \overline{P} = 800/1.0 = 800.$$ **(10-28)**

This equation states that the Fed has fixed the nominal money supply at $\overline{M} = 800$, and the price level is fixed at $\overline{P} = 1.0$. Since the supply of real money balances is independent of the interest rate, it will be depicted as a vertical line. Draw this line on Graph 10-16 and label it $\overline{M}/\overline{P}$.

Graph 10-16

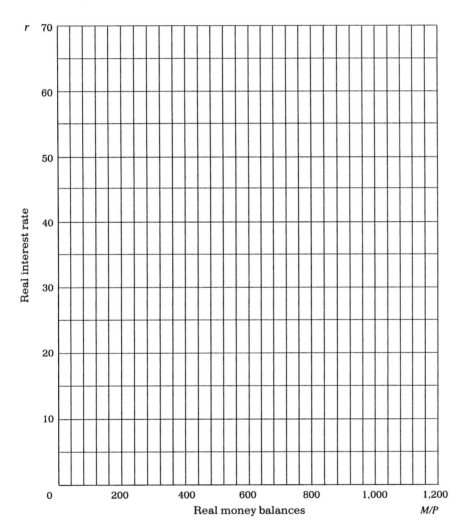

b. Suppose that the following equation describes the demand for real money balances:

$$(M/P)^d = L(r, Y) = 0.8Y - 16r. \qquad \text{(10-29)}$$

This equation states that the demand for real money balances depends on the level of real income Y and the interest rate r. (In Chapter 10 of the textbook, footnote 6 notes that money demand actually depends on the nominal interest rate i, rather than on the real interest rate r, and that this difference will be explored more fully in Chapter 11.) Using Equation 10-29, complete Table 10-4.

Table 10-4

(1) Real Income Y	(2) Interest Rate r (%)	(3) Real Money Demand $(M/P)^d = 0.8Y - 16r$
1,100	55	_____
1,100	25	_____
1,100	10	_____
1,100	5	_____
1,100	0	_____

Plot these points on Graph 10-16, draw the resulting money demand curve, and label it $L(r, Y = 1,100)$.

c. From Graph 10-16 and Table 10-4, it can be seen that if real income $Y = 1,100$, the supply of real money balances is equal to the demand for real money balances when $r = $ _____ percent.

d. Now suppose that real income increases to $Y = 1,200$. Complete Table 10-5.

Table 10-5

(1) Real Income Y	(2) Interest Rate r (%)	(3) Real Money Demand $(M/P)^d = 0.8Y - 16r$
1,200	60	_____
1,200	50	_____
1,200	25	_____
1,200	10	_____
1,200	5	_____

Plot these points on Graph 10-16, draw the resulting money demand curve, and label it $L(r, Y = 1,200)$. When Y increases, the real money supply curve remains unchanged at $M/P = 800$, but the real money demand curve shifts to the left/right. Consequently, the interest rate at which the supply of real money balances is equal to the demand for real money balances rises/falls to $r = $ _____ percent.

e. Finally, suppose that real income increases to $Y = 1,400$. Complete Table 10-6.

Table 10-6

(1) Real Income Y	(2) Interest Rate r (%)	(3) Real Money Demand $(M/P)^d = 0.8Y - 16r$
1,400	70	_____
1,400	50	_____
1,400	25	_____
1,400	10	_____
1,400	0	_____

Plot these points on Graph 10-16, draw the resulting money demand curve, and label it $L(r, Y = 1,400)$. When Y increases again, the real money supply curve remains unchanged at $M/P = 800$, but the real money demand curve again shifts to the left/right. Consequently, the interest rate at which the supply of real money balances is equal to the demand for real money balances rises/falls to

$r = $ _____.

f. The LM curve depicts the combinations of r and Y for which a given supply of real money balances is equal to real money demand. Throughout Exercise 6, the supply of real money balances has been fixed at $M/P = $

_____. From Table 10-4, we learned that when $Y = 1,100$, real money supply equals real money demand at $r = $ _____.
From Table 10-5, we learned that when $Y = 1,200$, real money supply equals real money demand at $r = $ _____. And from Table 10-6 and Graph 10-16, we learned that when $Y = 1,400$, real money supply equals real money demand at $r = $ _____. Plot and draw a curve for these three points on Graph 10-17 and label it LM_1.

g. Along each LM curve, a constant real money supply is equal to real money demand. As Y increases, real money demand will increase/decrease if the interest rate remains constant. Since the real money supply has remained unchanged, the interest rate must rise/fall to keep real money demand equal to the unchanged real money supply.

Graph 10-17

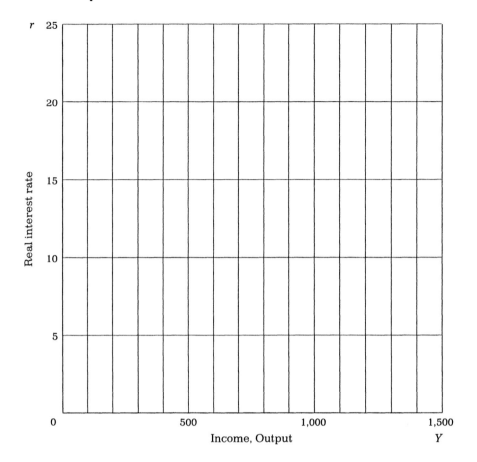

h. Now let us derive the equation for our *LM* curve. Along the LM_1 curve, the real money supply equals _____ and this value is equal to real money demand. Thus, along the LM_1 curve,

$$\overline{M} / \overline{P} = \underline{\hspace{2cm}} = 0.8Y - 16r.$$

Since *r* appears on the vertical axis on Graph 10-17, it is useful to rearrange this equation and solve for *r*.

$$r = \underline{\hspace{4cm}} + \underline{\hspace{4cm}}Y.$$

The *y* intercept of this *LM* curve is _____ and the slope of the *LM* curve is _____.

7.   Monetary Policy and the *LM* Curve *In this exercise, we show how changes in monetary policy shift the LM curve.*

a.   Refer to the initial money supply and money demand equations:

$$(M^s/P) = \overline{M} / \overline{P} = 800 / 1.0 = 800 \tag{10-30}$$

$$(M/P)^d = 0.8Y - 16r. \tag{10-31}$$

By setting money supply equal to money demand and solving for r, the equation for the *LM* curve in Exercise 6h can be derived:

$$r = \underline{\hspace{4cm}} + \underline{\hspace{4cm}} Y.$$

Draw the curve for this equation on Graph 10-18 and label it LM_1.

Graph 10-18

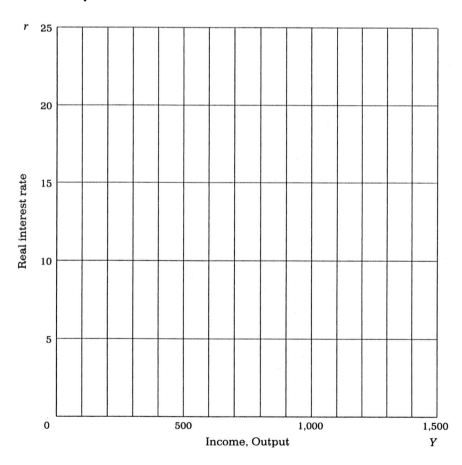

b. Following the example given in Chapter 10 of the textbook, suppose that the Fed decreased the money supply to $(M^s/P) = 640$. Set this new money supply equal to the money demand equation, Equation 10-31, and solve for r to derive the equation for the new LM curve.

$r = $ _____ $+$ _____ Y.

Plot and draw the new LM curve from this equation on Graph 10-18 and label it LM_2. The slope of LM_2 is greater than/less than/equal to the slope of LM_1. The y intercept of LM_2 is greater than/less than the y intercept of LM_1. (Be careful about your signs.) Consequently, a reduction in the real money supply will shift the LM curve to the right (downward)/left (upward).

c. For the money market to remain in equilibrium, a reduction in the real money supply must be matched by an equal reduction in money demand. This match can be accomplished by a(n) increase/decrease in r at each level of Y and/or a(n) increase/decrease in Y at each level of r. Consequently, a decrease in the real money supply will shift the LM curve to the right (downward)/left (upward). Conversely, an increase in the real money supply will shift the LM curve to the right (downward)/left (upward).

8. **Short-Run Equilibrium** *In this exercise, we use the models developed in the preceding exercises to illustrate the short-run* IS-LM *equilibrium.*

   a. Consider the model of the economy from Exercise 4, in which planned investment depends on the interest rate:

$$Y = C + I + G \tag{10-32}$$
$$C = C(Y - T) = 125 + 0.75(Y - T) \tag{10-33}$$
$$I = 200 - 10r \tag{10-34}$$
$$G = \overline{G} = 150 \tag{10-35}$$
$$T = \overline{T} = 100. \tag{10-36}$$

As we saw in Exercise 4, the equation for the *IS* curve can be derived by setting total planned expenditure, $E = C + I + G$, equal to Y and solving for r:

$$E = 125 + 0.75(Y - 100) + (200 - 10r) + 150 = Y. \tag{10-37}$$

$$r = \underline{\hspace{6cm}} - \underline{\hspace{6cm}}Y.$$

Plot and draw the *IS* curve from this equation on Graph 10-19 and label it IS_1.

Graph 10-19

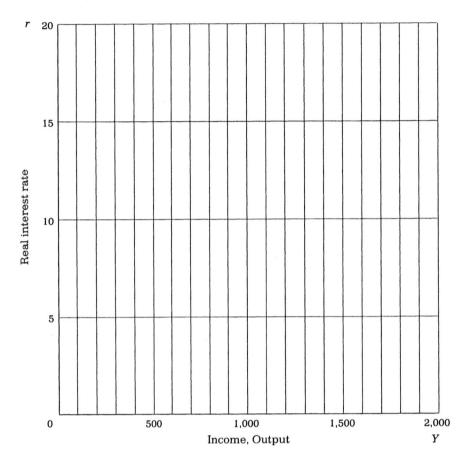

b. In Exercise 6, we derived the equation for the *LM* curve by setting the money supply equation equal to the money demand equation and solving for *r*:

$$(\overline{M} / \overline{P}) = 800 = (M / P)^d = 0.8Y - 16r$$
$$800 = 0.8Y - 16r.$$

(10-38)

$r =$ _____ + _____ Y.

Plot and draw the *LM* curve for this equation on Graph 10-19 and label it LM_1.

c. The equilibrium of the economy occurs at the intersection of the *IS* curve and the *LM* curve. This point gives the interest rate *r* and the level of income *Y* at which actual expenditure equals planned expenditure, and the supply of real money balances equals the demand for real money balances. Compute the equilibrium values of *Y* and *r* by setting the equation for the *IS* curve equal to the equation for the *LM* curve and solving for *Y* and *r*.

The equilibrium value of *Y* = _____ and the equilibrium value of *r* = _____ percent. Locate these values on Graph 10-19 and label them Y_1 and r_1, respectively.

Problems

Answer the following problems on a separate sheet of paper.

1. Assume the following model of the economy:

$$C = 180 + 0.8(Y - T)$$
$$I = 190$$
$$G = 250$$
$$T = 150.$$

   a. What is the value of the *MPC* in this model?

   b. Draw the planned expenditure curve and indicate its slope and *y* intercept.

   c. Compute the equilibrium level of income.

   d. Calculate the level of unplanned inventory accumulation when *Y* = 3,000.

2. Consider the same model as in Problem 1:

$$C = 180 + 0.8(Y - T)$$
$$I = 190$$
$$G = 250$$
$$T = 150.$$

a. Compute the initial equilibrium level of income.

b. If government purchases were to increase by 10 to 260, what would happen to each of the following? State the amount as well as the direction of the changes.

   i.   the planned expenditure curve
   ii. the equilibrium level of income
   iii. the level of consumption
   iv. the government budget deficit

c. Starting over again at $G = 250$, suppose that taxes increased by 10 to 160. What would happen to each of the following? State the amount as well as the direction of the changes.

   i.   the planned expenditure curve
   ii. the equilibrium level of income
   iii. the level of consumption
   iv. the government budget deficit

d. Starting over one last time at $G = 250$ and $T = 150$, suppose that government expenditures and taxes were both increased by 10 to 260 and 160, respectively. What would happen to each of the following? This time, draw the consumption, government purchases, and planned expenditure graphs to indicate the amount as well as the direction of the changes.

   i.   the planned expenditure curve
   ii. the equilibrium level of income
   iii. the level of consumption
   iv. the government budget deficit

3. Consider the following model of the economy:

$$C = 170 + 0.6(Y - T)$$
$$I = 250$$
$$G = 300$$
$$T = 200.$$

a. What is the value of the marginal propensity to consume?

b. What is the value of the government budget *deficit*?

c. Calculate the equilibrium level of GDP.

d. What is the value of the government-purchases multiplier?

e. Use your answer to Part d to calculate the amount by which government purchases of goods and services would have to rise in order to increase the equilibrium level of GDP by 50.

4. Consider the following model of the economy:

$$C = 20 + 0.75(Y - T)$$
$$I = 380$$
$$G = 400$$
$$T = 0.20Y$$
$$Y = C + I + G$$

   a. What is the value of the *MPC* in this model?

   b. The equation for taxes indicates that when *Y* rises by $100, taxes rise by $20. Consequently, when *Y* rises by $100, disposable income *Y* – *T* rises by $80 and consumption rises by 0.75(80) = $60. Draw the consumption and planned expenditure curves as a function of *Y* and label their slopes and *y* intercepts.

   c. Compute the equilibrium level of income.

   d. At the equilibrium level of income, what is the value of the government budget surplus?

   e. Increase *G* by 10 to 410, calculate the government-purchases multiplier, and explain why it no longer equals 1/(1 – *MPC*).

5. Suppose that the following equations describe an economy. (*C*, *I*, *G*, *T*, and *Y* are measured in billions of dollars, and *r* is measured as a percent; for example, *r* = 10 = 10%):

$$C = 170 + 0.6(Y - T)$$
$$T = 200$$
$$I = 100 - 4r$$
$$G = 350$$
$$(M/P)^d = L = 0.75Y - 6r$$
$$M^S/P = \overline{M}/\overline{P} = 735.$$

   a. Derive the equation for the *IS* curve. (*Hint:* It is easier to solve for *Y* here.)

   b. Derive the equation for the *LM* curve. (*Hint:* Again, it is easier to solve for *Y*.)

   c. Now express both the *IS* and *LM* equations in terms of *r*. Graph both curves and calculate their slopes.

   d. Use the equations from Parts a and b to calculate the equilibrium levels of real output, the interest rate, planned investment, and consumption.

   e. At the equilibrium level of real output, calculate the value of the government budget surplus.

6.
a. Rather than being independent of changes in Y, suppose that planned investment increases as real income Y rises and decreases as Y falls. Briefly explain why this situation might occur. Then draw the planned investment curve.

b. Compared to the case in which investment is independent of Y, how would the situation in Part a affect each of the following?

   i.   the slope of the planned expenditure curve
   ii. the government-purchases multiplier
   iii. the shapes of the *IS* and/or *LM* curves

7. Suppose that there is a sudden increase in the demand for money—that is, at the same levels of r and Y people want to hold more money. What would happen to the money demand curve and the *LM* curve?

8. How would each of the following changes affect the shape of the *IS* curve?

   a. the *MPC* gets bigger

   b. investment becomes more sensitive to changes in the interest rate (for example, investment now rises by a bigger amount whenever the interest rate falls by one percentage point)

9. In his State of the Union Address in January, 2002, President Bush announced that he would ask Congress to approve substantial increases in defense spending to counter terrorism and significant reductions in taxes. If these policy changes are enacted:

   a. What would the short-run effects be on the planned expenditure curve and the equilibrium level of GDP?

   b. What would be the effects on the *IS* and/or *LM* curves? Be as precise as you can about the exact shifts.

Data Questions

Locate the necessary economic data and apply them to answer the following data questions. All of the relevant data may be found in the Economic Report of the President.

1. **a.** Complete Table 10-7.

Table 10-7

(1) Year	(2) Nominal $M2$ ($ in billions)	(3) % Change in $M2$	(4) GDP Deflator (1996 = 100)	(5) Real $M2$ $M2/P$	(6) % Change in $M2/P$
1979	————		————	————	
1980	————	————	————	————	————
1981	————	————	————	————	————
1982	————	————	————	————	————
1983	————	————	————	————	————

    b. Given your calculations, would you characterize monetary policy in *each* of these four periods as expansionary, neutral, or contractionary? Which is the most appropriate measure of changes in monetary conditions: changes in the real or nominal money supply? (*Hint*: What happened to the economy in this period?)

Questions to Think About

1. Which definition of the money supply, $M1$ or $M2$, is more appropriate to use to derive the LM curve?

2. Banks now pay interest on checking deposits, although the interest rates they pay are usually less than those paid on government bonds. Given this, does the liquidity preference theory of money still make sense? If so, what variable should appear on the vertical axis of the money demand and LM curves?

3. Many companies do not need to borrow in order to invest because they have ample retained earnings from past profits. Why will their investment decisions still depend on the interest rate?

Aggregate Demand II

Fill-in Questions

Use the key terms below to fill in the blanks in the following statements. Each term may be used more than once.

debt-deflation theory   monetary transmission mechanism
liquidity trap   Pigou effect

1. A lower price level implies higher real money balances. According to the
    _____, consumers then feel wealthier and, therefore, spend
    more.

2. According to the _____, unexpected deflation hurts debtors
    and benefits creditors. Consequently, national income will fall if debtors have a
    higher propensity to spend than creditors.

3. The process by which an increase in the money supply induces greater spending is
    called the _____.

4. Some economists believe that Japanese interest rates have fallen so low that Japan
    may now be in a _____, in which expansionary monetary
    policy may be unable to stimulate the economy.

Multiple-Choice Questions

1. An increase in government purchases will shift the:
    a. *IS* curve to the left and decrease both the interest rate and the level of income.
    b. *IS* curve to the right and increase both the interest rate and the level of income.
    c. *IS* curve to the right and increase the level of income but decrease the interest
        rate.
    d. *LM* curve downward (to the right) and increase the level of income but decrease
        the interest rate.

2. An increase in taxes will shift the:

    a. *IS* curve to the left and decrease both the interest rate and the level of income.

    b. *IS* curve to the right and increase both the interest rate and the level of income.

    c. *IS* curve to the right and increase the level of income but decrease the interest rate.

    d. *LM* curve downward (to the right) and increase the level of income but decrease the interest rate.

3. An increase in the money supply will shift the:

    a. *IS* curve to the left and decrease both the interest rate and the level of income.

    b. *LM* curve downward (to the right) and increase both the interest rate and the level of income.

    c. *IS* curve to the right and increase the level of income but decrease the interest rate.

    d. *LM* curve downward (to the right) and increase the level of income but decrease the interest rate.

4. If real income rose and the interest rate fell following an increase in government purchases, the:

    a. *IS* curve must be vertical.

    b. *LM* curve must be vertical.

    c. Fed must have increased the money supply at the same time.

    d. Fed must have decreased the money supply at the same time.

5. If the Fed decreases the money supply at the same time as taxes increase, the:

    a. interest rate will definitely rise.

    b. interest rate will definitely fall.

    c. equilibrium level of income will definitely rise.

    d. equilibrium level of income will definitely fall.

6. The *IS* curve will shift to the right if:

    a. consumer confidence in the economy improves.

    b. firms become more optimistic about the economy and decide to invest more at each interest rate.

    c. the government increases transfer payments.

    d. all of the above.

7. If people suddenly wish to hold more money at each interest rate:

    a. the money demand curve will shift to the right.

    b. the *LM* curve will shift upward (to the left).

    c. real income will fall.

    d. all of the above.

8. Which of the following statements explains why the aggregate demand curve is downward-sloping?

   a. A lower price level increases real balances. Consequently, the *LM* curve shifts downward (to the right) and the level of income increases.

   b. A lower price level forces the Fed to increase the money supply. Consequently, the *LM* curve shifts down (to the right) and the level of income increases.

   c. A lower price level induces the government to reduce taxes. Consequently, the *IS* curve shifts to the right and the level of income increases.

   d. all of the above.

9. As we move along a stationary aggregate demand curve, one factor that is held constant is:

   a. real income.

   b. the aggregate price level.

   c. the (nominal) money supply.

   d. real money balances.

10. All of the following will shift the aggregate demand curve to the right EXCEPT a(n):

    a. increase in government purchases.

    b. reduction in transfer payments.

    c. increase in the (nominal) money supply.

    d. reduction in taxes.

11. The FALSE statement below is:

    a. the classical assumption that output reaches its natural rate is best used to describe the long run.

    b. in the short run, output may deviate from its natural rate.

    c. in the *IS-LM* model, the price level is assumed to be sticky in the short run.

    d. in the *IS-LM* model, aggregate demand is never equal to the natural rate of output even in the long run.

12. If income is initially less than the natural rate of output, the price level:

    a. will gradually fall, shifting the *LM* curve downward (to the right).

    b. will gradually rise, shifting the *LM* curve upward (to the left).

    c. will fall, shifting the *IS* curve to the right.

    d. is stuck at this level even in the long run.

13. According to adherents of the money hypothesis, the Great Depression was caused by a:

    a. sharp decline in the money supply.

    b. decline in business confidence.

    c. decline in consumer confidence.

    d. sharp decline in real money balances.

14. According to adherents of the spending hypothesis, the Great Depression was caused by:
    a. a reduction in business and consumer confidence.
    b. a contractionary (leftward) shift in the *IS* curve.
    c. the stock market crash.
    d. all of the above.

15. According to the Pigou effect:
    a. for a given supply of money, a lower price level shifts the *LM* curve outward, which leads to a higher level of income.
    b. since consumers will buy more of a good as its price falls, real output will rise during a depression.
    c. as prices fall and real balances rise, consumers will feel wealthier and spend more.
    d. all of the above.

16. According to the debt-deflation theory, unexpected deflation hurts debtors and benefits creditors. Consequently, national income will fall if:
    a. both groups have the same spending propensities.
    b. debtors have a higher propensity to spend than creditors.
    c. creditors have a higher propensity to spend than debtors.
    d. the *MPC* for both groups is less than 1.

17. The following statement is FALSE:
    a. money demand depends on the nominal interest rate.
    b. investment demand depends on the real interest rate.
    c. *IS-LM* analysis is unable to incorporate changes in expected inflation.
    d. an expected deflation causes the real interest rate to rise at each level of the nominal interest rate, which leads to a contractionary (leftward) shift of the *IS* curve.

18. Most economists believe that a Great Depression is less likely today than it was during the 1930s because:
    a. our knowledge of monetary and fiscal stabilization policies has improved.
    b. the system of federal deposit insurance makes widespread bank failures less likely.
    c. we now have more automatic stabilizers, such as the income tax.
    d. all of the above.

19. If an economy is in a liquidity trap, then:
    a. the interest rate is so low that fiscal policy cannot stimulate the economy.
    b. the interest rate is so low that monetary policy cannot stimulate the economy.
    c. the budget deficit is so high that fiscal policy cannot stimulate the economy.
    d. all of the above.

20. If investment becomes very sensitive to the interest rate, the:
    a. *IS* curve becomes steeper.
    A b. *IS* curve becomes flatter.
    c. *LM* curve becomes steeper.
    d. *LM* curve becomes flatter.

21. A smaller marginal propensity to consume leads to:
    a. a steeper planned expenditure curve.
    A b. a smaller government-purchases multiplier.
    c. a flatter *IS* curve.
    d. all of the above.

22. If money demand is not very sensitive to the level of income:
    a. the money demand curve does not shift very far to the right as income rises.
    A b. only a small change in the interest rate is necessary to offset the increase in money demand caused by a change in income.
    c. the *LM* curve is relatively flat.
    d. all of the above.

23. If the quantity of money demanded is very sensitive to the interest rate:
    a. the money demand curve will be relatively flat.
    A b. a shift in money demand due to a change in income leads to a small change in the equilibrium interest rate.
    c. the *LM* curve is relatively flat.
    d. all of the above.

24. The aggregate demand curve will be relatively flat if:
    a. the *MPC* is large.
    A b. the multiplier is small.
    c. investment is not very sensitive to changes in the interest rate.
    d. all of the above.

25. If money demand is relatively insensitive to changes in the interest rate, the:
    A a. *IS* curve will be relatively flat, and changes in monetary policy will have a large effect on real income.
    b. *IS* curve will be relatively steep, and changes in monetary policy will have a small effect on real income.
    c. *LM* curve will be relatively steep, and changes in fiscal policy will have a small effect on real income.
    d. *LM* curve will be relatively flat, and changes in fiscal policy will have a large effect on real income.

Exercises

1. **Shifts in the *IS* and *LM* Curves and Short-Run Changes in the Equilibrium Level of Income** *In this exercise, we review the policy and nonpolicy changes that shift the* IS *and* LM *curves, and we graphically illustrate the short-run changes in the equilibrium level of income. A review of Exercises 4 and 7 in Chapter 10 would be very helpful.*

    a. Examine the initial equilibrium shown at Point A on Graph 11-1.

    Graph 11-1

    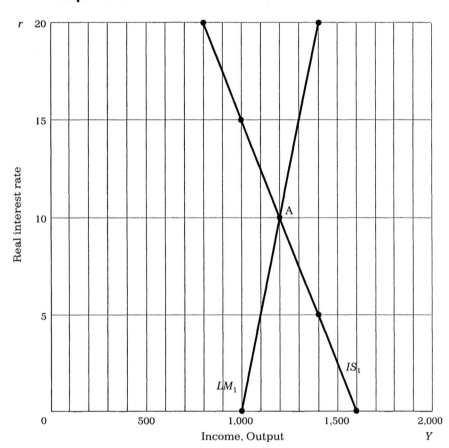

    Recall that the *IS* curve depicts the relationship between the interest rate *r* and the equilibrium value of income that results from the investment function and the Keynesian cross. The *LM* curve depicts the combinations of *r* and *Y* for which a given supply of real money balances is equal to real money demand. At the initial situation illustrated in Graph 11-1, the initial equilibrium level of income equals _____, and the initial equilibrium interest rate equals _____ percent. This occurs at Point A.

    b. Starting from the initial equilibrium illustrated on Graph 11-1, suppose that government purchases increase by $100 (billion). As a result, the planned expenditure curve (which is not shown) will shift <u>upward/downward</u> by $_____ billion. If the *MPC* equals 0.75, the *IS* curve will shift to the <u>right/left</u> by $100 billion × the government-purchases multiplier, or by $_____ billion. Draw this *IS* curve on Graph 11-1 and label it *IS*$_2$.

c. As income rises, money demand rises/falls. To keep real money demand equal to a constant real money supply, any increase in income must be accompanied by a(n) increase/decrease in the interest rate. As a result of this change in the interest rate, firms will increase/decrease investment, which partially offsets the effect of the increase in government purchases. Consequently, the equilibrium level of income rises by less/more than the horizontal shift in the *IS* curve. Locate the new equilibrium on Graph 11-1 and label it Point B.

d. Starting again from Point A, suppose that taxes increased by $100 billion. If the *MPC* = 0.75, the expenditure curve will shift upward/downward by $_____ billion, and the *IS* curve will shift to the right/left by $_____ billion. Draw this curve on Graph 11-1 and label it *IS*$_3$.

e. As income falls, money demand rises/falls. To keep real money demand equal to a constant real money supply, any decrease in income must be accompanied by a(n) increase/decrease in the interest rate. This, in turn, leads to a(n) increase/decrease in investment, which partially offsets the effect of the increase in taxes. Consequently, the equilibrium level of income falls by more/less than the horizontal shift in the *IS* curve. Locate the new equilibrium on Graph 11-1 and label it Point C.

f. Now examine Graph 11-2, which again illustrates the initial equilibrium.

Graph 11-2

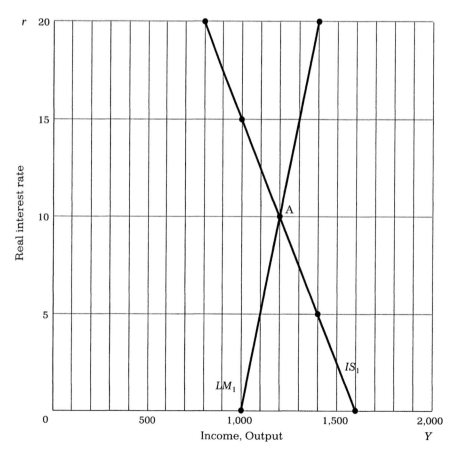

If the Federal Reserve were to increase the money supply, the *LM* curve would shift upward (to the left)/downward (to the right). Draw this shift on Graph 11-2. Label the new curve LM_2 and the new equilibrium Point D. As a result of this increase in the money supply, the equilibrium interest rate would rise/fall and the equilibrium level of income would rise/fall. When the Federal Reserve increases the money supply, at the initial interest rate people have more money than they want to hold. Consequently, they start depositing the extra money in banks or buy more bonds, which tends to raise/lower the interest rate until people want to hold all the extra money created by the Fed. This change in the interest rate increases/decreases planned investment, which increases/decreases planned expenditure and the equilibrium level of income. If, instead, the Fed reduced the money supply, the *LM* curve would shift upward (to the left)/ downward (to the right), the equilibrium interest rate would rise/fall, and the equilibrium level of income would rise/fall.

g. Nonpolicy changes can also shift the *IS* and/or *LM* curves. If firms suddenly feel more optimistic about the future and decide to invest more at every interest rate, the *IS/LM* curve would shift _____, the equilibrium level of income would rise/fall, and the equilibrium interest rate would rise/fall. If households became more pessimistic about the future and decided to consume less at every level of disposable income, the *IS/LM* curve would shift _____, the equilibrium level of income would rise/fall, and the equilibrium interest rate would rise/fall. Finally, if the amount of real money demanded increases substantially at each interest rate and level of income, the money demand curve will shift to the right/left and the *IS/LM* curve would shift _____. Consequently, the equilibrium level of income would rise/fall and the equilibrium interest rate would rise/fall.

2. **The Aggregate Demand Curve** *In this exercise, we examine the changes in the* IS-LM *equilibria as the price level varies and derive the aggregate demand curve.*

   a. Graph 11-3 illustrates the initial equilibrium in the basic model presented in the exercises for Chapter 10 of this workbook.

      The real money supply initially is equal to $800 billion, and the initial equilibrium is at Point A. If the real money supply increases to $1,040 billion, the *LM* curve will shift upward (to the left)/downward (to the right). Locate the appropriate curve on Graph 11-3, label it LM_2, and label the new equilibrium Point B.

   b. If, on the other hand, the real money supply falls to $560 billion, the *LM* curve will shift upward (to the left)/downward (to the right). Locate this curve on Graph 11-3, label it LM_3, and label the corresponding equilibrium Point C.

   c. The aggregate demand curve can now be derived using Graphs 11-3 and 11-4. As we saw in Part a, the *LM* curve will shift downward (to the right) whenever there

Graph 11-3

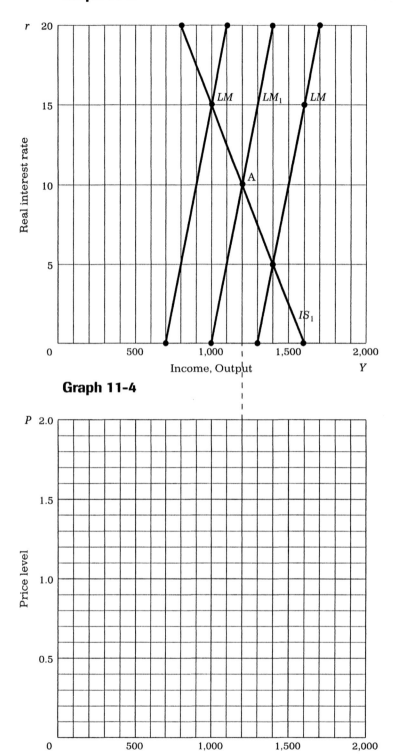

Graph 11-4

is an increase in the real money supply. This can be accomplished if the Fed increases the nominal money supply M, holding the aggregate price level P constant. It can also be accomplished by reducing P, while holding M constant. Using this information, a more general and realistic aggregate demand curve than the one introduced in Chapter 9 can be derived. This aggregate demand curve plots the relationship between the price level and the level of income that arises from the *IS-LM* model. On Graph 11-3, Point A represents the *IS-LM* equilibrium when the real money supply equals $800 billion. If the nominal money supply $M = \$800$ billion and the real money supply equals M/P, the aggregate price level $P =$ _____. From Graph 11-3, note that real income Y at Point A = _____. Use this information to plot one point on what will become the aggregate demand curve on Graph 11-4 and label this Point A.

d. Similarly, Point B on Graph 11-3 represents the *IS-LM* equilibrium when the real money supply equals 1,040. If M remains equal to 800, this occurs as a result of a change in the price level. Thus, $M/P = 800/P = 1{,}040$. Calculate P (round off to two decimal places).

$P =$ _____.

Real income at Point B on Graph 11-3 = _____. Use this information about P and Y to plot another point on the aggregate demand curve on Graph 11-4 and label this Point B.

e. Finally, Point C on Graph 11-3 represents the *IS-LM* equilibrium when the real money supply equals 560. If, instead of a decrease in the nominal money supply, this situation occurs as a result of a change in the price level, then $M/P = 800/P = 560$. Calculate P (round off to two decimal places).

$P = $ _____.

Real income at Point C = _____. Use this information about P and Y to plot another point on the aggregate demand curve on Graph 11-4, and label this Point C. Now connect all three points on Graph 11-4 to draw the aggregate demand curve.

f. Summarizing Parts a–e, the aggregate demand curve slopes downward because as the aggregate price level falls, real money balances <u>increases/decreases</u>. This shifts the *IS/LM* curve _____, <u>increases/decreases</u> the interest rate, and <u>increases/decreases</u> planned investment. As a result, the equilibrium level of income at the intersection of the *IS* and *LM* curves <u>increases/ decreases</u>. Note that, as we move along a stationary aggregate demand curve, government purchases, taxes, and the nominal money supply all remain constant.

3. **Fiscal Policy and the Aggregate Demand Curve** *In this exercise, we show how changes in fiscal policy shift the aggregate demand curve.*

On Graphs 11-5 and 11-6, the aggregate demand curve is derived for arbitrary *IS-LM* curves.

Graph 11-5

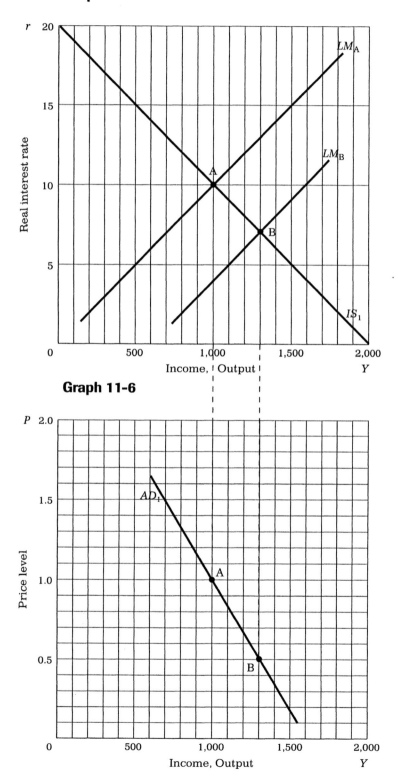

a. Assume that LM_A is drawn for a nominal money supply equal to 800 (billion dollars) and a price level equal to 1.0. Thus, at the initial equilibrium Point A, $P = $ _____ and $Y = $ _____. (Find Y from Graph 11-5.) Point A is also depicted on Graph 11-6. If the price level fell to 0.5, the real money supply would increase to $M/P = 800/0.5 = $ _____. This is reflected on Graph 11-5 by a shift in the LM curve to LM_B. The goods and money markets reach a new equilibrium at Point B, at which $Y = $ _____. This change is also reflected on Graph 11-6 by a movement along AD_1 to Point B.

b. Start again at Point A with $M/P = 800/1.0 = 800$, and let government purchases rise by 100. If the marginal propensity to consume equals 0.75 (or 3/4), the government-purchases multiplier $= 1/(1 - MPC) = $ _____. Consequently, if government purchases rise by 100, the IS curve shifts to the right/left by _____. Draw this new IS curve on Graph 11-5 and label it IS_2.

c. Because the LM curve has a positive slope, Y would rise by more/less than the horizontal shift in the IS curve. Starting at Point A on Graph 11-5, find the new equilibrium level of income if P remains equal to 1.0 and label it Point C. Find the corresponding point on Graph 11-6 and also label it Point C. (It will no longer lie on AD_1.)

d. Now start at Point B on Graph 11-5, with $M/P = 800/0.5 = 1,600$. Find the new equilibrium level of income if P remains equal to 0.5 after government purchases rise by 100 and label it Point D. Find the corresponding point on Graph 11-6 and also label it Point D. (It will no longer lie on AD_1.)

e. Connect Points C and D on Graph 11-6 to draw the new aggregate demand curve and label it AD_2. Compare Points C and A in both graphs. At Point C, real income is higher than/lower than/equal to real income at Point A, and the price level at Point C is higher than/lower than/equal to the price level at Point A. Now compare Points D and B. At Point D, real income is higher than/lower than/equal to real income at Point B, and the price level is higher than/lower than/equal to the price level at Point B.

f. Consequently, an increase in government purchases will shift the IS curve to the right/left and the aggregate demand curve to the right/left. A reduction in taxes will shift the IS curve to the right/left and the aggregate demand curve to the right/left.

4. **Monetary Policy and the Aggregate Demand Curve** *In this exercise, we show how changes in monetary policy shift the aggregate demand curve.*

On Graphs 11-7 and 11-8, the aggregate demand curve is derived for arbitrary *IS-LM* curves.

Graph 11-7

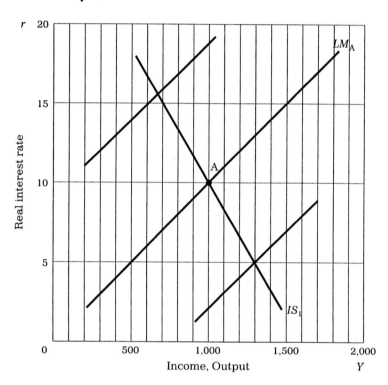

Graph 11-8

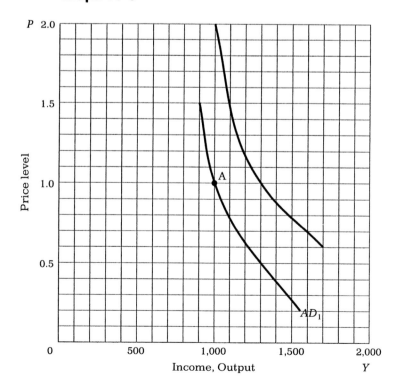

a. Assume that LM_A is drawn for a (nominal) money supply equal to 800 (billion dollars) and a price level equal to 1.0. Thus, at the initial equilibrium Point A, $P =$ _____ and $Y =$ _____. (Find Y from Graph 11-7.) Point A is also illustrated on Graph 11-8.

b. If the Fed were to double the nominal money supply to 1,600 and the price level remained constant, the real money supply would rise to $M/P = 1,600/1.0 =$ _____. This would shift the LM curve on Graph 11-7 upward (to the left)/downward (to the right). Locate the new LM curve on Graph 11-7 and label it LM_E. Locate the point on Graph 11-7 at which the goods and money markets reach a new equilibrium and label it Point E. Find the corresponding point on Graph 11-8 and also label it Point E (Point E does *not* lie on AD_1).

c. Note that, at Point E on Graph 11-8, real income is higher than/lower than/equal to real income at Point A, whereas the price level at Point E is higher than/lower than/equal to the price level at Point A. Consequently, an increase in the nominal money supply will shift the aggregate demand curve to the right/left. Conversely, a decrease in the nominal money supply will shift the aggregate demand curve to the right/left.

d. Finally, suppose that the nominal money supply remained equal to 1,600 while the price level rose to 2.0. The real money supply would then equal $M/P = 1,600/2.0 =$ _____. Consequently, the LM curve would shift all the way back to LM_A, and Y would equal _____ (even though the price level is now 2.0). Locate the new equilibrium points on both Graphs 11-7 and 11-8 and label them Points F. Note that Point F is the same as Point A on Graph 11-7 but not the same as Point A on Graph 11-8. This situation occurs because an increase in the nominal money supply will shift the aggregate demand curve, but the LM curve is affected only by changes in real money balances.

5. **The *IS-LM* Model in the Short Run and the Long Run** *In this exercise, we start from an* IS-LM *equilibrium level of income that is lower than the long-run equilibrium level and illustrate how reductions in the aggregate price level will shift the* LM *curve toward the long-run equilibrium.*

a. Assume the following equation for an economy's *IS* curve:

$$r = 40 - 0.025Y.$$

Plot and draw this curve on Graph 11-9 and label it IS_1.

Graph 11-9

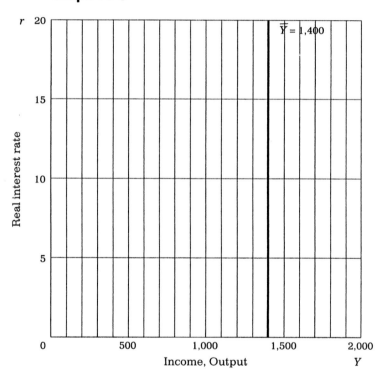

b. Assume the following money demand curve for this economy:

$$M/P = 0.8Y - 16r.$$

If $M = 800$ and $P = 1.0$, derive the equation for the economy's *LM* curve by setting real money balances equal to real money demand and solving for r.

$r =$ _____ + _____ Y.

Plot and draw this curve on Graph 11-9 and label it $LM(P_1 = 1.0)$.

c. Solve the *IS* and *LM* equations simultaneously. The initial equilibrium level of income and the initial interest rate are:

$Y =$ _____; $r =$ _____.

Label the initial equilibrium Point A on Graphs 11-9 and 11-10. Remember that the initial price level is assumed to be 1.0.

Graph 11-10

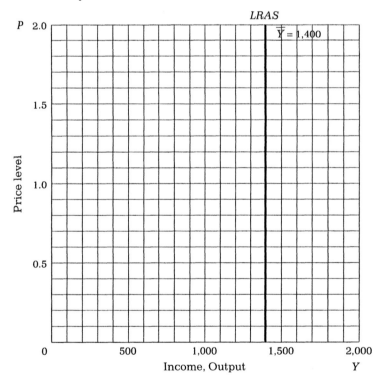

d. As you can see from Graphs 11-9 and 11-10, the natural rate of output $\overline{Y}$, which is also the long-run equilibrium level of income, is assumed to equal 1,400. Consequently, the initial level of income is <u>more/less</u> than the long-run equilibrium level of income. Point A is a short-run equilibrium level because the price level is assumed to be <u>sticky/flexible</u> in the short run, leading to a <u>horizontal/vertical</u> short-run aggregate supply curve.

e. In the long run, however, prices are sticky/flexible. Thus, as time goes by, the price level will rise/fall. This change will increase/decrease the real money supply, thereby shifting the *LM* curve upward (to the left)/downward (to the right) until it intersects the *IS* curve at the natural rate of output. Draw the long-run position of the *LM* curve on Graph 11-9 and label it $LM(P_2)$. Label the final equilibrium Point B on both Graphs 11-9 and 11-10.

f. The final price level can be computed in the following way. In the long run, $Y = $ 1,400, and we lie on the original *IS* curve. Substitute $Y = 1,400$ into the *IS* equation and solve for *r*.

$r = $ _____.

Given our long-run values for *Y* and *r*, use the money demand equation to compute real money demand.

$M/P = $ _____.

Since *M* is still equal to 800, this increase in *M/P* must come from a decrease in the price level. Solve the preceding equation for *P* (round off to two decimal places).

$P = $ _____.

g. Conversely, if the initial *IS–LM* equilibrium level of income were higher than the natural rate of output, over time the aggregate price level would rise/fall, there-by shifting the *IS/LM* curve _____ until the *IS* and *LM* curves intersected at the long-run equilibrium.

6. **Changes in Expected Inflation in the *IS-LM* Model** *In this exercise, we illustrate how a change in expected inflation will change the* IS-LM *equilibrium.*

   a. Investment is a function of the real interest rate r, whereas money demand is a function of the nominal interest rate i. Consequently, the *IS* curve should be drawn as a function of r, and the *LM* curve should be drawn as a function of i. Assume that the equations for the *IS* and *LM* curves are:

   $$IS \text{ curve: } r = 40 - 0.025Y \text{ and}$$
   $$LM \text{ curve: } i = -50 + 0.05Y.$$

   Recall that $r = i - \pi^e$. Assume that expected inflation equals zero so that $r = i$, and it does not matter which variable we put on the vertical axis. We'll put the nominal interest rate i on the vertical axis. Draw these two curves on Graph 11-11, label them IS_1 and LM_1, and label the initial equilibrium Point A.

   Graph 11-11

   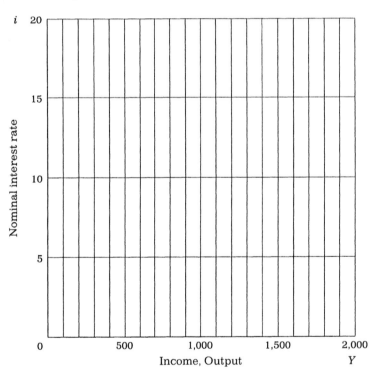

   b. The initial equilibrium occurs at $Y =$ _____ and $i =$ _____ percent. Since $\pi^e = 0$, $r =$ _____ percent.

c. Now suppose that we have deflation and expected inflation falls to –7.5 percent. As a result of this decrease in expected inflation, the real interest rate at the initial value of the nominal interest rate will rise to $r = i - \pi^e =$ _____ $- (-7.5) =$ _____. Consequently, at each level of i, r will now be higher/lower than it was before the expected deflation. Since the *LM* curve is a function of the nominal interest rate, it will not shift. The *IS* curve, on the other hand, is a function of the real interest rate. From the *IS* equation, it is known that $Y = 1,200$ when $r =$ _____. When $\pi^e = 0$, this value of r occurs when $i =$ _____. Now that $\pi^e = -7.5$ percent, this level of r will occur when $i = r + \pi^e =$ _____ + _____ = _____ percent. Thus, the same level of investment will occur only if i falls by _____ percentage points. Consequently, the *IS* curve shifts upward/downward by _____ percentage points. Draw the new *IS* curve on Graph 11-11, label it IS_2, and label the new equilibrium Point B.

d. The equation for the new *IS* curve when $\pi^e = -7.5$ percent is $i = 32.5 - 0.025Y$. Set this equal to the equation for the *LM* curve, and compute the new equilibrium values of Y and i:

   $Y =$ _____; $i =$ _____.

e. The decrease in expected inflation leads to a(n) increase/decrease in Y and a(n) increase/decrease in i. The real interest rate $r = i - \pi^e$ was initially equal to _____ – _____ = _____ but now equals _____ – _____ = _____. Consequently, the real interest rate rises/falls.

7. **Determinants of the Steepness of the *IS* Curve** *In this exercise, we examine how the slope of the IS curve is affected by the marginal propensity to consume and the sensitivity of planned investment to changes in the interest rate.*

   a. Recall from Chapter 10, Exercise 4e, that when planned investment increases by 50, the planned expenditure curve shifts upward by _____, and income Y rises by the shift in the planned expenditure curve multiplied by the government-purchases multiplier, or by _____ × $1/(1 - MPC)$. In our example, $MPC = 0.75$, so Y rose by _____ × $1/(1 -$ _____$) =$ _____.

   b. Now suppose that the MPC were larger. If, for example, it were 0.9, the government-purchases multiplier would equal $1/(1 - MPC) = 1/(1 -$ _____$) =$ _____. This is larger/smaller than the multiplier in Exercise 4e.

   c. If $MPC = 0.9$, the government-purchases multiplier = _____, and an increase in planned investment of 50 would increase the equilibrium level of Y by $50 × 1/(1 - MPC) =$ _____. This increase is larger/smaller than the increase in Y in Part a.

   d. According to our original investment equation, $I = 200 - 10r$. To increase investment by 50, as in Parts a–c, the interest rate would have to decrease by _____ percentage points. In Part a, this reduction in r increased the equilibrium level of Y by _____. In Part c, this same reduction in r increased the equilibrium level of Y by _____ because the multiplier, or round-by-round effects on consumption, were larger/smaller. Thus, as the MPC grows larger, the increase in Y resulting from a reduction in r becomes larger/smaller and the IS curve becomes steeper/flatter.

   e. Now suppose that the MPC remains equal to 0.75. Our original investment equation, $I = 200 - 10r$, implies that whenever the interest rate falls by 1 percentage point, planned investment increases by _____. This investment curve is illustrated on Graph 11-12.

Graph 11-12

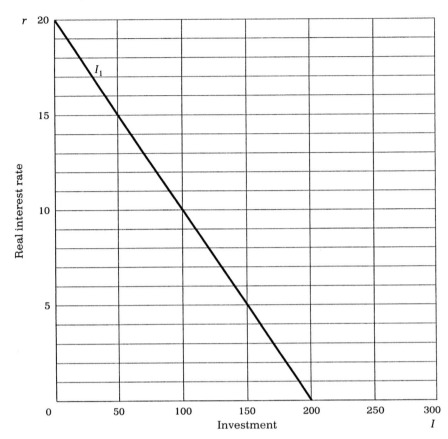

f. Suppose, instead, that $I = 300 - 20r$. According to this second equation, whenever the interest rate falls by 1 percentage point, planned investment increases by _____. Consequently, investment would be <u>more/less</u> sensitive to changes in the interest rate than in Part e. Graph this second investment equation on Graph 11-12 and label it I_2. I_2 is <u>steeper/flatter</u> than I_1.

g. Note that the two investment curves on Graph 11-12 intersect when $r = 10$ and $I =$ _____. Since all of the other parameters are the same, when $r = 10$, the equilibrium value of Y will be the same as before—that is, $Y = 1,200$.

h. Suppose that the MPC is still 0.75 and the interest rate falls by 5 percentage points. Using our original investment equation $I = 200 - 10r$, planned investment will rise by $5 \times$ _____ $= 50$, and the equilibrium level of Y will rise by $50 \times 1/(1 - MPC) = 50 \times$ _____ $=$ _____. With our new investment equation, planned investment will rise by $5 \times$ _____ $=$ _____, and the equilibrium level of Y will rise by _____ $\times 1/(1 - MPC) =$ _____. Consequently, the *IS* curve will be <u>steeper/flatter</u> when planned investment becomes more sensitive to changes in the interest rate.

8. **Determinants of the Steepness of the *LM* Curve** *In this exercise, we examine how the slope of the LM curve is affected by the sensitivity of money demand to changes in real income and the sensitivity of money demand to changes in the interest rate.*

   a. In Chapter 10, Exercise 6, the *LM* curve was derived from the following equations for real money supply and real money demand:

   $$\overline{M}/\overline{P} = 800 \text{ (money supply equation)} \qquad \text{(11-1)}$$
   $$(M/P)^d = 0.8Y - 16r \text{ (money demand equation).} \qquad \text{(11-2)}$$

   Now suppose that money demand were more sensitive to changes in *Y*, so that the coefficient on *Y* were equal to 1.0, rather than 0.8:

   $$(M/P)^d = 1.0Y - 16r. \qquad \text{(11-3)}$$

   If this were the case, an increase in *Y* would increase money demand by <u>more/less</u> than in Chapter 10, Exercise 7. To keep real money demand equal to the fixed real money supply, the interest rate would have to increase by <u>more/less</u> than in Exercise 7 of Chapter 10. This change would make the *LM* curve <u>steeper/flatter</u> than in Exercise 6.

   b. As an example, suppose that *Y* increased by 160. In Equation 11-2, if the interest rate were to remain constant, money demand would increase by 0.8(160) = _____. To keep real money demand equal to the fixed supply, the interest rate would have to increase by _____/16 = _____. In Equation 11-3, however, if *r* were to remain constant, money demand would increase by 1.0(160) = _____. To keep real money demand equal to the fixed supply, *r* would have to increase by _____/16 = _____. Consequently, when *Y* increases by 160, the interest rate rises by more when money demand is <u>more/less</u> sensitive to changes in *Y*, and, hence, the *LM* curve is <u>steeper/flatter</u>.

   c. Refer to the original money demand equation, Equation 11-2. According to this equation, whenever *r* increases by 1 (percentage point), money demand falls by _____. Now compare this equation with one in which money demand is more sensitive to changes in the interest rate:

   $$(M/P)^d = 0.8Y - 32r. \qquad \text{(11-4)}$$

   According to Equation 11-4, whenever *r* increases by 1 percentage point, the quantity of money demanded falls by _____.
   Consequently, money demand is now <u>more/less</u> sensitive to changes in the interest rate, and the money demand curve would be <u>steeper/flatter</u>.

d. Suppose that Y again increased by 160. In Equations 11-2 and 11-4, if the interest rate were to remain constant, money demand would increase by 0.8(160) = _____. To keep real money demand equal to the fixed supply in Equation 11-2, the interest rate would have to increase by _____/16 = _____. In Equation 11-4, however, the interest rate would have to increase by _____/32 = _____. Consequently, when Y increases by 160, the interest rate rises by more when money demand is more/less sensitive to changes in the interest rate, and the LM curve will be steeper/flatter.

9. **Determinants of the Steepness of the Aggregate Demand Curve** *In this exercise, we examine how the slope of the aggregate demand curve is affected by the slope of the* IS *curve and the sensitivity of money demand to changes in the interest rate.*

Using Graphs 11-13 and 11-14, we derive the aggregate demand curve for a steep IS curve and a flat IS curve. Assume that the initial equilibrium at Point A is the same in both situations.

a. Assume that the money demand function and the nominal money supply M are held constant. Use the information from Graph 11-13 to plot and draw Points A, B, and C on the aggregate demand curve corresponding to the flat IS curve on Graph 11-14. Connect the points and label the curve AD_1. Now use the information from Graph 11-13 to plot Points A, D, and E on the aggregate demand curve corresponding to the steep IS curve on Graph 11-14. Connect the points and label the curve AD_2. Note that AD_2 is flatter/steeper than AD_1.

b. Consequently, when the IS curve is flat, the AD curve will be flat/steep. Intuitively, as the price level falls and real balances increase, real income rises by more when the IS curve is flat/steep. An IS curve can be flat (as opposed to steep) for several reasons. Planned investment, for example, may be very/not be very sensitive to changes in the interest rate. Alternatively, the marginal propensity to consume may be large/small, resulting in a large/small multiplier.

Graph 11-13

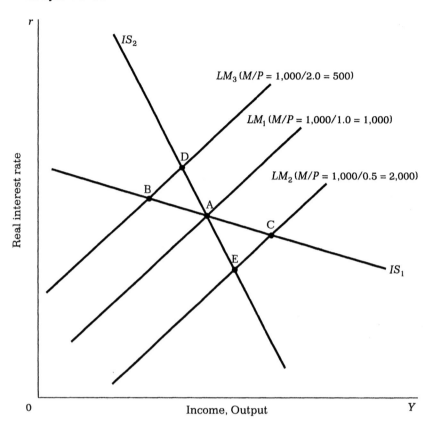

Graph 11-14

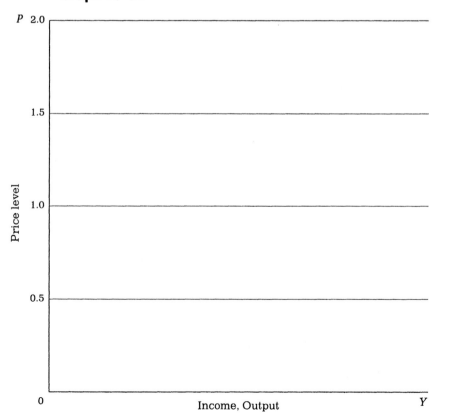

c. Graph 11-15 illustrates an initial equilibrium for one *IS* curve and two *LM* curves
CH (one flat *LM* curve and one steep *LM* curve). Assume that the initial equilibrium,
Point A, is the same in both situations. Recall that an *LM* curve can be flat for
several reasons. Assume that the flat *LM* curve results from money demand
<u>being very/not being very</u> sensitive to changes in the interest rate.

Graph 11-15

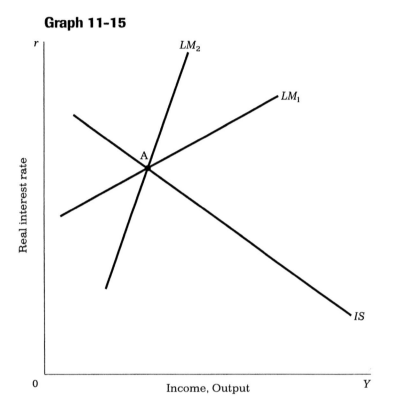

d. Suppose that the price level falls by one-half. This fall would double the real
CH money supply and shift both *LM* curves <u>upward (to the left)/downward (to the
right)</u>. The horizontal shift in the *LM* curve depends on the increase in real
money balances and the sensitivity of money demand to changes in income.
Assume that these are equal in both situations so that the horizontal shift in
both *LM* curves will be equal. Draw the new *LM* curves and label the flat curve
LM_3 and the steep curve LM_4. Label the new equilibrium for the flat *LM* curve
Point B and the new equilibrium for the steep *LM* curve Point C. When the price
level falls, real income rises by more when money demand is <u>very/not very</u> sensitive to changes in the interest rate. Thus, the aggregate demand curve will be
relatively flat when money demand is <u>very/not very</u> sensitive to changes in the
interest rate. (Since both the slope and the horizontal shift in the *LM* curve
depend on the sensitivity of money demand to changes in income, one cannot
determine the relationship between the slope of the aggregate demand curve
and the sensitivity of money demand to changes in income merely by examining
the relative slopes of the *LM* curves.)

Problems

Answer the following problems on a separate sheet of paper.

1. (Parts a–e of this problem are the same as Problem 5 in Chapter 10 of this workbook.) Suppose that the following equations describe an economy (C, I, G, T, and Y are measured in billions of dollars and r is measured in percent; for example, $r = 10$ means $r = 10$ percent):

$$C = 170 + 0.6(Y - T)$$
$$T = 200$$
$$I = 100 - 4r$$
$$G = 350$$
$$(M/P)^d = L = 0.75Y - 6r$$
$$M^s/P = \overline{M}/\overline{P} = 735.$$

   a. Derive the equation for the *IS* curve. (*Hint:* It is easier to solve for real output Y here.)

   b. Derive the equation for the *LM* curve. (*Hint:* Again, it is easier to solve for real output Y.)

   c. Now express both the *IS* and *LM* equations in terms of r. Plot and graph both curves and calculate their slopes.

   d. Use the equations from Parts a and b to calculate the equilibrium levels of real output Y, the interest rate r, planned investment I, and consumption C.

   e. At the equilibrium level of real output Y, calculate the value of the government budget surplus.

   f. Suppose that G increases by 36 to 386. Derive the new *IS* and *LM* equations and plot and draw these curves on the graph you drew for Part c.

   g. What is the horizontal shift in the *IS* curve and/or the *LM* curve in Part f (that is, if r remains constant, by how much does Y increase on each curve)?

   h. Refer to the *IS* and *LM* equations you derived in Part f. With Y on the left-hand side of the equations, calculate the new equilibrium levels of real output Y, the interest rate r, planned investment I, and consumption C.

   i. Instead of increasing G, suppose that the Fed sought to achieve the equilibrium **CH** level of real output Y in Part h through expansionary monetary policy alone. By how much would the Fed have to increase the money supply? (*Hint:* Start by drawing the appropriate shifts in the *IS* curve and/or the *LM* curve in Parts f and i.)

   j. Compare the equilibrium levels of consumption C, government spending G, and planned investment I in Parts h and i. Based on this comparison, why might some economists prefer expansionary fiscal policy while others prefer expansionary monetary policy?

2. As a result of the dramatic events in Eastern Europe in the 1990s, many Americans felt less threatened by Russia and called for massive reductions in the defense budget as a "peace dividend."

   a. Suppose that the defense budget had been cut by one-third, or about $100 billion. If no other policy changes are enacted, use the *IS-LM* model to analyze what would happen to real GDP and the interest rate. Illustrate the changes that would occur by graphing the *IS* and *LM* curves and indicating their shift(s).

   b. Now suppose that defense spending had been cut by the same $100 billion, but government transfers were raised by the same amount ($100 billion) to alleviate poverty and subsidize education and day care. Draw the appropriate shifts in the *IS* and/or *LM* curves on your graph for Part a and predict what would happen to real GDP and the interest rate.

   c. Compare the sizes of the changes in Parts a and b.

   d. Finally, start over and suppose that defense spending had been cut by $100 billion and the government used the money to give unrestricted grants to the struggling economies of Eastern Europe. Assuming that this action does not change the money supply, what does the *IS-LM* model predict would be the change in U.S. GDP relative to the changes described in Parts a and b? Explain briefly.

3. Many economists believe that consumption expenditures depend on household wealth in addition to disposable income.

   a. If this were true, how would the U.S. stock market decline in 2000 and 2001 have affected the consumption expenditure curve and the planned expenditure curve?

   b. Draw representative *IS* and *LM* curves on a graph and illustrate the consequent shift(s) in the *IS* curve and/or the *LM* curve. Indicate the predicted (directional) changes in real output *Y* and the interest rate *r*.

4. In 1993, President Clinton proposed reducing the federal budget deficit by increasing
   ☐ net taxes and reducing government spending. Some economists claimed that this policy would reduce interest rates and increase real GDP as well as cut the deficit.

   a. Draw *IS-LM* graphs to analyze the effects of this mix of fiscal policies on the deficit, interest rates, and real GDP. (Assume that taxes are lump sum, that is, taxes are an absolute amount that is unrelated to the level of income.) Are these results consistent with the economists' predictions?

   b. Most economists who believe that an increase in taxes and a reduction in government spending would both increase GDP and cut the deficit implicitly assume that the Fed would change its monetary policy if this deficit-reduction plan were enacted. Draw *IS-LM* graphs on a separate sheet of paper to show what kind of monetary policy must accompany this mix of fiscal policy changes in order to decrease the deficit and interest rates, while increasing GDP.

   c. What happens to the aggregate demand curve in Parts a and b?

5. Suppose two countries differ only in the size of their *MPC*. In Country A, the *MPC* is large, and in Country B, the *MPC* is small.

   a. Draw representative *IS* and *LM* curves for each country and label them IS^A and LM^A for Country A and IS^B and LM^B for Country B. Compare the shapes of the *IS* and *LM* curves in the two countries and explain your results.

   b. In which country will an increase in the money supply be more effective in changing real output? Illustrate using the graph you drew in Part a.

6. Suppose that private spending (for example, *C* or *I*) is volatile and unpredictable. This situation implies that the *IS* curve would frequently shift to the right and to the left.

   a. Assume that the Fed decided to keep the real money supply constant. Draw *IS-LM* curves to illustrate how real output *Y* would respond to the instability in private spending.

   b. Now suppose that the Fed tried to keep the interest rate constant at its initial level even if this required frequent changes in the real money supply. Draw a money supply and demand diagram to show what the Fed would have to do to the real money supply when *Y* increases (because of a shift in the *IS* curve to the right). What would this monetary response do to the *IS* curve and/or *LM* curve?

   c. Similarly, if the Fed tried to keep the interest rate *r* constant, what would the Fed have to do to the real money supply when the *IS* curve shifts to the left and *Y* falls? What would this response do to the *IS* curve and/or *LM* curve?

   d. Using your answers to Parts b and c, explain which of the two policies (keeping *M/P* constant or keeping *r* constant) would stabilize the economy better (by minimizing the fluctuations in real GDP) if the main source of instability in the economy were fluctuations in private spending.

7. a. During the 1960s, President John F. Kennedy's tax cuts were enacted. Draw the appropriate graphs to indicate what would happen to the *IS*, *LM*, aggregate demand, and short-run aggregate supply curves, and indicate any short-run changes in the equilibrium levels of *r*, *I*, *C*, *G*, *Y*, and *P* if the Fed had not changed any of its policies.

   b. During this period, the Fed actually pursued expansionary monetary policy and kept interest rates nearly constant. Redraw your diagrams from Part a and indicate what actually happened to the *IS* curve, *LM* curve, aggregate demand curve, short-run aggregate supply curve, and the levels of *r*, *I*, *C*, *G*, *Y*, and *P*. How do they compare with the levels in Part a?

8. Suppose policymakers want to raise investment but keep real GDP constant. Use the *IS-LM* model to describe and illustrate what *mix* of monetary and fiscal policies would achieve this goal.

9. In addition to depending on disposable income, suppose household consumption were also a function of the interest rate. In particular, assume that households consume more (i.e., save less) when the interest rate falls.

   a. Explain how this situation would influence the shapes of the *IS* and/or *LM* curves relative to the case in which consumption is not a function of the interest rate.

   b. Now use *IS-LM* curves to illustrate how this situation would influence the short-run effectiveness of monetary policy.

   c. What, if anything, would this modification do to the shape of the aggregate demand curve?

10. a. Suppose the economy were initially in long-run and short-run equilibrium. Illustrate this position by drawing an *IS-LM* graph and, directly below it, the aggregate supply-aggregate demand graph.

    b. Now suppose that oil prices increase dramatically. On the same graphs that you drew in Part a, illustrate what happens in both the short run and the long run to the *IS* curve, *LM* curve, short-run aggregate supply curve, long-run aggregate supply curve, and the equilibrium levels of *Y* and *P*. Explain the changes depicted in the graphs.

11. Some economists believe that the Japanese economy entered a liquidity trap in the late 1990s as interest rates fell almost to zero. One proposed solution was an announced, long-term expansionary monetary policy that increased both the nominal money supply and inflationary expectations. Draw *IS-LM* curves using the nominal interest rate on the vertical axis and illustrate how a successful implementation of this policy would affect the equilibrium levels of *i*, *Y*, and *r*.

12. In the Case Study about the U.S. recession that began in 2001, the textbook cites the decline in the stock market and the declining perceptions of the profitability of new technologies (largely involving the Internet and telecommunications) as two causes of the slump. Use *IS-LM* curves to illustrate and explain how the preceding rise in the stock market and optimistic perceptions of the profitability of new technologies had contributed to the long economic expansion during the 1990s.

13. a. Draw an *IS* curve and an *LM* curve using the real interest rate *r* on the vertical axis, assuming that expected inflation is 0 percent.

    b. Illustrate how the *IS* and/or *LM* curves you drew in Part a would shift if expected inflation fell to −10 percent. What happens to *Y*, *r*, and *i*? Compare your answer to the analysis presented in the textbook.

14. Several economists believe that the money supply *M* tends to increase as the interest rate increases. Draw a money-supply, money-demand graph, and, next to it, derive the *LM* curve to illustrate how this tendency would affect the slope of the *LM* curve.

Data Questions

Locate the necessary economic data and apply them to answer the following data questions. All of the relevant data may be found in the Economic Report of the President.

1. a. Complete Table 11-1 on the following page (all values are in billions of dollars except for the GDP deflator).

Table 11-1

(1) Year	(2) Real GDP in billions of 1996 dollars	(3) % Change in Real GDP	(4) $M1$ (Dec.)	(5) GDP Deflator (1996 = 100)	(6) Real $M1$ (= $M1/P$)	(7) % Change in Real $M1$
1979	————		————	————	————	
		————				————
1980	————		————	————	————	
		————				————
1981	————		————	————	————	
		————				————
1982	————		————	————	————	

b. Compare the percentage changes in real GDP and real money balances during this period with those that occurred during the Great Depression. (The Depression data are presented in Table 11-2 in your textbook.)

2. a. Complete Table 11-2.

Table 11-2

(1) Year	(2) Real GDP in billions of 1996 dollars	(3) % Change in Real GDP	(4) Interest Rate on 10-Year U.S. Treasury Securities
1960	————		————
		————	
1965	————		————

b. Between 1960 and 1965, the government pursued expansionary fiscal policy by increasing government purchases and reducing taxes. These fiscal policies caused the *IS* curve to shift to the right. Given this information plus the data in Table 11-2, what do you conclude about the Fed's policy during this period and why? Draw an *IS-LM* diagram on a separate sheet of paper and illustrate the joint effects of the fiscal and monetary policies pursued during this period on the *IS* curve and the *LM* curve, and on the equilibrium levels of real income and the interest rate.

Questions to Think About

1. Based on the discussion presented in Chapter 11 of the textbook, do you think the Great Depression was caused primarily by a shock to the *LM* curve or a shock to the *IS* curve? What evidence do you find most convincing and why?

2. What does the experience of the Great Depression imply about the downward flexibility of prices and the speed with which the economy moves to the natural rate of output after an aggregate demand shock?

CHAPTER *12* TWELVE

Aggregate Demand in the Open Economy

Fill-in Questions

Use the key terms below to fill in the blanks in the following statements. Each term may be used more than once.

devaluation   Mundell-Fleming model
fixed exchange rates   revaluation
floating exchange rates

1. Under a system of _____, the exchange rate is allowed to fluctuate freely in response to changing economic conditions.

2. Under a system of _____, a central bank buys or sells the domestic currency for foreign currencies at a predetermined price.

3. Under a system of _____, monetary policy is dedicated to the single goal of keeping the exchange rate at the announced level. Consequently, one argument in favor of _____ is that they allow monetary policy to be used for other purposes.

4. In a fixed-exchange-rate regime, a reduction in the value of the currency is called a(n) _____; an increase in the value of the currency is called a(n) _____.

5. In the _____, a(n) _____ shifts the LM^* curve to the right, whereas a(n) _____ shifts the LM^* curve to the left.

6. Proponents of _____ argue that this policy reduces some of the uncertainty in international business transactions.

Multiple-Choice Questions

1. The exchange rate is defined as the amount of foreign currency needed to buy one unit of domestic currency (for example, 100 yen per dollar). A higher exchange rate:

   a. makes domestic goods less expensive relative to foreign goods.
   b. stimulates exports and depresses imports.
   c. leads to a decrease in net exports.
   d. leads to higher income.

2. In the conventional *IS-LM* model, real income *Y* and the real interest rate *r* appear on the axes. When the exchange rate increases:

   a. investment increases and the *IS* curve shifts to the right.
   b. net exports increase and the *IS* curve shifts to the right.
   c. investment decreases and the *IS* curve shifts to the left.
   d. net exports decrease and the *IS* curve shifts to the left.

3. All of the following statements about the Mundell-Fleming model drawn with aggregate income *Y* and the exchange rate *e* on the axes are true EXCEPT:

   a. the interest rate is fixed at the world interest rate.
   b. the *LM** curve is vertical because the exchange rate does not enter the money demand or money supply equations.
   c. the *IS** curve slopes downward because a lower exchange rate stimulates investment.
   d. the intersection of the *IS** and *LM** curves determines the equilibrium exchange rate.

4. In a small open economy with a floating exchange rate, fiscal policy will be ineffective because:

   a. monetary policy will completely offset it.
   b. the exchange rate will remain constant.
   c. a fall in net exports will offset any increases in government purchases or consumption.
   d. the exchange rate will rise by the same amount as the interest rate.

5. In a small open economy with a floating exchange rate, monetary expansion does all of the following EXCEPT:

   a. lower the interest rate.
   b. increase the equilibrium income level.
   c. decrease the exchange rate.
   d. cause net exports to rise.

6. Trade restrictions have no effect on income under floating exchange rates because:

   a. net exports increase but investment decreases.
   b. the exchange rate rises to offset the initial increase in net exports.
   c. the fall in imports equals the rise in exports.
   d. all of the above.

7. If the current yen-to-dollar exchange rate (for example, 200 yen per dollar) is above the fixed exchange rate set by the Fed (for example, 150 yen per dollar), arbitragers can make profits by:
   a. buying yen in foreign exchange markets and selling them to the Fed.
   b. buying yen from the Fed and selling them in foreign exchange markets.
   c. buying dollars in foreign exchange markets and selling them to the Fed.
   d. none of the above.

8. The profit-making actions described in Question 7 will cause the money supply to:
   a. rise, thereby shifting the LM^* curve to the left.
   b. rise, thereby shifting the LM^* curve to the right.
   c. fall, thereby shifting the LM^* curve to the left.
   d. fall, thereby shifting the LM^* curve to the right.

9. If the current yen-to-dollar market exchange rate (for example, 100 yen per dollar) is below the fixed exchange rate set by the Fed (for example, 150 yen per dollar), arbitragers can make profits by:
   a. buying yen from the Fed and selling them in foreign exchange markets.
   b. buying dollars in foreign exchange markets and selling them to the Fed.
   c. buying dollars from the Fed and selling them in foreign exchange markets.
   d. both a and b.

10. The profit-making actions described in Question 9 will cause the money supply to:
    a. rise, thereby shifting the LM^* curve to the left.
    b. rise, thereby shifting the LM^* curve to the right.
    c. fall, thereby shifting the LM^* curve to the left.
    d. fall, thereby shifting the LM^* curve to the right.

11. Under a gold standard, if the Fed sells an ounce of gold for $100, and the Bank of England sells an ounce of gold for 50 pounds, then the equilibrium exchange rate would be fixed at:
    a. 2 pounds per dollar.
    c. 1.5 pounds per dollar.
    b. 0.5 pounds per dollar.
    d. 5 pounds per dollar.

12. An expansionary fiscal policy under fixed exchange rates will:
    a. force the Fed to increase the money supply in order to prevent the exchange rate from falling.
    b. increase real income.
    c. eventually lead the IS^* and LM^* curves to shift to the right.
    d. all of the above.

13. If the Fed tries to increase the money supply under fixed exchange rates:
    a. national income will be unaffected.
    b. the initial increase in the money supply will be offset if the Fed maintains the original fixed exchange rate.
    c. the LM^* curve on a $Y - e$ graph will shift first to the right and then to the left, back to its original position.
    d. all of the above.

14. If the value of the currency is reduced via a devaluation, the:
    a. LM^* curve shifts to the right, and both net exports and income rise.
    b. LM^* curve shifts to the right, net exports fall, and income rises.
    c. LM^* curve shifts to the left, and both net exports and income fall.
    d. IS^* and LM^* curves both shift to the right.

15. A restrictive trade policy under a fixed exchange rate will:
    a. have the same effect as under a floating exchange rate.
    b. raise the equilibrium level of national income.
    c. shift the IS^* curve to the right and the LM^* curve to the left on a $Y - e$ graph.
    d. lead to a devaluation of the currency.

16. In the Mundell-Fleming model:
    a. both fiscal and monetary policy will have greater effects on national income if the exchange rate is fixed rather than flexible.
    b. both fiscal and monetary policy will have greater effects on national income if the exchange rate is flexible rather than fixed.
    c. fiscal policy will have a greater effect on national income if the exchange rate is fixed rather than flexible, whereas monetary policy will be more potent if the exchange rate is flexible.
    d. fiscal policy will have a greater effect on national income if the exchange rate is flexible rather than fixed, whereas monetary policy will be more potent if the exchange rate is fixed.

17. The risk premium in a country's interest rate will rise if:
    a. people expect the country's exchange rate to fall.
    b. fears arise that the government may not pay all of its debt.
    c. the country's foreign exchange reserves are quickly being depleted.
    d. all of the above.

18. An increase in a country's perceived risk premium will:
    a. shift its IS^* and LM^* curves to the right, resulting in an appreciation of its exchange rate.
    b. shift its IS^* and LM^* curves to the left, resulting in a depreciation of its exchange rate.
    c. shift its IS^* curve to the left and its LM^* curve to the right, resulting in a depreciation of its exchange rate.
    d. shift its IS^* curve to the right and its LM^* curve to the left, resulting in an appreciation of its exchange rate.

19. An argument in favor of floating exchange rates is that they:
    a. reduce uncertainty and promote international trade.
    b. allow monetary policy to be used for purposes other than maintaining exchange rates.
    c. reduce the volatility of exchange rates.
    d. all of the above.

20. Suppose the initial level of income is less than the long-run equilibrium level. Then, in the Mundell-Fleming model with a changing price level, the price level will:
    a. fall, shifting the *IS** curve to the right.
    b. rise, shifting the *IS** curve to the left.
    c. rise, shifting the *LM** curve to the left.
    d. fall, shifting the *LM** curve to the right.

21. In the short-run model for a large open economy presented in the appendix to
A Chapter 12, a reduction in the domestic interest rate:
    a. increases net capital outflow and lowers both net exports and the exchange rate.
    b. increases net capital outflow and net exports, and reduces the exchange rate.
    c. reduces net capital outflow, net exports, and the exchange rate.
    d. reduces net capital outflow and net exports, and increases the exchange rate.

22. Fiscal policy will have the largest short-run effect on the equilibrium level of na-
A tional income in a:
    a. small open economy with a flexible exchange rate.
    b. large open economy with a flexible exchange rate.
    c. closed economy.
    d. small open economy with a fixed exchange rate.

Exercises

1. **The Effect of the Exchange Rate on the *IS* Curve** *In this exercise, we add net exports to the expenditure curve and illustrate the effects of changes in the exchange rate on the expenditure and IS curves.*

    a. Consider the following model of the economy:

$$E = C + I + G + NX \qquad (12\text{-}1)$$
$$C = 125 + 0.75(Y - T) \qquad (12\text{-}2)$$
$$I = 200 - 10r \qquad (12\text{-}3)$$
$$G = 100 \qquad (12\text{-}4)$$
$$T = 100 \qquad (12\text{-}5)$$
$$NX = 150 - 50e. \qquad (12\text{-}6)$$

This model is very similar to the one presented in the Student Guide exercises for Chapters 10 and 11, except that net exports *NX* are now included. As in Chapter 5 of the textbook, *NX* is negatively related to the nominal exchange rate *e*. Since both the domestic and foreign price levels are held fixed in Chapter 12 of the textbook, changes in the nominal exchange rate *e* are proportional to changes in the real exchange rate ε, so we can focus on changes in *e*.

b. Suppose that the nominal exchange rate e is initially equal to 2.0 (for example, 2 euros per dollar). Consequently, $NX = 150 - 50($ _____ $) =$ _____. Substitute this value of net exports NX into Equation 12-1, along with Equations 12-2 to 12-5, and simplify to obtain the equation for aggregate expenditure E in terms of the interest rate r and aggregate income Y:

$E =$ _____ $+$ _____ $Y -$ _____ r.

c. Recall that, in equilibrium, $E = Y$. Derive the equation for the IS curve by setting the preceding expenditure equation equal to Y and solving for r.

$r =$ _____ $-$ _____ Y.

Graph this equation on Graph 12-1 and label it $IS(e = 2)$.

Graph 12-1

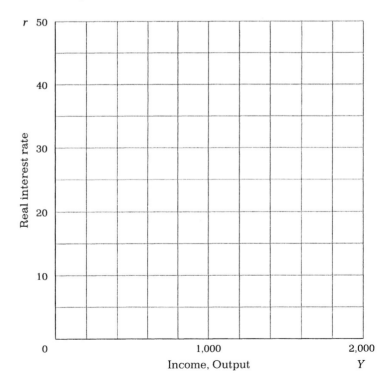

d. Now suppose that the exchange rate falls to $e = 1.0$ (for example, 1 euro per dollar). This exchange rate reflects a(n) <u>appreciation/depreciation</u> of the dollar relative to the euro. As a result, U.S. net exports would <u>rise/fall</u> to $NX = 150 - 50(\underline{\hspace{1.5cm}}) = \underline{\hspace{1.5cm}}$. Substitute this new value of net exports NX, along with Equations 12-2 to 12-5, into Equation 12-1, set the result equal to Y, and derive the equation for the new IS curve.

$r = \underline{\hspace{2cm}} - \underline{\hspace{2cm}} Y.$

Graph this equation on Graph 12-1 and label the curve $IS(e = 1)$.

e. Summarizing the results, we see that a reduction in the exchange rate reflects a(n) <u>appreciation/depreciation</u> of the dollar, which will <u>increase/decrease</u> net exports. This reduction shifts the aggregate expenditure curve <u>upward/downward</u> and thereby shifts the IS curve to the <u>right/left</u>. In this example, the reduction in the exchange rate e from 2 to 1 increases net exports NX by $\underline{\hspace{4cm}}$. This increase in NX shifts the expenditure curve <u>upward/downward</u> by $\underline{\hspace{4cm}}$ and shifts the IS curve to the <u>left/right</u> by the shift in the expenditure curve multiplied by the (government purchases) multiplier, or by $\underline{\hspace{1.5cm}} \times \underline{\hspace{1.5cm}} = \underline{\hspace{1.5cm}}$. Conversely, an increase in the exchange rate reflects a(n) <u>appreciation/depreciation</u> of the dollar, which will <u>increase/decrease</u> net exports. This change shifts the aggregate expenditure curve <u>upward/downward</u> and thereby shifts the IS curve to the <u>left/right</u>.

2. **The Mundell-Fleming Model on a Y - e Graph** *In this exercise, we derive the Mundell-Fleming model on a graph with aggregate income Y and the exchange rate e on the axes.*

a. On Graph 12-1, each IS curve represents the combinations of the interest rate r and aggregate income Y for which the goods market is in equilibrium, holding the exchange rate e fixed. As Chapter 12 of the textbook indicates, one can also draw an IS curve, called IS^*, which represents the combinations of the exchange rate e and aggregate income Y for which the goods market is in equilibrium, holding the interest rate r fixed at the world interest rate r^*. Consider the same model utilized in Exercise 1:

$$E = C + I + G + NX \qquad (12\text{-}7)$$
$$C = 125 + 0.75(Y - T) \qquad (12\text{-}8)$$
$$I = 200 - 10r \qquad (12\text{-}9)$$
$$G = 100 \qquad (12\text{-}10)$$
$$T = 100 \qquad (12\text{-}11)$$
$$NX = 150 - 50e. \qquad (12\text{-}12)$$

Suppose that $r^* = 10$ percent. If $e = 2.0$, then $NX =$ _____. An examination of Graph 12-1 reveals that the goods market will be in equilibrium when $Y =$ _____. Locate this point on Graph 12-2 and label it Point A.

b. Now suppose that e falls to 1.0. Graph 12-1 shows that when $e = 1.0$ and $r = 10$, the goods market is in equilibrium when $Y =$ _____. Locate this point on Graph 12-2 and label it Point B. Connect Points A and B and label the resulting curve $IS^*(r = 10)$. Intuitively, as the exchange rate falls, net exports rise/fall, the aggregate expenditure curve shifts upward/downward, and the level of income increases/decreases.

Graph 12-2

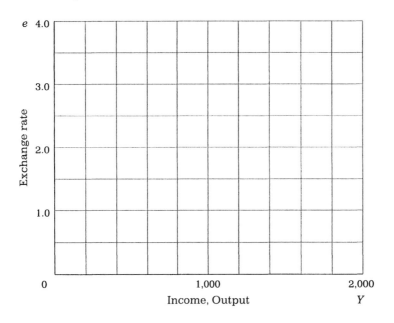

c. The LM curve is unaffected by changes in e because neither money demand nor money supply depends on the exchange rate. Alternatively, there is only one level of income for which the LM curve intersects the $r = r^*$ curve, regardless of the level of e. Suppose that when $r^* = 10$, the money market is in equilibrium when $Y = 1,200$. Draw a vertical LM^* curve on Graph 12-2 at this level of Y.

d. Graph 12-2 now illustrates the combinations of e and Y for which the goods market is in equilibrium (along the IS^* curve), and the combinations of e and Y for which the money market is in equilibrium (along the LM^* curve), assuming that $r^* = 10$. The levels of e and Y at which both the goods and money markets are in equilibrium are at $e =$ _____ and $Y =$ _____. This equilibrium occurs at Point _____ on Graph 12-2.

3. **The Small Open Economy with a Floating Exchange Rate** *In this exercise, we explore the effects of fiscal and monetary policies for a small open economy with a flexible exchange rate.*

a. Graph 12-3 depicts an initial equilibrium using the IS^* and LM^* curves introduced in Exercise 2.

The *IS** and *LM** curves indicate that the initial equilibrium levels of the exchange rate *e* and aggregate income *Y* are at *e* = _____
and *Y* = _____. Locate this point on Graph 12-3 and label it Point A.

Graph 12-3

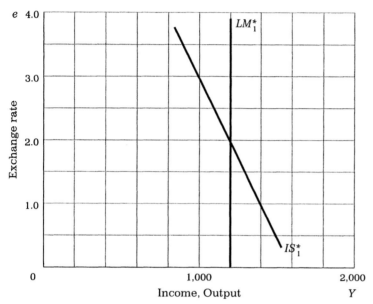

b. Now suppose that the government pursues an expansionary fiscal policy either by <u>increasing/decreasing</u> government purchases *G* or by <u>increasing/decreasing</u> taxes *T*. If the exchange rate *e* is held constant, this policy will <u>increase/decrease</u> aggregate income *Y*. Thus, the *IS** curve will shift to the <u>left/right</u>. Draw the new *IS** curve on Graph 12-3 and label it IS_2^*. Locate the point on the IS_2^* curve at which *e* = 2.0 and label it Point B.

c. At Point B on Graph 12-3, the demand for money is <u>greater than/less than/ equal to</u> the supply of money. Since money demand is unrelated to the exchange rate *e*, equilibrium can be achieved in the money market only if aggregate income *Y* <u>increases/decreases/remains constant</u> from Point B. This situation is achieved through a(n) <u>increase/decrease</u> in *e*. As *e* <u>rises/falls</u>, net exports *NX* <u>increase/decrease</u>, and the economy moves along the IS_2^* curve until the new equilibrium is achieved when money demand once again equals the initial money supply. Locate this point on Graph 12-3 and label it Point C. The upward pressure on *e* occurs because expansionary fiscal policy tends to <u>increase/decrease</u> the interest rate. Yet, whenever the domestic interest rate <u>rises above/falls below</u> the world interest rate, U.S. and foreign investors buy more U.S. assets, which <u>increases/decreases</u> the exchange rate *e*. This assumption of perfect capital mobility (from Chapter 5) results in a constant real world interest rate *r**.

d. Comparing Points A and C on Graph 12-3, note that in a small open economy with a flexible exchange rate, expansionary fiscal policy <u>increases/decreases/has no effect</u> on the equilibrium level of aggregate income Y and <u>increases/decreases/has no effect</u> on the equilibrium exchange rate e. Consequently, net exports NX will <u>rise/fall/remain constant</u>. Conversely, contractionary fiscal policy <u>increases/decreases/has no effect</u> the equilibrium level of Y and <u>increases/decreases/has no effect</u> e.

e. The results in Part d occur because the LM^* curve is vertical; only one level of income will equilibrate the money market as long as the money supply is unchanged. Now start again at Point A on Graph 12-4.

Graph 12-4

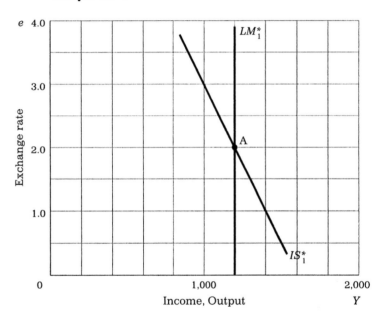

An increase in the money supply will shift the conventional LM curve drawn with r and Y on the axes to the <u>left (upward)/right (downward)</u>. If the interest rate r is constant at the real world interest rate r^*, then the level of aggregate income Y at which this higher money supply equals money demand will <u>rise/fall</u>. As a result, the LM^* curve on Graph 12-4 will shift to the <u>left/right</u>. Draw a new LM^* curve on Graph 12-4 and label it LM_2^*. Obviously, the equilibrium level of income <u>increases/decreases/remains constant</u>. and the equilibrium exchange rate e <u>increases/decreases/remains constant</u>. Thus, net exports NX will <u>rise/fall/remain constant</u>.

f. In both a closed economy and a small open economy with a flexible exchange rate, expansionary monetary policy will lead to a(n) <u>increase/decrease</u> in the equilibrium level of national income. There are, however, some important differences. In a closed economy, an increase in the money supply increases investment (and, hence, GDP) by reducing _____. In a small open economy with a flexible exchange rate, the interest rate remains fixed at the world interest rate. As soon as the domestic interest rate falls a little, capital flows <u>into/out of</u> the domestic economy. This causes the exchange rate to <u>appreciate/depreciate</u>, which <u>increases/decreases</u> net exports and, hence, GDP.

4. Managing a Fixed Exchange-Rate System *In this exercise, we illustrate how the maintenance of a fixed exchange rate requires adjustments in the money supply.*

a. Graph 12-5 depicts a hypothetical situation in which the IS^* and LM^* curves intersect at an equilibrium exchange rate of $e = 3$ at Point A. This situation implies, for example, that people could exchange 3 euros per dollar on the international currency markets.

Graph 12-5

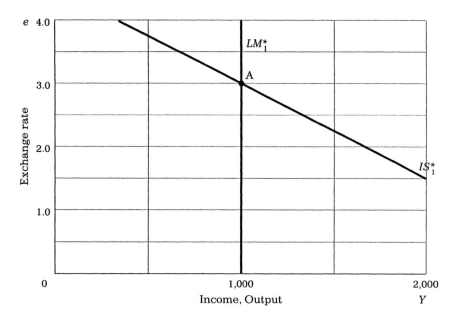

Suppose that the United States committed itself to maintaining a fixed exchange rate of $e = 2$, or _____ euros per dollar. Draw a horizontal line on Graph 12-5 to show this exchange rate, and label it e_{Fixed}. The Fed would establish this exchange rate by holding a reserve of euros and selling them for 2 euros per dollar. It would also commit itself to buying euros for 2 euros per dollar. It is *critical* to note that whenever these transactions occurred, the Fed would be changing the U.S. money supply by buying or selling dollars.

b. In Part a, note that the initial equilibrium exchange rate is greater than/less than the fixed exchange rate. As Chapter 12 of the textbook indicates, this situation cannot prevail for long because it creates opportunities for arbitrage. At $e = 3$, people would profit by buying euros on the international currency markets and selling them to the Fed at its fixed exchange rate. For example, at $e = 3$, people would trade \$1 for _____ euros on the international currency markets. They would then sell these _____ euros to the Fed and receive \$1 for every 2 euros or

   [\$1/(2 euros)] × _____ euros = \$_____.

They would continue to profit by this kind of arbitrage as long as the equilibrium exchange rate exceeded the fixed exchange rate.

c. In Part b, the Fed buys euros with newly created dollars. This action increases/decreases the U.S. money supply and shifts the LM^* curve to the left/right. The LM^* curve will continue to shift until $e = e_{Fixed}$. Draw the final LM^* curve on Graph 12-5 and label it LM_2^*. Label the final equilibrium Point B. Consequently, under a fixed-exchange-rate regime, whenever $e > e_{Fixed}$, the domestic money supply will increase/decrease, and the LM^* curve will shift to the left/right until $e = e_{Fixed}$.

d. Now suppose that the equilibrium exchange rate is 1.0, while the Fed continues to maintain an official fixed exchange rate of 2. This initial situation is depicted on Graph 12-6 at Point C. Draw a horizontal line on Graph 12-6 at $e = 2$ and label it e_{Fixed}.

Graph 12-6

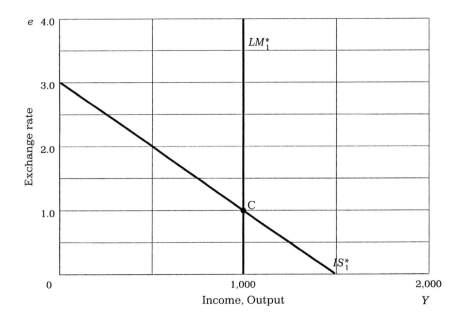

On Graph 12-6, the initial equilibrium exchange rate is greater than/less than the fixed exchange rate. This situation, too, creates opportunities for arbitrage. At $e = 1$, people would profit by buying dollars on the international currency markets and selling them to the Fed at its fixed exchange rate of $e_{Fixed} = 2$. For example, at $e = 1$, people would trade 1 euro for \$_____ on the international currency markets. They would then sell the \$_____ to the Fed at its fixed exchange rate and receive _____ euros. They would continue to profit by this kind of arbitrage as long as the fixed exchange rate exceeded the equilibrium exchange rate.

e. When the Fed is buying dollars in Part d, these dollars are retired from circulation and the U.S. money supply increases/decreases. This situation, in turn, shifts the LM^* curve to the left/right. The LM^* curve will continue to shift until $e = e_{Fixed}$. Draw the final LM^* curve on Graph 12-6, label it LM_3^*, and label the final equilibrium Point D. Consequently, under a fixed-exchange-rate regime, whenever $e < e_{Fixed}$, the domestic money supply will increase/decrease and the LM^* curve will shift to the left/right until $e = e_{Fixed}$.

5. **The Small Open Economy with a Fixed Exchange Rate** *In this exercise, we explore the effects of fiscal and monetary policies for a small open economy with a fixed exchange rate.*

a. Graph 12-7 depicts a situation in which the equilibrium exchange rate is equal to the fixed exchange rate of 2. Draw a horizontal line on Graph 12-7 at $e = 2$ and label it e_{Fixed}.

Graph 12-7

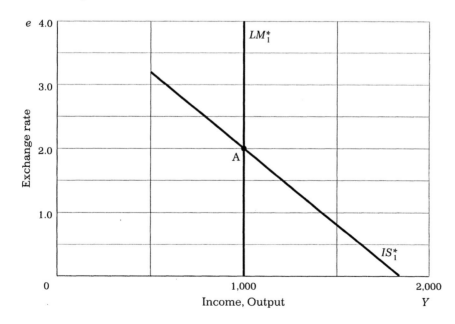

Starting from Point A, suppose that the government pursued expansionary fiscal policy. As in Exercise 3, this policy would shift the IS^* curve to the left/right. Draw the new IS^* curve on Graph 12-7 and label it IS^*_2.

b. In Exercise 3, we found that under a flexible-exchange-rate regime, expansionary fiscal policy will increase/decrease/have no effect on real output Y and increase/decrease/have no effect on the exchange rate e. If, on the other hand, the exchange rate is fixed, as we saw in Exercise 4, the Fed will have to increase/decrease the money supply, shifting the LM^* curve to the left/right until $e = e_{\text{Fixed}} = $ _____. Draw the new LM^* curve on Graph 12-7, label it LM^*_2, and label the new equilibrium Point B. Thus, under a fixed-exchange-rate regime, expansionary fiscal policy will increase/decrease/have no effect on real output Y and increase/decrease/have no effect on the exchange rate e. This situation occurs because the Fed will be forced to change the money supply in order to maintain the fixed exchange rate at $e = 2$.

c. Now start again at Point A on Graph 12-8 with $e = e_{\text{Fixed}}$.

Graph 12-8

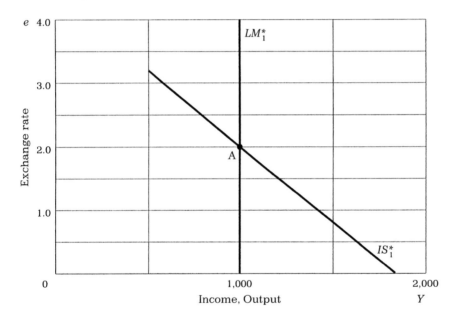

Expansionary monetary policy will initially shift the LM^* curve to the left/right. Draw this new LM^* curve on Graph 12-8 and label it LM^*_3. In Exercise 3 we found that under a flexible-exchange-rate regime, expansionary monetary policy will increase/decrease/have no effect on real output Y and increase/decrease/have no effect on the exchange rate e. If, on the other hand, the exchange rate is fixed, as the equilibrium exchange rate rises above/falls below the fixed exchange rate, the Fed will find itself buying/selling euros and buying/selling dollars. This activity will increase/decrease the money supply and will shift the LM^* curve to the left/right until $e = e_{\text{Fixed}} = $ _____. Draw the final LM^* curve on Graph 12-8, label it LM^*_4, and label the new equilibrium Point C. (Note the relationship between LM_1^* and LM_4^*.) Thus, under a fixed-exchange-rate regime, expansionary monetary policy will increase/decrease/have no effect on real output Y and will increase/decrease/have no effect on the exchange rate. This situation occurs because the final money supply will be greater than/less than/equal to the initial money supply. The normal power of monetary policy to change income is lost because the money supply is dedicated to maintaining the fixed exchange rate. Finally, since the exchange rate does not change, net exports NX will rise/fall/remain constant.

d. Starting over once again at Point A on Graph 12-8, suppose that the United States devalued the dollar by reducing the fixed exchange rate from 2 to 1. If the initial equilibrium exchange rate were 2, the Fed would find itself buying/selling euros and buying/selling dollars. This activity would increase/decrease/ have no effect on the money supply and would shift the LM^* curve to the left/right until $e = 1$. As a result, Y would increase/decrease/remain constant. Conversely, a revaluation of the dollar to $e = 3$ would shift the LM^* curve to the left/right, and Y would increase/decrease/remain constant.

6. **Incorporating Risk Premiums in the Mundell-Fleming Model** *In this exercise, we use the Mundell-Fleming model to analyze the effects of changes in a country's perceived risk premium.*

a. Real interest rates may differ among countries for a variety of reasons. One reason is that assets in one country (for example, government bonds) may be viewed as riskier than similar asssets in another country if the first country is politically or economically unstable. To induce international investors to purchase their assets, the domestic interest rate in countries that are seen as more risky will be higher/lower.

Graph 12-9

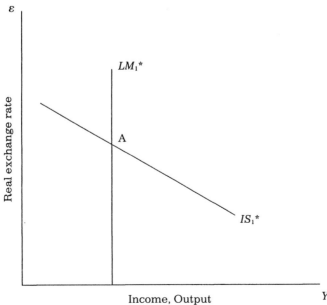

b. Point A in Graph 12-9 depicts an initial equilibrium in a small open economy. If new political turmoil raises this country's perceived risk, its domestic interest rate r rises/falls. This change in the interest rate would increase/decrease investment and thereby shift the IS^* curve to the left/right. Draw this new IS^* curve in Graph 12-9 and label it IS_2^*.

c. This change in the interest rate would also increase/decrease the demand for money. Because this allows a higher level of income for any given money supply, the LM^* curve would shift to the left/right. Draw the new LM^* curve in Graph 12-9, label it LM_2^*, and label the new equilibrium Point B.

d. Comparing Points A and B, we see that an increase in a country's perceived risk premium will lead to a(n) appreciation/depreciation of its exchange rate and a(n) increase/decrease in its real income.

e. Even though higher domestic interest rates reduce investment, national income rises because the change in the exchange rate increases/decreases net exports by an even greater amount. In those countries that have experienced perceived increases in risk, however, national income has often declined for one of several reasons. First, the central banks have occasionally reduced the money supply in order to counteract the exchange rate depreciation, which shifts the IS^*/LM^* curve to the left/right. Second, the depreciation causes the price of imported goods to rise, which may increase the domestic price level P. This would increase/decrease the real money supply and shift the IS^*/LM^* curve to the left/right. Finally, domestic residents may increase their demand for money because money is a liquid and relatively safe asset. This would shift the IS^*/LM^* to the left/right.

7. **The Mundell-Fleming Model with a Changing Price Level** *In this exercise, we show how the long-run price adjustments that move the economy toward its long-run equilibrium operate within the Mundell-Fleming model's flexible-exchange-rate regime.*

a. In Chapter 9 of the textbook, we saw how shifts in the aggregate supply curve move the economy toward its long-run equilibrium. The same phenomenon also occurs in the Mundell-Fleming model, although the aggregate demand curve is somewhat different. Points A in Graphs 12-10 and 12-11 depict an initial equilibrium at which output is greater than/equal to/less than the long-run natural rate of output $\overline{Y}$.

Note that the vertical axis in Graph 12-10 now measures the real exchange rate ε. Recall that $\varepsilon = e(P/P^*)$, where e represents the nominal exchange rate and P/P^* represents the ratio of domestic to foreign prices. It was not necessary to make this adjustment in Exercises 2–5 because the price levels there were assumed to increase/remain constant/decrease. Since ε is on the vertical axis in Graph 12-10, however, a change in P will not shift the IS^* curve.

b. When the short-run equilibrium level of output is less than Y, the short-run aggregate supply $SRAS$ curve will shift upward/downward over time, just as in a closed economy. (Although the $SRAS$ curve is depicted as a horizontal line in Graph 12-11, one can derive the same results from a positively sloped $SRAS$

Graph 12-10

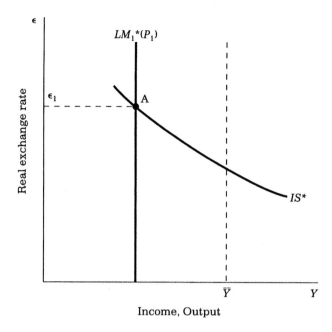

Graph 12-11

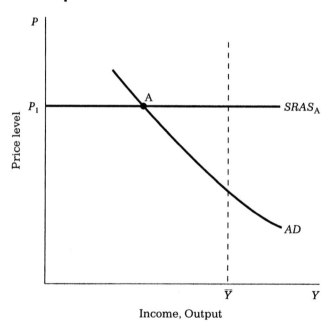

curve.) As this *SRAS* curve shifts, the domestic price level *P* will rise/fall and output will rise/fall. Draw the final *SRAS* curve in Graph 12-11, label it $SRAS_2$, and label the long-run equilibrium Point Z.

c. Returning to Graph 12-10, the reduction in the domestic price level will increase/decrease real money supply/demand. This will shift the *IS*/LM** curve to the right/left since the exchange rate is flexible. Hence, the real exchange rate will rise/fall and net exports will rise/fall. Draw the final *LM** curve, label it

LM_2^*, and label the final equilibrium Point Z. Comparing Points Z and A, output rises/falls/remains the same and net exports rises/falls/remains the same. Investment rises/falls/remains the same because the real interest rate rises/falls/remains the same

8. **The Large Open Economy** *In this exercise, we examine the short-run model of the large open economy derived in the appendix to Chapter 12 to illustrate why the IS curve in a large open economy with international capital flows is flatter than the IS curve in a closed economy, assuming that net exports are unrelated to income.*

Graph 12-12

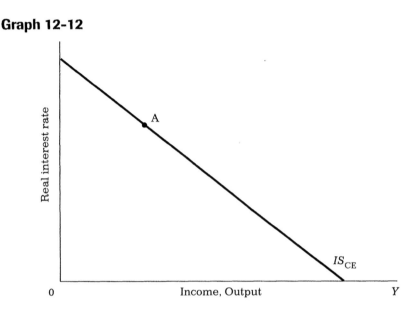

a. Graph 12-12 depicts a simple *IS* curve for a closed economy that is labeled IS_{CE}.

Recall that the *IS* curve for a closed economy has a negative slope because, as the real interest rate *r* falls, investment *I* increases/decreases/remains constant. This situation has both a direct and multiplier effect on *Y*. Consequently, starting at Point A, as *r* falls, *Y* increases/decreases/remains constant.

b. Recall from the appendix to Chapter 5 of the textbook that a large open economy differs from a small open economy because its domestic interest rate is not fixed by world financial markets. Thus, in a large open economy, as in a closed economy, as the real interest rate falls, investment rises/falls. Furthermore, recall that net capital outflow *CF* is the amount that domestic investors lend abroad minus the amount foreigners lend here. As the domestic interest rate falls, net capital outflow rises/falls. Since $CF = NX$, this increase/decrease in *CF* leads to a corresponding increase/decrease in the trade balance *NX*, which must be accompanied by a(n) appreciation/depreciation of the exchange rate.

c. In Part b, a reduction in the real interest rate will increase/decrease investment and increase/decrease net exports. Consequently, *Y* will now increase by more/less than in the closed economy analyzed in Part a, and the *IS* curve for a

large open economy will be flatter/steeper than the *IS* curve in a closed economy. Starting from Point A, draw the *IS* curve for a large open economy on
Graph 12-12 and label it *IS*$_{\text{LOE}}$.

d. Recall that a flatter *IS* curve will make monetary policy more/less potent in
changing *Y* and it will make fiscal policy more/less potent in changing *Y*.

Problems

Answer the following problems on a separate sheet of paper.

1. Explain why a monetary contraction for a small open economy under fixed
exchange rates will have no effect on real income.

2. During the fall of 1992, Great Britain decided to leave the European Monetary
System, in which members agreed to limit fluctuations in the exchange rates among
their currencies. Describe the advantages and disadvantages of such a move.

3. Not all countries in Europe are currently participating in the move to a single
European currency, called the euro.

    a. How will monetary unification change the ability of each country that is currently
    a participant to conduct independent countercyclical monetary and fiscal policy?

    b. How will the introduction of the euro and monetary unification change the ability
    of each European country that is not a participant (but typically has a floating
    exchange rate) to conduct independent countercyclical monetary and fiscal
    policy?

4. If a small open economy with a flexible exchange rate is experiencing a recession,
what will automatically happen over time to its trade balance, foreign exchange
rate, and national output?

5. Suppose the government in a small developing economy places restrictions on agri-
cultural *exports* in order to increase the domestic food supply and lower food prices.
Use the Mundell-Fleming model to analyze the short-run effects of this policy on the
exchange rate and real GDP if the country has a:

    a. flexible exchange rate.

    b. fixed exchange rate.

6. Use the Mundell-Fleming model to illustrate the short-run effects of the Mexican
crisis in a small open economy with a fixed exchange rate.

7. In 1997, 1998, and 1999, the risk premiums associated with several countries in
Southeast Asia rose dramatically. Since that time many of these countries have
regained economic stability by reducing their foreign debt burdens and more effi-
ciently managing their economies. Use the Mundell-Fleming model to illustrate the
effects of renewed stability on these countries' domestic interest rates, exchange
rates, and real GDP under a regime of flexible exchange rates.

8. As the textbook states, Argentina introduced a currency board in the early 1990s. Under this arrangement the Argentine central bank held one U.S. dollar for every outstanding Argentine peso and maintained a fixed dollar-peso exchange rate of 1:1. Although the Argentine economy initially responded well to this innovation, it ran into severe difficulties by the late 1990s and was forced to abandon the currency board in 2002. One of the reasons for its difficulties was the fact that many of Argentina's major trading partners, most notably Brazil, allowed their currencies to fall in value relative to the U.S. dollar during the late 1990s. Because Argentina maintained a fixed dollar-peso exchange rate, the devaluation of Brazil's and other neighbors' currencies, essentially shifted the Argentine net export curve to the left below:

Graph 12-13

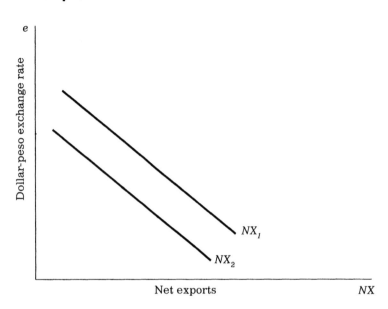

a. Treating Argentina as a small, open economy, use the Mundell–Fleming model to illustrate the effects of this de-facto shift in its net export curve on Argentina's domestic interest rate and real GDP if Argentina adhered to its fixed exchange rate relative to the dollar. (This is largely what happened.)

b. Now use the appropriate graphs to show what the effects of this shift in net exports would have been on Argentina's dollar-peso exchange rate and real GDP if Argentina had allowed its dollar-peso exchange rate to fluctuate freely following Brazil's devaluation. (While many economists believe this is what Argentina should have done, others believe that earlier abandonment of the currency board would have created other difficulties by reducing the credibility of Argentina's central bank.)

9. The United States is certainly a large open economy. Suppose consumer confidence
    suddenly plummets so that consumption falls at each level of disposable income.
    Use the Mundell-Fleming model for a large open economy with a flexible exchange
    rate to illustrate the short-run effects of this development on:

    a. the *IS* and/or *LM* curve(s).

    b. the domestic real interest rate.

    c. U.S. net capital outflow and net exports.

    d. the U.S. foreign exchange rate.

10. Suppose political stability in the United States as seen from abroad deteriorates and
    U.S. assets become less attractive to foreign investors. Assume that the United
    States is a large open economy; state and show graphically what would happen in
    the short run to each of the following:

    a. the U.S. net capital outflow curve.

    b. the U.S. trade balance and foreign exchange rate at the original real interest
        rate.

    c. the *IS* and *LM* curves.

    d. the domestic real interest rate.

    e. the *level* of U.S. net capital outflow and net exports after the change in the real
        interest rate.

    f. U.S. national income and output.

11. In a large open economy, suppose policymakers wanted to increase output in the
    short run without affecting the real exchange rate. What *mix* of monetary and/or fis-
    cal policies would be required to achieve this objective? Briefly explain and use the
    appropriate graphs to illustrate.

Questions to Think About

1. Would you advise the leader of a small open economy in Africa to adopt a fixed or
    floating exchange rate? Would your answer be different if the country were in
    Europe? Why or why not?

2. Why do policymakers in small open countries with floating exchange rates pursue
    countercyclical fiscal policies?

3. Would the world economy be better off with just one currency? Why or why not?

Aggregate Supply

Fill-in Questions

Use the key terms below to fill in the blanks in the following statements. Each term may be used more than once.

adaptive expectations
cost-push inflation
demand-pull inflation
hysteresis
imperfect-information model
NAIRU

natural-rate hypothesis
Phillips curve
rational expectations
sacrifice ratio
sticky-price model
sticky-wage model

1. The _____ explains that the short-run aggregate supply curve slopes upward because in the short run nominal wages are fixed. Therefore, if the price level unexpectedly rises, the real wage falls below its expected level, and firms hire more workers and increase production.

2. The _____ assumes that all markets clear, but that short-run and long-run aggregate supply curves differ because of short-run misperceptions about prices. Therefore, when prices unexpectedly rise, suppliers infer that their relative prices have risen, which induces them to produce more output.

3. The _____ assumes that firms do not instantly adjust the prices they charge in response to changes in demand. It states that the slope of the short-run aggregate supply curve depends on the proportion of firms in the economy that have flexible prices.

4. The graph of the negative relationship between inflation and unemployment, holding expected inflation constant, is called the _____.

5. When the Phillips curve is written as $\pi = \pi_{-1} - \beta(u - u^n) + v$, the natural rate of unemployment is sometimes called the _____.

6. When unemployment falls below the natural rate, inflation tends to rise. This type of inflation is called _____.

7. Rising inflation due to an adverse supply shock is called _____.

8. According to the assumption of _____, people form their expectations of inflation based solely on recently observed inflation.

9. According to the assumption of _____, people form their expectations by optimally using all of the available information, including information about current policies, to forecast the future.

10. The _____ is the number of percentage points of a year's real GDP that must be foregone to reduce inflation by 1 percentage point. It will tend to be lower if people have _____ rather than _____.

11. According to the _____, the economy returns in the long run to the levels of output, employment, and unemployment described by the classical model. In the short run, however, output and unemployment are affected by fluctuations in aggregate demand.

12. _____ is the term used to describe the long-lasting influence of history on the natural rate of unemployment. For example, a recession can have permanent effects on output and unemployment if it eventually reduces the skills of those who become unemployed.

Multiple-Choice Questions

1. The three models of the short-run aggregate supply curve presented in Chapter 13 of the textbook include all of the following EXCEPT the:
   a. sticky-wage model.
   b. sticky-price model.
   c. industry-misperception model.
   d. imperfect-information model.

2. The factor that is sticky in the sticky-wage model is:
   a. the real wage.
   b. the nominal wage.
   c. output.
   d. inflation.

3. In the sticky-wage model, when GDP increases and there are no supply shocks, real wages:

   a. rise.

   b. fall.

   c. remain constant.

   d. may rise, fall, or remain constant.

4. The sticky-wage model predicts that:

   a. the short-run aggregate supply curve is vertical.

   b. the short-run aggregate supply is unrelated to the price level.

   c. firms move along a stationary labor demand curve.

   d. none of the above.

5. According to the imperfect-information model, when prices unexpectedly rise, suppliers infer that their relative prices have _____, which induces them to _____ output.

   a. increased; increase

   b. decreased; decrease

   c. increased; decrease

   d. decreased; increase

6. In the sticky-price model:

   a. all firms adjust prices instantly in response to changes in demand.

   b. no firms adjust prices instantly in response to changes in demand.

   c. some firms adjust prices instantly in response to changes in demand while others do not.

   d. output is constant.

7. If all firms in the economy have fixed prices in the short run:

   a. the short-run and long-run aggregate supply curves will be identical.

   b. the short-run aggregate supply curve will be vertical.

   c. the short-run aggregate supply curve will be horizontal.

   d. none of the above will be true.

8. The sticky-price model can explain why countries with variable aggregate demand have short-run aggregate supply curves that are:

   a. flat.

   b. steep.

   c. horizontal.

   d. vertical.

9. All three models of aggregate supply discussed in Chapter 13 of the textbook predict:

    a. an upward-sloping *SRAS* curve.

    b. a vertical *LRAS* curve.

    c. that the actual level of output is equal to its natural rate in the long run.

    d. all of the above.

10. According to the Phillips curve, the inflation rate depends on:

    a. expected inflation.

    b. the difference between the actual and natural rates of unemployment.

    c. supply shocks.

    d. all of the above.

11. When unemployment is below the natural rate and inflation rises, it is characterized as:

    a. demand-pull inflation.

    b. cost-push inflation.

    c. a supply shock.

    d. stagflation.

12. Compared with the assumption of adaptive expectations, the assumption of rational expectations implies that the transition to the new long-run equilibrium following a credible change in monetary or fiscal policy will take:

    a. less time.

    b. more time.

    c. the same amount of time.

    d. any of the above.

13. The Phillips curve immediately shifts upward whenever:

    a. inflation rises.

    b. unemployment falls.

    c. an adverse supply shock, such as an oil price increase, occurs.

    d. all of the above.

14. A typical estimate of the sacrifice ratio is about 5. Thus, if the inflation rate were to be lowered by 2 percentage points, the amount of one year's GDP we must give up is:

    a. 2 percent.

    b. 2.5 percent.

    c. 5 percent.

    d. 10 percent.

15. According to the hypothesis of unemployment hysteresis, a prolonged recession will:

    a. increase the natural rate of unemployment.
    b. decrease the natural rate of unemployment.
    c. have no effect on the natural rate of unemployment.
    d. never occur.

Exercises

1. **The General Short-Run Aggregate Supply Curve** *In this exercise, we discuss the general short-run aggregate supply equation that is derived later from three different models. We graph this equation and discuss the changes that will shift the aggregate supply curve.*

    a. All three models of aggregate supply discussed in Chapter 13 of the textbook result in an aggregate supply equation of the following form:

    $$Y = \overline{Y} + \alpha(P - P^e),$$

    where Y is output, $\overline{Y}$ is the natural rate of output, P is the price level, and P^e is the expected price level. This equation implies that output will be at its natural rate when the actual price level is <u>greater than/less than/equal to</u> the expected price level. Output exceeds its natural rate $(Y > \overline{Y})$ only when the actual price level is <u>greater than/less than/equal to</u> the expected price level.

    b. It is easier to graph this equation if we isolate P on the left-hand side. Subtracting $\overline{Y}$ from both sides of the equation and rearranging yields

    $$\alpha P - \alpha P^e = Y - \overline{Y},$$
    $$\alpha P = \alpha P^e + (Y - \overline{Y}), \text{or}$$
    $$P = P^e + \left(\frac{1}{\alpha}\right)(Y - \overline{Y}). \tag{13-1}$$

    Equation 13-1 indicates that when $Y = \overline{Y}$, $P = P^e$. Graph this equation on Graph 13-1, label the curve *AS*, and label the slope of the line.

Graph 13-1

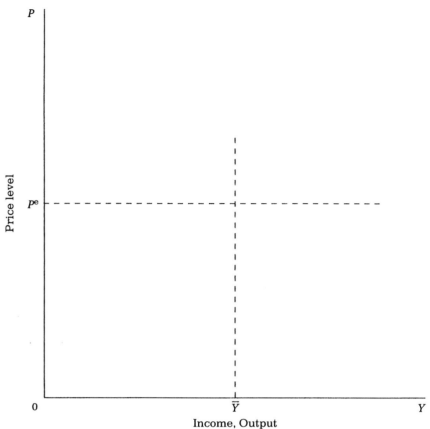

c. Equation 13-1 and Graph 13-1 indicate that an increase in the expected price level will shift the aggregate supply curve <u>upward (to the left)/downward (to the right)</u>. An increase in the natural rate of output will shift the aggregate supply curve <u>upward (to the left)/downward (to the right)</u> because the level of Y at which output will equal its natural rate (and P will equal P^e) will <u>increase/decrease</u>. The next three exercises illustrate how we can derive this aggregate supply curve from three different models of aggregate supply.

2. **The Sticky-Wage Model** *In this exercise, we derive the aggregate supply curve using the nominal sticky-wage model. You may find it useful to review Exercises 1 and 2 of Chapter 3.*

   a. In this exercise, we use the production function and labor demand curve that were introduced in Exercises 1 and 2 of Chapter 3, except now we assume that they refer to the entire economy. On Graphs 13-2 and 13-3, this labor demand curve and production function are illustrated.

      According to these graphs, when the real wage is equal to 16, the quantity of labor demanded is equal to 2, and total output is equal to 36. If the real wage falls to 8, the quantity of labor demanded equals _____ and total output equals _____. Finally, if the real wage falls to 4, the quantity of labor demanded equals _____, and total output equals _____. Recall that firms hire labor until the real wage is equal to the _____.

   b. According to the sticky-wage model, workers and firms agree on a nominal wage before they know what the actual price level will be when the bargain takes effect. They set the nominal wage W so that the expected real wage W/P^e will be equal to a target real wage ω:

      $$W/P^e = \omega.$$

      Because of union power, efficiency wages, and other factors, this target real wage may be greater than or equal to the equilibrium real wage at which the demand for labor is equal to the supply of labor. If $P = P^e$, then the actual real wage W/P will be greater than/less than/equal to the target real wage, and unemployment and output will both be at their natural rates.

   c. Suppose that $P^e = 1.0$ and $\omega = 16$. Workers and firms will set the nominal wage W so that

      $$W/P^e = \omega \qquad \text{or} \qquad W/1.0 = 16.$$

      Consequently, workers and firms will set the nominal wage W equal to _____. Find the points that they are trying to attain on Graphs 13-2 and 13-3 and label them both Point A.

   d. Given the value of W in Part c, when $P = P^e = 1.0$, $W/P = $ _____ and $Y = \overline{Y} = $ _____. Find this point on Graph 13-4 and label it Point A($P^e = 1.0$).

Graph 13-2

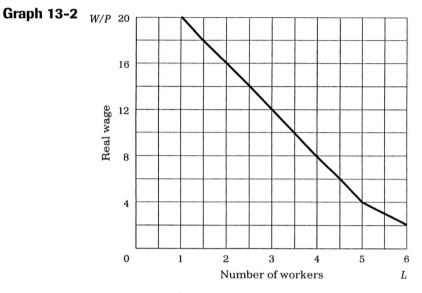

Graph 13-3

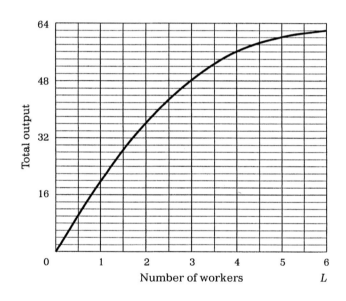

Graph 13-4

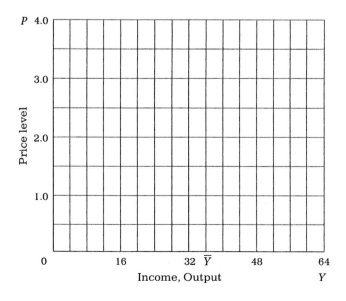

e.   Now suppose again that $P^e = 1.0$ and, hence, $W = $ _____, so
     that $W/P^e = \omega$. The actual price level, however, exceeds expectations, and $P = 2.0$.
     Since the nominal wage is already fixed at _____, the
     actual real wage <u>rises/falls</u> to $W/P = $ _____$/2.0 =$
     _____. Consequently, we see from Graphs 13-2 and 13-3
     that the quantity of labor demanded will <u>rise/fall</u> to $L = $ _____,
     and total output Y will <u>rise/fall</u> to $Y = $ _____. Find the cor-
     responding points on Graphs 13-2 and 13-3 and label them Point B. Find the cor-
     responding point on Graph 13-4 and label it Point B($P^e = 1.0$). Connect the two
     points on Graph 13-4 and label this curve $AS(P^e = 1.0)$.

f.   From Part e, we see that when the actual price level rises above the expected
     price level and the nominal wage is fixed in advance, the actual real wage will
     <u>rise above/fall below</u> the target real wage. This, in turn, will <u>increase/decrease</u>
     real output <u>above/below</u> the natural rate of output, resulting in a positively
     sloped aggregate supply curve.

g.   Now suppose that the expected price level P^e rose to 2.0. If the target real wage
     remains equal to 16, workers and firms will set the nominal wage so that

$$W/P^e = \omega \qquad \text{or} \qquad W/2.0 = 16.$$

     Consequently, workers and firms will set the nominal wage W equal to
     _____. Since W/P^e remains equal to 16, the target real
     wage is still attained at Point A on Graphs 13-2 and 13-3. On Graph 13-4, however,
     P^e no longer equals 1.0. Instead, P^e now equals _____,
     and the target real wage and the natural rate of output will be achieved only if
     the actual price level P equals _____. Find this point on
     Graph 13-4 and label it Point C($P^e = 2.0$).

h.   Now suppose again that $P^e = 2.0$ and $\omega = 16$, so that $W = $ _____. This time,
     however, let $P = 4.0$. Consequently, $W/P = $ _____$/4.0 = $ _____. The quan-
     tity of labor demanded rises to _____, and output rises to _____. Find
     these points on Graphs 13-2 and 13-3 and label them Point D. Find this point
     on Graph 13-4 and label it Point D($P^e = 2.0$). Connect Points C and D on Graph
     13-4 and label this curve $AS(P^e = 2.0)$.

i.   From Parts g and h, we see that an increase in the expected price level will lead
     to a(n) <u>increase/decrease</u> in the nominal wage, which will shift the aggregate
     supply curve <u>upward/downward</u>. Conversely, a decrease in the expected price
     level will lead to a(n) <u>increase/decrease</u> in the nominal wage, which will shift the
     aggregate supply curve <u>upward/downward</u>.

3. **The Imperfect-Information Model** *In this exercise, we develop the aggregate supply curve using the imperfect-information model.*

a. In the imperfect-information model, all markets clear, and output again deviates from its natural rate whenever prices deviate from their expected levels. Following the simple example presented in Chapter 13 of the textbook, consider a wheat farmer in an imperfectly competitive wheat market. This wheat farmer will increase her production of wheat only if she thinks that the price of wheat relative to all other goods and services—that is P_{wheat}/P—has increased. Although the farmer can easily see when the price of wheat rises, she does not immediately get information about the aggregate price level. Consequently, she makes a forecast of the aggregate price level P^e. As a result, the production of wheat will be positively related to P_{wheat}/P^e. This relationship is graphed on Graph 13-5.

Graph 13-5

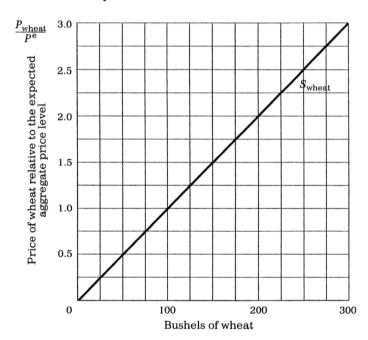

b. Assume that the equilibrium price of wheat equals $1. If the expected aggregate price level P^e = 1.0, and the actual price of wheat P_{wheat} = $1, then the expected relative (or real) price of wheat = P_{wheat}/P^e =

_____ / _____ = _____.

From Graph 13-5, we see that the quantity of wheat produced will equal _____ bushels. Label this Point A.

c. Suppose for the moment that the expected price level remains equal to 1.0, but that the farmer suddenly finds that the price of wheat has risen to $3. As a result, the farmer thinks that the relative price of wheat has risen to P_{wheat}/P^e = $_____/_____ = _____.

From Graph 13-5, we see that the quantity of wheat produced will <u>rise/fall</u> to _____ bushels. Label this Point B.

d. In the imperfect-information model, however, farmers realize that part of the increase in the price of wheat probably reflects an increase in the aggregate price level. Thus, they respond to the increase in the price of wheat by increasing both the quantity of wheat produced and P^e. On Graph 13-6, Point A reflects the situation in which P_{wheat} = $1 and P^e = 1.0. Thus, at Point A, the expected relative price of wheat = P_{wheat}/P^e = _____/_____ = _____.

From Graph 13-5, we see that when this occurs, the quantity of wheat supplied will equal _____ bushels.

Graph 13-6

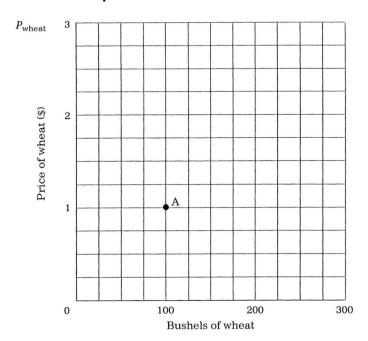

e. Starting from $1, suppose that the farmer again finds that the price of wheat has risen to $3. This represents an increase in P_{wheat} of _____ percent. Now, however, the farmer estimates that half of this percentage increase represents an increase in the aggregate price level. Consequently, her estimate of P^e rises by 0.5 × _____ percent = _____ percent, that is, P^e rises from 1.0 to _____. The new expected relative price of wheat is now $P_{wheat}/P^e = \$3/$_____ = _____. From Graph 13-5, we see that at this expected relative price, the quantity of wheat supplied will equal _____ bushels. Label this Point C on Graph 13-5. Locate the point on Graph 13-6 that corresponds to this quantity and price of wheat ($3) and also label it Point C. Connect Points A and C on Graph 13-6 and label the curve AS_1. (In reality, of course, GDP includes more than just wheat.)

f. Extending this story to the entire economy, each producer will increase production only if she thinks that the price of the commodity she produces has risen relative to the aggregate price level. The price of all commodities taken together is merely the aggregate price level P. In long-run equilibrium, $P = P^e$, so that P/P^e = _____, and output will be at its equilibrium or natural rate. If $P > P^e$, output will be <u>greater/less</u> than its natural rate, and if $P < P^e$, output will be <u>greater/less</u> than its natural rate. These conditions result in an upward-sloping short-run aggregate supply curve.

g. Now suppose that there has been a great deal of inflation in the recent past. **CH** Consequently, when P_{wheat} rises from $1 to $3, or by _____ percent, our farmer assumes that 70 percent of this increase represents an increase in the aggregate price level. Thus, the farmer's P^e rises by 0.70 × _____ percent = _____ percent, that is, from $P^e = 1.0$ to $P^e =$ _____. The new expected relative price of wheat is now $P_{wheat}/P^e = \$3/$_____ = _____. From Graph 13-5, we see that at this expected relative price, the quantity of wheat supplied will equal _____ bushels. Locate this quantity and this price of wheat ($3) on Graph 13-6 and label it Point D. Connect Points A and D on Graph 13-6 and label your curve AS_2. AS_2 is <u>flatter/steeper</u> than AS_1. Thus, if firms believe that most of any increase in the price of their output is the result of general inflation, the aggregate supply curve will be relatively <u>flat/steep</u>. In the extreme case in which all increases in P_{wheat} are assumed to result from general inflation, P_{wheat}/P^e will always equal _____, the quantity of wheat supplied will always equal _____ bushels, and the aggregate supply curve will be <u>horizontal/vertical</u>.

4. **The Sticky-Price Model** *In this exercise, we derive the aggregate supply curve using the sticky-price model.*

   a. In the sticky-price model, the prices of some firms or products may be sticky because of long-term contracts or because of the way that markets are structured. The prices of other firms or products, however, will be flexible. As a result, the slope of the aggregate supply curve, reflecting the degree of price stickiness in the entire economy, will depend on the proportion of firms (or products) that have sticky prices.

   b. Let us first consider a firm with flexible prices. This firm will set its price p so that

$$p = P + a(Y - \overline{Y}).$$

   If the aggregate price level P rises, this firm's costs will rise/fall, and it will raise/lower its own price p. If aggregate income rises above its natural rate, the demand curve for the firm's product will also increase/decrease, resulting in a(n) increase/decrease in price.

   c. The firms with sticky prices have to set their prices before the aggregate price level and level of income become known. Therefore, they must set their prices according to their expectations of these variables:

$$p = P^e + a(Y^e - \overline{Y}^e).$$

   If s represents the fraction of all firms with sticky prices, and $(1 - s)$ represents the fraction with flexible prices, then the overall price level will be a weighted average of the prices of flexible and sticky-price firms:

$$P = s[P^e + a(Y^e - \overline{Y}^e)] + (1 - s)[P + a(Y - \overline{Y})].$$

   Now suppose that aggregate income is expected to be at its natural rate—that is, $Y^e = \overline{Y}^e$. Consequently, $Y^e - \overline{Y}^e = $ _____, and

$$P = sP^e + (1 - s)[P + a(Y - \overline{Y})], \text{ or}$$
$$P = sP^e + P - sP + [(1 - s)a(Y - \overline{Y})], \text{ or}$$
$$sP = sP^e + [(1 - s)a(Y - \overline{Y})], \text{ or}$$
$$P = P^e + [(1 - s)a/s](Y - \overline{Y}). \quad \text{(13-2)}$$

   Equation 13-2 indicates that income will equal its natural rate, that is, $Y = \overline{Y}$, whenever the aggregate price level is greater than/less than/equal to the expected price level. Output (income) will exceed its natural rate only if the aggregate price level is greater than/less than/equal to the expected price level. As the proportion of firms with sticky prices rises, s rises. The rise in s increases/decreases the numerator of the coefficient of Y and increases/decreases the denominator. Consequently, the coefficient of Y increases/decreases. This increases/decreases the slope of the aggregate supply curve; hence, the aggregate supply curve becomes flatter/steeper. In Chapter 9 of the textbook, for example, the short-run aggregate supply curve was horizontal/vertical, the implicit value of s was _____, and all/no firms were assumed to have sticky prices in the short run.

5. **Short-Run and Long-Run Effects of an Increase in Aggregate Demand** *In this exercise, we link the aggregate supply and aggregate demand curves developed in Chapters 10 and 11 of the textbook with the long-run aggregate supply curve presented in Chapter 9 of the textbook.*

    a. On Graph 13-7, we put the aggregate supply and aggregate demand curves together to depict an initial equilibrium at Point A.

    Graph 13-7

    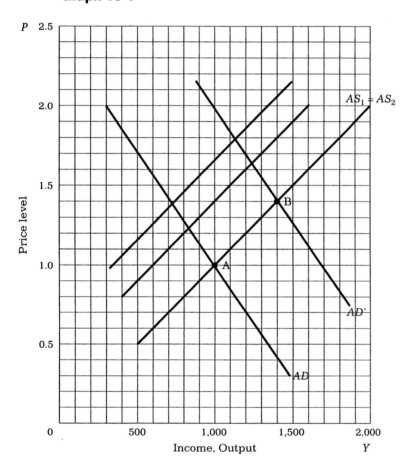

    Recall that the aggregate demand curve slopes downward because as the aggregate price level falls, real money balances <u>increase/decrease</u>. This change in real money balances shifts the *IS/LM* curve _____.
    Consequently, the equilibrium level of income at the intersection of the *IS* and *LM* curves <u>increases/decreases</u>. The short-run aggregate supply curve slopes upward because output increases above its natural rate only if the price level <u>rises above/falls below</u> the expected price level. Finally, the long-run aggregate supply curve is vertical because in the long run all prices and wages are <u>sticky/flexible</u>, and in the long run output will always be <u>greater than/less than/equal to</u> its natural rate, regardless of the price level.

b. At Point A, output is equal to the natural rate of output, which we arbitrarily set equal to 1,000. Consequently, the aggregate price level P must be greater than/less than/equal to its expected level P^e. If P^e does not change, it must therefore equal _____ all along the short-run aggregate supply curve AS_1.

c. Now suppose that the aggregate demand curve shifts to the right, to AD', in the second period. This shift could result from a(n) increase/decrease in government purchases, a(n) increase/decrease in taxes, a(n) increase/decrease in the money supply, or a variety of other reasons. If the expected price level does not change (this is an important assumption), it will remain equal to _____. Consequently, in the second period, the short-run aggregate supply curve will not immediately shift (and, as on Graph 13-7, $AS_1 = AS_2$), and we will move to Point B. At Point B, output $Y =$ _____ and $P =$ _____. (These numbers must be read from the graph itself.)

d. If the policy change is a one-time, permanent change, the aggregate demand curve will not shift again. Nevertheless, the economy will not stay at Point B forever because, at Point B, the actual price level is greater than/less than/equal to the expected price level. Consequently, in the next period, the expected price level will increase/remain the same/decrease.

e. Suppose that the expected price level in any period is equal to the last period's actual price level—that is, $P^e = P_{-1}$. Since the actual price level P in Period 2 = _____, the expected price level in Period 3 will equal _____. This change will shift the short-run aggregate supply curve upward/downward because, in Period 3, output will equal its natural rate only if $P = P^e =$ _____. Label as AS_3 the curve on Graph 13-7 that depicts the short-run aggregate supply curve in Period 3.

f. Consequently, in Period 3 the economy moves to the intersection of AD' (since AD' remains stationary) and AS_3. Label this Point C on Graph 13-7. At Point C, $Y =$ _____ and $P =$ _____. (Again, read these data from the graph; round off if necessary.) Between Periods 2 and 3, output has risen/fallen, whereas the price level has risen/fallen.

g. At Point C, the actual price level is greater than/less than/equal to the expected price level. Consequently, in the next period, the expected price level will increase/remain the same/decrease. If $P^e = P_{-1}$ and the actual price level in Period 3 = _____, then the expected price level in Period 4 will rise to _____. This rise in P^e will shift the short-run aggregate supply curve upward/downward so that, in Period 4, output will equal its natural rate only if $P = P^e =$ _____. Label as AS_4 the curve on Graph 13-7 that depicts the short-run aggregate supply curve in Period 4. Label as Point D the point that represents the short-run equilibrium in Period 4.

h. At Point D on Graph 13-7, the actual price level is <u>greater than/less than/equal to</u> the expected price level. Consequently, in the next period, the expected price level will <u>increase/remain the same/decrease</u>, and this change will shift the short-run aggregate supply curve <u>upward/downward</u>. The short-run aggregate supply curve will continue to shift in each successive period as long as $P > P^e$. This shift will occur as long as actual output is <u>greater than/less than</u> the natural rate of output. The short-run aggregate supply curve will stop shifting when $P = P^e$, which occurs when $Y = \overline{Y}$. At this point, the short-run aggregate supply curve will intersect the aggregate demand curve at a point along the long-run aggregate supply curve. Label the long-run equilibrium on Graph 13-7 Point F. At Point F, $Y = $ _____ and $P = $ _____.
Draw the short-run aggregate supply curve that corresponds to this long-run equilibrium on Graph 13-7 and label it AS_F. At Point F, the expected price level $P^e = $ _____, and this is equal to the actual price level. The equilibrium level of output Y is also equal to the natural rate of output $\overline{Y}$. Consequently, there are no forces pushing the economy away from Point F.

i. Comparing Points A and F, the long-run effects of the increase in aggregate demand were <u>an increase/no change/a decrease</u> in output and <u>an increase/no change/a decrease</u> in the price level.

j. Now suppose that we start again at Point A, and the aggregate demand curve once again shifts to AD'. Since this shift occurred unexpectedly, the economy would move to point B. In Period 3, however, people (particularly those who have taken an intermediate macroeconomics course) may begin to realize that prices will continue to rise. Consequently, they may try to revise their expectations of the future price level to take this into account. If they did, the expected price level would rise more rapidly than indicated in Parts e through h, and the short-run aggregate supply curve would shift upward <u>more/less</u> rapidly, provided that wages and prices could change as rapidly as price expectations. As a result, the economy would reach its long-run equilibrium <u>more/less</u> rapidly.

6. The Phillips Curve *In this exercise, we use the Phillips curve to analyze the short-run and long-run effects of changes in macroeconomic policies.*

a. The Phillips curve is an alternative way to analyze the interactions between aggregate supply and aggregate demand. The Phillips curve equation is

$$\pi = \pi^e - \beta(u - u^n) + v, \tag{13-3}$$

where π equals the actual inflation rate, π^e equals expected inflation, u and u^n equal the actual and natural rates of unemployment, v represents the effects of supply shocks that shift the Phillips curve, and β is greater than zero. According to Equation 13-3, when the unemployment rate exceeds the natural rate of unemployment and there are no supply shocks, $\beta(u - u^n)$ is <u>positive/negative</u> Thus, actual inflation, $\pi = \pi^e - \beta(u - u^n)$, will be <u>greater/less</u> than expected inflation.

b. Suppose that the Phillips curve equation was

$$\pi = \pi^e - 0.4(u - u^n) + v.$$

Suppose, in addition, that expected inflation was 8 percent, the natural rate of unemployment was 5 percent, and there were no supply shocks. Consequently, the Phillips curve equation corresponding to this situation would be

$$\pi = 8 - 0.4(u - 5).\qquad\qquad\textbf{(13-4)}$$

Solve this equation for π.

$\pi =$ _____ − _____ $u.$

Note that in Equation 13-4, inflation and unemployment are expressed as percentages rather than decimals. Plot and draw Equation 13-4 on Graph 13-8 and label it PC_1.

Graph 13-8

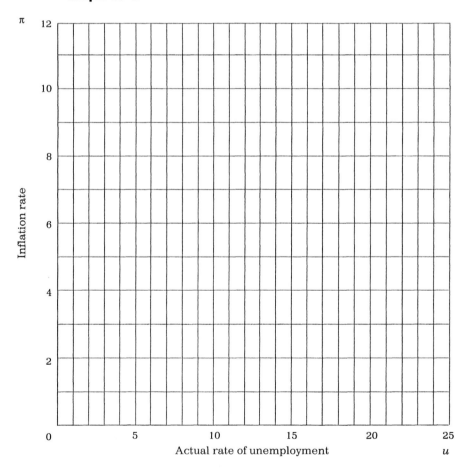

Note that on Graph 13-8, when $u = u^n$, actual inflation is greater than/
less than/equal to the expected inflation rate of 8 percent.

c. Suppose that the economy was initially at the natural rate of unemployment. Find the point along PC_1 on Graph 13-8 at which the unemployment rate is equal to the natural rate of unemployment and label it Point A. If the Fed and/or the government thought that inflation must be reduced, they could decrease aggregate demand in the second period by increasing/decreasing government purchases, increasing/decreasing taxes, and/or increasing/decreasing the money supply. If expected inflation does not change (this is an important assumption), it will remain equal to _____ percent. Consequently, in the second period, the Phillips curve will not shift, and we will move along PC_1 to the left/right. Since the Phillips curve did not shift, change the label of PC_1 on Graph 13-8 to $PC_1 = PC_2$.

d. Suppose that these policies increased the unemployment rate to 10 percent. Find this point on your Phillips curve on Graph 13-8 and label it Point B. At Point B, $u =$ _____ percent and $\pi =$ _____ percent.

e. At Point B, actual inflation is greater than/less than/equal to expected inflation. Consequently, in the next (third) period, expected inflation will rise/fall and the Phillips curve will shift upward/downward.

f. Suppose that expected inflation in any period was equal to actual inflation during the preceding period, that is,

$$\pi^e = \pi_{-1}.$$

In Period 2, we found that $\pi =$ _____ percent.
Consequently, in Period 3, $\pi^e =$ _____ percent. This value will change the Phillips curve equation to

$$\pi = \pi^e - 0.4(u - 5) = \underline{\hspace{3cm}} - 0.4(u - 5). \tag{13-5}$$

Solve this equation for π.

$\pi =$ _____ $-$ _____ u.

Plot and draw Equation 13-5 on Graph 13-8 and label the curve PC_3.

g. In Period 3, suppose that the government and/or the Fed continued their policies and kept the unemployment rate at 10 percent. Find this point on PC_3 on Graph 13-8 and label it Point C. At Point C, $u =$ _____ percent and $\pi =$ _____ percent.

h. At Point C, actual inflation is <u>greater than/less than/equal to</u> expected inflation. Consequently, in the next (fourth) period, expected inflation will <u>rise/fall</u> and the Phillips curve will shift <u>upward/downward</u>. Since actual inflation in Period 3 = _____ percent, expected inflation in Period 4 will equal _____ percent. Once again, this value will change the Phillips curve equation to

$$\pi = \pi^e - 0.4(u - 5) = \underline{\hspace{4cm}} - 0.4(u - 5). \qquad \textbf{(13-6)}$$

Solve this equation for π.

$$\pi = \underline{\hspace{5cm}} - \underline{\hspace{5cm}} u.$$

Plot and draw Equation 13-6 on Graph 13-8 and label the curve PC_4.

i. In Period 4, suppose that the government and the Fed eased their policies and allowed the unemployment rate to resume its natural rate of 5 percent. Find this point on PC_4 on Graph 13-8 and label it Point D. At Point D, $u =$ _____ percent, $\pi =$ _____ percent, and actual inflation is <u>greater than/less than/equal to</u> expected inflation. Consequently, in the next (fifth) period, expected inflation will <u>rise/stay the same/fall</u>, and the Phillips curve will <u>shift upward/remain stationary/shift downward</u>. Thus, Point D represents a new long-run equilibrium.

j. In this exercise, it took two periods of excess unemployment to reduce inflation from 8 percent to _____ percent. If each period lasted for one year, it took two years of unemployment that exceeded the natural rate by $10 - 5 =$ _____ percentage points, or a total of $2 \times$ _____ = _____ percentage-point years of cyclical unemployment, to reduce inflation by $8 -$ _____ _____ = _____ percentage points. For each percentage-point reduction in inflation, it took _____ percentage-point years of cyclical unemployment. According to Okun's law (see Chapter 2 of the textbook), each percentage-point year of cyclical unemployment represents 2 percentage points in lost GDP. Consequently, in our example, it took _____ percentage points in lost GDP to reduce inflation by 1 percentage point. This is called the _____ ratio.

k. Now suppose that we start over at Point A, and unemployment again rises to 10 percent. Since this rise occurs unexpectedly, the economy would move to Point B. In Period 3, however, people may realize that inflation will continue to fall. As a result, they may try to revise their expectations of future inflation to take this into account. If they did, expected inflation would fall more rapidly than indicated in Parts c through i, and the Phillips curve would shift downward <u>more/less</u> rapidly, provided that wages and prices could change as rapidly as inflationary expectations. As a result, the economy would reach its long-run equilibrium <u>more/less</u> rapidly and the sacrifice ratio would be <u>higher/lower</u> than in Part j.

l. The path depicted in Parts c through i is only one of several ways to reduce inflation, even if expected inflation changes slowly. On Graph 13-9, the initial Phillips curve and the initial equilibrium have been redrawn.

Graph 13-9

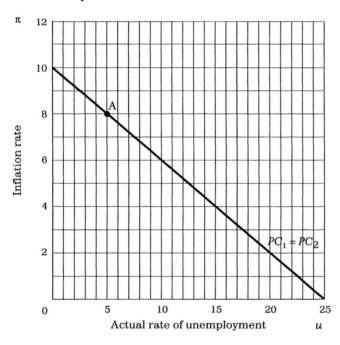

At Point A, $\pi^e = 8$, $u =$ _____ percent, and $\pi =$ _____ percent. Now suppose that the Fed and/or the government thought it necessary to reduce inflation more rapidly than in Part c. Consequently, they pursued more restrictive policies and increased unemployment to 15 percent in the second period. Find this point on the Phillips curve on Graph 13-9 and label it Point B. At Point B, $u =$ _____ percent and $\pi =$ _____ percent. (Note that π^e has not yet changed.) If expected inflation in the third period is equal to actual inflation in the second period, π^e would fall to _____ percent. Consequently, the Phillips curve equation would change to

$$\pi = \pi^e - 0.4(u - 5) = \text{_____} - 0.4(u - 5). \qquad \textbf{(13-7)}$$

Solve this equation for π.

$$\pi = \text{_____} - \text{_____}\, u.$$

Plot and draw Equation 13-7 on Graph 13-9 and label the curve PC_3. In Period 3, suppose that the government and the Fed eased their policies and allowed the unemployment rate to resume its natural rate of 5 percent. Find this point on PC_3 on Graph 13-9 and label it Point C. At Point C, $u =$ _____ percent, $\pi =$ _____ percent, and actual inflation is <u>greater than/less than/equal to</u> expected inflation. Consequently, Point C represents a new long-run equilibrium. This situation shows that inflation could be reduced more quickly if a more restrictive policy were enacted that increased unemployment more drastically. Note, however, that it took _____ percentage-point years of cyclical unemployment here to reduce inflation by _____ percentage points, which is <u>more than/less than/equal to</u> the amount it took in Parts c through i.

m. Finally, suppose that we start again at Point A on Graph 13-9 and that there is an adverse supply shock, such as a substantial increase in oil prices. In this case, the Phillips curve would shift <u>shift upward/remain stationary/shift downward</u> even if expected inflation did not change.

Problems

Answer the following problems on a separate sheet of paper.

1. Suppose that the aggregate production function were equal to $Y = 2(K^{1/2}L^{1/2})$, where
   C Y equals real GDP, K equals the total capital stock, and L equals total labor
   employed. Furthermore, suppose that $K = 100$.

   a. Derive the labor demand function by differentiating the aggregate production
   function with respect to L to get the marginal product of labor, setting this value
   equal to the real wage W/P and solving for L.

   b. Derive the equation that expresses output as a function of the real wage by substituting the labor demand function into the aggregate production function.

   c. Suppose that the nominal wage W initially equals $4, the actual and expected
   price levels equal 1.0, and the target real wage equals 4. Calculate the initial
   level of output and the natural rate of output.

   d. In accordance with the sticky-wage model, suppose that the nominal wage is
   fixed at $W = $4. Derive the aggregate supply equation by substituting $W = $4 in
   the equation you derived in Part b and solving for Y as a function of P.

   e. Invert the equation you derived in Part d by solving for P. Draw a graph showing
   the short-run aggregate supply curve when $P^e = 1.0$ and $W = $4.

2. a. Suppose that the economy is initially at the natural rate of output, and the
   ◻ expected price level in any period is equal to the actual price level in the preceding period. If the Fed makes a credible, permanent reduction in the money
   supply, draw a graph to illustrate the path of the economy in both the short run
   and the long run, using aggregate supply and aggregate demand curves.

   b. Explain how and why your answer to Part a would be different if expectations
   were static—that is, if the expected price level were unaffected by current and
   past price levels.

   c. Explain how and why your answer to Part a would be different if expectations
   were rational and all wages and prices were flexible.

3. If the economy is initially at the natural rate of output and inflation rises, what additional macroeconomic data would enable one to determine whether the inflation
   was demand-pull or cost-push? Explain.

4. As the textbook notes, real wages tend to be procyclical; that is, they increase
   during business expansions and decrease during recessions.

   a. Explain why this empirical finding contradicts the sticky-wage model of aggregate
   supply if variations in output are due primarily to shifts in aggregate demand.

   b. Now explain why this finding does not contradict the sticky-wage model if variations in output are due primarily to aggregate supply shocks, such as an oil price
   shock.

5. It is ironic that workers and firms typically bargain over nominal wages, rather than
   indexing wages to the CPI, GDP deflator, or an industry price index and then bar-
   gaining over real wages. One explanation is that workers and firms would probably
   disagree about the specific price index to which wages should be indexed.

   a. Which index do you think workers would choose? Why?

   b. Which index do you think firms would choose? Why?

6. In April 1997, Senator Connie Mack of Florida and 10 other senators sponsored a bill
☐ in Congress that would require the Federal Reserve to "establish an explicit numerical definition of 'price stability,' and maintain a monetary policy that effectively promotes long-term price stability."

   a. Use aggregate supply and aggregate demand curves to illustrate the short-run and long-run effects on real GDP if Senator Mack's resolution was adopted and it involved an immediate reduction in the money supply.

   b. How would the speed with which the economy moves to the new long-run equilibrium depend on the following factors—rational expectations, wage and price flexibility, and policy credibility?

7. a. Draw an appropriately labeled Phillips curve and illustrate the current position of the U.S. economy. Somewhere in your graph clearly indicate each of the following: the current actual unemployment rate, the (approximate) natural rate of unemployment, the actual rate of inflation, and the (approximate) expected rate of inflation.

   b. Illustrate what will happen over time if no new macroeconomic policies are implemented.

8. What does the hysteresis theory of unemployment imply about the effects of a recession on the long-run aggregate supply curve? Briefly explain.

Data Questions

Locate the necessary economic data and apply them to answer the following data questions. All of the relevant data may be found in the Economic Report of the President.

1. a. Complete Columns 1–5 of Table 13-1.

Table 13-1

(1) Year	(2) Real GDP (billions of 1996 dollars)	(3) % Change in Real GDP	(4) Civilian Unemployment Rate (%)	(5) Actual Change in Unemployment Rate	(6) Predicted Change in Unemployment Rate
1997	_____		_____		
		_____		_____	_____
1998	_____		_____		
		_____		_____	_____
1999	_____		_____		
		_____		_____	_____
2000	_____		_____		
		_____		_____	_____
2001	_____		_____		

   b. Recall from Chapter 2 of the textbook that Okun's law can be written as:

Percent Change in Real GDP = 3% – 2 × Change in the Unemployment Rate.

Use this equation and the data in Column 3 of Table 13-1 to calculate the predicted change in the unemployment rate and enter the answers in Column 6.

c. Compare your predictions in Column 6 with the actual change in Column 5. What do you conclude about the accuracy of Okun's law?

Questions to Think About

1. Although the GDP deflator is reported by the government only every three months, most of the other major aggregate price indices, such as the consumer price index and the producer price index, are reported every month. In addition, the current prices for many commodities are available daily in the *Wall Street Journal* and other publications. What does the frequency with which prices are readily available to the public imply about the length of time during which people are ignorant about actual prices? What does this imply about the applicability of each of the three models of aggregate supply presented in Chapter 13 of the textbook?

2. Aside from the issue discussed in Problem 5, why else do workers and firms bargain over nominal wages rather than real wages?

Stabilization Policy

Fill-in Questions

Use the key terms below to fill in the blanks in the following statements. Each term may be used more than once.

automatic stabilizers

index of leading indicators

inside lag

Lucas critique

monetarists

outside lag

political business cycle

time inconsistency

1. The _____ is the time between a shock to the economy and the policy action responding to that shock.

2. The _____ is the time between a policy action and its ultimate influence on the economy.

3. Fiscal policy has a relatively long _____; monetary policy has a relatively long _____.

4. _____ are policies that stimulate or depress the economy when necessary without any deliberate policy changes.

5. The _____ is composed of 10 data series that signal future changes in real output. Economists use this measure to forecast future economic conditions.

6. The _____ argues that traditional methods of policy evaluation did not adequately take into account the impact of policy on expectations.

7. The manipulation of the economy by politicians in an attempt to gain reelection is called the _____.

8. The phenomenon of _____ implies that policymakers can sometimes better achieve their own goals by having their discretion taken away from them.

9. _____ advocate that the Fed keep the money supply growing at a steady rate as a method of preventing most large fluctuations in real output.

10. _____ may be viewed as fiscal policy without any inside lag.

Multiple-Choice Questions

1. The outside lag is the time between a:

    a. shock to the economy and the policy action responding to that shock.
    b. policy action and its influence on the economy.
    c. shock to the economy and the realization that some policy action needs to be taken.
    d. decision to implement a policy and the enactment of that policy.

2. The following statement is TRUE:

    a. monetary policy has an especially long outside lag.
    b. fiscal policy has an especially long inside lag.
    c. automatic stabilizers eliminate part of the inside lag in the conduct of fiscal policy.
    d. all of the above.

3. Arguments against the use of active stabilization policy include all of the following EXCEPT the:

    a. existence of long inside and outside lags.
    b. limited ability of economic forecasters to predict future economic conditions accurately.
    c. responsiveness of labor force participation rates to changes in national output.
    d. historical view that ill-advised policy choices were the cause of the Great Depression.

4. The system of unemployment insurance can be used to illustrate:

    a. the time inconsistency of policy.
    b. the way that the economy is automatically stabilized in the event of a shock.
    c. the Lucas critique.
    d. long inside lags in policy implementation.

5. Countries with more independent central banks tend to have:

    a. lower unemployment rates.
    b. lower inflation rates.
    c. higher rates of economic growth.
    d. all of the above.

6. Suppose that the index of leading indicators falls. Economic forecasters will expect all of the following to occur EXCEPT:

    a. the unemployment rate will increase.

    b. real output growth will decrease.

    c. inflation will increase.

    d. tax revenue growth will decrease.

7. According to the Lucas critique:

    a. traditional methods of policy evaluation do not adequately account for the impact of policy changes on expectations.

    b. traditional estimates of the sacrifice ratio are unreliable.

    c. economists cannot be completely confident when they make assessments about the effects of alternative economic policies.

    d. all of the above.

8. Comparing the time period before World War I with the period after World War II, Christina Romer found that:

    a. real GDP and unemployment have been much more stable in the later period.

    b. real GDP and unemployment have been much less stable in the later period.

    c. real GDP and unemployment have been slightly more stable in the later period.

    d. the levels of real GDP and unemployment have been approximately equal in the two periods.

9. All of the following are examples of a policy conducted by rule EXCEPT:

    a. the Fed automatically increases the money supply every year by 3 percent.

    b. the federal government is required, by a constitutional amendment, to balance the budget every year.

    c. the Fed adopts the following monetary policy for the indefinite future:
    % Change in $M = 3\% + 2 \times$ (Actual Unemployment Rate $- 5.5\%$).

    d. after a decline in private spending, Congress debates and then decides to stimulate aggregate demand by reducing taxes.

10. The following statement is FALSE:

    a. a policy that is active cannot be conducted by rule.

    b. the problem of time inconsistency is especially relevant to policy conducted by discretion.

    c. the conflicting interests of politicians reduce the desirability of policy conducted by discretion compared with policy conducted by rule.

    d. monetary policy currently is conducted by discretion.

11. If the Fed conducts monetary policy by setting a targeted unemployment rate of 5.5 percent, then the:

    a. unemployment rate will never fall above or below 5.5 percent.

    b. natural rate of unemployment will converge to the Fed's target.

    c. Fed will increase the growth rate of the money supply whenever unemployment exceeds this targeted rate.

    d. Fed will adjust its target whenever unemployment deviates from this rate.

12. Which of the following policies might lead to suboptimal results in the long run because of time inconsistencies?

    a. negotiation with terrorists who have taken hostages after a policy of nonnegotiation has been announced

    b. the enactment of a temporary "tax amnesty" for tax evaders

    c. the use of discretionary monetary policy rather than monetary rules

    d. all of the above

13. The best argument against the monetarists' view that a steady growth in the money supply would prevent most large fluctuations in output and unemployment is that:

    a. steady growth in the money supply would prevent fluctuations in output only if the aggregate price level is constant.

    b. steady growth in the money supply need not stabilize aggregate demand because the velocity of money is not always stable.

    c. large fluctuations in the money supply do not occur because there is a limited amount of money available in the economy.

    d. fluctuations in output and unemployment are best treated by fiscal policy because the federal government has a more direct control over the economy through its use of the tax system.

14. In the 1990s, the volatility of real GDP growth and inflation were:

    a. much greater than before.

    b. about the same as before.

    c. much less than before.

    d. close to zero.

Exercises

1. **Active versus Passive Macroeconomic Policies** *In this exercise, we review the arguments for active and passive policy responses to fluctuations in real output.*

   a. Suppose that the economy is initially at Point A on Graph 14-1.

Graph 14-1

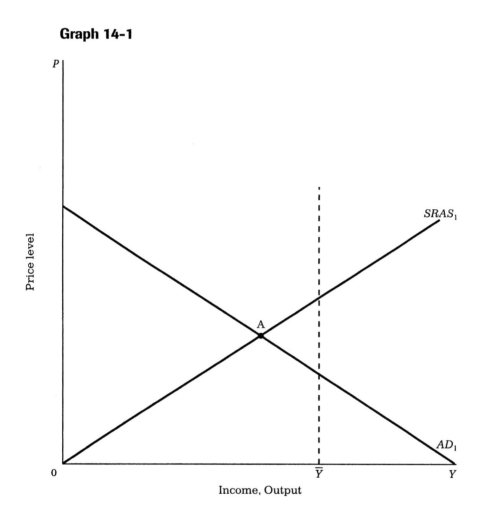

   Clearly, at Point A, real output Y is <u>greater than/equal to/less than</u> the natural rate of output $\overline{Y}$. Consequently, the actual price level P must be <u>greater than/equal to/less than</u> the expected price level P^e.

   b. In future years, therefore, P^e will <u>rise/fall/remains the same</u>. If macroeconomic policies remain unchanged, the change in P^e will shift the short-run aggregate supply curve <u>upward/downward</u> until eventually actual output is <u>greater than/equal to/less than</u> the natural rate of output. Draw the final short-run aggregate supply curve on Graph 14-1 and label it $SRAS_F$. Label the final equilibrium Point F. Comparing Points A and F, one can conclude that if no policy response is taken, real output will eventually <u>rise/fall/remains the same</u>, and the price level will <u>rise/fall/remain the same</u>.

c. The initial equilibrium from Graph 14-1 is redrawn on Graph 14-2.

Graph 14-2

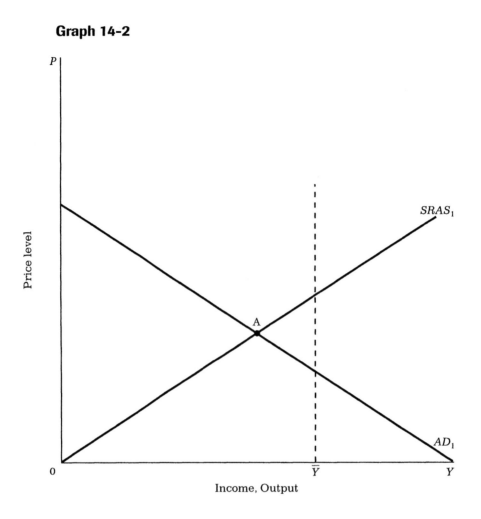

If policymakers wanted to increase output to the natural rate quickly, they could increase/decrease the money supply, increase/decrease government purchases, or increase/decrease taxes. These policies would shift the aggregate demand curve to the left/right. Draw the new aggregate demand curve on Graph 14-2, label it AD_2, and label the new equilibrium Point B. Comparing Points A and B, one can conclude that if an active policy response is taken, real output will rise/fall/remain the same, and the price level will rise/fall/remain the same.

d. In Parts a and b, the economy eventually reaches the natural rate of output. If an active policy response is taken, however, the eventual price level is greater than/ equal to/less than the eventual price level if no policy response is taken.

The case for an active policy response to fluctuations in output relies partially on the belief that the transition back to the natural rate will be longer/shorter if expansionary monetary and fiscal policies are pursued than if no new policies are pursued. It also relies on the belief that policymakers will be able and willing to implement the appropriate policies.

e. In Chapter 13 of the textbook, there is a discussion of some of the issues that determine the speed with which the economy approaches the natural rate of output when policy is passive. Instead of assuming that expected inflation is equal to last year's actual rate of inflation, suppose that inflationary expectations are rational. Then real output will return to its natural rate <u>more/less</u> rapidly. If wages and prices are flexible rather than sticky, real output will return to its natural rate <u>more/less</u> rapidly. If the duration of wage and price contracts is relatively long rather than short, real output will return to its natural rate <u>more/less</u> rapidly.

f. In Chapter 14 of the textbook, there is a discussion of several problems that commonly arise when active policy measures are taken to stabilize output. One limitation of active policy concerns the fact that fiscal policy has a relatively long <u>inside/outside</u> lag, whereas monetary policy has a relatively long <u>inside/outside</u> lag. Another limitation is that the track record of economic forecasters has not been especially good. Finally, policymakers occasionally seem to be unwilling or unable to implement the appropriate macroeconomic policies because of political considerations.

2. **The Lucas Critique** *In this exercise, we use a simple Phillips curve example to illustrate the Lucas critique.*

    a. Suppose that the following equation represents the Phillips curve for an imaginary economy:

    $$u = u^n - \beta\,(\pi - \pi^e) = 6 - 0.2(\pi - \pi^e). \tag{14-1}$$

    According to Equation 14-1, the natural rate of unemployment is _____ percent. Furthermore, whenever the actual inflation rate exceeds the expected rate of inflation by 1 percentage point, the unemployment rate is _____ percentage points <u>above/below</u> the natural rate of unemployment.

    b. During the nineteenth century, suppose that the actual rate of inflation was +5 percent half the time and –5 percent the remaining half. In the absence of any prior information, the average or expected rate of inflation for any year would be

    $$\pi^e = 0.5 \times 5\% + 0.5 \times (-5\%) = \underline{\hspace{2cm}}\%.$$

    During those years in which the actual rate of inflation turned out to be +5 percent, the Phillips curve equation indicates that the actual unemployment rate was 6 – 0.2(_____ – _____) = _____ percent. On the other hand, during those years in which the actual rate of inflation was –5 percent, the actual rate of unemployment was 6 – 0.2 (_____ – _____) = _____ percent. Since each of the two rates occurred half of the time, the average unemployment rate during the entire century was _____ percent.

c. After a century of this pattern, advisers recommended policies designed to keep the inflation rate equal to +5 percent in every year. It was the advisers' hope that people's expectations of inflation would remain equal to the last century's expected inflation rate of _____ percent, so that the unemployment rate would be 6 – 0.2(_____ – _____) = _____ percent in every year.

d. Alas, after several years of these new policies and persistent 5 percent inflation, people soon increased their forecast of inflation to 5 percent. As a result, unemployment thereafter equaled 6 – 0.2(_____ – _____) = _____ percent in every year, which was more than/less than/equal to the average during the preceding century.

e. This example illustrates the Lucas critique, whereby an evaluation of a change in economic policy must take into account the impact of the policy change on people's expectations of the future. Several economists believe that the imaginary economy in this exercise resembles the experience of the U.S. economy during the past two centuries. Finally, the more quickly people changed their expectations in response to the more inflationary policies, the more quickly/slowly unemployment returned to its natural rate.

3. **Rules versus Discretion** *In this exercise, we present and evaluate several rules for the conduct of monetary policy.*

a. As stated in Exercise 1, many observers are wary about the ability and/or willingness of policymakers to implement the appropriate macroeconomic policies. Some economists believe that monetary policy should be governed by a set of rules or formulas. One example is the constant-growth-rate rule, advocated by many monetarists, in which the Fed would increase the money supply by a fixed percentage each year. Suppose, for example, that the goal of monetary policy is to fuel noninflationary long-run economic growth. Recall the quantity equation presented in Chapter 4 of the textbook.

$$MV = PY \tag{14-2}$$

The percentage change version of the quantity equation is

% Change in M + % Change in V = % Change in P + % Change in Y.

The long-run rate of growth of output is about 3 percent per year. If velocity were constant, growth that kept the price level stable would require that % Change in M = % Change in P + % Change in Y – % Change in V or

_____ + _____ – _____ = _____%.

b. One frequently mentioned problem with the constant-growth-rate rule is that large fluctuations in velocity would lead to large fluctuations in aggregate demand. As a result, some economists advocate a money-growth rule that sets a target for nominal income PY. Suppose that the target growth rate for nominal income is 3 percent per year. If velocity were constant, this target growth rate would require a _____ percent annual increase in the money supply M. Suppose, however, that nominal income increases by 7 percent in one year. If the money supply continued to grow by _____ percent, then velocity must have increased/decreased by _____ percent. Following a nominal-income targeting rule, the Fed would then reduce the growth rate of the money supply to dampen aggregate demand. If, on the other hand, nominal income increased by 1 percent in one year and the money supply continued to grow at its initial rate, then velocity must have increased/decreased by _____ percent. The Fed would then increase the growth rate of the money supply to spur aggregate demand. In this way, the Fed would have the ability and the authority to offset fluctuations in the velocity of money.

c. A third group of economists believes that price stability should be the sole goal of monetary policy. Consequently, they advocate a money-growth rule that is based on a target price level. If the actual price level were to exceed the target, money growth would increase/decrease. If the actual price level were less than the target, money growth would increase/decrease.

Problems

Answer the following problems on a separate sheet of paper.

1. Suppose you do not know the exact natural rate of unemployment, but you are confident that it is between 4.5 and 6 percent. Given the evidence cited in the textbook concerning the accuracy of economic forecasts and policy time lags, what might you reasonably conclude about the appropriate changes in monetary and fiscal policies if:

    a. the actual unemployment rate is 6.1 percent? Explain.

    b. the actual unemployment rate is 10.1 percent? Explain.

2. Explain why you agree or disagree with the following statement: The acceptance of rational expectations *totally* discredits the notion that policy activism should be pursued if output lies below its natural rate.

3. Table 14-1 in the textbook illustrates that there is usually a recession in the second year of Republican presidential administrations but not in the second year of Democratic administrations.

    a. Use the aggregate supply, aggregate demand model presented in Chapters 11 and 13 of the textbook to explain what differences in the conduct of monetary and/or fiscal policy by Republicans and Democrats would explain these differences in economic growth.

    b. If people have rational expectations and the imperfect-information model of the economy is correct, what differences in the conduct of monetary and/or fiscal policy would explain these differences in economic growth?

4. As the textbook notes, countries with more independent central banks tend to have lower average inflation rates. Nevertheless, the average unemployment rates among countries is unrelated to the degree of central bank independence. How would one explain this finding using the Phillips curve?

5.   **a.** According to what measure has real GDP become much less variable (volatile) in the post-World War II period relative to its variability in the 40-year period prior to World War II?

    b. According to what measure has the volatility of real GDP been roughly the same in these two periods?

    c. Why is this issue important for the debate concerning the desirability of pursuing macroeconomic stabilization policies when the economy is in a boom or a recession?

6.   **a.** Many economists advocate a reduction in the capital gains tax in order to stimulate saving and investment. (See Exercise 8 in Chapter 4 of the Student Guide for a discussion of the capital gains tax.) Briefly explain these economists' reasoning.

    b. Other economists believe that a capital gains tax reduction on past acquisitions would reduce tax revenues without stimulating additional saving and investment. Briefly explain their reasoning.

    c. Instead, this second group of economists suggests that saving and investment could be stimulated more by focusing all of the tax reduction on new acquisitions. This action would allow the tax rates on additional saving and investment to be reduced even more. Explain how the problem of time inconsistency might be used to dispute their assertion.

7. According to the Taylor rule, what is the optimal real federal funds rate if:

    a. inflation is 4 percent and GDP is 2 percent below its natural-rate level?

    b. inflation is zero and unemployment is at its natural rate?

8. In early 2002, inflation was about 2 percent and the Fed acted to reduce the nominal federal funds rate to 1.75 percent.

    a. What was the real federal funds rate?

b. If the Fed was acting in accordance with Taylor's rule, what was the implied GDP gap?

c. Most economists believe that the actual GDP gap at the time was substantially less than that implied in Part b. If so, why did the Fed set the federal funds rate so low?

9. Suppose a central banker was concerned *only* about price stability, resulting in the loss function $L(\pi) = \pi^2$.

    a. Use calculus to derive the optimal level of inflation for this central banker. (The answer should not be surprising.)

    b. What will be the resulting rate of unemployment in the long run? Explain.

Questions to Think About

1. a. Are inflationary expectations rational?

    b. What empirical tests would prove or disprove the hypothesis that expectations are rational?

2. As the textbook illustrates, different economists believe in different models of the economy. In what sense, then, can everyone have a rational expectation of the effects of various policies on real output?

3. If policymakers decided to conduct monetary policy by a rule, should they be allowed to change the rule? If so, under what circumstances?

4. If monetary policy is governed by a rule, but policymakers are allowed to change this rule, how can one apply the problem of time inconsistency to the debate about whether policy should be conducted by rules or by discretion?

5. How might policymakers make a commitment to a policy rule? Might the policymakers' reputation be a form of commitment?

6. If you believe that democracy is the best form of government, how could you justify greater central bank independence from a political perspective?

CHAPTER *15* FIFTEEN

Government Debt

Fill-in Questions

Use the key terms below to fill in the blanks in the following statements. Each term may be used more than once.

capital budgeting   government debt

cyclically adjusted budget deficit   Ricardian equivalence

generational accounts   traditional view of government debt

1. When the conventionally measured government budget deficit is positive, there is an increase in the nominal value of the _____.

2. Some economists believe that the budget deficit should measure changes in the real value of the _____.

3. A budget procedure that accounts for assets as well as liabilities is sometimes called _____.

4. The _____ measures what the budget deficit would be if the economy were operating at its natural rate of output and employment.

5. _____ measure the impact of fiscal policy on the lifetime incomes of different generations.

6. According to the _____, a tax cut that is unaccompanied by current or expected future reductions in government spending stimulates current consumption.

7. According to the _____ hypothesis, a tax cut that is unaccompanied by current or expected future reductions in government spending has no effect on current consumption.

Multiple-Choice Questions

1. Compared with the percentages of other industrial countries, the gross U.S. national debt as a percentage of its GDP is:

   a. very high.

   b. very low.

   c. about average.

2. The ratio of federal government debt to GDP:

   a. has never been higher than it is today.

   b. peaked during the Civil War years.

   c. has never been lower than it has been during the past 15 years.

   d. is much smaller today than it was at the end of World War II.

3. If no changes are made to Social Security and Medicare, projected demographic changes will:

   a. worsen our budgetary problems in the next 50 years.

   b. alleviate our budgetary problems in the next 50 years.

   c. have little effect on our budgetary problems in the next 50 years.

4. The government budget deficit is equal to:

   a. $G - T$.

   b. $T - G$.

   c. $G + T$.

   d. $- G$.

5. The stock of government debt is equal to:

   a. the current government budget deficit.

   b. the total debt of all individuals in the nation.

   c. the outstanding debt of the government.

   d. government expenditures minus the tax revenues.

6. Most economists believe that the budget deficit should measure the change in the government's:

   a. nominal debt.

   b. real debt.

   c. tax revenues.

   d. fiscal policy.

7. During periods of inflation, the official measure of the budget deficit:

   a. overstates the change in the government's real indebtedness.

   b. understates the change in the government's real indebtedness.

   c. equals the change in the government's real indebtedness.

   d. should equal the expected rate of inflation.

8. Economists argue that the official measure of the budget deficit is an incomplete measure of the change in the government's overall indebtedness because it:

   a. measures the change in the nominal debt rather than the real debt.

   b. does not consider any changes in the value of government assets.

   c. excludes the accrual of future pension benefits that must be paid to government employees.

   d. all of the above.

9. During recessions the:

   a. actual budget deficit will be smaller than the cyclically adjusted budget deficit.

   b. actual budget deficit will be greater than the cyclically adjusted budget deficit.

   c. actual budget deficit will be equal to the cyclically adjusted budget deficit.

   d. cyclically adjusted budget deficit will always be positive.

10. According to the traditional view of government debt, a tax cut will lead to all of the following in the short run EXCEPT a(n):

    a. increase in consumption.

    b. increase in private saving.

    c. increase in investment.

    d. decrease in public saving.

11. According to the traditional view of government debt, a tax cut will lead to all of the following in the long run EXCEPT a:

    a. decrease in public saving.

    b. decrease in national saving.

    c. decrease in net exports.

    d. depreciation of the foreign exchange rate.

12. According to the Ricardian view of government debt, consumers will treat a current tax cut as an increase in:

    a. their wealth.

    b. the sum of their current and expected future income.

    c. their current disposable income accompanied by a future tax increase.

    d. public saving.

13. According to the Ricardian view of government debt, consumers will respond to a current tax cut by:

    a. increasing their current consumption.

    b. increasing their private saving by the amount of the tax cut.

    c. increasing their future consumption.

    d. decreasing their private saving by the amount of the tax cut.

14. According to the Ricardian view of government debt, a current tax cut will:

    a. decrease public saving.

    b. increase private saving.

    c. have no effect on national saving.

    d. all of the above.

15. According to the Ricardian view of government debt, the relevant decision-making unit is the:

    a. infinitely lived family.
    b. finitely lived family.
    c. finitely lived individual.
    d. infinitely lived world community.

16. During the early 1980s, taxes were cut substantially, and national saving fell. This evidence by itself would seem to support:

    a. the traditional view of government debt.
    b. the Ricardian view of government debt.
    c. neither view of government debt.
    d. the view that government debt is neutral.

17. The events of the early 1980s, when taxes were cut and national saving fell, are consistent with the Ricardian view of government debt if:

    a. people suddenly became less optimistic about future economic growth.
    b. people expected future reductions in government spending.
    c. people expected that the tax cuts were temporary.
    d. the tax cuts were unexpected.

18. High budget deficits may:

    a. encourage excessively expansionary monetary policy.
    b. increase the risk of government default on its debt.
    c. reduce a nation's political influence throughout the world.
    d. all of the above.

19. If higher deficits raise fears of default on a country's national debt:

    a. domestic interest rates will rise.
    b. the foreign exchange rate will depreciate.
    c. capital flight may occur.
    d. all of the above.

20. Indexed government bonds:

    a. have higher interest rates than nonindexed bonds.
    b. reduce the government's incentive to produce surprise inflation.
    c. were introduced in the United States in 1946.
    d. all of the above.

21. Adherence to a balanced-budget rule by the federal government results in:

    a. an inability to use monetary policy to stimulate the economy when it slips into a recession.
    b. persistent inflation.
    c. an inability to lower tax rates to stimulate the economy when it slips into a recession.
    d. all of the above.

Exercises

1. **Adjusting the Budget Deficit for Inflation** *In this exercise, we illustrate how inflation can lead to an overestimate of the correctly measured budget deficit and how the inclusion of real, rather than nominal, interest payments in government expenses overcomes this problem.*

   Consider Table 15-1.

   Table 15-1

(1)	(2) Country A	(3) Country B
Initial debt (in billions of dollars)	$2,000	$2,000
Nominal government outlays (made near the end of the year), excluding interest payments (in billions of dollars)	$200	$200
Price level at the beginning of the year	1.0	1.0
Annual inflation rate	0	0.10
Nominal interest rate	0.03	0.13
Nominal taxes (in billions of dollars)	$260	$260

   Countries A and B are identical, except that Country B has 10 percent more inflation and, therefore (assuming that real interest rates are 3 percent in both economies), a 10 percent higher nominal interest rate than Country A.

   a. Using these data, we see that government (nominal) interest payments during the year in Country A = 0.03 × $2,000 = $_____ billion. In Country B, however, government (nominal) interest payments during the year = _____ × $2,000 = $_____ billion.

   b. The official government deficit in each country is equal to nominal government outlays, *including* nominal interest payments minus nominal taxes. In Country A, this amount equals $200 + (0.03 × $2,000) − $260 = $_____ billion. In Country B, however, the official government budget deficit equals $_____ + (_____ × $2,000) − $_____ = $_____ billion.

   c. The nominal value of outstanding government debt at the end of the fiscal year is equal to the initial value of debt plus any additional nominal budget deficits during the year. Consequently, the nominal value of outstanding government debt at the end of the fiscal year in Country A equals $2,000 + $_____ = $_____ billion, whereas in Country B it equals $_____ + $_____ = $_____ billion.

   d. Given the initial price level of 1.0 in both countries and the different inflation rates in Table 15-1, the price level at the end of the fiscal year is _____ in

Country A and _____ in Country B. The real value of outstanding government debt at the end of the fiscal year in Country A is equal to the nominal debt at the end of the year divided by the aggregate price level at the end of the year, or $_____/_____ = $_____ billion. The real value of outstanding government debt at the end of the fiscal year in Country B is equal to $_____/_____ = $_____ billion. The real value of government debt at the end of the year in Country A is greater than/less than/equal to the real value of government debt at the end of the year in Country B. If deficits truly measured changes in the real value of outstanding government debt, the budget deficits in both countries would equal $_____ billion. Thus, during periods of high inflation, as in Country B, official deficit measures tend to understate/overstate the true value of the deficit.

e. Suppose that one counts only *ex post* real interest payments in the deficit. The *ex post* real interest rate is _____ (or _____ percent) in Country A and _____ in Country B. Consequently, real interest payments are $_____ billion in Country A and $_____ billion in Country B. The adjusted budget deficit would then equal nominal government outlays excluding interest payments plus real interest payments minus nominal taxes. This adjusted budget deficit would equal $_____ + $_____ − $_____ = $_____ billion in both countries. Thus, one way to eliminate the distortionary effects of inflation on the deficit is to include in the budget only real interest payments on the government debt.

2. The Traditional View of Government Debt *In this exercise, we review the short- and long-run effects of tax cuts according to the traditional view of government debt.*

a. In a closed economy in the short run, a tax cut will shift the *IS/LM* curve to the left/right. This shift will increase/decrease real income, increase/decrease consumption, and increase/decrease the real interest rate. As a result, investment will rise/fall and the tax cut partially crowds out government purchases/investment.

b. In an open economy, the short-run effects of the tax cut will depend upon whether the country is small or large and whether its foreign exchange rate is fixed or floating. If the country is a small open economy, the real interest rate will increase/decrease/remain constant. If the foreign exchange rate is floating, a tax cut will lead to a(n) appreciation/depreciation of the domestic currency and national income will increase/decrease/remain constant. Disposable income and consumption, however, will increase/decrease/remain constant, and the tax cut will completely crowd out investment/government purchases/net exports. If the foreign exchange rate is fixed, the tax cut will increase/decrease/have no effect on real income and increase/decrease/have no effect on consumption. To maintain the fixed exchange rate, the Fed will have to increase/decrease the money supply.

c. If the country is a large open economy, the short-run effects of a tax cut
    CH will be an increase/a decrease/no change in real income and an increase/
    a decrease/no change in consumption. Since the *IS* curve for a large open
    economy is flatter/steeper than the *IS* curve for a closed economy, the changes
    in income and consumption following a tax cut will be larger/smaller than those
    in a closed economy.

d. In the long run, output will be at its natural rate. According to the traditional
    view of government debt, if the steady-state capital stock is unaffected, then in a
    closed economy the tax cut will increase/decrease/have no effect on national
    saving in the long run and increase/decrease/have no effect on consumption.

e. If the steady-state capital stock is affected and the economy starts from a
    CH position below the Golden Rule level of capital, the tax cut will increase/
    decrease/have no effect on the saving rate. Consequently, the steady-state level
    of the capital stock will increase/decrease/remain constant, and the steady-
    state levels of output and consumption will rise/fall/remain constant.

3. **The Ricardian View of Government Debt** *In this exercise, we present the Ricardian
    view that tax cuts will increase saving and have no effect on current consumption.*

    a. According to the Ricardian view of government debt, a tax cut does not stimu-
        late consumption because it does not affect the current and expected future
        income of current citizens and their descendants. Let us begin by analyzing a
        simple two-period model. Suppose that the government cuts taxes by $1,000 in
        Period 1. If this tax cut represents an increase in current and expected future
        income, consumers will respond by increasing/decreasing/not changing
        consumption.

    b. Now suppose that the government finances the tax cut by issuing a bond
        for $1,000 plus interest of 10 percent. When the government pays back its
        loan in Period 2, it will pay $1,000 + 0.10($1,000) = $_____.
        To pay this amount, it will have to increase taxes in Period 2 by
        $_____. If in Period 1 you had saved all of the money you
        received from the initial tax cut and put it into the bank at an interest rate of
        10 percent, you would have $1,000 + 0.10($1,000) = $_____ in
        Period 2. Consequently, after you pay the tax increase in Period 2, you will be
        better off/worse off/equally well off compared with your situation before the
        initial tax cut in Period 1. As a result, the early tax cut and the later tax increase
        will increase/decrease/have no effect on the sum of your current and expected
        future income, and consumption in Period 1 will increase/decrease/remain
        constant.

    c. Ricardians expand this simple model to include many periods in the distant
        future. Any tax reduction in the current period unaccompanied by current or
        future reductions in government spending will eventually lead to a tax increase
        in the future that is equal to the amount of money that will accumulate if current
        citizens save all of the current tax reduction. (Alternatively, the "present value"

of the future tax increase is equal to the initial tax cut.) Consequently, if the indefinite future is considered, an early tax cut and a later tax increase will increase/decrease/<u>have no effect</u> on the sum of current and expected future income, and consumption in Period 1 will increase/decrease/<u>remain constant</u>.

4. **Fiscal Policy Rules** *Chapter 14, Exercise 3 examined policy rules for monetary policy. In this exercise we present and evaluate several rules for the conduct of fiscal policy.*

   a. The most well-known rule for fiscal policy is one that requires the federal budget to be balanced in each year, that is, $G - tY = 0$ where t is the tax rate. This balanced-budget rule would obviously reduce the ability of policymakers to use fiscal policy to offset fluctuations in real output. It might even exacerbate these fluctuations. If, for example, the economy slipped into a recession, tY would increase/remain constant/<u>decrease</u>. To keep the budget balanced, policymakers might then have to <u>increase</u>/decrease G or increase/<u>decrease</u> the tax rate t. Either change would shift the aggregate demand curve to the <u>left</u>/right and thereby magnify the reduction in output.

   b. As the textbook states, policymakers should avoid large changes in tax rates in order to minimize the distortion of incentives caused by the tax system. Relatively constant tax rates, however, would lead to government surpluses/<u>deficits</u> during recessions and <u>surpluses</u>/deficits during economic booms. Finally, budget deficits may be the appropriate way to shift a portion of the burden of a current government expenditure to future generations if they, too, benefit from the expenditure.

   c. To avoid the first problem mentioned in Part a, the reduction in the ability of policymakers to use fiscal policy to offset fluctuations in real output, some economists have advocated a rule that balances the "cyclically adjusted budget deficit," which is the budget deficit that would occur if $Y = \overline{Y}$. (See Problem 5 in Chapter 15 of the textbook.) This amount is roughly equal to $G - t\overline{Y}$. Consequently, if the economy slipped into a recession, tax rates would/<u>would not</u> have to be increased because the cyclically adjusted budget deficit would/<u>would not</u> increase.

Problems

Answer the following problems on a separate sheet of paper.

1. How does an increase in Social Security taxes, unaccompanied by any changes in Social Security benefits or changes in government spending, affect current consumption in a closed economy, according to the traditional and Ricardian views of government debt? Explain.

2. Suppose the government cuts taxes by $100 billion. According to Ricardian equivalence, indicate what will happen to each of the following and briefly explain your answer.

    a. current consumption

    b. current private saving

    c. current national saving

3. Suppose that the assumptions behind the Ricardian view of government debt are true, and you are planning to emigrate to another country with your family next year. How would you respond to a tax reduction in this year? If the Ricardian view of government debt is true, how would the economy as a whole respond?

4. How does an expected future reduction in government purchases affect current consumption and current private saving, according to the traditional and Ricardian views of government debt? Explain.

5. Consider Table 15-2.

Table 15-2

(1)	(2) Country A	(3) Country B
Initial debt (in billions of dollars)	$2,000	$2,000
Nominal government outlays (made near the end of the year), excluding interest payments (in billions of dollars)	$200	$200
Price level at the beginning of the year	1.0	1.0
Annual inflation rate	0	−0.05
Nominal interest rate	0.07	0.02
Nominal taxes (in billions of dollars)	$340	$340

Countries A and B are identical, except that Country B has 5 percent less inflation and, therefore (assuming that the real interest rate is 7 percent in both economies), a 5 percent lower nominal interest rate than Country A.

    a. What is the nominal value of government interest payments in each economy?

    b. What are the official government deficits in each economy?

    c. Calculate the nominal value of outstanding government debt at the end of the fiscal year in each economy.

    d. Show that the real value of outstanding government debt at the end of the fiscal year is the same in both economies, so that the difference in official deficits does not reflect any real difference in the governments' net debt positions.

    e. Show that, if one counts only *ex post* real interest payments in the deficit, then Country A's and Country B's deficits are equal.

    f. During deflationary periods, do official deficit measures tend to understate or overstate the true value of the deficit? Explain.

6. Suppose a president facing budget deficits asked his economic advisers to solve the following dilemma: he would like to reassure the "financial markets" that he is serious about proposing a long-run plan that will eventually reduce the federal budget deficit further, but he is concerned that any contractionary fiscal policy might push the economy into a recession. One adviser suggests that the president propose (and Congress pass) legislation *now* that will raise taxes, *starting four years from now*. Assume throughout this problem that everyone believes that taxes will indeed rise four years from now.

   a. Why would the simple Keynesian consumption function predict that this strategy would work?

   b. Many of the president's economists argue that the legislation will affect the economy now even if taxes do not increase for another four years. Explain their reasoning and the theory (or theories) they use.

   c. A small group of economists argues that the tax increase will have no effect on real GDP, regardless of when it takes effect. Why?

   d. Even if the theory cited by economists in Part c is correct, other economists argue that the tax increase will still affect consumption when it takes effect if people have liquidity constraints. Explain their reasoning.

7. During the Mexican crisis of 1994–1995, the U.S. government guaranteed up to $50 billion of Mexican government debt. This guarantee helped to calm the crisis, and the Mexican government did not default. Explain what the effect of a U.S. guarantee for another country's debt (for example, Brazil) would be on the U.S. budget deficit.

8. Many people associate high budget deficits with high real interest rates and rising prices. Taxes in the United States are primarily linked to income. Throughout this problem assume that $T = ty$, where t is the net tax rate.

   a. Use *IS-LM* and *AS-AD* graphs to illustrate and explain whether this association (that is, high budget deficits with high real interest rates and rising prices) is true in the short run if the deficits are primarily due to expansionary fiscal policies (like increases in government purchases).

   b. Use *IS-LM* and *AS-AD* graphs to illustrate and explain whether this association is true in the short run if there is a sudden decline in consumer or business confidence.

Data Questions

Locate the necessary economic data and apply them to answer the following data questions. All of the relevant data may be found in the Economic Report of the President.

1. **a.** Complete Table 15-3 (the data in Columns 2–5 should be in billions of current dollars).

Table 15-3

(1) Fiscal Year	(2) Total Federal Government Receipts	(3) Total Federal Government Outlays	(4) Official Federal Budget Surplus	(5) Gross Federal Debt Held by the Public (end of year)
1995	——	——	——	——
1996	——	——	——	——
1997	——	——	——	——
1998	——	——	——	——
1999	——	——	——	——

b. Now complete Columns 2–4 of Table 15-4, noting the difference between Column 4 in Table 15-4 and Column 5 in Table 15-3.

Table 15-4

(1) Calendar Year	(2) Price Deflator for GDP (1996 = 100)	(3) Percentage Change	(4) Gross Federal Debt Held by Public (end of *preceding* fiscal year) ($ in billions)	(5) Approximate "True" Federal Budget Surplus ($ in billions)
1996	——		——	——
		——		
1997	——		——	——
		——		
1998	——		——	——
		——		
1999	——		——	——
		——		
2000	——			

c. As the textbook states, many economists believe that one should adjust the official budget deficit or surplus to account for the reduction in the real value of government debt that results from inflation. Calculate the approximate "true" budget surplus in Column 5 by multiplying the inflation rate for each calendar year (expressed as a decimal) by the amount of outstanding federal debt held by the public at the end of the preceding fiscal year and adding this amount to the official (negative or positive) budget surplus for the current year, which is given in Column 4 of Table 15-3. For example, multiply the inflation rate for 1996–1997 by the debt held at the end of fiscal year 1995 (that is, September 30, 1995) and add this to the official (negative) budget surplus for 1996 to approximate the "true" surplus for fiscal year 1996.

Questions to Think About

1. Would your own spending change in response to a tax cut that was not linked to current or future changes in government spending? Explain.

2. Why does the government have to pay off its debt at some point in the future? Can debt continue to grow at any rate indefinitely? Examine two cases, one in which the real interest rate on government debt exceeds the economy's long-run rate of growth of real output, and a second in which the economy's long-run growth rate exceeds the real interest rate.

3. Under what circumstances do you think indexed bonds would be especially attractive?

Consumption

Fill-in Questions

Use the key terms below to fill in the blanks in the following statements. Each term may be used more than once.

average propensity to consume	marginal rate of substitution
borrowing constraint	normal good
budget constraint	permanent income
discounting	permanent-income hypothesis
income effect	precautionary saving
indifference curve	random walk
intertemporal budget constraint	substitution effect
life-cycle hypothesis	transitory income
marginal propensity to consume	

1. The amount that an individual consumes out of an additional dollar of (disposable) income is called the _____.

2. According to the Keynesian consumption function, as income rises an individual's _____ falls. Over time, however, as income per person increases, the _____ actually remains relatively constant. This phenomenon can be explained by both the _____ and the _____.

3. All consumers face a(n) _____, which is a limit on how much they can spend in the current period.

4. When consumers are deciding how much to consume today versus how much to save for future consumption, they face a(n) _____.

5. Since saving earns interest, one should compare future income with current income by _____, which reduces the value of $10,000 of income received in the future below the value of $10,000 of current income.

6. In Irving Fisher's model of consumption, a(n) _____ shows the combinations of first-period consumption and second-period consumption that make the consumer equally happy.

7. The slope of the indifference curve equals the _____, which represents the amount of second-period consumption the consumer requires to be compensated for a one-unit reduction in first-period consumption.

8. If a consumer wants to consume more of a good when his or her income rises, that good is said to be a(n) _____.

9. When the real interest rate changes, the change in consumption can be divided into two components. The change in consumption resulting from the movement to a higher indifference curve is called the _____. The change in consumption arising from the change in the relative price of consumption between different periods is called the _____.

10. When the interest rate rises for someone who saves part of her income, the _____ tends to make consumers choose more consumption in all periods, and the _____ tends to make consumers choose less consumption in the current period and more consumption in future periods.

11. A consumer who wishes to consume more than her current income may be unable to borrow against her future income if she faces a(n) _____.

12. The _____ suggests that people save their income in order to smooth their consumption over their entire adult lifetime. In reality, the elderly do not dissave to the extent predicted by this model, possibly because of _____, which is additional saving that arises from uncertainty.

13. The _____ distinguishes between two types of income that affect consumption. _____ is the part of income that people expect to persist in the future. The part of income that people do not expect to persist is called _____.

14. The combination of the permanent-income hypothesis and rational expectations implies that consumption follows a(n) _____. A(n) _____ is the term that economists use to describe the path of a variable whose changes are unpredictable.

Multiple-Choice Questions

1. According to the Keynesian theory of consumption, when individuals experience an increase in their income their:
   a. consumption will rise by the total amount of the increase in income.
   b. consumption will rise by less than the increase in income.
   c. average propensity to consume will increase.
   d. marginal propensity to consume will increase.

2. According to the Keynesian theory of consumption, the primary determinant of consumption is the:

   a. interest rate.

   b. wealth of the consumer.

   c. consumer's ability to borrow.

   d. consumer's income.

3. According to Fisher's model of consumption, all of the following statements about the intertemporal budget constraint are true EXCEPT:

   a. if current consumption rises, the resources available for future consumption will fall.

   b. consumption in Period 1 must be less than or equal to consumption in Period 2.

   c. in the first period, saving is equal to first-period income minus consumption.

   d. consumers take into account both current income and expected future income when making consumption choices.

4. In the Fisher model, if the real interest rate is positive:

   a. second-period consumption costs less in terms of first-period income than the same amount of first-period consumption.

   b. second-period income is worth more than an equal amount of first-period income.

   c. consumers will be unwilling to borrow money, so their consumption in Period 1 will be less than their income in Period 1.

   d. all of the above.

5. All of the following statements about indifference curves are true EXCEPT:

   a. if first-period consumption is decreased, second-period consumption must be increased in order for the consumer to remain equally satisfied.

   b. the slope is equal to the marginal rate of substitution.

   c. the greater the decrease in first-period consumption, the less second-period consumption must increase to keep the consumer's utility constant.

   d. the consumer prefers to be on a higher indifference curve than a lower one.

6. According to the Fisher model, the optimal level of consumption for a consumer occurs when the marginal rate of substitution:

   a. equals one.

   b. equals zero.

   c. equals the slope of the budget line.

   d. is maximized.

7. An increase in the real interest rate leading to an increase in consumption in all periods because of a movement to a higher indifference curve is an example of:

   a. the substitution effect.

   b. the income effect.

   c. the life-cycle hypothesis.

   d. the permanent-income hypothesis.

8. Which of the following may NOT occur when the real interest rate increases?

    a. The income effect works to increase consumption in both Periods 1 and 2 for consumers who initially save part of their income in Period 1.

    b. Consumption rises in all periods.

    c. A consumer who saves part of her income in Period 1 will move to a higher indifference curve.

    d. The substitution effect works to increase second-period consumption and reduce first-period consumption.

9. If a consumer wishes to consume more than his current income in Period 1:

    a. he will be unable to consume anything in Period 2.

    b. the real interest rate must be greater than one.

    c. the decision to consume more must satisfy both his budget constraint and his borrowing constraint.

    d. none of the above.

10. If a consumer faces a borrowing constraint:

    a. she will be unable to consume anything in the second period.

    b. she may or may not be less satisified than if she was able to borrow.

    c. consumption in the first period must be less than consumption in the second period.

    d. all of the above.

11. The life-cycle consumption function takes into account all of the following EXCEPT the:

    a. amount of wealth.

    b. government budget deficit.

    c. expected number of working years.

    d. expected number of years of retirement.

12. According to the life-cycle hypothesis, a person who expects to work 40 more years before retiring and who expects to live a total of 50 more years will have the following consumption function:

    a. $C = 0.2W + 0.6Y$.

    b. $C = 0.2W + 0.8Y$.

    c. $C = 0.04W + 0.8Y$.

    d. $C = 0.02W + 0.8Y$.

13. Under the life-cycle hypothesis, the consumption function, $C = 0.025W + 0.5Y$, implies that:

    a. the individual expects to live 40 more years.

    b. half of the person's expected remaining life will be spent in retirement.

    c. for every additional dollar of wealth, consumption increases by 2.5 cents.

    d. all of the above.

14. An example of precautionary saving is when:

    a. a newly married couple saves to buy a house in 10 years.

    b. high interest rates cause a business professional to reduce investment.

    c. an individual automatically deposits a fraction of his weekly income in a Christmas Club to save for the coming holiday.

    d. an individual increases her saving in preparation for retirement because she fears that poor health may lead to added expenses.

15. According to the permanent-income hypothesis:

    a. the average propensity to consume is the ratio of transitory income to current income.

    b. consumption depends equally on permanent and transitory income.

    c. people use saving to smooth consumption in response to transitory changes in income.

    d. none of the above.

16. A change in permanent income occurs when a(n):

    a. Florida resort owner enjoys unusually good business during a particularly harsh winter.

    b. individual wins $10,000 in a lottery.

    c. injured worker receives workers' compensation benefits for six months.

    d. tenured college professor receives a $10,000 increase per year in her salary.

17. Which of the following statements is TRUE?

    a. Studies indicate that households with high incomes tend to have low average propensities to consume.

    b. Over long periods of time, the average propensity to consume is fairly constant.

    c. The life-cycle and permanent-income hypotheses can explain most of the empirical facts about the average propensity to consume.

    d. all of the above

18. According to the permanent-income hypothesis, an artist whose income fluctuates from year to year will:

    a. have a higher average propensity to consume in years of lower income.

    b. have a higher average propensity to consume in years of high income.

    c. have a constant average propensity to consume every year.

    d. never save any of her income.

19. According to the permanent-income hypothesis, which of the following is likely to happen if Congress enacts a temporary tax cut?

    a. Consumers will view the year as a temporarily good one and will increase their saving by almost the full amount of the tax cut.

    b. Consumers will increase their consumption by the full amount of the tax cut.

    c. The tax cut will have a large effect on aggregate demand.

    d. both b and c are true

20. When a consumer borrows money to allow for greater consumption, he is:

    a. increasing his total income.

    b. escaping his intertemporal budget constraint.

    c. borrowing against his future income.

    d. able to increase his consumption in all periods.

Exercises

1. **The Keynesian Consumption Function** *In this exercise, we use a Keynesian consumption function to illustrate the algebraic and graphical differences between the marginal and average propensities to consume.*

    a. Consider the simple consumption function

$$C = 125 + 0.75(Y - T), \tag{16-1}$$

where T = taxes and $Y - T$ = disposable income. If $T = 0$, we may write

$$C = 125 + 0.75Y, \tag{16-2}$$

where Y is both national income and disposable income. Graph this equation on Graph 16-1 and label the curve C.

Graph 16-1

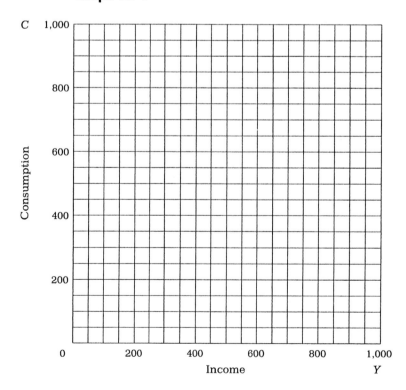

b. The marginal propensity to consume (*MPC*) is defined as:

The value of the *MPC* in this model is _____. This fraction is also equal to the slope of the consumption function in Graph 16-1. As *Y* increases in this model, the value of the *MPC* <u>increases/decreases/remains constant</u>. Furthermore, Keynes postulated that the *MPC* would always be greater than _____ but less than _____.

c. The average propensity to consume (*APC*) is defined as the ratio of consumption to disposable income, which, when *T* = 0 as in this model, is equal to *Y*. Thus, in this model, *APC* = *C/Y*. Substituting Equation 16-2 into the numerator of the *APC* and simplifying yields

$APC = $ _____ + _____ × (1/*Y*).

When *Y* = 250, $APC = $ _____ + _____ × (1/250) = _____.

When *Y* = 500, $APC = $ _____ + _____ × (1/500) = _____.

When *Y* = 1,000, $APC = $ _____ + _____ × (1/1,000) = _____.

This example illustrates that as *Y* increases, the value of the *APC* <u>increases/ decreases/remains constant</u>.

d. The value of the *APC* can also be illustrated on Graph 16-1. Suppose that *Y* = 1,000. According to Equation 16-2, when *Y* = 1,000, *C* = _____. Locate this point on Graph 16-1, label it Point A, and draw a line between Point A and the origin. The slope of this line is equal to the rise over run, or _____ / _____ = _____. This is equal to the <u>*MPC/APC*</u> when *Y* = 1,000. Consequently, the slope of the line connecting the origin to any point on the consumption function is equal to the <u>*MPC/APC*</u> at that level of income. Note that the slope of this line <u>increases/decreases/remains constant</u> as *Y* increases.

2. **The Short-Run and Long-Run Consumption Functions** *In this exercise, we review the cross-section and time-series evidence concerning the average propensity to consume and discuss the resulting short-run and long-run consumption functions.*

    a. Data collected from various households at any one point in time, called *cross-sectional data,* confirm the basic implications of the Keynesian consumption function. In these studies, the *MPC* is greater than _____ and less than _____. Furthermore, people with higher incomes tend to save a greater percentage of their income, which is another way of saying that the *APC* increases/decreases/remains constant as *Y* increases. Aggregate (economywide) data over short time periods also confirm these implications.

    b. Aggregate data collected over long periods of time, called *time-series data,* however, seem to contradict some of the implications of the Keynesian consumption function. Greater amounts of inputs and improved technology lead to rising income over time. As income rises, the Keynesian consumption function predicts that the *APC* will increase/decrease/remain constant. Economists who have studied the data, however, find that the *APC* tends to increase/decrease/remain constant over long periods of time despite substantial increases in *Y.*

    c. These contradictory findings have led economists to conclude that the aggregate short-run consumption function is different from the aggregate long-run consumption function. The short-run consumption function is very similar to the Keynesian consumption function: the *MPC* lies between _____ and _____, and the *APC* increases/decreases/remains constant as *Y* increases. Draw an arbitrary line on Graph 16-2 that satisfies these properties and label it *SRCF* (short-run consumption function). As stated in Part b, in the long run, the *APC* tends to increase/decrease/remains constant as *Y* increases. Draw an arbitrary line on Graph 16-2 that satisfies these properties and label it *LRCF* (long-run consumption function). (You may find it useful to review Part d of Exercise 1.) Note that any positively sloped straight line with a *y* intercept of _____ will satisfy the properties of the *LRCF.*

3. **Present and Future Value** *In this exercise, we present the concepts of present and future value.*

    a. Suppose you have $100 and the bank interest rate is 5 percent. If you put this $100 in the bank, at the end of one year you would have $100 + 0.05 ($100) = $_____. Note that we can express this algebraically as:

$$FV_1 = PV + i(PV) = PV(1 + i) \tag{16-3}$$

    where FV_1 is the future value at the end of year 1, *PV* represents the present (initial) value, and *i* represents the annual interest rate.

Graph 16-2

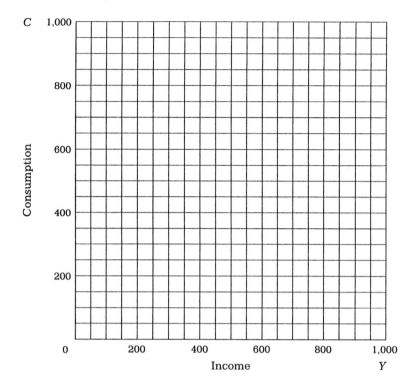

b. Conversely, if you knew you could get $\$FV_1$ at the end of one year and the interest rate is i, you could calculate the "present value" of this option by solving Equation 16-3 for PV:

$$PV = FV_1/(1 + i) \qquad\qquad\qquad \textbf{(16-4)}$$

As you might expect, the present value of receiving $105 at the end of one year with an interest rate of 5 percent is therefore $\$$_____$/(1 + 0.05) =$ $\$$_____ .

c. If you keep your original $100 in the bank, you would earn interest in the second year on the full amount of money you had at the end of the first year. Consequently, at the end of two years, you would have $105 + 0.05(\$105) =$ $\$$_____ . Note that this can be written as $1[\$100(1 + i)] + i[\$100(1 + i)]$ or $(1 + i)\$100(1 + i)$, which is also equal to $\$100(1 + i)^2$. Thus, we can write:

$$FV_2 = PV(1 + i)^2 \qquad\qquad\qquad \textbf{(16-5)}$$

d. Conversely, if you knew you could get $\$FV_2$ at the end of two years and the annual interest rate is i, you could calculate the "present value" of this option by solving Equation 16-5 for PV:

$$PV = FV_2/(1 + i)^2 \tag{16-6}$$

As you might expect, the present value of receiving $\$110.25$ at the end of two years with an interest rate of 5 percent is therefore $\$\underline{\hspace{3cm}}/$ $(1 + 0.05)^2 = \$\underline{\hspace{2cm}}.$

e. Using the results from Parts a–d, you may surmise that the formula for determining the amount you would have if you left your money in the bank for T years at annual interest rate i is $\underline{\hspace{3cm}}$. Conversely, if you know the future value in year T, FV_T, and the interest rate i, the formula for determining the present value is $\underline{\hspace{3cm}}$.

4. **The Intertemporal Budget Constraint** *In this exercise, we use a simple two-period model to derive the intertemporal budget constraint.*

a. Suppose that a typical consumer named Jennifer lives for two consumption periods. Her real income in each of Periods 1 and 2, Y_1 and Y_2, equals 12. Designate consumption during Periods 1 and 2 as C_1 and C_2, respectively. The portion of Jennifer's income in Period 1 that she does not consume in Period 1 is her saving S. Obviously,

$$S = Y_1 - C_1 = \underline{\hspace{4cm}} - C_1. \tag{16-7}$$

Assume that any saving from Period 1 earns interest at a real interest rate of 50 percent, or 0.50. Since Jennifer knows she will die at the end of Period 2, she does not save in the second period. Consequently, her consumption in Period 2, C_2, is equal to her income in Period 2, $(Y_2 = 12)$, plus any saving from Period 1 plus accumulated interest:

$$C_2 = Y_2 + S + rS = Y_2 + (Y_1 - C_1) + r(Y_1 - C_1) = \tag{16-8}$$

$$\underline{\hspace{2cm}} + (\underline{\hspace{2cm}} - C_1) + \underline{\hspace{2cm}} (\underline{\hspace{2cm}} - C_1), \text{ or}$$

$$C_2 = \underline{\hspace{3cm}} - \underline{\hspace{3cm}} C_1.$$

Graph this equation on Graph 16-3 and label it *IBTC* (intertemporal budget constraint).

Graph 16-3

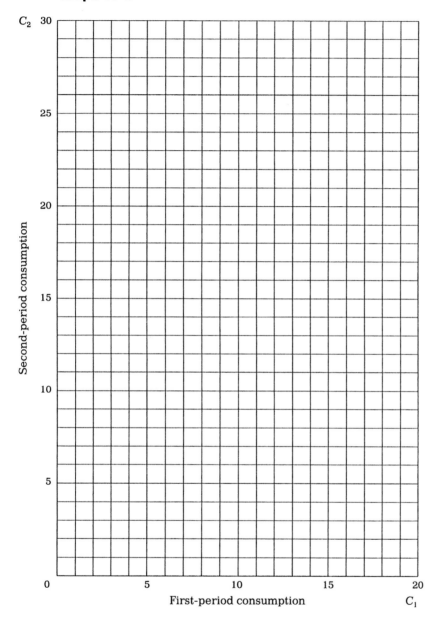

b. The line you drew on Graph 16-3 is called the *intertemporal budget constraint*. Given Jennifer's income and the real interest rate, the intertemporal budget constraint depicts the combinations of C_1 and C_2 that are available to her. The slope of this line is equal to $-(1 + r) = -(1 +$ _____) = $-$_____. This number indicates that each unit of consumption in Period 1 can be transformed into _____ units of consumption in Period 2 because any saving earns interest at the rate of _____ percent.

c. Although Jennifer can consume at any point along her intertemporal budget constraint, three points are worth noting. Locate the point on Graph 16-3 at which Jennifer consumes all of her current income in each of the two periods and label it Point A. At Point A, $C_1 = Y_1 =$ _____. Consequently, during Period 1, saving $S =$ _____, and $C_2 = Y_2 =$ _____. Now locate the point on Graph 16-3 at which Jennifer saves all of her income in Period 1 in order to maximize C_2 and label it Point B. At Point B, $C_1 =$ _____. Consequently, during Period 1, $S =$ _____ and $C_2 = Y_2 + S + rS =$ _____ + _____ + _____ × _____ = _____. Graph 16-3 can also be used to illustrate the situation in which Jennifer borrows at the same real interest rate to finance a level of consumption during Period 1 that exceeds her income in Period 1. Locate the point on Graph 16-3 at which Jennifer maximizes C_1 by borrowing against all of her income in Period 2 and label it Point C. At Point C, $C_2 =$ _____ and $C_1 = Y_1 + [Y_2/(1 + r)] =$ _____ + [_____ / _____] = _____.

5. **The Consumer's Optimal Levels of Consumption** *In this exercise, we derive a set of indifference curves from a specific utility function and illustrate the optimal consumption pattern given the intertemporal budget constraint in Exercise 3.*

a. Suppose that Jennifer, the same consumer from Exercise 3, lives for two periods and derives pleasure from her consumption in each of them. Assume, furthermore, that the amount of her total satisfaction is given by this utility function:

$$U = C_1 \times C_2 = C_1 C_2. \qquad (16\text{-}9)$$

Given this utility function, complete Table 16-1. Round off your answers to one decimal place.

Table 16-1

(1)	(2)	(3)	(4)	(5)	(6)	(7)	(8)
C_1	8.0	9.0	_____	_____	12.0	14.0	16.0
C_2	18.0	16.0	14.4	13.09	_____	_____	_____
$U = C_1 C_2$	_____	_____	144.0	144.00	144.0	144.0	144.0

b. Plot the numbers from Columns 2–8 on Graph 16-4, connect them (try to make the curve smooth), and label this curve $IC_{U=144}$.

Inasmuch as Jennifer's levels of utility at these seven combinations of C_1 and C_2 all equal _____, Jennifer is indifferent among them. Hence, $IC_{U=144}$ is called the indifference curve for a level of utility equal to 144.

c. Now complete Table 16-2, which lists all the combinations of C_1 and C_2 for which Jennifer's level of utility would equal 150.

Graph 16-4

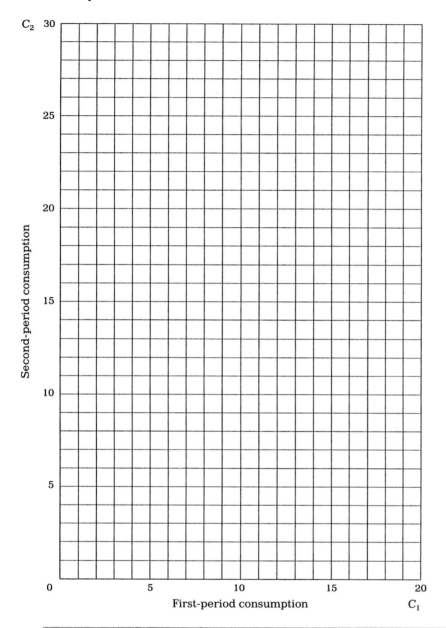

Table 16-2

(1)	(2)	(3)	(4)	(5)	(6)	(7)	(8)
C_1	8.00	9.00	10.0	_____	_____	14.0	16.00
C_2	18.75	16.67	_____	13.64	12.5	_____	_____
$U = C_1 C_2$	_____	_____	150.0	150.00	150.0	150.0	150.00

Plot the numbers from Table 16-2 on Graph 16-4, connect them (again, try to make the curve smooth), and label this curve $IC_{U=150}$.

d. Finally, complete Table 16-3, which lists the combinations of C_1 and C_2 for which Jennifer's level of utility would equal 162.

Table 16-3

	(1)	(2)	(3)	(4)	(5)	(6)	(7)	(8)
C_1	8.00	9.0	10.0	_____	_____		14.0	16.0
C_2	20.25	18.0	_____	14.73	13.5		_____	_____
$U = C_1 C_2$	_____	_____		162.0	162.00	162.0	162.0	162.0

Plot the numbers on Graph 16-4, connect them (again, try to make the curve smooth), and label this curve $IC_{U=162}$.

e. Along each indifference curve, the level of utility is held constant. As the level of utility increases, the entire indifference curve shifts to the left (downward)/ right (upward) because, in order to achieve the higher level of utility, consumption in one or both periods must increase/decrease. The slope of the indifference curve at any point shows how much second-period consumption Jennifer requires to be compensated for a one-unit reduction in first-period consumption and remain equally satisfied. This slope is called the _____ between first-period consumption and second-period consumption.

f. Suppose that Jennifer faces the same intertemporal budget constraint that she did in Exercise 3 (that is, $C_2 = 30 - 1.5C_1$). Graph this equation on Graph 16-4 and label it *ITBC*.

g. If Jennifer follows Polonius's advice to Laertes ("neither a borrower nor a lender be") and decides to consume all of her current income in each period, then $C_1 = Y_1 =$ _____ and $C_2 = Y_2 =$ _____. Locate this point on Graph 16-4 and label it Point A. Because Point A lies on the indifference curve labeled _____, Jennifer's level of utility at Point A equals _____.

h. Note, however, that Jennifer can move to a higher indifference curve and a higher level of utility by saving some of her income in Period 1 and increasing her consumption in Period 2. Indeed, she can move up to the indifference curve labeled _____ on Graph 16-4 and achieve a level of utility equal to _____ by reducing C_1 to 10 and thereby saving _____ in Period 1. If this amount of saving is put in a bank and earns interest of 50 percent, it will grow to _____ by Period 2, at which time Jennifer can add it to her income in Period 2 to obtain $C_2 = Y_2 + (1 + r)S =$ _____ + _____ = _____. Locate this point on Graph 16-4 and label it Point D. At Point D, $U = C_1 C_2 =$ _____ × _____ = _____. Also note that at Point D, Jennifer's indifference curve is just tangent to her intertemporal budget constraint line, which means that the slopes of these two curves are equal. Thus, at her optimal levels of consumption, Jennifer's marginal rate of substitution is equal to $1 + r$. All indifference curves corresponding to a still higher level of utility, such as $IC_{U=162}$, lie to the <u>left (below)/right (above)</u> of Jennifer's intertemporal budget constraint line and are consequently unattainable.

6. **The Effects of Changes in Income and the Real Interest Rate on the Consumer's Optimal Levels of Consumption** *In this exercise, we graphically illustrate the effects of increases in income and the real interest rate on the consumer's optimal levels of consumption and discuss the income and substitution effects.*

   a. Graph 16-5 illustrates Jennifer's initial optimal levels of consumption at Point D from Exercise 4 and the indifference curves corresponding to utility levels of 150 and 162, respectively. The real interest rate equals 50 percent. The curve labeled $ITBC_1$ represents Jennifer's initial intertemporal budget constraint. Suppose that Jennifer's income in Period 1 rises to 12.78, while Y_2 remains equal to 12. Consequently, Jennifer's intertemporal budget constraint would change to the following:

$$C_2 = Y_2 + S + rS = Y_2 + (Y_1 - C_1) + r(Y_1 - C_1)$$
$$= 12 + (12.78 - C_1) + 0.50(12.78 - C_1), \text{ or}$$

$C_2 =$ _____ $-$ _____ C_1.

Graph this new intertemporal budget constraint on Graph 16-5 and label it $ITBC_2$.

Graph 16-5

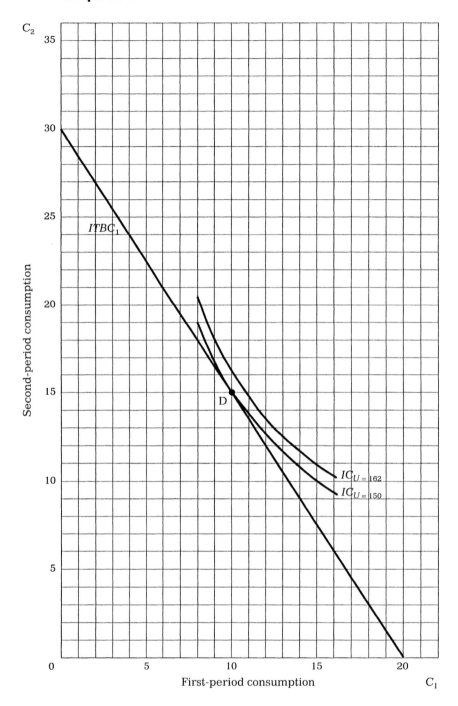

This shift of the intertemporal budget constraint curve could have also occurred from an increase in income in Period 2 or from increases in income in both periods. The slope of $ITBC_2$ is <u>greater than/less than/equal to</u> the slope of $ITBC_1$.

b. As a result of her increase in income, Jennifer is now able to move to a higher indifference curve. Indeed, the new optimum occurs at the tangency of $ITBC_2$ with $IC_{U=162}$, indicating that Jennifer is able to increase her level of utility to _____. Locate this point on Graph 16-5 and label it Point E.

At Point E, $C_1 = 10.39$. Since $U = C_1C_2$ and $U =$ _____, $C_2 =$ $U/C_1 =$ _____. We can see that consumption during each period has increased/decreased. The changes in consumption between Points D and E are the result of the income effect, which measures the change in consumption resulting from the movement to a higher indifference curve, holding the slope of the intertemporal budget constraint (whose absolute value is equal to 1 plus the real interest rate) constant.

c. Finally, suppose that Jennifer's income in each period returns to its former level of 12 and that the real interest rate rises to 100 percent, or 1.0. Jennifer's intertemporal budget constraint becomes

$$C_2 = Y_2 + S + rS = Y_2 + (Y_1 - C_1) + r(Y_1 - C_1), \text{ or}$$
$$C_2 = \underline{\hspace{1cm}} + (\underline{\hspace{1cm}} - C_1) + 1.0(\underline{\hspace{1cm}} - C_1), \text{ or}$$

$$C_2 = \underline{\hspace{5cm}} - \underline{\hspace{4cm}} C_1.$$

Graph Jennifer's new intertemporal budget constraint on Graph 16-5 and label it $ITBC_3$. Once again, Jennifer is able to move to a higher indifference curve. Indeed, the new optimal levels of consumption occur at the tangency of $ITBC_3$ with $IC_{U=162}$, which is where the new intertemporal budget constraint just touches $IC_{U=162}$ and has the same slope. Thus, Jennifer is again able to increase her level of utility to _____. Plot this point on Graph 16-5 and label it Point F. At Point F, $C_1 = 9$. Since $U = C_1C_2$ and $U =$ _____, $C_2 = U/C_1 =$ _____.

d. The changes in consumption between Points D and F resulting from the increase
CH in the real interest rate can be decomposed into two different effects. The first reflects the change in consumption resulting from Jennifer's ability to move to a higher indifference curve while holding the real interest rate constant. This effect is called the income/substitution effect, and it is represented by a hypothetical movement from Point D to Point E (since Point E lies on the new indifference curve but would be the equilibrium only if the slope of the intertemporal budget constraint had remained unchanged, as in Part b). The change in consumption from Point E to Point F reflects the second effect, called the income/substitution effect. This represents the change in consumption arising from the change in the relative price of consumption in the two periods. As the interest rate increases from 50 percent to 100 percent, Jennifer must now give up less first-period consumption to obtain an extra unit of second-period consumption. Comparing Points E and F, Jennifer responds to this change in the relative price of consumption in the two periods by increasing/decreasing C_1 and increasing/decreasing C_2.

e. In Part d, the income effect increases/decreases C_1 and increases/decreases C_2, while the substitution effect increases/decreases C_1 and increases/decreases C_2. The combination of these two effects will always increase/decrease C_2. Depending on the specific circumstance, however, C_1 can either increase or decrease. In this example, C_1 obviously increases/decreases.

7. **The Life-Cycle Hypothesis** *In this exercise, we develop a simple life-cycle model of consumption and derive some of its implications.*

a. The life-cycle hypothesis is based on the assumption that people try to smooth their consumption over their (adult) lifetimes. Assume that a typical adult named Tanya expects to live for another T years. She intends to work for R years, earning an annual real income equal to Y, and then retire for $(T - R)$ years. If Tanya wishes to smooth her annual consumption C over her remaining lifetime, she will plan to spend her lifetime earnings $(R \times Y)$ over her remaining T years in equal amounts so that

$$C \times T = R \times Y, \tag{16-10}$$

or $C = Y \times ($\underline{\hspace{4cm}}$/$\underline{\hspace{4cm}}$)$. This equation implies that Tanya will consume a fraction of her income during her working years and save the remaining portion to fund her consumption during her retirement. (Although the real interest rate is implicitly assumed to equal zero here, a positive real interest rate could easily be incorporated into the model.)

b. Suppose that Tanya begins working at age 20, intends to retire at age 65 after working for 45 years, and expects to live until age 80. Thus, $T = 80 - 20 =$ \underline{\hspace{2cm}}, $R = 65 - 20 =$ \underline{\hspace{2cm}}, and $T - R =$ \underline{\hspace{2cm}}. If $Y = \$40,000$, then Tanya's annual consumption will be $C = \$$\underline{\hspace{2cm}}$ \times ($\underline{\hspace{2cm}}$/$\underline{\hspace{2cm}}$) =$ $\$$\underline{\hspace{2cm}}. During each of her working years, Tanya will consume $\$$\underline{\hspace{2cm}}, or \underline{\hspace{2cm}}/\underline{\hspace{2cm}} of her income, and will save $\$$\underline{\hspace{2cm}}, or \underline{\hspace{2cm}}/\underline{\hspace{2cm}} of her income. During her working years, therefore, Tanya's consumption function will be $C =$ \underline{\hspace{2cm}} Y. An extra dollar of annual income would raise consumption by \underline{\hspace{2cm}} cents.

c. Draw a rectangle on Graph 16-6 whose height is equal to $Y = \$$\underline{\hspace{2cm}} and whose width is equal to $R =$ \underline{\hspace{2cm}} years. The area of this rectangle represents Tanya's total lifetime earnings and is equal to $\$$\underline{\hspace{3cm}}. Now draw a second rectangle whose height is equal to C and whose width is equal to T. The area of this second rectangle, representing Tanya's total lifetime consumption, is equal to $\$$\underline{\hspace{3cm}}. Now shade in the area of a third rectangle, labeled saving, which represents Tanya's total saving during her working years and a fourth rectangle, labeled dissaving, which represents her total consumption during retirement. The size of the shaded rectangle representing Tanya's total saving is greater than/less than/equal to the size of the shaded rectangle representing her total consumption during retirement.

Graph 16-6

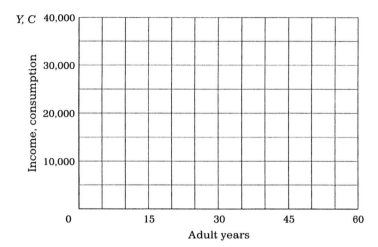

d. Now suppose that Tanya begins her adult life with an initial wealth equal to W. Consequently, the total amount that she will now have available to spend during her lifetime will equal $RY + W$. If Tanya still wishes to consume equal amounts in every year,

$$C \times T = (R \times Y) + W, \hspace{2cm} \text{(16-11)}$$

or $C = [(\underline{\hspace{1.5cm}}/\underline{\hspace{1.5cm}}) \times Y] + W/\underline{\hspace{1.5cm}}$. Substituting from Part c the values for $T = \underline{\hspace{1cm}}$ and $R = \underline{\hspace{1cm}}$, we obtain Tanya's new consumption function, $C = \underline{\hspace{1cm}}Y + \underline{\hspace{1cm}}W$. An extra dollar of wealth raises consumption by \underline{\hspace{1cm}} cents. Draw this consumption function on Graph 16-7 and label it C. The y intercept of this line is \underline{\hspace{1cm}}W, and the slope of the line equals \underline{\hspace{1cm}}.

Graph 16-7

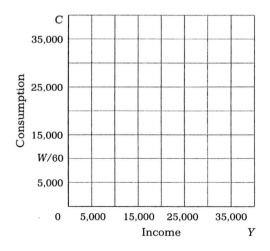

e. As Chapter 16 of the textbook states, the life-cycle model can explain the cross-sectional evidence concerning the average propensity to consume. Dividing the consumption function in Part d by Y yields $APC = C/Y =$ _____ + _____ × (W/Y). Suppose that $W = \$120,000$ and $Y = \$40,000$. Then $APC =$ _____ + _____ (_____ / _____) = _____. As Chapter 16 of the textbook explains, in the short run, wealth does not vary with income from person to person or from year to year. Consequently, if Y rises to $\$80,000$ and W remains equal to $\$120,000$, $APC =$ _____ + _____ (_____ / _____) = _____. Obviously, as income rises, APC rises/falls. Conversely, if Y falls to $\$20,000$ and W remains equal to $\$120,000$, $APC =$ _____.

f. The life-cycle model can also explain the time-series evidence concerning the relative constancy of the economy's APC in the long run. Over long periods of time, wealth and income grow together. If $W = 3Y$ in the long run, then, in this model, $APC =$ _____.

8. **The Permanent-Income Hypothesis** *In this exercise, we present the permanent-income model of consumption and discuss its implications.*

a. According to the permanent-income hypothesis, current income Y is the sum of permanent income Y^P plus transitory income Y^T, or $Y = Y^P + Y^T$. Permanent income is a measure of expected or average income. Transitory income is the random difference between current income Y and permanent income Y^P that occurs because of unexpected and temporary increases or decreases in income. On average, however, transitory income equals zero. Consumption is a function of permanent income. For example, assume the following:

$$C = aY^P = 0.75Y^P. \qquad (16\text{-}12)$$

Equation 16-12 suggests that people consume _____ percent of their permanent income; the remainder is saved, presumably for retirement.

b. Let us examine the consumption patterns of three people: a college professor having a typical year; an artist who is experiencing an especially good year, having just sold several paintings; and another artist who is having a dry spell, having sold only two paintings during the year. Assume that the average or permanent income of each of these three people equals $\$40,000$ and that $C = 0.75Y^P$. Now complete Table 16-4.

Table 16-4

(1)	(2) Y^P	(3) $C = 0.75Y^P$	(4) Y	(5) $APC = C/Y$	(6) Y^T
College professor	$80,000	_____	$ 80,000	_____	_____
Artist in a good year	$80,000	_____	$100,000	_____	_____
Artist in a bad year	$80,000	_____	$ 60,000	_____	_____

c. The data in Table 16-4 indicate that changes in transitory income will increase/decrease/not change consumption. Consequently, if a person's actual current income temporarily rises above her permanent income, then her consumption will increase/decrease/not change. This situation will increase/decrease/not change her *APC*. Conversely, if a person's actual current income temporarily falls below her permanent income, her consumption will increase/decrease/not change but her *APC* will increase/decrease/not change.

d. As stated previously, cross-sectional household data indicate that the average propensity to consume tends to increase/decrease/remain constant as income increases. If, at any one time, people who have high incomes are generally having temporarily good years and those who have low incomes are generally having temporarily bad years, data in Table 16-4 indicate that the *APC* will increase/decrease/remain constant as current income *Y* increases.

e. This theory can also be used to explain short-term variations in the average propensity to consume. If the economy slips into a recession and the majority of the population is having a bad year, the *APC* will increase/decrease/remain constant. If, on the other hand, the economy is in a temporary boom and the majority of the population is having a good year, the *APC* will increase/decrease/remain constant.

f. Alternatively, if the government enacts a temporary tax cut, everyone will experience a temporarily good year, but the *APC* will increase/decrease/remain constant and most of the tax cut will be consumed/saved. If, on the other hand, the government enacts a permanent tax cut, everyone will experience an increase in permanent/transitory, and most of the tax cut will be consumed/saved.

g. Over time, the good and bad years will cancel out. In the long run, as the economy grows, permanent income also grows. Thus, if the economywide permanent income Y^P equals actual income *Y* in the long run, the *APC* will increase/decrease/remain constant, just as the time-series evidence indicates.

Problems

Answer the following problems on a separate sheet of paper.

1. Consider the Keynesian consumption function $C = 100 + 0.8(Y - T)$.

   a. If $T = 0$, calculate the value of the marginal propensity to consume (*MPC*) and the formula for the average propensity to consume (*APC*).

   b. Choose two values of *Y* and compute the directional changes in the *MPC* and *APC* when *Y* increases.

2. Suppose someone offers you a piece of paper (a bond) that will pay you a (coupon) payment of $100 at the end of *each* of the next three years. You will also get an additional $1,000 at the end of the third year.

    a. Calculate the present value of this bond if the prevailing interest rate is 5 percent per year.

    b. Calculate the present value of this bond if the prevailing interest rate rises to 15 percent per year.

    c. Consequently, what do you conclude about the relationship between the present value of a bond and the prevailing interest rate?

3. a. Suppose that income in each of two periods is equal to 100 and the interest rate is 10 percent per year. Draw a graph of the intertemporal budget constraint and calculate its slope.

    b. On the same graph, draw a hypothetical indifference curve that is tangent to this intertemporal budget constraint at a point at which saving in the first period is positive, and label it IC_1. Label the initial equilibrium Point A.

    c. Suppose that the interest rate rises to 25 percent. Draw the new budget line on your graph. Draw a new indifference curve that is tangent to this budget line and label it IC_2. Label the new equilibrium Point B.

    d. On the same graph, illustrate both the income and substitution effects of this
    CH   increase in the interest rate.

    e. From your answer to Part d, under what circumstances might an increase in the
    CH   interest rate lead to an *increase* in C_1 and hence a *reduction* in saving?

4. Suppose that Bart has the following utility function: $U = C_1 C_2 = (C_1 C_2)^{1/2}$, where C_1
C and C_2 are Bart's levels of consumption in Periods 1 and 2, respectively. Suppose
    that his income is $120 in Period 1 and $100 in Period 2, and the real interest rate is
Q 25 percent.

    a. Calculate Bart's optimal levels of consumption in Periods 1 and 2 and his saving in Period 1. (You may wish to use a Lagrange multiplier to solve this problem, but it isn't necessary.)

    b. Suppose that the real interest rate increases to 50 percent. Calculate Bart's new optimal levels of consumption in Periods 1 and 2 and his saving in Period 1.

5. Consider the Keynesian consumption function, $C = a + b(Y - T)$, where a and b are
C constants.

    a. Let $T = 0$ and calculate the value of the marginal propensity to consume and the formula for the average propensity to consume.

    b. Differentiate your answers to Part a with respect to income Y to calculate the directional changes in the *MPC* and *APC* when Y increases.

6. What does the life-cycle model of consumption predict about the relative saving
Q rates between:

    a. a country with a rapidly increasing population and a country with a steady population, all other things being equal? Explain.

    b. a country where real GDP per capita is growing rapidly and a country with a stagnant economy, all other things being equal? Explain.

7. People who support an active role for macroeconomic policymakers occasionally argue that policy activism is necessary to buffer the economy from extreme fluctuations in private spending. What do the life-cycle and permanent-income models of consumption imply about this argument, especially as it relates to consumption, which is by far the largest component of private spending? Explain.

8. Suppose that Jan expects to live for 25 more years and work for 10 of those years.

   a. Derive Jan's consumption function in terms of her annual income Y and initial wealth W according to the life-cycle model.

   b. Suppose that Jan expects her income to be $50,000 per year until she retires. In addition, she has accumulated $250,000 in wealth. Calculate her annual level of consumption.

9. Many economists advocate a reduction in tax rates on interest and dividends to stimulate saving and investment. What does the Fisher model of consumption imply about the effects of such a tax reduction on saving?

10. In 1981, Congress passed President Reagan's proposed tax cuts. This legislation called for a permanent reduction in tax *rates* by 5 percent in 1981, another 10 percent in 1982, and an additional 10 percent in 1983. If people had rational expectations, fully expected all of the tax cuts to occur (which they did), and incorporated these expectations into their estimates of their permanent incomes, in what years would the permanent-income hypothesis predict that the greatest *change* in consumption would occur? Explain.

11. In 2001 Congress passed President Bush's proposed tax cuts. Over the following decade taxes were scheduled to be cut by $1.6–$2.0 trillion. Only a small portion of the total, however, took effect in 2001 and 2002. Critics complained that the tax cut was not well-suited to combat the recession that began in 2001 because of this "backloading."

   a. Explain how these critics used Keynesian consumption function to support their criticism.

   b. Now explain how defenders of the cuts might use the permanent income or life cycle hypothesis to argue that the timing of the tax cuts was not critical in changing consumption in 2001–2002 as long as they were implemented within the decade.

   c. Even if one accepted the theoretical arguments presented in Part b, how might considerations of borrowing constraints weaken their argument?

   d. Finally, how would proponents of the Ricardian equivalence proposition respond to the two economists in Parts a and b?

12. As the recession deepened in late 2001, President Bush proposed that Congress speed up (or accelerate) the implementation of his income tax cuts so that they all became effective much earlier. Given that the phased-in tax cuts had already been passed by Congress in 2001, explain how the acceleration would affect consumption in the year 2002 according to:

   a. the Keynesian consumption function?

   b. the permanent income hypothesis?

Data Questions

Locate the necessary economic data and apply them to answer the following data questions. All of the relevant data may be found in the Economic Report of the President.

1.   **a.**   Use the real (deflated) values of the following variables to complete Table 16-5.

Table 16-5

(1) Year	(2) Consumption Expenditures ($ in billions)	(3) Disposable Income ($ in billions)	(4) Average Propensity to Consume (APC)*
1960	_____	_____	_____
1980	_____	_____	_____
2000	_____	_____	_____

*Round off to three decimal places.

b.   Calculate the total percentage changes in real disposable income and the *APC* between 1960 and 2000.

c.   What do you conclude about the stability of the *APC* over long periods of time?

2. **a.** Use the nominal values of the following variables to complete Table 16-6.

Table 16-6

(1) Year	(2) Consumption Expenditures ($ in billions)	(3) Disposable Income ($ in billions)	(4) Average Propensity to Consume (APC)*
1967	_____	_____	_____
1968	_____	_____	_____
1970	_____	_____	_____

*Round off to three decimal places.

b. Use the permanent-income hypothesis and the facts about fiscal policy presented in Chapter 16 of the textbook to explain the temporary rise in the APC in 1968.

Questions to Think About

1. **a.** Which aspects of your family's consumption behavior are described by each of the four models of consumption presented in Chapter 16 of the textbook? Which aspects are not described by these theories?

   b. Which of the four models is the most appropriate for describing your family's consumption behavior? Explain.

2. Does the life-cycle model of consumption accurately explain the consumption behavior of your grandparents? Why or why not?

3. If you won $10,000,000 in the lottery, how and when would you spend it? Which of the four models of consumption presented in Chapter 16 of the textbook would be consistent with your behavior?

Investment

Fill-in Questions

Use the key terms below to fill in the blanks in the following statements. Each term may be used more than once.

accelerator model

business fixed investment

corporate income tax

depreciation

financing constraints

inventories as a factor of production

inventory investment

investment tax credit

neoclassical model of investment

net investment

production smoothing

real cost of capital

residential investment

stock market

stock-out avoidance

Tobin's *q*

work in process

1. Economists distinguish among three types of investment spending: _____ includes the new housing that people buy to live in and that landlords buy to rent out; _____ includes the equipment and structures that businesses buy to use in production; and _____ includes materials, supplies, and finished goods that businesses put aside in storage.

2. The _____ examines the benefit and cost to firms of owning capital goods by showing how investment is related to the marginal product of capital, the interest rate, and the tax rules affecting firms.

3. As capital ages, it undergoes wear and tear, which decreases its value. This process is called _____.

4. The cost of buying and renting out a unit of capital, measured in units of the economy's output, is called the _____.

5. The change in the capital stock is called _____. Recall from Chapter 2 of the textbook that it is equal to gross investment minus _____.

6. According to the _____, firms find it profitable to add to their capital stock if the marginal product of capital exceeds the _____.

7. The _____ is a tax on corporate profits.

8. Many economists believe that the _____ may discourage investment because it does not define profit as the rental price of capital minus the cost of capital.

9. The _____ reduces a firm's taxes by a certain amount for each dollar that the firm spends on capital goods. It works as a subsidy on investment.

10. According to one theory of investment, firms base their investment decisions on the ratio of the market value of installed capital divided by the replacement cost of installed capital. This ratio is known as _____.

11. According to the q-theory of investment, net investment will be positive whenever managers can raise their firm's market value by buying more capital. More precisely, if the _____ value of capital exceeds its replacement cost, _____ will exceed 1.0, and net investment will be positive.

12. When firms are limited in the amount that they can raise in financial markets, they are said to face _____.

13. Firms have several motives for holding inventories. One motive, called _____, exists when it is cheaper for a firm to produce goods at a steady rate when that firm experiences temporary booms and busts in sales. Firms can also view _____ when inventories increase output by improving efficiency. A third motive, called _____, exists when firms hold inventories to avoid running out of goods when sales are unexpectedly high. A final motive exists because many goods take time to produce, so they are counted as part of a firm's inventory when they are only partly completed. These inventories are called _____.

14. According to the _____, investment depends on the firm's level of output. When output is increasing, investment will be greater than when output is decreasing.

Multiple-Choice Questions

1. According to the neoclassical model of investment:
   a. investment falls as the real interest rate rises.
   b. investment falls as the real interest rate falls.
   c. an increase in the marginal product of capital causes the investment function to shift to the left.
   d. both a and c are true.

2. In equilibrium, the real rental price of capital is equal to:
   a. 1.0.
   b. the marginal product of capital.
   c. the price of output.
   d. all of the above.

3. In a Cobb-Douglas production function, the equilibrium rental price of capital increases as:
   a. the stock of capital used by the firm falls.
   b. the amount of labor employed by the firm rises.
   c. technology improves.
   d. all of the above.

4. The cost of capital is determined by all of the following EXCEPT the:
   a. rate of depreciation.
   b. corporate profit rate.
   c. interest rate.
   d. price of capital and its rate of change.

5. Assume that the price of capital goods rises at the same rate as the price of other goods. If the price of capital is $1,500 per unit, the real interest rate is 4 percent, and the depreciation rate is 6 percent, then the cost of capital equals:
   a. $30.   b. $300.   c. $150.   d. $100.

6. If the price of capital goods rises at the same rate as the price of other goods, the real cost of capital may be written as:
   a. $(P_K/P)(r + \delta)$.   b. $(P_K/P)(r - \delta)$.   c. $(P/P_K)(i + \delta)$.   d. $(P/P_K)(r - \delta)$.

7. Firms find it profitable to add to their capital stock if the:
   a. real cost of capital exceeds the marginal product of capital.
   b. marginal product of capital exceeds the real cost of capital.
   c. marginal product of capital exceeds the real interest rate.
   d. rental price of capital exceeds the marginal product of capital.

8. Expansionary monetary policy spurs investment in the short run via:
   a. a decrease in inflation.
   b. a decrease in the cost of capital.
   c. an increase in the rental price of capital.
   d. all of the above.

9. An event that decreases the marginal product of capital will:
   a. shift the investment function to the left.
   b. shift the investment function to the right.
   c. raise the real cost of capital.
   d. raise the rate of depreciation.

10. The corporate income tax discourages investment because it:
   a. defines profit as the rental price of capital minus the cost of capital.
   b. taxes profits at an exorbitant rate of 60 percent.
   c. does not appropriately take inflation into account in calculating depreciation and profit.
   d. all of the above.

11. All of the following statements about the investment tax credit are true EXCEPT:

    a. it stimulates investment.

    b. most of the benefits go to unprofitable corporations.

    c. it reduces the after-tax cost of capital.

    d. it operates as an indirect subsidy for investment.

12. All of the following statements about the q-theory of investment are true EXCEPT:

    a. Tobin's q is equal to the market value of installed capital divided by the replacement cost of installed capital.

    b. if Tobin's q is greater than 1.0, firms will allow their capital to wear out without replacing it.

    c. it assumes that stock prices play an influential role in investment decisions.

    d. it implies that investment depends on the current and expected future profits from installed capital.

13. Residential investment depends on:

    a. the relative price of housing P_H/P.

    b. the real interest rate.

    c. the size of the adult population.

    d. all of the above.

14. Some firms hold inventories in order to avoid changing production frequently in response to fluctuations in sales. This motive is called:

    a. holding inventories as a factor of production.

    b. production smoothing.

    c. stock-out avoidance.

    d. holding inventories as work in process.

15. According to the accelerator model of investment, investment:

    a. is high when the real interest rate is low.

    b. remains fairly constant at all times.

    c. is high when output grows rapidly.

    d. is high when corporate profits are high.

Exercises

1. **The Demand for Capital** *In this exercise, we use a numerical example to illustrate how the demand for capital is related to the real rental price of capital. Note: Students may wish to review Exercises 1–3 in Chapter 3 of this Study Guide.*

    a. The owners of Acme Car Wash must decide how many units of capital to rent. They have the data shown in Columns 1 and 2 of Table 17-1 to help them in making a decision. (All data are for a given number of workers.)

Table 17-1

(1) Units of Capital	(2) Number of Cars Washed per Hour	(3) Marginal Product of Capital
0	0	
		_____
1	20	
		_____
2	35	
		_____
3	45	
		_____
4	50	

Recall that the marginal product of capital *MPK* is the extra output produced when one unit of capital is added. Thus, the *MPK* for the first unit of capital is equal to 20 – 0 = _____. Use this information to complete Column 3 in Table 17-1. Then use the data from Columns 1 and 3 to plot and draw the *MPK* curve on Graph 17-1, and label it *MPK*.

Graph 17-1

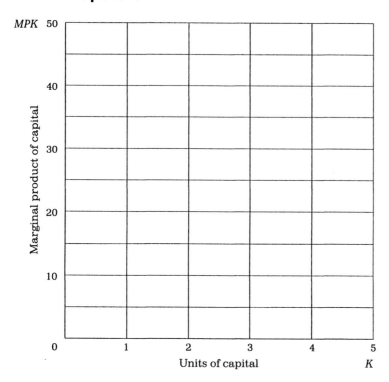

b. To maximize profits, firms rent capital until *MPK* is equal to the real rental price of capital, where the latter is defined as the rental rate of capital *R* divided by the price of the firm's output *P*, or *R/P*. Thus, in equilibrium, *R/P* = *MPK*. Using the data from Table 17-1, if *R/P* = 15, Acme will want to rent _____ units of capital because this is the point at which *R/P* = *MPK*. Remember that this will occur if *R* = \$15 and *P* = \$1 or if *R* = \$30 and *P* = \$2. (*Note:* Review the exercises in Chapter 3 if this is not clear.) If *R/P* = 5, Acme will want to rent _____ units of capital because this is now the point at which *R/P* = *MPK*. Thus, the demand curve for capital is the same as the *MPK* curve. Consequently, add *R/P* as an additional label for the vertical axis on Graph 17-1, and add Capital demand as an additional label for the *MPK* curve. Obviously, as the real rental price of capital falls, firms will want to rent more/fewer units of capital.

c. You can construct an aggregate *MPK* and an aggregate capital demand curve for the entire economy in a similar way. One such curve is depicted on Graph 17-2. On this graph, *P* represents the aggregate price level, which can also be viewed as the price of output for a representative firm.

Graph 17-2

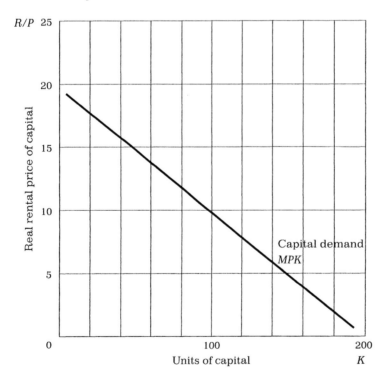

In the short run, the total amount of capital in the economy is fixed at $\overline{K}$. Suppose that $\overline{K}$ = 100. Draw a vertical capital supply curve at $\overline{K}$ = 100 on Graph 17-2, and label it Capital supply. In this case, the equilibrium real rental price of capital *R/P* will equal _____ in the short run because at this price the supply of capital equals the demand for capital.

d. Several factors can affect the equilibrium real rental price of capital R/P. Chapter 17 of the textbook illustrates some of these factors using the Cobb-Douglas production function, but one can also present them intuitively. If the capital stock were to increase suddenly, the capital supply curve would shift to the left/right and the equilibrium real rental price of capital would rise/fall. If capital and labor both became more productive, the marginal product of each unit of capital would be higher/lower, thereby shifting the capital demand curve to the left/right and increasing/decreasing the equilibrium real rental price of capital. If more workers were employed, each unit of capital would probably become more productive, thereby increasing the MPK at each level of capital, shifting the capital demand curve to the left/right, and increasing/decreasing the equilibrium real rental price of capital.

2. The Cost of Capital *In this exercise, we derive the cost of capital.*

a. Following the simplification introduced in Chapter 17 of the textbook, assume that the firms in Exercise 1 rent capital from other firms that own it. The nominal rent received by these other firms per unit of capital is R; the real rent is R/P, where P is the aggregate price level. As Chapter 17 of the textbook illustrates, the nominal cost of one unit of capital per period to the firm that owns it is

$$\text{(Nominal) Cost of Capital} = iP_K - \Delta P_K + \delta P_K, \qquad \text{(17-1)}$$

where i equals the nominal interest rate, P_K equals the purchase price of a unit of capital, ΔP_K equals the change in the price of (new) capital, and δ equals the rate of physical or technological depreciation. The first term on the right-hand side of Equation 17-1, iP_K, represents the foregone interest revenue the firm could have earned had it put its money in the bank or purchased bonds instead of purchasing capital. The second term, ΔP_K, represents the amount by which capital prices increase, and the third term, δP_K, reflects the amount by which the capital is reduced by depreciation. The minus sign before ΔP_K indicates that the cost of capital to firms that own it falls when capital prices increase, because the capital can then be sold to other firms that own capital for a higher price. Factoring P_K from the right-hand side of Equation 17-1 by P_K yields

$$\text{(Nominal) Cost of Capital} = P_K[i - \Delta P_K/P_K + \delta], \qquad \text{(17-2)}$$

where $\Delta P_K/P_K$ equals the rate at which capital prices are changing.

Now complete Table 17-2.

Table 17-2

(1) Price of Capital P_K	(2) Nominal Interest Rate i	(3) Rate of Growth of Capital Prices	(4) Rate of Depreciation δ	(5) Cost of Capital
$100	0.05	0.05	0.10	_____
$100	0.10	0.05	0.10	_____
$100	0.10	0.08	0.10	_____
$100	0.10	0.08	0.20	_____
$200	0.10	0.08	0.20	_____
$100	_____	0.08	0.20	$15

b. Equation 17-2 and the data in Table 17-2 indicate that an increase in the nominal interest rate will increase/decrease the cost of capital, and an increase in the rate of growth of capital prices will increase/decrease the cost of capital. Finally, an increase in the rate of depreciation will increase/decrease the cost of capital because the capital now wears out more quickly/slowly, thereby lasting for a longer/shorter period of time.

c. If capital prices are rising at the same rate as the aggregate price level, then $\Delta P_K/P_K = \pi$, and Equation 17-2 becomes

$$\text{(Nominal) Cost of Capital} = P_K[i - \pi + \delta] = P_K[r + \delta], \qquad \textbf{(17-3)}$$

where r is the real interest rate. Given this assumption, the real interest rate in the first row of Table 17-2 is _____ percent, and the real interest rate in the second row of Table 17-2 is _____ percent.

d. Finally, recall that the nominal rental cost of capital R for the firms that rent capital must be divided by the price level to obtain the real rental cost of capital R/P. Similarly, the real cost of capital to the firms that own the capital is $(P_K/P)(r + \delta)$. An increase in the real interest rate will increase/decrease the real cost of capital, and an increase in the rate of depreciation will increase/decrease the real cost of capital.

3. **The Determinants of Investment** *In this exercise, we combine the results from Exercises 1 and 2 to illustrate the determinants of investment.*

a. In Exercise 1, it was shown that firms rent additional units of capital until the marginal product of capital *MPK* is greater than/less than/equal to the real rental cost of capital *R/P*. In Exercise 2, it was also shown that if capital prices rise at the same rate as the aggregate price level, the real cost of capital to the firms that own it is $(P_K/P)[$_____ + _____$]$. Consequently, the real profit rate from owning one unit of capital and renting it is

$$\text{Profit Rate} = MPK - (P_K/P) \times (\underline{\qquad} + \underline{\qquad}).$$ **(17-4)**

If the profit rate is positive, firms that own capital will add to/subtract from their capital stock, resulting in positive/negative net investment. If the profit rate is negative, firms that own capital will add to/subtract from their capital stock, leading to positive/negative net investment. Total, or gross, business fixed investment is equal to net investment plus replacement investment, where the latter is equal to δK. Consequently, total investment may be positive even if net investment is negative.

b. In competitive long-run equilibrium, *MPK* is greater than/less than/equal to the real cost of capital $(P_K/P)(r + \delta)$, and the profit rate is positive/zero/negative. Starting from equilibrium, a reduction in the real interest rate *r* (resulting from either a(n) increase/decrease in the nominal interest rate or a(n) increase/decrease in the rate of inflation) will increase/decrease the real cost of capital and hence increase/decrease the profit rate from owning capital. As a result, firms that own capital will add to/subtract from their capital stock, resulting in a(n) increase/decrease in investment. Thus, as *r* falls, investment rises/falls. This result is similar to/different from that obtained in earlier textbook chapters. As capital is added and lent out, firms move along the aggregate *MPK* curve, and the marginal product of capital will rise/fall until it equals the new real cost of capital.

c. Starting from equilibrium again, a technological innovation that increases the marginal product of capital will increase/decrease/have no immediate effect on the real cost of capital, but it will increase/decrease the profit rate from owning capital. As a result, firms that own capital will add to/subtract from their capital stock, resulting in a(n) increase/decrease in investment. As capital is added/subtracted and lent out, firms move along the aggregate *MPK* curve, and the marginal product of capital will rise/fall until it equals the real cost of capital.

d. As Chapter 17 of the textbook indicates, many provisions of the tax code encourage or discourage the accumulation of capital by firms. Most economists believe that a reduction in the corporate income tax on accounting profits will increase/decrease investment. The investment tax credit reduces a firm's taxes by a certain amount for each dollar the firm spends on investment goods. An increase in the investment tax credit would increase/decrease the real after-tax cost of capital and thereby increase/decrease investment.

4. Residential Investment *In this exercise, we discuss the supply and demand for housing and residential investment.*

a. Graph 17-3 depicts an initial equilibrium in the housing market at Point A. Housing demand, labeled D_1, is negatively related to the relative price of housing P_H/P. Housing supply, labeled S_1, is fixed in the short run. If the residential construction industry is perfectly competitive, economic profits will be positive/negative/zero.

Graph 17-3

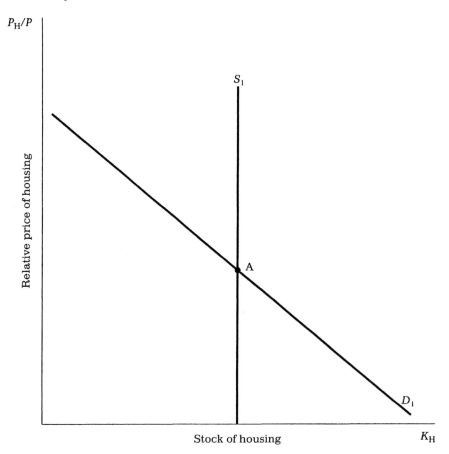

b. An economic boom that increases households' income will shift the housing demand curve to the left/right. Draw the new demand curve on Graph 17-3, label it D_2, and label the new short-run equilibrium Point B. Obviously, the relative price of housing will increase/decrease. This trend will induce the residential construction industry to increase/decrease the production of new houses, which will increase/decrease residential investment. This change in residential investment will eventually shift the housing supply curve on Graph 17-3 to the left/right. As it shifts, the relative price of housing will rise even more/fall from Point B.

c. Starting again at Point A, an increase in mortgage interest rates will shift the housing demand curve to the left/right. Draw the new demand curve on Graph 17-3, label it D_3, and label the new short-run equilibrium Point C. Obviously, the relative price of housing will increase/decrease, and residential investment will increase/decrease.

5. **The Accelerator Model** *In this exercise, we present a numerical example of the accelerator model to illustrate how changes in output can affect investment.*

a. The accelerator model has been used to analyze several types of investment, especially inventory investment. In this model, investment I is a function of the change in output ΔY from one period to another:

$$I = \beta(\Delta Y) = \beta(Y - Y_{-1}). \tag{17-5}$$

When output Y rises, firms want to hold more inventories, so they invest in them. When Y falls, firms want to hold fewer inventories, so they run them down, and inventory investment is negative. If $\beta = 0.2$, complete Table 17-3.

Table 17-3

(1) Period	(2) Output Y	(3) Change in Y	(4) % Change in Y	(5) $I = 0.2(\Delta Y)$ $= 0.2(Y - Y_{-1})$	(6) % Change in I
0	1,000				
		100	_____		
1	1,100			20	
		_____	_____		_____
2	1,200			_____	
		_____	_____		_____
3	1,300			_____	
		_____	_____		_____
4	1,350			_____	
		_____	_____		_____
5	1,350			_____	

b. Compare the percentage changes in output Y in each period from Period 2 through Period 5 with the comparable percentage changes in investment I. One of the major implications of the accelerator model is that relatively small changes in the growth rate of output Y lead to even smaller/much larger changes in the growth of investment I. Consequently, investment I is likely to be very stable/unstable.

Problems

Answer the following problems on a separate sheet of paper.

1. In Chapters 10 and 11 of the textbook, it was assumed that investment I depends on the real interest rate r but is independent of changes in real output Y. Now suppose that I also increases as Y rises and decreases as Y falls.

    a. Draw an investment curve that illustrates this relationship between I and Y.

    b. Explain why I might be an increasing function of Y.

    c. If I increases as Y rises and decreases as Y falls, what would happen to the:

        i.   slope of the planned expenditure curve? Explain.
        ii. government-purchases multiplier? Explain using the round-by-round story.
        iii. slopes of the *IS* and *LM* curves?
        iv. slopes of the *AD* and *SRAS* curves?

2. a. Consider a harvester that costs $10,000. If harvester prices are rising at 3 percent per year, the interest rate is 6 percent, and harvesters depreciate by 20 percent per year, calculate the cost of capital on this investment.

    b. Now consider a computer that costs $10,000. Once again, assume that the interest rate is 6 percent and computers depreciate by 20 percent per year. Computer prices, however, *fall* by 15 percent per year. Calculate the cost of capital on this investment.

3. Suppose that there were large increases in the prices of certain basic commodities, such as oil and food. Consequently, the prices of capital goods increase by less than the overall rate of inflation. Would the use of the real interest rate in the cost-of-capital equation over- or underestimate the true cost of capital? Explain.

4. Consider the following Cobb-Douglas production function:
    C $Y = 12(K^{1/3}L^{2/3})$. Assume that labor $L = 64$.

    a. Derive the equation for the marginal product of capital *MPK*.

    b. Find the specific values for *MPK* when capital $K = 1, 8, 27$, and 64. Plot these values of *MPK* on a graph and draw the resulting capital demand curve.

    c. Now suppose that L rises to 125, and repeat Parts a and b.

5. Suppose that there is a reduction in personal income taxes. Use the *IS-LM* model and the relevant sections in Chapter 17 of the textbook to illustrate what happens to investment according to the:

    a. neoclassical (cost-of-capital) model of investment.

    b. accelerator model of investment.

6. During the 1980s, the enormous baby-boom generation provided much of the new demand for residential investment. In the 1990s, the baby-bust generation, which is a much smaller cohort than the baby boomers, provided much of the new demand for housing. What were the effects of this demographic change on the demand for housing, the relative price of housing, and investment in housing?

7. Mortgage interest payments are tax deductible in the United States. Many economists have argued for the elimination of this provision. What would the effects of an elimination on the tax deductibility on mortgage interest payments be on the demand for housing, the relative price of housing, investment in housing, and the profits of residential construction firms in the short run?

8. a. Define what is meant by an investment tax credit of 8 percent.

    b. Assume that the United States is a closed economy and Congress enacts an investment tax credit of 8 percent. If the aggregate price level is held constant, what happens to the *IS* and/or *LM* curves in the short run? Briefly explain.

    c. Now assume that the United States is a large open economy. If the price level is still held constant and Congress enacts an 8 percent investment tax credit for domestic firms only, explain what happens to each of the following in the short run:

        i. the *IS* and/or *LM* curves.
        ii. U.S. net foreign investment.
        iii. the U.S. trade surplus and the U.S. real foreign exchange rate.

    d. In these models, does the investment tax credit have a greater short-run effect on output in a closed economy or in a large open economy? Where does it have the greater effect on investment? Explain your answers intuitively.

Data Questions

Locate the necessary economic data and apply them to answer the following data questions. All of the relevant data may be found in the Economic Report of the President.

1. a. Complete Table 17-4 (in billions of 1996 dollars), which presents data about various forms of real private gross investment. (To locate the data in Column 5 you may have to look in tables on the components of GDP.)

Table 17-4

(1) Year	(2) Real Nonresidential Investment in Structures	(3) Real Nonresidential Investment in Equipment and Software	(4) Real Residential Investment	(5) Real Change in Business Inventories
1990	————	————	————	————
1995	————	————	————	————
2000	————	————	————	————

   b. Calculate the percentage change in each category of investment between its highest and lowest values. What do you conclude about the relative volatility of the different components of investment?

Questions to Think About

1. Why do you think banks use the nominal interest rate in determining the creditworthiness of their potential customers?

2. Many economists support the introduction of investment tax credits during recessions to spur investment. Critics argue, however, that investment may merely get crowded into recessions in anticipation of the subsidies—that is, critics suggest that firms may wait until recessions to invest in order to receive the investment subsidy. How might one control for this potential effect in an academic study?

CHAPTER *18* EIGHTEEN

Money Supply and Money Demand

Fill-in Questions

Use the key terms below to fill in the blanks in the following statements. Each term may be used more than once.

100-percent-reserve banking	high-powered money
balance sheet	monetary base
Baumol-Tobin model	money multiplier
currency-deposit ratio	near money
discount rate	open-market operation
dominated asset	portfolio theories
excess reserves	reserve-deposit ratio
federal funds rate	reserve requirements
financial intermediation	reserves
fractional-reserve banking	transactions theories

1. A bank's _____ is a statement of its assets and liabilities.

2. The deposits that banks receive but do not lend out are called _____. Under a(n) _____ system, banks hold all deposits as reserves and are, therefore, unable to create money by making loans.

3. Under a(n) _____ system, banks keep a fraction of their deposits in reserve.

4. The _____ represent(s) the fraction of deposits banks keep in reserve. The _____ reflects the preferences of the public about how to apportion their money holding between currency and deposits.

5. Institutions that act as go-betweens for those individuals who wish to save some of their income for future consumption and those individuals who wish to borrow engage in _____.

6. The _____ is the sum of currency and bank reserves. It can be easily controlled by the Fed, and it is sometimes called _____.

7. The money supply is equal to the monetary base multiplied by the _____, where the latter is equal to (one plus the _____) divided by (the _____ plus the _____).

8. The Fed uses three tools to control the money supply. The tool most often used is a(n) _____, by which the Fed purchases and sells government bonds. The Fed may also alter the _____, which regulate(s) the minimum reserve-deposit ratio. Finally, the Fed may change the _____, which is the interest rate it charges banks that wish to borrow reserves from the Fed.

9. When the reserve-deposit ratio exceeds the reserve requirements, banks are holding _____.

10. Money demand theories that emphasize the role of money as a store of value are called _____. Some economists question the usefulness of these theories for studying money demand because money is a(n) _____, that is, there are other financial assets that are equally safe and offer a higher return.

11. _____ of money demand emphasize the role of money as a medium of exchange. The _____ of cash management is perhaps the most prominent model of this type.

12. In the _____, people compare the opportunity costs of holding currency with the benefits resulting from making fewer trips to the bank.

13. Nonmonetary assets that have acquired some of the liquidity of money are called _____.

14. Since 1993 the Fed's principal target in setting monetary policy has been the _____.

Multiple-Choice Questions

1. The money supply as defined by $M1$ is roughly equal to currency held by the:
   a. public.
   b. public plus demand deposits.
   c. public plus bank reserves.
   d. public plus bank loans.

2. In a 100-percent-reserve banking system, if a bank receives $500 in new deposits:
   a. the bank's assets will increase by $500.
   b. the bank's liabilities will increase by $500.
   c. the bank's loans will remain equal to zero.
   d. all of the above.

3. The monetary base is equal to:

   a. currency held by the public plus bank reserves.

   b. currency held by the public plus bank deposits.

   c. *M*1.

   d. total bank deposits.

4. In a 100-percent-reserve banking system, the money multiplier equals:

   a. 0.   **c.** 10.

   b. 1.   **d.** 100.

5. In a fractional-reserve banking system, if the reserve-deposit ratio is 30 percent and the currency-deposit ratio is 40 percent, then the money multiplier equals:

   a. 1.   **c.** 1.5.

   b. 0.5.   **d.** 2.

6. If the monetary base is $60 billion and the money multiplier is 3, then the money supply equals:

   a. $20 billion.   **c.** $63 billion.

   b. $60 billion.   **d.** $180 billion.

7. If the monetary base doubles and both the currency-deposit and reserve-deposit ratios remain constant, the money supply will:

   a. fall by half.

   b. remain constant.

   c. double.

   d. increase by a factor of $2 \times [(1 + cr)/(cr + rr)]$.

8. An increase in the currency-deposit ratio leads to a(n):

   a. increase in the money supply.

   b. decrease in the money supply.

   c. increase in the money multiplier.

   d. increase in the reserve-deposit ratio.

9. An open-market operation occurs when:

   a. there is an emergency appendectomy at the farmers' market.

   b. the Fed buys government bonds from the public.

   c. the Fed sells government bonds to the public.

   d. both b and c.

10. A reduction in reserve requirements will not significantly affect the money supply if:

   a. banks do not change their reserve-deposit ratios.

   b. the currency-deposit ratio does not change.

   c. the amount of excess reserves held by banks does not change.

   d. the monetary base does not change.

11. The discount rate is the:

   a. difference between the price of a good sold at Walmart and the price of the same good at Bloomingdale's.

   b. interest rate charged by banks on loans to their best customers.

   c. interest rate charged by the Fed to banks that borrow reserves from the Fed.

   d. difference between the interest rate on Treasury bonds and the prime rate of interest.

12. If the Fed wishes to increase the money supply, it may:

   a. perform an open-market purchase.

   b. decrease the discount rate.

   c. decrease the reserve requirements.

   d. all of the above.

13. A decrease in the discount rate will increase the money supply by:

   a. increasing the money multiplier.

   b. increasing the amount of reserves banks borrow from the Fed.

   c. decreasing the reserve-deposit ratio.

   d. increasing the currency-deposit ratio.

14. A decrease in the reserve-deposit ratio will increase the money supply by:

   a. increasing the monetary base.

   b. increasing the money multiplier.

   c. decreasing the currency-deposit ratio.

   d. decreasing the discount rate.

15. Between 1929 and 1933, during the Great Depression, the money supply fell for all of the following reasons EXCEPT the:

   a. reserve-deposit ratio increased.

   b. currency-deposit ratio increased.

   c. monetary base decreased.

   d. money multiplier decreased.

16. According to portfolio theories of money demand, all of the following affect money demand EXCEPT the:

   a. expected real return on bonds.

   b. usefulness of money in making transactions.

   c. expected rate of inflation.

   d. expected real return on stocks.

17. According to transactions theories of money demand, the demand for money is primarily a result of the:

   a. risk involved in buying stocks and bonds.

   b. unpredictability of the inflation rate.

   c. desire of individuals to engage in illegal activities such as the drug trade.

   d. convenience of money in making purchases.

18. The Baumol-Tobin model of money demand considers all of the following factors EXCEPT:

    a. the return on stocks.

    c. the interest rate.

    b. expenditures.

    d. the cost of going to and from the bank.

19. According to the Baumol-Tobin model, average money holding will rise if:

    a. the fixed cost of going to and from the bank falls.

    b. the inflation rate rises.

    c. the interest rate falls.

    d. expenditures fall.

20. Each of the following will result in a decrease in the fixed cost of going to the bank (denoted by F in the Baumol-Tobin model of money demand) EXCEPT:

    a. a decrease in banking fees.

    b. a decrease in real wages.

    c. the spread of safety deposit boxes.

    d. a reduction in downtown traffic.

21. Empirical studies indicate that the actual elasticities of money demand with respect to income and the interest rate are:

    a. equal to those predicted by the Baumol-Tobin model.

    b. larger than they would be if the Baumol-Tobin model were completely correct.

    c. different from what they would be if the Baumol-Tobin model were completely correct. The estimated interest elasticity is larger (in absolute value) and the estimated income elasticity is smaller.

    d. different from what they would be if the Baumol-Tobin model were completely correct. The estimated interest elasticity is smaller (in absolute value) and the estimated income elasticity is larger.

Exercises

1. **Fractional-Reserve Banking** *In this exercise, we illustrate how money is created by an open-market purchase in a fractional-reserve banking system.*

    a. Imagine an economy with three banks, each of which has the following initial balance sheet:

Initial Balance Sheet of
First, Second, and Third National Banks

Assets		Liabilities	
Reserves	$250 million	Deposits	$1,000 million
Loans	$750 million		

If there is no currency held outside the three banks, the total initial money supply will equal total deposits, or 3 × $_____ million = $_____ million. The reserve-deposit ratio in this economy is _____ percent. Note that this percentage may or may not equal the discount rate/reserve requirements, which mandate the minimum legal reserve-deposit ratio.

b. Suppose that the Fed makes an open-market purchase of $10 million by buying $10 million in government bonds from Tara, a typical citizen. It pays Tara with a $10 million check, which Tara takes to her bank, the First National Bank. When the bank presents the check to the Fed, the Fed credits the First National Bank with an additional $10 million in reserves, and Tara's deposits at the First National Bank officially increase by the amount of the check, or $_____ million. At that point, the bank's balance sheet will be:

First National Bank

Assets			Liabilities		
Reserves	$_____ million		Deposits	$_____ million	
Loans	$_____ million				

The balance sheets of the two remaining banks have not yet changed.

c. If the First National Bank wishes to maintain its initial reserve-deposit ratio of _____ percent, it must keep _____ percent of the additional $_____ million in reserves, and it can lend out the remaining $_____ million. Suppose it lends all this money to Fred, who is not a depositor at the bank. When it makes the loan, its reserves fall and its loans rise by the same amount, and its deposits do not change. Thus, the First National Bank's balance sheet becomes:

First National Bank

Assets			Liabilities		
Reserves	$_____ million		Deposits	$_____ million	
Loans	$_____ million				

d. Now suppose that Fred takes his $_____ million loan and either deposits it in the Second National Bank or buys a minor league baseball team, and the seller of the team deposits the proceeds in the Second National Bank. In either case, both the reserves and deposits of the Second National Bank will rise by $_____ million above their initial levels in Part a, and its balance sheet will be:

Second National Bank

Assets			Liabilities		
Reserves	$_____ million		Deposits	$_____ million	
Loans	$_____ million				

e. If the Second National Bank wishes to maintain its initial reserve-deposit ratio of _____ percent, it must keep _____ percent of the additional $_____ million in deposits (and reserves) obtained from Fred, and it can lend out the remaining $_____ million. Suppose it lends this amount to Eileen, who is not a depositor at the bank. Consequently, its reserves fall and its loans rise by the same amount, and the Second National Bank's balance sheet becomes:

Second National Bank

Assets		Liabilities	
Reserves	$_____ million	Deposits	$_____ million
Loans	$_____ million		

f. Eileen takes her $_____ million loan and either deposits it in the Third National Bank or donates it to her college, and the college deposits it in the Third National Bank. In either case, both the reserves and deposits of the Third National Bank will rise by $_____ million above their initial levels in Part a, and its balance sheet will be:

Third National Bank

Assets		Liabilities	
Reserves	$_____ million	Deposits	$_____ million
Loans	$_____ million		

g. The money supply has now grown by more than the $10 million open-market purchase that the Fed made in Part b. From Parts c, e, and f, total deposits in the three banks now equal $_____ million, compared with the initial level of 3 × $_____ million = $_____ million. Thus, the money supply has increased by $_____ million.

h. The process is not yet over. The Third National Bank will now increase its loans, and deposits at one of the three banks will rise even more when the borrower deposits the proceeds of his or her loan in the bank. According to the textbook, the total increase in deposits is equal to the initial infusion of reserves, or $10 million, multiplied by $1/rr$, where rr is the reserve-deposit ratio expressed as a decimal. (In this exercise, we implicitly assume that the currency-deposit ratio equals zero.) In this exercise, $rr =$ _____; thus, deposits (and the money supply) will eventually increase by $_____ million.

i. Note that reserves in all three banks increased by a total of
$_____ million above its initial level. Thus, when $cr = 0$,
an open-market purchase of $10 million will increase bank reserves by <u>more
than/exactly/less than</u> $10 million, while it eventually increases the money sup-
ply by <u>more than/exactly/less than</u> $10 million.

2. **The Money Multiplier** *In this exercise, we review the determinants of the money
multiplier.*

According to the model of the money supply presented in Chapter 18 of the textbook, the money supply can be written as

$$M = [(cr + 1)/(cr + rr)] \times B, \qquad \qquad \text{(18-1)}$$

where M equals the money supply, B is the monetary base, and the term in brackets
is called the money multiplier.

a. The money supply consists of currency plus <u>reserves/deposits/loans</u>. The monetary base consists of currency plus <u>reserves/deposits/loans</u>, and it is sometimes
called high-powered money. The reserve-deposit ratio is equal to rr, and cr is
the currency-deposit ratio.

b. Complete Table 18-1.

Table 18-1

(1) Currency-Deposit Ratio cr	(2) Reserve-Deposit Ratio rr	(3) Money Multiplier $[(cr + 1)/(cr + rr)]$
0.2	0.2	_____
0.2	0.4	_____
0.6	0.4	_____
0.2	1.0	_____
0.6	1.0	_____
0	0.2	_____

c. From Table 18-1, note that an increase in the reserve-deposit ratio rr will
<u>increase/decrease</u> the money multiplier, and an increase in the currency-
deposit ratio cr will <u>increase/decrease</u> the money multiplier in a fractional-
reserve banking system. If $rr = 1.0$, all deposits are held as reserves, there are no
loans, and we have a 100-percent-reserve banking system. In this case, the
money multiplier is equal to _____, and the money supply
is <u>greater than/less than/equal to</u> the monetary base. Finally, if cr equals 0, the
formula for the money multiplier becomes _____. In this
case, the entire money supply would be in the form of <u>currency/deposits</u>.

3. **The Three Instruments of Monetary Policy** *In this exercise, we describe the three instruments of monetary policy and discuss their effects on the money supply.*

    a. As Chapter 18 of the textbook states, the Fed has three instruments of monetary policy: open-market operations, reserve requirements, and the discount rate. If the Fed buys $1 million in bonds from the public, it makes an open-market pur-chase/sale of $1 million. If bank deposits initially increase by an amount equal to $1 million, then total bank deposits will eventually increase/decrease by an amount that is greater than/less than/equal to $1 million, and the money supply increases/decreases by an amount that is greater than/less than/equal to $1 million. Conversely, when the Fed sells existing government bonds to the public, total reserves, deposits, and the money supply will rise/fall/remain constant.

    b. A reduction in reserve requirements lowers the minimum reserve-deposit ratio. If banks respond by reducing the actual reserve-deposit ratio, they will increase/decrease the amount of loans, and both deposits and the money supply will increase/decrease/remain constant. Conversely, an increase in reserve requirements will increase/decrease the money supply, if banks respond by increasing the actual reserve-deposit ratio.

    c. The discount rate is the interest rate that the Fed charges when it makes loans to banks. If the Fed reduces the discount rate, banks will usually borrow more/fewer reserves from the Fed. Consequently, total bank reserves will rise/fall/remain constant, total deposits will eventually increase/decrease/remain constant, and the money supply will increase/decrease/remain constant.

Problems

Answer the following problems on a separate sheet of paper.

1. In the simple fractional-reserve model of the banking system, how much would the money supply rise if someone received an additional $1,000 in currency and the reserve-deposit ratio were 0.10? Explain.

2. Calculate the money multiplier for the following values of the currency-deposit ratio *cr* and the reserve-deposit ratio *rr*:

    a. $cr = 0.5$; $rr = 0.25$.

    b. $rr = 1.0$; $cr =$ any fraction. Explain this result.

3. a. Differentiate the formula for the money multiplier with respect to *rr*, and determine whether an increase in the reserve-deposit ratio will increase or decrease the money supply.

    b. Differentiate the formula for the money multiplier with respect to *cr*, and determine whether an increase in the currency-deposit ratio will increase or decrease the money supply.

4. According to the Baumol-Tobin model of cash management, the combined opportu-
   [C] nity and transactions cost of holding currency is $C = FN + iY/2N$.

   a. Differentiate C with respect to N.

   b. Find the first-order condition for the optimal value of N, that is, N^*.

   c. Check the second-order condition to confirm that total costs are minimized at
      the N^* you calculated in Part b.

5. Suppose that the nominal interest rate i was 10 percent per year, the cost of each
   round-trip to and from the bank F was \$25, and total annual expenditure Y was
   \$72,000.

   a. Calculate the optimal number of withdrawals N^* according to the Baumol-Tobin
      model of cash management.

   b. How often would an optimizing individual go to the bank, and how much would
      she withdraw from the bank each trip?

   c. Calculate the average money holding.

6. Use the formula for the optimal value of N in the Baumol-Tobin model of cash man-
   [O] agement to show that at the optimal N (that is, N^*), the opportunity cost of holding
   money $iY/2N$ is equal to the cost of foregone trips to the bank FN.

7. Recall from Chapter 4 of the textbook that the elasticity of money demand with
   [C] respect to the interest rate is $|(dM/di)| \times (i/M)$, and the income elasticity of money
   demand is $(dM/dY) \times (Y/M)$. Show that both the interest and income elasticity of
   money demand equal 1/2 in the Baumol-Tobin model of the transactions demand for
   money.

Data Questions

Locate the necessary economic data and apply them to answer the following data questions. All of the relevant data may be found in the Economic Report of the President.

1. **a.** Complete Columns 2, 3, and 5 of Table 18-2 in billions of current dollars.

Table 18-2

(1) Year	(2) Monetary Base ($ in billions)	(3) $M1$ ($ in billions)	(4) $M1$ Money Multiplier	(5) $M2$ ($ in billions)	(6) $M2$ Money Multiplier
1980	_____	_____	_____	_____	_____
1990	_____	_____	_____	_____	_____
2000	_____	_____	_____	_____	_____

b. Now compute the money multipliers in Columns 4 and 6.

c. If the Fed has preset targets for $M1$ and $M2$, how did the changes in the money multipliers between 1990 and 2000 complicate its job?

Questions to Think About

1. The discount rate is frequently far below the interest rate banks receive on new loans. During these periods, why don't banks increase their profits by borrowing an infinite amount (or extremely large finite amounts) from the Fed and increasing the money supply infinitely?

2. To estimate the cost of traveling to and from the bank, the textbook multiplied the wage rate by the travel time. This method is commonly used by economists to estimate the opportunity cost of time. What is the reasoning behind this method? Under what conditions is it valid? When might it be invalid?

CHAPTER 19 NINETEEN

Advances in Business Cycle Theory

Fill-in Questions

Use the key terms below to fill in the blanks in the following statements. Each term may be used more than once.

aggregate demand externality
coordination failure
intertemporal substitution of labor
labor hoarding

menu costs
new Keynesian economics
real-business-cycle theory
Solow residual

1. Adherents of _____ believe that one can explain short-run economic fluctuations while maintaining the assumptions of the classical model. According to this theory, short-term fluctuations in output are solely the result of real changes in the economy (such as a change in technology) and are not caused by changes in nominal variables (such as the money supply).

2. In real-business-cycle theory, the willingness to reallocate work over one's lifetime is called the _____.

3. The _____ is the percentage change in output minus the percentage change in inputs, where the different inputs are weighted by their factor shares. It is often used as a measure of the rate of technological progress in the economy.

4. _____ occurs when firms keep workers whom they do not need during recessions so that they will have these workers when the recession is over.

5. The goal of _____ is to put the traditional Keynesian approach to economic fluctuations on a firmer theoretical foundation. Much of its research is aimed at explaining why wages and prices are not flexible in the short run.

6. When a firm changes its prices, it may need to send out new catalogs, distribute new price lists, or print new menus. The costs of these price adjustments, called _____ , cause firms to adjust prices intermittently rather than continuously.

7. The macroeconomic impact of one firm's price adjustment on the demand for all other firms' products is called a(n) _____ .

8. If society fails to reach an optimal outcome as a result of the decisions of many agents who act separately but who must anticipate the actions of other agents, it may be the result of _____ .

Multiple-Choice Questions

1. All of the following are real variables, as opposed to nominal variables, EXCEPT:

    a. output.
    b. the price level.
    c. employment.
    d. consumption.

2. According to real-business-cycle theory, real GDP is always:

    a. greater than the natural rate of output.
    b. equal to the natural rate of output.
    c. less than the natural rate of output.
    d. less than or equal to the natural rate of output.

3. All of the following are characteristics of real-business-cycle theory EXCEPT:

    a. prices are sticky.
    b. the economy behaves according to the assumptions of the classical model.
    c. all unemployment is voluntary.
    d. real wages are flexible.

4. In the Robinson Crusoe parable, changes in real GDP were due to:

    a. changes in aggregate demand, such as changes in the money supply.
    b. changes in aggregate supply, such as technology shocks and the weather.
    c. changes in neither aggregate demand nor aggregate supply.
    d. inflation.

5. At the heart of the debate over the relevance of real-business-cycle theory are all of the following EXCEPT:

    a. the importance of intertemporal substitution of labor.
    b. the importance of technology shocks.
    c. progressive income taxation.
    d. the neutrality of money.

6. According to real-business-cycle theory, output rises when the real interest rate increases because of:
   a. changes in technology.
   b. the intertemporal substitution of labor.
   c. changes in the amount of real money balances.
   d. price and wage stickiness.

7. A new classical economist might explain that the reduction in output during a recession is caused by:
   a. a low real interest rate, which causes workers to choose leisure now and postpone working until some future period.
   b. a deterioration in the available production technology.
   c. an increase in unemployment insurance benefits, which leads workers to choose more leisure.
   d. all of the above.

8. According to real-business-cycle theory, all of the following statements regarding employment are true EXCEPT:
   a. people are always operating on their labor supply curves.
   b. fluctuations in employment reflect changes in the amount that people want to work at the market wage.
   c. real wages are perfectly flexible so that the labor market always clears.
   d. people vary the amount of labor that they wish to supply in response to changes in nominal wages even though real wages remain constant.

9. The Solow residual reflects:
   a. deviations from the natural rate of unemployment.
   b. changes in real wages.
   c. the intertemporal substitution of labor.
   d. changes in technology.

10. If the measured Solow residual is negative, it may reflect:
    a. technological regress.
    b. bad weather.
    c. increases in energy prices that adversely affect technology.
    d. all of the above.

11. The existence of labor hoarding makes the measured Solow residual:
    a. more cyclical than actual changes in the production technology.
    b. less cyclical than actual changes in the production technology.
    c. positive.
    d. greater than one.

12. According to real-business-cycle theory, an increase in the money supply will:
    a. decrease the real interest rate.
    b. increase the real interest rate.
    c. have no effect on the real interest rate.
    d. either decrease or have no effect on the real interest rate.

13. Which of the following have *not* been used as evidence of the non-neutrality of money:
    a. the death of Benjamin Strong and the subsequent Great Depression.
    b. the relationship between shifts in Federal Reserve policy and subsequent changes in GDP.
    c. the traditional coin flips that precede meetings of the Open Market Committee.
    d. All of the above have been used as evidence of non-neutrality..

14. According to real-business-cycle theory, the positive relationship between GDP and the money supply is probably caused by:
    a. increases in the money supply that lead to reductions in the real interest rate, increases in investment, and increases in output.
    b. increases in output that lead to increases in money demand and accommodating increases in money supply.
    c. increases in the money supply that lead to inflation, lower real wages, and increases in the quantity of labor demanded and GDP.
    d. all of the above.

15. According to new Keynesian economists, sticky wages and prices in the short run are the result of:
    a. rational expectations.
    b. changes in the money supply by the Fed.
    c. menu costs and staggered wage and price settings.
    d. perfect competition.

16. An aggregate demand externality occurs when firms do not take into account the effects of their price reductions on:
    a. inflation.
    b. output.
    c. government spending.
    d. real money balances.

17. Recessions may be caused by coordination failures if:
    a. nobody in the economy is athletically inclined.
    b. firms keep their own prices constant because they expect that other firms will also keep their prices constant.
    c. firms form cartels to coordinate prices.
    d. firms promise to coordinate but ultimately cheat.

18. The economists who are most likely to support the use of expansionary monetary and fiscal policy during recessions are the:
    a. classical economists.
    b. new classical economists.
    c. new Keynesian economists.
    d. monetarists.

19. The most frequently cited reason firms give for their reluctance to change prices more frequently is:
    a. their belief that this would be unfair to customers.
    b. their desire to wait until other firms change their prices first.
    c. the fact that changing prices is costly.
    d. their fear that customers will mistake price cuts for reductions in product quality.

Exercises

1. **The Economy under Flexible Prices in the Short Run** *In this exercise, we illustrate how the* LM *curve responds if prices are flexible in the short run.*

   a. Graph 19-1 depicts one *IS* curve and three *LM* curves.

   Graph 19-1

   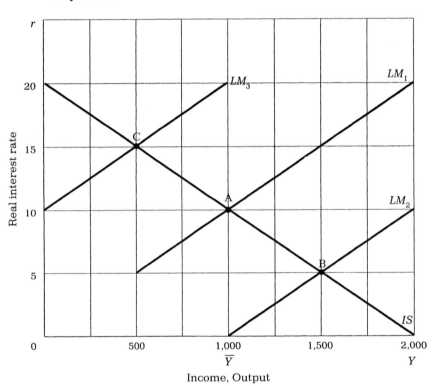

   Suppose that the initial equilibrium is at Point A on the LM_1 curve on Graph 19-1. At Point A, real output Y is greater than/less than/equal to the natural rate of output $\overline{Y}$. If prices are completely flexible in the short run, the aggregate price level P will rise/fall/remain constant and real output Y will rise/fall/remain constant.

b. Now suppose that the initial equilibrium is at Point B on the LM_2 curve on Graph 19-1. At Point B, real output Y is greater than/less than/equal to the natural rate of output $\overline{Y}$. If prices are completely flexible in the short run, the aggregate price level P rises/falls/remains constant As it does so, the LM curve shifts to the left (upward)/right (downward) until the LM curve intersects the IS curve at a point greater than/less than/equal to the natural rate of output $\overline{Y}$. This intersection occurs at Point _____.

c. Now suppose that the initial equilibrium is at Point C on the LM_3 curve on Graph 19-1. At Point C, real output Y is greater than/less than/equal to the natural rate of output $\overline{Y}$. If prices are completely flexible in the short run, the aggregate price level P rises/falls/remains constant. As it does so, the LM curve shifts to the left (upward)/right (downward) until the LM curve intersects the IS curve at a point greater than/less than/equal to the natural rate of output $\overline{Y}$. This intersection occurs at Point _____.

d. If there is complete price flexibility in the short run, actual output will always be greater than/less than/equal to the natural rate of output $\overline{Y}$. This situation implies that the short-run aggregate supply curve is horizontal/vertical

2. **Intertemporal Substitution and Labor Supply** *In this exercise, we utilize a two-period model to illustrate the effects of changes in the real interest rate on labor supply. For simplicity, we assume that there is no expected inflation.*

a. Suppose that Wendy expects to retire after two more years. When she retires, she would like to have enough money to make a down payment on a condominium in Florida. In addition, she must take one of the next two years off from work in order to have surgery. Consequently, she is faced with the decision of working this year or working next year. Suppose that her current wage rate $W_1 =$ $10 per hour. If she works for 2,000 hours this year, she will earn $_____. If she then takes all of this money, puts it in the bank, and earns 10 percent interest while she has her operation, when she is ready to buy the condominium one year later, she will have $(1 + 0.10) \times \$$_____ $= \$$_____.

b. On the other hand, if Wendy has her surgery this year, she expects to earn $W_2 = \$11$ per hour when she returns to work in one year. If she works for 2,000 hours next year, she will earn $_____, which she can then use as a down payment on the condominium. The amount of money she will have for a down payment if she works next year is greater than/less than/equal to the amount of money she will have if she works this year and earns interest for one year. This amount is also reflected in Wendy's intertemporal relative price of $(1 + r)W_1/W_2$, which, in this example, is equal to $(1 +$ _____ $)$ _____ $/$ _____ $=$ _____.

c. In Parts a and b, Wendy would be indifferent between working this year or next year. Suppose, however, that her expected wage next year W_2 rose to $15 per hour, while her current wage W_1 remained equal to $10 per hour. If Wendy works 2,000 hours next year, she will then have \$_____ for her condominium's down payment. Consequently, she would probably decide to work this/next year and have her operation this/next year.

d. On the other hand, suppose that Wendy's expected wage next year W_2 remained equal to $11 per hour while her current wage W_1 rose to $15 per hour. If Wendy works 2,000 hours this year, she will earn \$_____. If she put this money in the bank at 10 percent interest, she will have \$_____ for her condominium's down payment, compared with \$_____ if she works 2,000 hours next year at $11 per hour. Obviously, in this case, Wendy would decide to work this/next year and have her operation this/next year.

e. Finally, suppose that Wendy's current wage W_1 and expected wage next year W_2 returned to their initial levels of $10 and $11 per hour, respectively, but the real interest rate r rose to 20 percent. If Wendy works 2,000 hours this year, she will earn \$_____. If she put this money in the bank at 20 percent interest, she will have \$_____ for her down payment. If, instead, she works 2,000 hours next year at $11 per hour, she will have \$_____ for her down payment. Thus, as the real interest rate increases, Wendy is more likely to work this/next year and have her operation this/next year.

f. In reality, people do not typically work all of one year and none of the next. Nevertheless, the same principles of intertemporal substitution of labor apply. If the current wage rises, people will decide to work more/less now, which will increase/decrease the current amount of labor supplied and hence will increase/decrease the natural rate of output $\overline{Y}$ at which labor is fully employed. If the expected future wage rises, people will decide to work more/less now and work more/less later, which will increase/decrease the current amount of labor supplied and hence increase/decrease the natural rate of output $\overline{Y}$.

g. Finally, if the real interest rate r rises, people will work more/less now, as Part e illustrated. This will increase/decrease the current amount of labor supplied and hence increase/decrease the natural rate of output $\overline{Y}$.

Problems

Answer the following problems on a separate sheet of paper.

1. Suppose that the economy were initially described by the following equations:

$$L^s = 100(r) \quad = \text{current labor supply,} \qquad (19\text{-}1)$$
$$Y = 10\,K^{1/2}L^{1/2} = \text{the aggregate production function,} \qquad (19\text{-}2)$$
$$K = 81 \quad = \text{supply of capital, and} \qquad (19\text{-}3)$$
$$r = 4\,(\%) \quad = \text{real interest rate.} \qquad (19\text{-}4)$$

   a. Explain why current labor supply is positively related to the real interest rate.

   b. Solve for the initial equilibrium levels of labor L and real output Y. Note that $r = 4$ and *not* 0.04 in Equation 19-1.

   c. In real-business-cycle theory, changes in fiscal policy affect real GDP by changing the real interest rate and thereby changing labor supply. Suppose an increase in government spending increases the real interest rate to 6.25(%). Calculate the new equilibrium levels of labor L and real output.

   d. Suppose a technological improvement changes the aggregate production function to $Y = 12\,K^{1/2}L^{1/2}$. Calculate the new equilibrium levels of labor L and real output Y if the real interest rate is equal to 4.

2. Changes in monetary policy have no effect on real output in the real-business-cycle model. Illustrate how this result is obtained using an *IS-LM* diagram and the assumption of flexible prices.

3. Suppose the aggregate production function were

$$Y = AK^{1/3}L^{2/3}. \qquad (19\text{-}5)$$

   From one year to the next we observe that capital rises by 1 percent, labor rises by 1/2 percent, and output rises by 1 percent. Calculate the Solow residual. (See footnote 3 in the textbook. It may also be helpful to review the appendix to Chapter 8.)

4. Using the United States as a benchmark, would a new Keynesian economist expect recessions to be longer or shorter in countries in which labor contracts are synchronized so that almost all workers and firms negotiate wages at the same time?

5. Consider two countries whose conflicts with each other have led them to the brink of war. Country A and Country B both face the following options:

   Option 1: Neither country compromises and there is a war;
   Option 2: Country A gives in to Country B with no war;
   Option 3: Country B gives in to Country A with no war; and
   Option 4: Both countries compromise with no war.

   a. Under what circumstances would a war be the result of a coordination failure? (*Hint:* consider the costs of war to each side.)

   b. Under what circumstances would it not?

Questions to Think About

1.   Can you think of any occasions on which you or your parents' labor supply has been altered by a change in the real interest rate? Describe these occasions and explain how the change affected your or their labor supply.

2.   If fiscal policy affects real output in both the conventional model and the real-business-cycle model, why should it be used to stabilize output in the former model but not in the latter model?

3.   What portion of the unemployed do you think cannot get any job? What portion do you think cannot get a job at the prevailing wage for individuals with the same level of skills, education, and experience? That is, do you think that many of the unemployed choose not to work because they do not want to work for the wages they are offered rather than because of a lack of jobs? What do these observations suggest about alternative theories of economic fluctuations?

4.   Courses in microeconomics emphasize that prices equilibrate supply and demand, and they rarely mention price stickiness. How does this observation relate to the debate over real-business-cycle theory?

5.   Cite three examples where coordination failures lead to suboptimal results.

Answers

CHAPTER 1

Fill-in Questions

1. Macroeconomics; Microeconomics
2. models
3. exogenous; endogenous
4. price flexibility; price stickiness
5. market-clearing

Multiple-Choice Questions

1. b   2. d   3. b   4. d   5. c

Exercises

1. **a.** 20 percent   **b.** 325 percent   **c.** −20 percent
2. **a.** $Y = 3.5$; $Y = 4.0$; $Y = 4.5$
   b. Graph 1-1

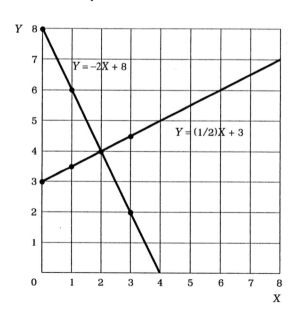

c. Slope = 1/2, or 0.5. Every time the value of X increases by 1 unit, the value of Y increases by 1/2.

d. Y intercept = 3. When $X = 0$, $Y = 3$.

e. $Y = 6$; $Y = 4$; $Y = 2$

f. See Graph 1-1.

g. Slope = -2; Y intercept = 8

h. $X = 2$ and $Y = 4$

i. By definition, the point of intersection must lie on both lines. This means that the values of X and Y at this point must satisfy both equations, that is, $Y = (1/2)X + 3$, and $Y = -2X + 8$. Consequently, at the intersection $(1/2)X + 3 = -2X + 8$.

3. a. 8; 9; 5

    b. 1/8; 1/3; 1/1,000

    c. $5^5 = 3{,}125 = 25 \times 125$; $6^2 = 36 = 216 \times 1/6$; $4^1 = 4 = 2 \times 2$

Problems

1. a. In a controlled experiment, researchers observe changes in two or more samples in which the only conditions that are different in the two samples are the variables whose effects are being tested. All other variables are held constant.

    b. In experiments that are not controlled, it is often difficult to attribute any differences in the results from the two (or more) samples to the differences in the variables that were purposefully changed because other influencing variables may have also changed.

    c. It is extremely difficult to hold constant all of the macroeconomic variables we would ideally like to hold constant. Even if it could be done, it would be very expensive and often politically impossible.

2. a. Graph for Problem 2a.

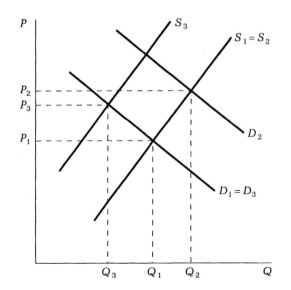

b. The demand curve for coal shifts to the right to D_2, and the supply curve does not shift. The equilibrium price of coal rises, and the equilibrium quantity of coal also rises.

c. The supply curve of coal shifts to the left to S_3, and the demand curve does not shift. The equilibrium price of coal rises and the equilibrium quantity of coal falls.

CHAPTER 2

Fill-in Questions

1. Nominal gross domestic product; Real gross domestic product
2. unemployment rate
3. Okun's law
4. consumer price index; Laspeyres
5. GDP deflator; nominal gross domestic product; real gross domestic product; Paasche
6. stock; flow
7. Depreciation
8. labor-force participation rate
9. disposable personal income
10. recession; unemployment rate
11. Nominal gross national product; Nominal gross domestic product

Multiple-Choice Questions

1. c   2. b   3. c   4. c   5. c   6. c   7. a   8. d   9. b   10. b
11. a   12. c   13. c   14. a   15. d   16. d   17. c   18. d   19. b   20. d

Exercises

1. a. intermediate; intermediate; final; final
    b. $1,500 million
    c. **Table 2-1**

	Value-Added per Unit	Number of Units	Company Value-Added
Intel	$200	1 million	$200 million
Princeton Graphics	$300	1 million	$300 million
IBM	$700	1 million	$700 million
Anheuser Busch	$1.50	200 million	$300 million
Total			$1,500 million

2. a. Nominal GDP in 1990 = $15 billion; nominal GDP in 2000 = $40 billion
    b. $15 billion

    c. $48 billion

    d. 220 percent

    e. Real GDP in 1990 using 2000 as base year = $21 billion; real GDP in 2000 using 2000 as base year = $40 billion.

    f. 90.5 percent

    g. In 1990, computers were expensive relative to automobiles. Consequently, when 1990 is used as the base year, the dramatic increase in the quantity of computers produced between 1990 and 2000 is multiplied by a big price ($6,000), resulting in a large increase in real GDP. In 2000, however, computers were cheap relative to automobiles. Consequently, when 2000 is used as the base year, the large change in the quantity of computers produced in the period is multiplied by a relatively low price ($2,000), resulting in a much smaller increase in real GDP.

3.   a. $48 billion

    b. $15 billion

    c. 220%; 3.20

    d. 90.5%

    e. 1.905

    f. 2.47; 147%

4.   a. 140

    b. 83.3

    c. $40 billion; 0.833; $48 billion

    d. Percentage change in CPI (1990 = 100) = 40 percent; percentage change in GDP deflator (1990 = 100) = −16.7 percent.

    e. In 1990, computers comprised a small portion of the consumer market basket. Therefore, in a Laspeyres index like the CPI, the dramatic reduction in the price of computers will be outweighed by the increase in the price of automobiles. For a Paasche index like the GDP deflator, however, the weight given to computers is much greater because they comprise a much larger portion of the GDP in 2000 than in 1990. Consequently, in this index the reduction in computer prices will outweigh the increase in automobile prices.

5.   a. and b.

Table 2-4

(1) Period	(2) Nominal GDP (PY)	(3) % Change in PY	(4) P	(5) % Change in P	(6) Y	(7) % Change in Y
1	100		1.00		100	
		5		2		3
2			1.02		103	

c. 2; 3; 5

d. 1.02; 103; 105.06; 105.06; 5.06

e. 2

f. minus; 3

6. **a. Table 2-5**

(1) Event	(2) Included in U.S. GNP	(3) Included in U.S. GDP
1. Michael Jackson performs a rock concert in New York	Yes	Yes
2. Michael Jackson performs a rock concert in London	Yes	No
3. The Rolling Stones perform a rock concert in New York	No	Yes
4. The Rolling Stones perform a rock concert in London	No	No
5. Toyota earns profits from its car factory in California	No	Yes
6. Ford earns profits from its car factory in England	Yes	No

7. **a. Graph 2-1**

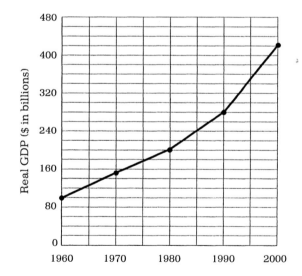

b. Graph 2-2

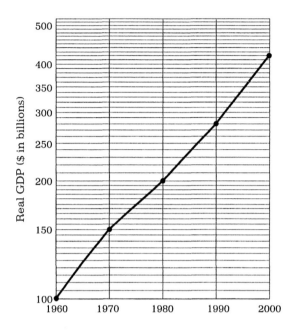

Problems

1. **a.** $8,619.5 billion
    b. $7,980.9 billion
    c. $8,319.2 billion
    d. $7,031.0 billion (Some additional minor items were included in related categories.)

2. Prices are a better measure than weight of the (marginal) value that consumers place on various goods and services.

3. Education may be viewed as an investment because part of its value lies in its ability to increase a student's future production, just like a new piece of equipment. Economists sometimes refer to education as an investment in human capital.

4. There are at least two reasons why the ratios in GDP per capita may overstate the true differences in standards of living between the United States, on the one hand, and Ethiopia, Tajikstan, and Bangladesh, on the other. First, many researchers think that nonmarketed household production, which is usually not included in the official GDP statistics, may be larger relative to measured GDP in these three countries than in the United States. Second, the official GDP per capita measures generally use the market exchange rates to convert different currencies. These exchange rates are usually determined by the flows of tradable goods, services, and assets among countries. If the relative prices of nontradable and tradable goods and services are not the same in all countries, this conversion will not accurately reflect differences in standards of living. Very few people, however, would deny that the standard of living in the United States is many times that in Ethiopia, Tajikstan, and Bangladesh.

5. a. Yes. It represents consumption.

    b. No. The purchase of a used computer from a friend does not increase GDP.

    c. No. Although many people think of stock purchases as investment, this is not true in the national income accounting sense.

    d. Yes. It represents investment.

    e. Yes. It represents investment.

    f. No. Your grandmother's Social Security check is a transfer payment.

    g. Yes. It represents a government purchase of a good.

6. Investment rises by $150,000, consumption rises by $6,000.

7. a. U.S. GNP falls.

    b. U.S. GDP remains unchanged.

8. a. $220,000

    b. $250,000

    c. 88

CHAPTER 3

Fill-in Questions

1. Factors of production
2. Factor prices
3. marginal product of labor; marginal product of capital
4. production function
5. constant returns to scale
6. competition; marginal product of labor; real rental price of capital
7. real wage
8. Accounting profit
9. Euler's theorem; economic profit
10. Cobb-Douglas production function
11. diminishing marginal productivity
12. consumption function; marginal propensity to consume
13. nominal interest rate; real interest rate
14. national saving
15. private saving
16. public saving; crowding out

Multiple-Choice Questions

1. c	2. d	3. b	4. c	5. a	6. a	7. a
8. b	9. b	10. a	11. c	12. d	13. d	14. a
15. c	16. d	17. c	18. b	19. b	20. c	21. c

Exercises

1. a. **Graph 3-1**

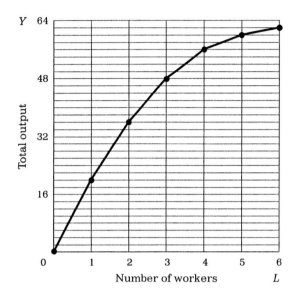

The positive slope indicates that as the number of workers employed increases, total output increases. The decreasing slope indicates that as more workers are hired, each additional worker adds less to total output.

b. **Table 3-1**

(1) No. of Workers (L)	(2) No. of Loaves Baked per Hour	(3) Marginal Product of Labor (MPL)	(4) Price per Loaf	(5) Price per Loaf × MPL	(6) Nominal Wage Rate (W)	(7) Real Wage Rate (W/P)
0	0				$8	8
		20	$1	$20		
1	20				$8	8
		16	$1	$16		
2	36				$8	8
		12	$1	$12		
3	48				$8	8
		8	$1	$8		
4	56				$8	8
		4	$1	$4		
5	60				$8	8
		2	$1	$2		
6	62				$8	8

c. **Graph 3-2**

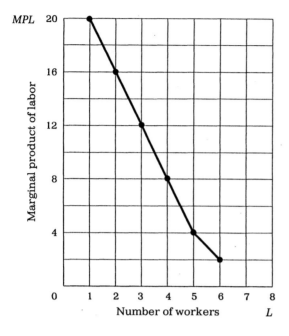

d. See Table 3-1 in Part b.

e. See Table 3-1 in Part b. The company hires four bakers.

f. **Graph 3-3**

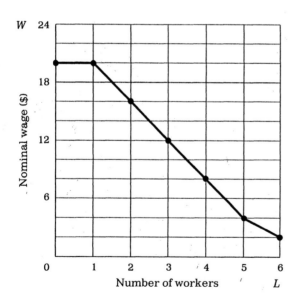

2. a. See Table 3-1 in the answer to Exercise 1.

    b. **Table 3-2**

(1)	(2)	(3)	(4)	(5)	(6)	(7)
No. of Workers (L)	No. of Loaves Baked per Hour	Marginal Product of Labor (MPL)	Price per Loaf	Price per Loaf × MPL	Nominal Wage Rate (W)	Real Wage Rate (W/P)
0	0				$16	8
		20	$2	$40		
1	20				$16	8
		16	$2	$32		
2	36				$16	8
		12	$2	$24		
3	48				$16	8
		8	$2	$16		
4	56				$16	8
		4	$2	$8		
5	60				$16	8
		2	$2	$4		
6	62				$16	8

    c. Four

    d. $32; right

    Graph 3-4

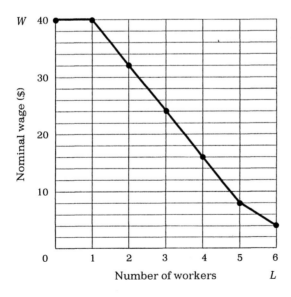

e. **Table 3-3**

(1) Nominal Wage (W)	(2) Price of Bread (P)	(3) Real Wage (W/P)	(4) Number of Bakers Hired
$20	$1	20	1
$40	$2	20	1
$16	$1	16	2
$32	$2	16	2
$12	$1	12	3
$24	$2	12	3
$ 8	$1	8	4
$16	$2	8	4
$ 4	$1	4	5
$ 8	$2	4	5

Graph 3-5

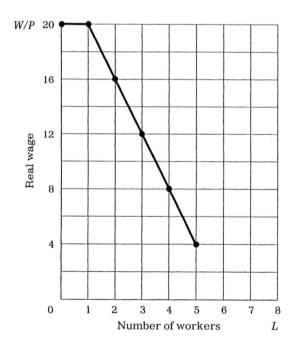

3. **a.** $Y = 50$

    b. Constant returns to scale refers to a production function in which an x percentage change in all inputs leads to the same x percentage change in output.

    Table 3-4

K	L	$Y = K^{1/2}L^{1/2}$
100	25	50
200	50	100
2,500	625	1,250

    doubled; increased 25-fold

    c. $MPL = 1$; equilibrium real wage $= 1$

    d. $MPK = 0.25$; equilibrium real rental price of capital $= 0.25$

    e. Step 1: 50

    Step 2: 1; 25

    Step 3: 1/2

    Step 4: 0.25; 25

    Step 5: 1/2

    Step 7: When $K = 100$ and $L = 625$, $Y = 250$, $MPL = W/P = 0.2$, $MPK = R/P = 1.25$, factor payments to labor $= 0.2(625) = 125$, factor payments to capital $= 1.25(100) = 125$, labor's share $=$ capital's share $= 1/2$.

    f. $25 + 25 = 50$

4. **a. Table 3-5**

(1) Disposable Income $(Y - T)$	(2) Consumption (C)
\$ 0	125
100	200
200	275
500	500
800	725
1,000	875

b. **Graph 3-6**

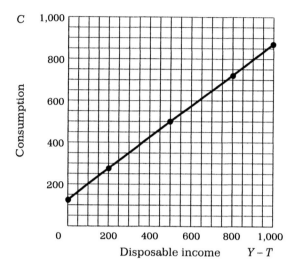

c. 125

d. 0.75; The slope is equal to the marginal propensity to consume here because it measures the change in consumption resulting from a $1 increase in disposable income.

5. a. 100; 50; −50

b. **Table 3-6**

(1) Net Taxes (T)	(2) Government Purchases (G)	(3) Budget Surplus	(4) Budget Deficit
200	100	100	−100
200	200	0	0
100	200	−100	100
−100	100	−200	200

6. **a.** 950

   b. 100; 100; $r = 10$

   c. Graph 3-7

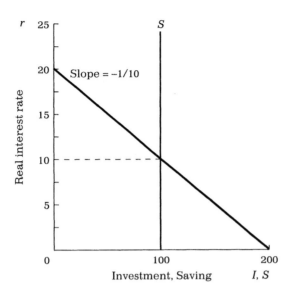

   d. public saving $= -50$; private saving $= 150$; national saving $= 100$

7. **a.** fall; 50; 50; left; 50

   Graph 3-8

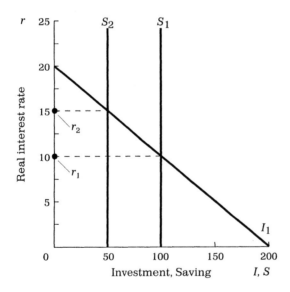

   b. fall; 50; 50; movement along; rise; $r = 15$

   c. decrease; increase; decrease

   d. increase; 965; decrease; 85; left; 15; fall; 15; 85; movement along; rise

e. right

Graph 3-9

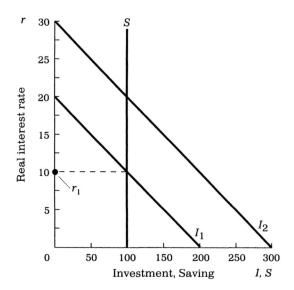

remain constant; not shift; rise; 100

f. positive; right

Graph 3-10

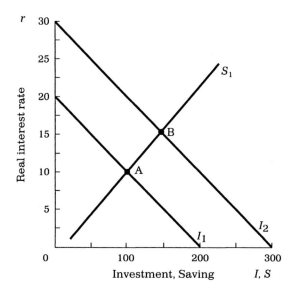

increase

8.　**a.**　decrease; left

Graph 3-11

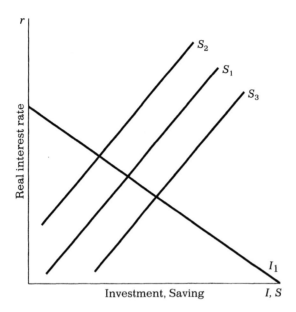

　　　rise; fall; negative

　　b.　increase; right; see Graph 3-11; fall; rise; negative

　　c.　right; increase; left; decrease; positive

　　d.　negative; positive

Problems

1. Graphs for Problem 1

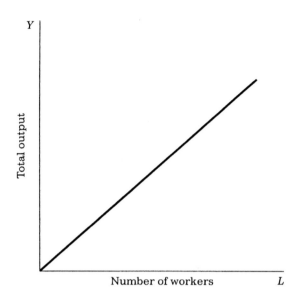

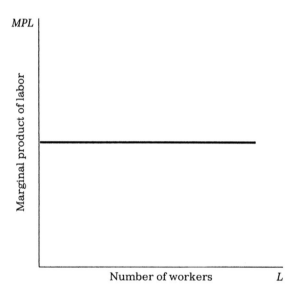

2. **a.** The profit-maximizing rule sets the real wage equal to the marginal product of labor. The average products of labor in California and Florida could be very different even if the marginal products of labor were equal.

   b. Once again, the average products of labor in California and Florida could be very different even if the marginal products of labor were equal. If all groves are maximizing profits, then the *MPL* is the same in all groves. Thus, the movement of a worker from Florida to California would reduce output in Florida by the same amount that output increased in California, resulting in no change in total orange production.

3. **a.** $Y = 960$; $Y = 1,920$; $Y = 2,880$. When all of the inputs were doubled, output doubled. When all of the inputs were tripled, output tripled. Consequently, these results illustrate the property of constant returns to scale.

   b. $MPL = 40K^{1/3}L^{-1/3} = 40(K/L)^{1/3}$

   c. $MPL = 80$; $W/P = 80$

   d. $MPK = 20K^{-2/3}L^{2/3} = 20(L/K)^{2/3}$

   e. $MPK = 5$; $R/P = 5$

   f. total real labor payments $= 640$;
   total real payments to capital $= 320$;
   labor's share $= 640/960 = 2/3$;
   capital's share $= 320/960 = 1/3$.

   g. Since $W/P = MPL$ and $R/P = MPK$, $(W/P)L = (MPL)L$ and $(R/P)K = (MPK)K$.
   $(MPL)L = 40(K/L)^{1/3}L = 40(K^{1/3}L^{2/3}) = (2/3)Y$.
   $(MPK)K = 20(L/K)^{2/3}K = 20(K^{1/3}L^{2/3}) = (1/3)Y$.

   h. $(W/P)L + (R/P)K = (MPL)L + (MPK)K = 40(K/L)^{1/3}L + 20(L/K)^{2/3}K =$
   $40(K^{1/3}L^{2/3}) + 20(K^{1/3}L^{2/3}) = 60K^{1/3}L^{2/3} = Y$.

4. **a.** The deficit would fall.

   b. Disposable income would fall by the full amount of the tax increase. Since consumption would fall by only a fraction (MPC) of this amount, private saving would also decrease. Public saving would increase by the amount of the tax increase plus the reduction in government spending. Consequently, national saving would increase.

   c. S would shift right to S_2. I would not shift. Consequently, the real interest rate would fall and investment would rise.
   Graph for Problem 4c

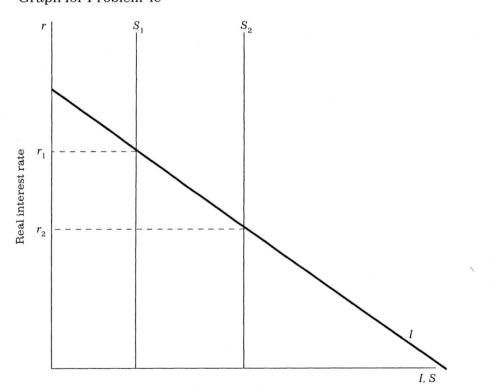

Investment, Saving

5. a. If both taxes and government purchases were reduced by equal amounts,
       the government budget surplus $T - G$, and hence public saving, would
       remain unchanged (at a negative value). The reduction in net taxes, however,
       would increase the amount of disposable income, $Y - T$, at the full employ-
       ment level of GDP, $\overline{Y}$, by the full amount of the tax cut. Consequently, the
       level of consumption would increase at $\overline{Y}$ by $MPC \times (\Delta T)$, since consumption
       rises with disposable income. Since $MPC < 1$, some of the additional dispos-
       able income will go toward increasing private saving. (Alternatively, note
       that $S_{PR} = (Y - T) - C$. Disposable income at $\overline{Y}$ rises by the full amount of
       the tax decrease while consumption rises by only a fraction of the increase.)
       Thus, the level of private saving would increase at $\overline{Y}$, along with the level of
       national saving S. This shifts the S curve to the right below. As a result, the
       equilibrium level of the real interest rate would fall and investment would rise.

    b. Graph for Problem 5b

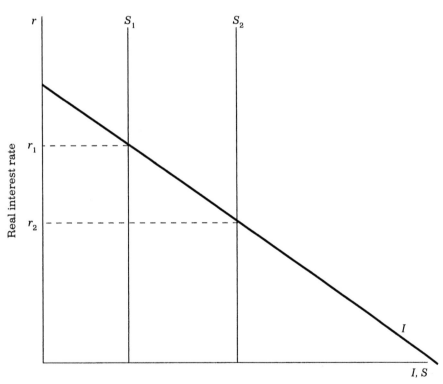

Investment, Saving

c. The increases in consumption and private saving at $\overline{Y}$ following an equal reduction in taxes and government purchases depend on the value of the marginal propensity to consume. The increase in disposable income at $\overline{Y}$ will equal the full amount of the tax reduction regardless of the value of MPC. If the MPC is large, that is, close to 1.0, the increase in consumption will be large, and the increases in private and national saving will be small. Consequently, the saving curve will shift only slightly to the right, the decline in the real interest rate will be small, and investment will rise by only a small amount. If, on the other hand, the MPC is small, the increase in consumption will be smaller and the increase in private saving will be larger. This will result in a large increase in national saving, a big shift to the right in the saving curve, a large decline in the real interest rate, and a big increase in investment.

6. a. The government surplus would fall by the increase in government spending plus the reduction in taxes.

b. Disposable income would rise by the full amount of the tax reduction. Consumption would rise by MPC times the reduction in taxes, and private saving would rise by (1 − MPC) times the reduction in taxes. Public saving would fall by the increase in government spending plus the reduction in taxes. Consequently, national saving would fall by the increase in government spending plus MPC times the reduction in taxes.

c. S would shift left to S_2. I would not shift. Consequently, the real interest rate would rise and investment would fall.
Graph for Problem 6c

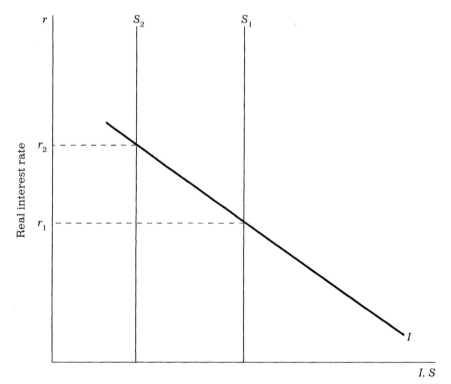

Investment, Saving

c. **Table 5-2**

(1)	(2)	(3)	(4)	(5)	(6)	(7)	(8)	(9)	(10)
					($ in billions)				
Case	Y	C	I	G	NX	T	Private Saving	Public Saving	National Saving
1.	5,000	3,000	700	1,000	300	900	1,100	−100	1,000
2.	5,000	3,200	900	1,000	−100	900	900	−100	800
3.	5,000	3,200	900	900	0	1,000	800	100	900

d. 300; 300; −100; −100; 0; 0

e. −100; 100

3. a. 950; 100; 150; 0; 0

   b. 1,100; 150; −50; 100; 0; 0

   c. **Graph 5-1**

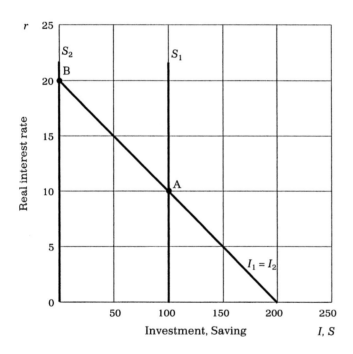

d. left; 100; not shift

e. 0; 0; 20

f. 100; −100; −100; fall; 100

g. increase; decrease; does not change; does not change; down; deficit

h. right; not shift

Graph 5-2

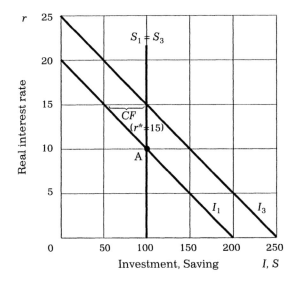

−50; −50

i.   increase; decrease; 50; not change; 50; 50

4. **a.**   **Table 5-3**

(1) Nominal Foreign Exchange Rate (euros per dollar)	(2) Price of IBM Computer in the U.S.	(3) Price of IBM Computer in Germany	(4) Price of Siemens Computer in Germany	(5) Price of Siemens Computer in the U.S
1.0	$10,000	10,000 euros	15,000 euros	$15,000
1.5	$10,000	15,000 euros	15,000 euros	$10,000
2.0	$10,000	20,000 euros	15,000 euros	$7,500

b.   increases; decrease

c.   remains constant; decreases; increase

d.   exports; imports; decrease

e.   decrease

5. a.   **Table 5-4**

(1) Nominal Foreign Exchange Rate (euros per dollar)	(2) Price of IBM Computer in the U.S.	(3) Price of IBM Computer in Germany	(4) Price of Siemens Computer in Germany	(5) Price of Siemens Computer in the U.S.
1.5	$10,000	15,000 euros	15,000 euros	$10,000
1.5	$12,000	18,000 euros	15,000 euros	$10,000

   b.   equal to; greater than; decrease

   c.   **Table 5-5**

(1) Nominal Foreign Exchange Rate (euros per dollar)	(2) Price of IBM Computer in the U.S.	(3) Price of IBM Computer in Germany	(4) Price of Siemens Computer in Germany	(5) Price of Siemens Computer in the U.S.
1.50	$10,000	15,000 euros	15,000 euros	$10,000
1.25	$12,000	15,000 euros	15,000 euros	$12,000

   20; 20; remain equal to; not change

   d.   0.67; 1.0; 1.0; 1.2; 1.33

   e.   decrease; increase; decrease; increases; increases; decreases

6. a.   decreases

   b.   **Graph 5-3**

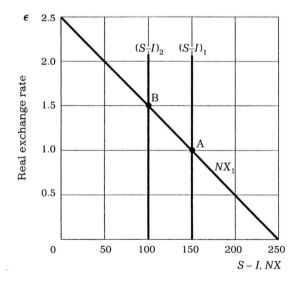

c. 150; 150; 1.0

d. decrease; 50; remains the same; decrease; 50; 100; left; 50; decrease; borrowing; decrease; 50; 100; 1.5; increase

e. **Graph 5-4**

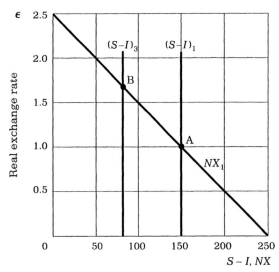

increase; decrease; increase; decrease; left; decrease; decrease; rise

7. a. % Change in $\varepsilon + \pi^* - \pi$; decrease; depreciate; increase; appreciates

b. 20; 100; 5

c. 40; 100; fall; 2.5

d. 200; increase; 10

e. **Table 5-7**

(1) Long-Run Nominal Foreign Exchange Rate (zlotys per dollar)	(2) U.S. Price Level	(3) Polish Price Level	(4) Long-Run Real Foreign Exchange Rate
5.0	20	100	1.0
2.5	40	100	1.0
10.0	20	200	1.0

1.0; horizontal

f. 1.0; 0; $\pi^* - \pi$; all

8. a. more; less; more; less; fall

b. fewer; more; fall

9. **a.** fall; 20; 1/5

   Graph 5-5

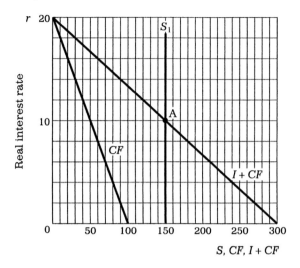

   b. vertical

   c. 300; 15; 20; 1/15; flatter

   d. 150; 150; 10; 100; 50

   e. 50

10. **a.** **Graph 5-6**

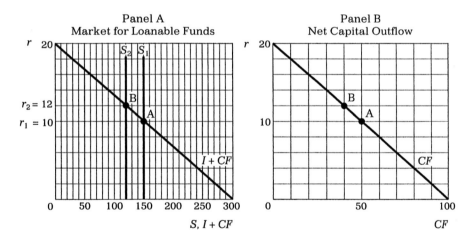

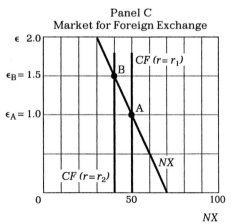

    b.   150; 150; 10; 50

    c.   1.0

    d.   falls; 30; 120; left; 30

    e.   12; 80; 40

    f.   rises; 1.5

    g.   decrease; increase; decrease; decrease; decrease; increase

    h.   shift right; not shift; rise; decrease; rise

Problems

1. **a.** U.S. investment would be low relative to our trading partners because relatively low U.S. saving would lead to a relatively high U.S. real interest rate, which would dampen U.S. investment.

    b. Net capital outflow has been negative; the United States has had a trade deficit.

2. **a.** The U.S. tax cuts and increased defense spending decreased world saving and, thereby, increased the world real interest rate.

       i.   As r^* increases, investment in Europe and Japan falls.

      ii. Since national saving in Europe and Japan remains constant, as investment falls, $S - I$ increases, and European and Japanese net capital outflow rises.

     iii. Recall that $S - I = NX$. As European and Japanese net capital outflow increases, their trade surpluses NX increase (or their trade deficits decrease).

      iv. For their trade surpluses to increase, the real exchange rates in Europe and Japan must decrease.

    b. The high Belgian budget deficits have had no effect on:

       i.   investment elsewhere in Europe and Japan.

      ii. net capital outflow elsewhere in Europe and Japan.

     iii. the trade balances elsewhere in Europe and Japan.

      iv. the real exchange rates elsewhere in Europe and Japan.

    c. The U.S. tax cuts and increased defense spending increase the world real interest rate because the United States is a "large" country in that it supplies a major part of total world saving. The Belgian budget deficits do not affect the world real interest rate because Belgium is a "small" country. It supplies a much smaller part of total world saving.

3. **a.** Under purchasing-power parity, the nominal exchange rate between any two countries can take on any value.

    b. It implies that the real exchange rate between any two countries will always equal 1.0.

    c. Purchasing-power parity, implies that almost all goods are freely and easily tradable among countries. Consequently, if the real exchange rate deviates from 1.0, all consumers will prefer to buy all commodities from one country and none from the other. This, of course, cannot occur. If the real exchange rate cannot deviate from 1.0, the answer to Part a follows directly from the definition of the real exchange rate $\varepsilon = eP/P^*$.

4. **a.** According to purchasing-power parity, the long-run real foreign exchange rate will eventually approach 1.0 and stay there. In the long run, according to the classical dichotomy, it is unaffected by nominal variables, such as the growth of the money supply.

   b. According to the Quantity Theory, velocity is constant in the long run and the long-run rate of inflation is equal to the growth of the money supply minus the long-run growth rate of real output (real GDP). Thus, a reduction in the growth rate of the money supply would reduce the rate of inflation in the United States below that prevailing abroad. The real foreign exchange rate can be written as:

$$\varepsilon = e(P/P^*).$$

The percentage change in the *nominal* foreign exchange rate can be written as:

$$\%\Delta e = \%\Delta\varepsilon + \%\Delta P^* - \%\Delta P.$$

According to purchasing-power parity, in the long run $\%\Delta\varepsilon = 0$. Thus, if foreign inflation exceeds domestic inflation, the nominal U.S. foreign exchange rate will increase.

5. **a.** According to the quantity equation, $MV = PY$.
   Taking percentage changes of both sides yields
   % Change in M + % Change in V = % Change in P + % Change in Y.
   If the money supply grows at 3 percent per year, velocity remains constant, and real GDP grows at 3 percent per year in the long run, then
   3% = % Change in P + 3%, or $\pi = 0\%$.
   If money supply growth rises to 10 percent per year,
   $\pi = 10\% - 3\% = 7\%$, that is, it rises by 7 percent (points) per year.

   b. According to the classical dichotomy, real variables, like the real interest rate, are not affected by nominal variables, like the money supply, in the long run. Instead, the real interest rate is typically determined by investment and saving. Consequently, the real interest rate would remain unchanged.

   c. Recall $i = r + \pi$. Because r remains constant in the long run and inflation rises by 7 percentage points, the nominal interest rate will also rise by 7 percentage points.

   d. Following the classical dichotomy, the real exchange rate will remain unchanged in the long run. This is also true if purchasing-power parity prevails.

   e. Because $\varepsilon = e (P/P^*)$,
   % Change in ε = 0 = % Change in e + % Change in P − % Change in P^*, or
   % Change in e = % Change in P^* − % Change in P.
   If foreign inflation is unaffected and U.S. inflation rises by 7 percentage points per year, the U.S. nominal exchange rate will fall by 7 percentage points per year.

f. Because investment is a function of the real interest rate, which is unchanged, investment will also be unchanged.

g. In the long run, real GDP is a function solely of technology and the amount of factor inputs, such as labor and capital. Because these are unchanged, real GDP will not be affected by the increase in money growth in the long run.

6. a. $\varepsilon = e\,(P/P^*) = 8.28$ yuan/\$1 $\times$ (\$2.42/Big Mac)/(9.90 yuan/Big Mac) = 2.02.

b. **i.** According to purchasing-power parity, the real exchange rate will eventually be 1.0. At any other real exchange rate, trade would theoretically go in only one direction.

ii. Recall $\varepsilon = e\,(P/P^*)$. Thus if $\varepsilon = 10$,

1.0 = e (\$2.42/Big Mac)/(9.90 yuan/Big Mac)

e = 9.90 yuan/\$2.42 = 4.09 yuan per dollar

7. a. In Germany net capital outflow would decrease, the German trade surplus would decrease, and the German foreign exchange rate would increase.

b. As German government spending increases, German saving would decrease, thereby decreasing net capital outflow and the German trade surplus even more, and increasing the German foreign exchange rate further.

8. a. In the long run, the tax increase will decrease disposable income by ΔT. Consumption will fall by $MPC\,(\Delta T)$. Private saving will fall by $(1 - MPC)\,\Delta T$. Public saving $T - G$ will rise by the increase in taxes plus the reduction in government spending. Thus, national saving will rise by the reduction in government spending plus MPC times the increase in taxes.

b. Graph for Problem 8b.

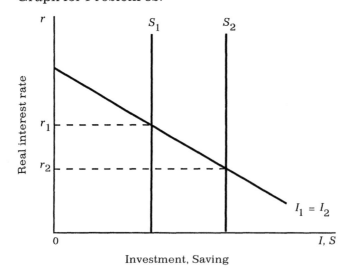

The increase in T and reduction in G would both shift the national saving curve to the right, from S_1 to S_2. In a closed economy $I = S$. Because the investment curve would not shift, the real interest rate would fall and the level of investment would rise.

c. Graph for Problem 8c.

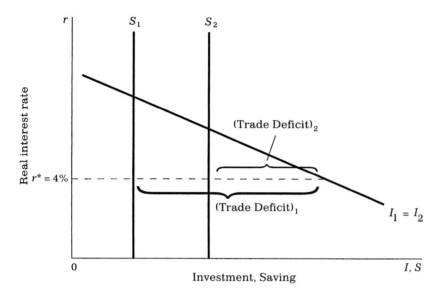

d. See graph for Part b.

In a small open economy, the real interest rate is unaffected by saving and investment decisions within the country. Although national saving will still increase, leading to the same shift in S to S_2, as in Part b, the real interest rate and the level of investment will remain constant. Consequently, $S - I$ will rise (or $I - S$ will fall) and the trade deficit will fall.

e. In the following graph, the $S - I$ curve shifts to the right following an increase in S. Consequently, the real exchange rate would fall, thereby increasing the quantity of net exports.

Graph for Problem 8e.

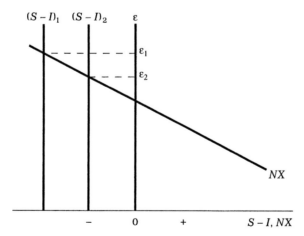

9. In a closed economy, saving and investment are equal. Consequently, investment will be low in a country with low saving and high in a country with high saving. In a small open economy, the levels of saving and investment are theoretically independent because a country can borrow unlimited amounts from abroad to finance any gaps between investment and saving at the world real interest rate. In a large open economy, a country can borrow more from abroad only if it raises its domestic real interest rate, which tends to reduce domestic investment. Consequently, low national saving will be associated with low investment.

11. **a.** Since both plans eliminate projected budget deficits that would occur in their absence, public saving $T - G$ will rise to zero in each plan.

$$\text{Private saving} = (Y - T) - C, \text{ where } C = f(Y - T).$$
$$\text{In the long run } Y = \overline{Y}.$$

In the Democratic plan, both Y and T are unaffected. Consequently, disposable income, consumption, and private saving are unaffected. In the Republican plan, taxes are cut, so disposable income is higher, and consumption rises by MPC times the increase in disposable income. As a result, private saving rises by MPS times the increase in disposable income.

In the Democratic plan, national saving will rise by the full amount of the deficit reduction. In the Republican plan, national saving will rise by this amount plus the increase in private saving.

b. If the United States were a closed economy, $I = S$ (see following graph). Consequently, both plans would shift the saving curve to the right, reduce the real interest rate r, and increase the amount of investment. Since S rises more in the Republican plan, r would fall by more, and the amount of investment would increase by more.

Graph for Problem 11b

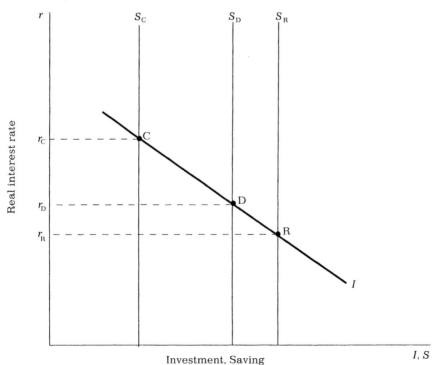

c. Graph for Problem 11c

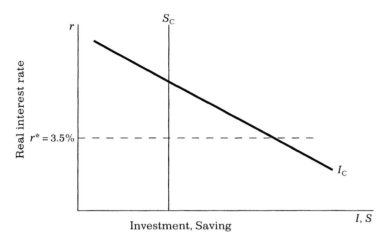

d. If the United States were a small open economy, the increase in national saving would have no effect on either the real interest rate r^* or the amount of investment. Since S rises by more under the Republican plan, both $S - I$ and NX would increase by more.

Graph for Problem 11d

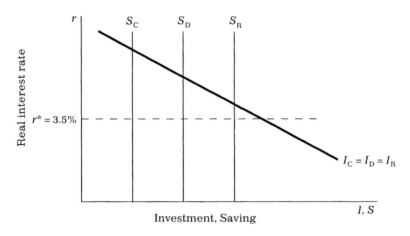

e. $S - I = NX$. In both plans $S - I$ and NX increase; consequently, both plans lead to a reduction in the real exchange rate. In the Republican plan $S - I$ and NX rise by more, so the real exchange rate falls by more.

Graph for Problem 11e

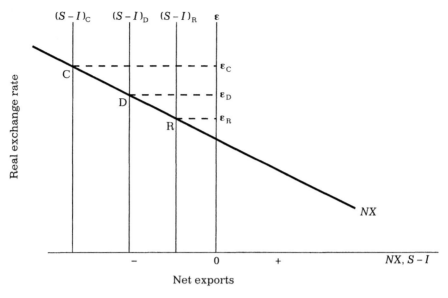

12. **a.** and **b.** The increased demand for Chilean wine will shift its *NX* curve to the right. Since neither *S*, *I*, nor (*S − I*) has changed, this would merely result in an increase in Chile's real exchange rate and no change in Chile's trade surplus.

Graph for Problem 12a and b

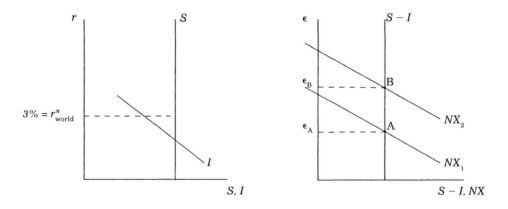

c. To keep Chile's real exchange rate unchanged the government could increase national saving by increasing taxes. The real interest rate would remain unchanged at the world real interest rate and Chilean investment would not change. Consequently, *NFI* = *S − I* would increase along with the trade surplus.

Graph for Problem 12c

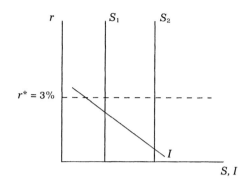

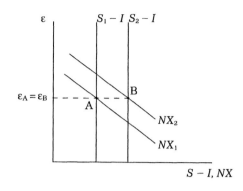

13. a. **i.** Because real GDP in the long run is a function solely of technology and factor inputs, it will be unaffected by the tax cuts.

ii. Public saving = $T - G$. Thus, public saving will fall by the reduction in taxes plus the increase in G.

iii. Private saving = $(Y - T) - C$.

Disposable income $Y - T$ will rise by the reduction in taxes.

Consumption will rise by MPC times the reduction in taxes.

Thus, private saving will rise by $(1 - MPC)$ times the reduction in taxes.

iv. National saving is the sum of public saving, which will fall by the reduction in taxes plus the increase in G, and private saving, which rises by $(1 - MPC)$ times the reduction in taxes. Thus, national saving falls by the increase in G plus MPC times the reduction in taxes.

b. In a small open economy, the real interest rate is fixed at the world real interest rate r^*. The tax cuts and increase in government spending will shift the S curve left and saving will fall. Neither the real interest rate nor investment (which depends on r) will be affected.

Graph for Problem 13b

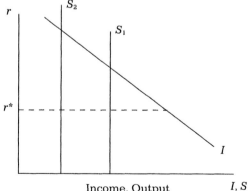

c. As S falls, $S - I$ also falls. Thus, the $S - I$ curve shifts left. This increases the real exchange rate and reduces net exports.
Graph for Problem 13c

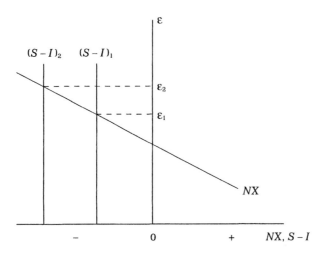

d. In the large open economy, a reduction in S raises the domestic real interest rate, which reduces both investment and net capital outflow. The reduction in CF increases the real exchange rate and reduces net exports.
Graph for Problem 13d

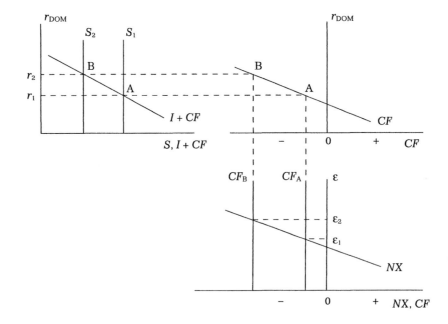

14. The initial equilibrium is represented by Points A in Panels A, B, and C below.
Graph for Problem 14

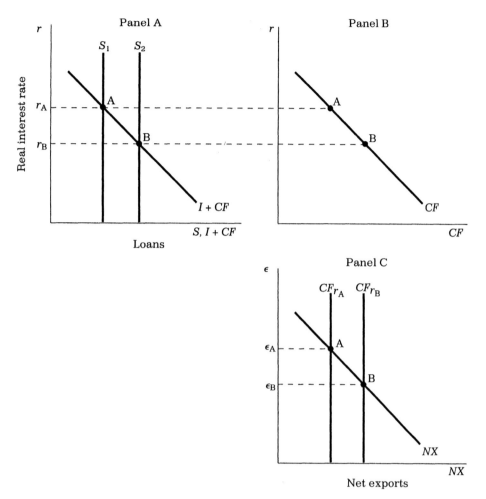

The increase in taxes and reductions in government spending would increase
national saving and shift the S curve right to S_2 in Panel A. The $I + CF$ curve
would not shift, so the domestic real interest rate would fall to Point B.
Consequently, the level of net capital outflow would rise in Panel B. Since net
capital outflow equals the trade surplus, the latter would also rise, implying a
decrease in the trade deficit. As NX rises, the real exchange rate will fall. As the
domestic real interest rate falls, investment will also rise.

16. The reduction in the perceived marginal product of capital will shift the
A Investment curve to the left. National saving and the *CF* curves are unaffected.
Consequently, the domestic real interest rate will fall to r_B. As r_{DOM} falls, the
amount of *CF* will increase to *B*. This increase will result in a reduction in the
real exchange rate and an increase in the amount of exports. Although the
reduction in the real interest rate would tend to increase investment, the *I* curve
originally shifted left. Investment will fall because $S = I + CF$, saving did not
change, and the net capital outflow has risen.
Graph for Problem 16

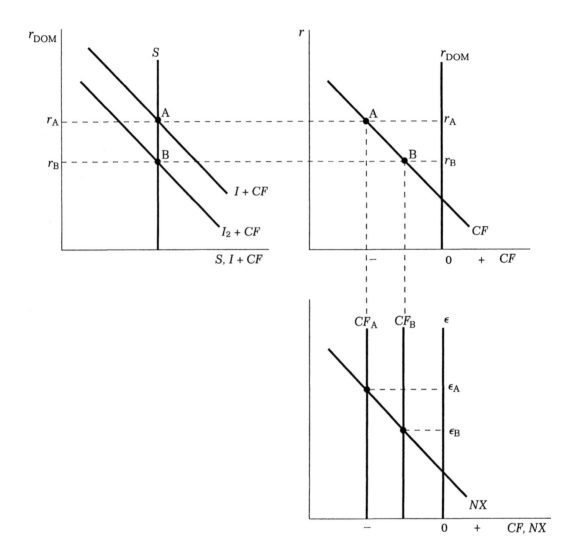

d.   **Graph 8-1**

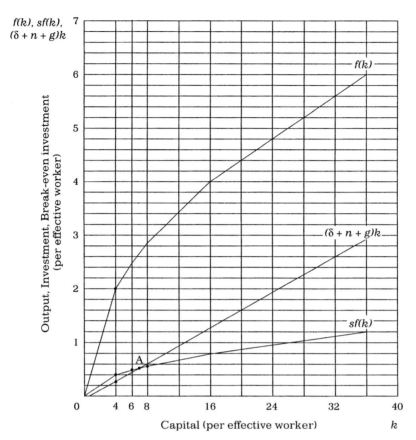

e.   0; $(\delta + n + g)k$; 6.25

f. g; technological change

g. n; g

h. $\delta + n + g$; δ; n; g

2.   a. Y/K

  b.   % Change in K; $\Delta Y/Y$; $\Delta K/K$

  c. sY/K; δ

  d.   A

  e. sA; δ

3.   a.   0.3; 0.7

  b.   % Change in Y – 0.3 × (% Change in K) – 0.7 × (% Change in L)

  c.   3.6; 1.2; 1.3; 1.1

Problems

1.   a. $y = f(k) = 10k^{1/4}$

  b. $k^* = 16$; $y = 20$; $c = 17.44$; saving per effective worker = $i = 2.56$; $\delta k^* = 1.6$

  c.   They all grow at $g = 2$ percent per year.

  d.   They all grow at $n + g = 6$ per year.

2. **a.** $sf(k) = (\delta + n + g)k$ In the steady state the amount of saving per effective worker equals the amount of capital per effective worker times the sum of the rates of depreciation, population growth and technological progress.

   b. consumption per effective worker in the steady state.

   c. $MPK = \delta + n + g$

3. **a.** $y = f(k) = 10k^{1/4}$

   b. $k^*_{gold} = 39.0625$; $s = 0.25$

   c. $y = 25$; saving per effective worker $= i = 6.25$; $c = 18.75$

4. In Chapter 3, $MPK = dY/dK$. In Chapter 8, $y = Y/EL = f(k)$, where $k = K/EL$. Thus, $Y = ELf(k)$. Using the chain rule, $dY/dK = ELdf(k)/dK = ELf'(k)(1/EL) = f'(k)$.

5. **a.** $y = f(k) = 10k^{1/4}$

   b. $MPK = f'(k) = 2.5\,(k)^{-3/4}$

   c. $f'(k^*_{gold}) = (\delta + n + g)(k^*_{gold})$; $k^*_{gold} = 39.0625$

6. **a.** $dk = [(EL)dK - k(EdL + LdE)]/E^2L^2$

   $= dK/EL - (K/EL)(dL/L) - (K/EL)(dE/E)$

   Since $dK/EL = i - \delta k$, $dL/L = n$, and $dE/E = g$,

   $dk = i - \delta k - nk - gk$

7. **a.** An increase in the saving rate will shift the $sf(k)$ curve up and increase the steady-state capital stock per effective worker.

   Graph for Problem 7a

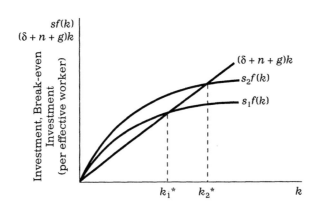

Graph 10-1

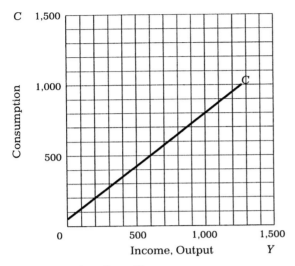

50; 0.75; −100; less than

c. **Graph 10-2**

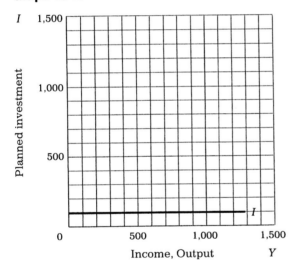

Graph 10-3

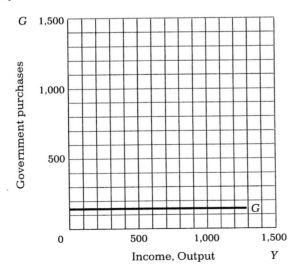

d. **Graph 10-4**

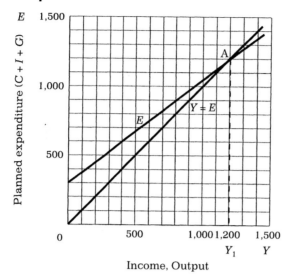

e. 50; 100; 150; 300; 0.75; 0; 0; 0.75

f. 300; 0.75

g. 1.0; 1,200

h. 1,500; 1,500; 100; lay off; decrease; fall; 1,200; 0

i. 1,050; 1,050; –50; hire more; increase; rise; 1,200; 0

2. a. 150; 151; 1

    b. 1

Graph 10-5

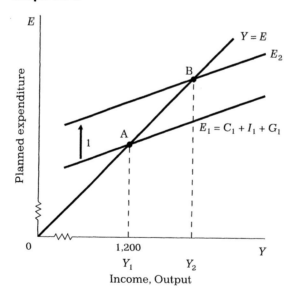

Graph 10-6

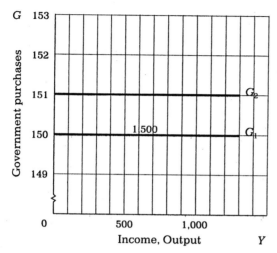

c.   301; 0.75

d.   301; 0.75; 1,204

e.   4

f. MPC^2; MPC^2; MPC^3; MPC^3; 0.75; 0.75; 4

3.   a.   0.75

b.   300.75; 0.75

c.   300.75; 0.75; 1,203

Graph 10-7

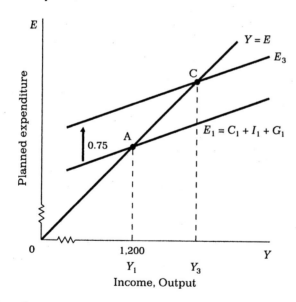

d.   3

e. MPC^2, MPC^2; MPC^3; MPC^3; 0.75; 0.75; 0.75; 3

f. $MPC/(1 - MPC)$

g.   upward; 1; downward; 0.75; upward; 0.25; rise, larger; 4; 3; decrease; 3; increase; 1

4. **a.** 10

Table 10-3

(1) Interest Rate (%)	(2) Planned Investment	(3) Equilibrium Level of Income
0	200	1,600
5	150	1,400
10	100	1,200
15	50	1,000
20	0	800

Graph 10-9

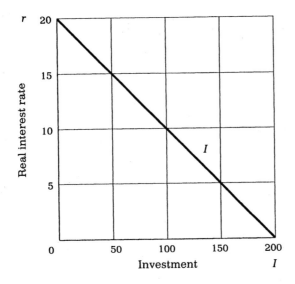

b. 400; 0.75; 10

c. 400; 0.75; 10; 1,600; 40

d. 100; 1,200

e. 50; 50

Graph 10-10

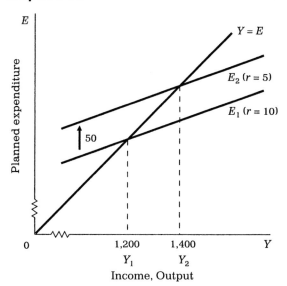

50; 50; 0.75; 50; 0.75; 200

f.   rises; upward

g.   **Graph 10-11**

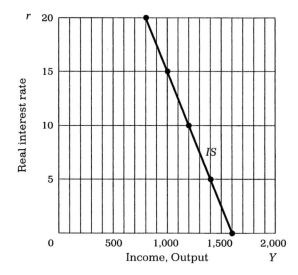

5. **a.**   100; 1,200; 0.75; 4; 1,204

    b.   **Graph 10-12**

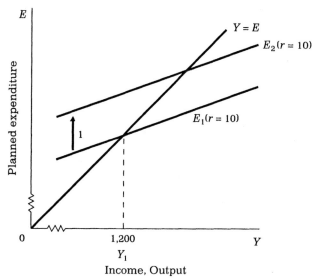

    c.   right; 4

    Graph 10-13

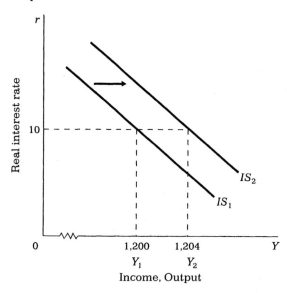

    d.   right; left; government-purchases multiplier
    e.   smaller; larger; larger; larger; larger
    f.   1; 0.75; 0.75; 3; 1,203

Graph 10-14

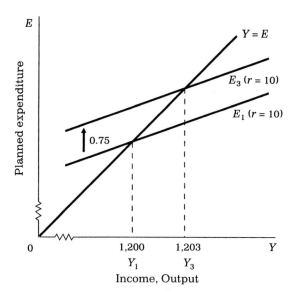

g. right; 3

Graph 10-15

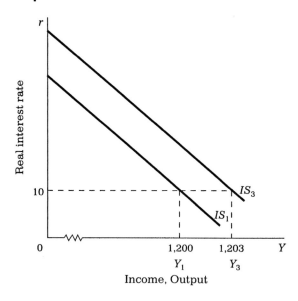

h. right; left; tax multiplier

i. larger; smaller; larger; larger; larger; larger; flatter

6. a. **Graph 10-16**

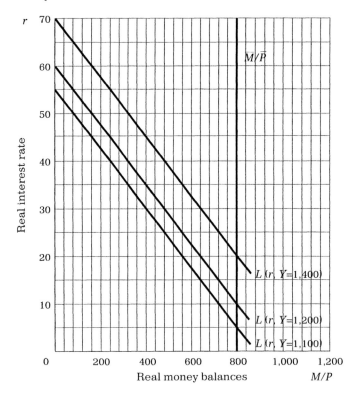

b. 0; 480; 720; 800; 880

c. 5

d. 0; 160; 560; 800; 880; right; rises; 10

e. 0; 320; 720; 960; 1,120; right; rises; 20

f. 800; 5; 10; 20

Graph 10-17

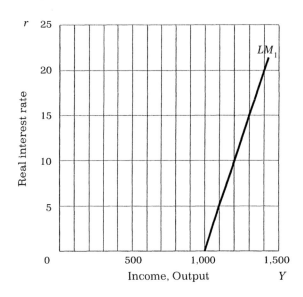

    g.   increase; rise

    h.   800; 800; −50; 0.05; −50; 0.05

7. **a.**   −50; 0.05

        Graph 10-18

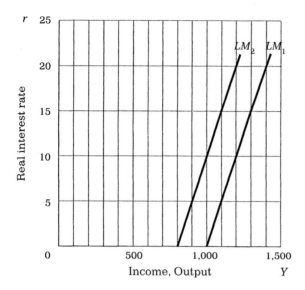

    b.   −40; 0.05; equal to; greater than; left (upward)

    c.   increase; decrease; left (upward); right (downward)

8. **a.**   40; −0.025

        Graph 10-19

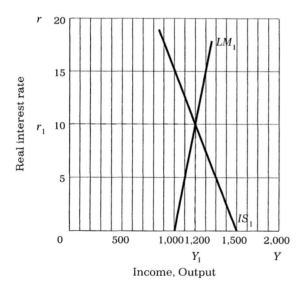

    b.   −50; 0.05

    c.   1,200; 10

Problems

1. **a.** 0.8

   b. Graph for Problem 1b

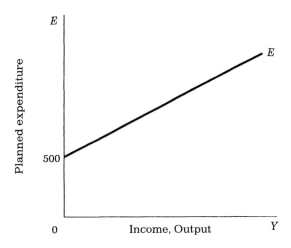

       slope $= 0.8$; y intercept $= 500$

   c. 2,500

   d. 100

2. **a.** 2,500

   b. **i.** The planned expenditure curve shifts upward by 10.

       ii. The equilibrium level of income increases by 50.

      iii. The level of consumption rises by 40.

      iv. The government budget deficit will rise by 10.

   c. **i.** The planned expenditure curve shifts downward by 8.

       ii. The equilibrium level of income decreases by 40.

      iii. The level of consumption decreases by 40.

      iv. The government budget deficit decreases by 10.

   d. **i.** The planned expenditure curve shifts upward by 2.

       ii. The equilibrium level of income increases by 10.

      iii. The level of consumption remains constant.

      iv. The government budget deficit remains unchanged.

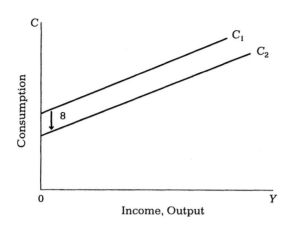

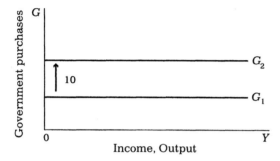

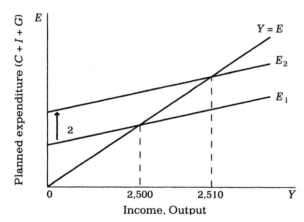

3. **a.** 0.6

    b. 100

    c. 1,500

    d. 2.5

    e. $50/2.5 = 20$

5. **a.** $Y = 1{,}250 - 10r$

    b. $Y = 980 + 8r$

    c. $r = 125 - (1/10)Y$ (*IS* curve equation)

    $r = -122.5 + (1/8)Y$ (*LM* curve equation)

Graphs for Problem 5c

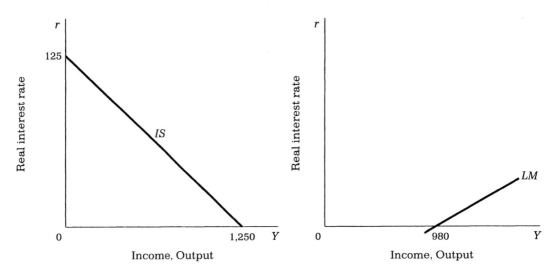

slope of *IS* curve = –1/10; slope of *LM* curve = 1/8

d. $r = 15$ (percent); $Y = 1,100$; $I = 40$; $C = 710$

e. –150

7. The money demand curve would shift to the right and the LM curve would shift to the left.

8. **a.** The *IS* curve becomes flatter.

   b. The *IS* curve becomes flatter.

9. **a.** The planned expenditure curve would shift up by the increase in government purchases plus *MPC* times the reduction in taxes. The equilibrium level of *GDP* would increase by the government purchases multiplier times the increase in *G* plus the tax multiplier times the reduction in *T* (or, by the shift in the planned expenditure curve times the government purchases multiplier).

   b. The *IS* curve would shift to the right by the government purchases multiplier times the increase in *G* plus the tax multiplier times the reduction in *T*. The *LM* curve would not shift.

CHAPTER 11

Fill-in Questions

1. Pigou effect
2. debt-deflation theory
3. monetary transmission mechanism
4. liquidity trap

Multiple-Choice Questions

1.	b	2.	a	3.	d	4.	c	5.	d	6.	d	7.	d
8.	a	9.	c	10.	b	11.	d	12.	a	13.	a	14.	d
15.	c	16.	b	17.	c	18.	d	19.	b	20.	b	21.	b
22.	d	23.	d	24.	a	25.	c							

Exercises

1. **a.** 1,200; 10
    b. upward; 100; right; 400
    Graph 11-1

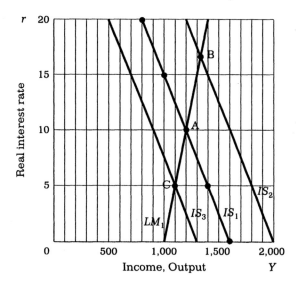

c. rises; increase; decrease; less

d. downward; 75; left; 300

e. falls; decrease; increase; less

f. downward (to the right); fall; rise; lower; increases; increases

Graph 11-2

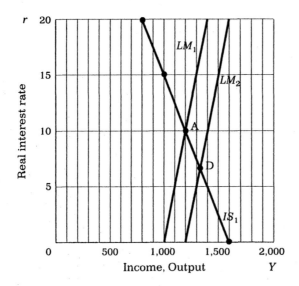

upward (to the left); rise; fall

g. *IS*; right; rise; rise; *IS*; left; fall; fall; right; *LM*; upward (to the left); fall; rise

2. **a.** downward (to the right)

Graph 11-3 and Graph 11-4

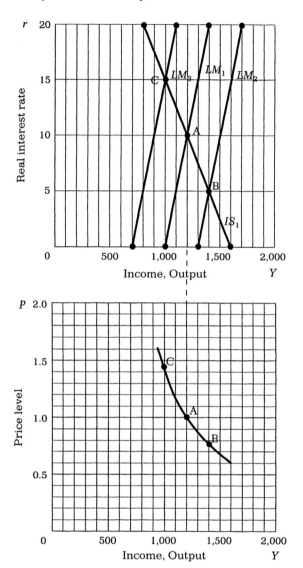

b. upward (to the left)

c. 1.0; 1,200

d. 0.77; 1,400

e. 1.43; 1,000

f. increase; *LM*; downward (to the right); decreases; increases; increases

3. a. 1.0; 1,000; 1,600; 1,300

Graph 11-5 and Graph 11-6

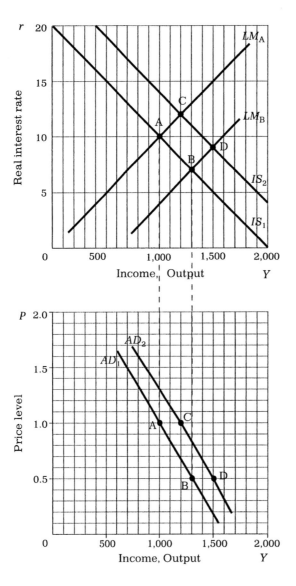

b. 4; right; 400

c. less

e. higher than; equal to; higher than; equal to

f. right; right; right; right

4. a. 1.0; 1,000

Graph 11-7

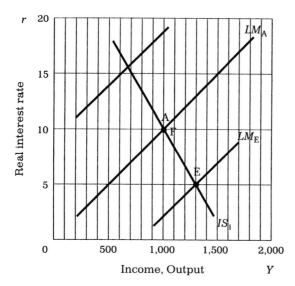

Graph 11-8

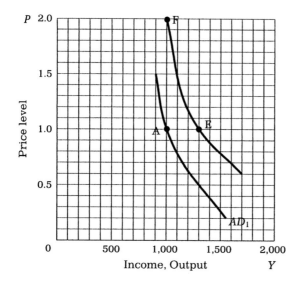

b. 1,600; downward (to the right)

c. higher than; equal to; right; left

d. 800; 1,000

5. a. **Graph 11-9**

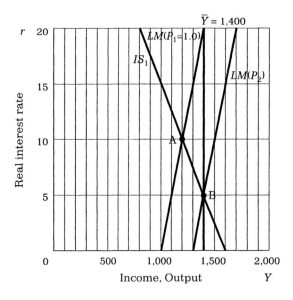

Graph 11-10

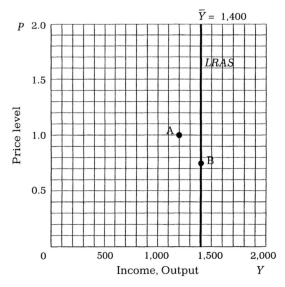

b. −50; 0.05

c. 1,200; 10

d. less; sticky; horizontal

e. flexible; fall; increase; downward (to the right)

f. 5; 1,040; 0.77

g. rise; *LM*; upward (to the left)

6. a. **Graph 11-11**

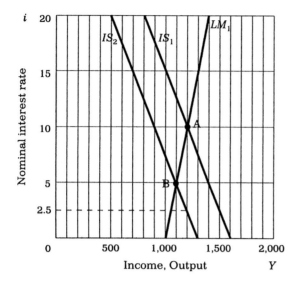

   b. 1,200; 10; 10
   c. 10; 17.5; higher; 10; 10; 10; −7.5; 2.5; 7.5; downward; 7.5
   d. 1,100; 5
   e. decrease; decrease; 10; 0; 10; 5; −7.5; 12.5; rises
7. a. 50; 50; 50; 0.75; 200
   b. 0.9; 10; larger
   c. 10; 500; larger
   d. 5; 200; 500; larger; larger; flatter
   e. 10
   f. 20; more

   Graph 11-12

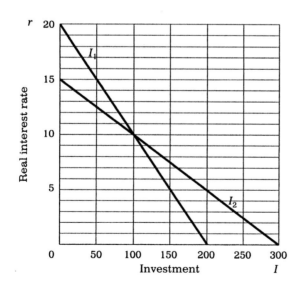

   flatter

    g.   100

    h.   10; 4; 200; 20; 100; 100; 400; flatter

8. **a.**   more; more; steeper

    b.   128; 128; 8; 160; 160; 10; more; steeper

    c.   16; 32; more; flatter

    d.   128; 128; 8; 128; 4; less; steeper

9. **a.**   **Graph 11-13 and Graph 11-14**

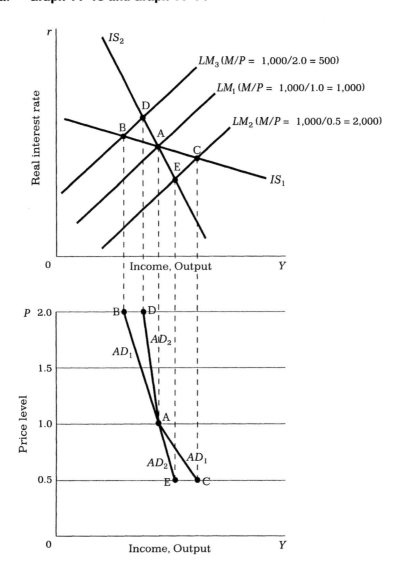

steeper

    b.   flat; flat; be very; large; large

c. being very

d. downward (to the right)

Graph 11-15

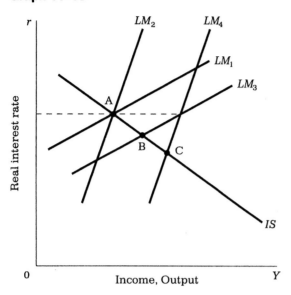

not very; not very

Problems

1. a. $Y = 1,250 - 10r$

   b. $Y = 980 + 8r$

   c. $r = 125 - (1/10)Y$ (*IS* curve equation)

      $r = -122.5 + (1/8)Y$ (*LM* curve equation)

      Graphs for Problem 1c

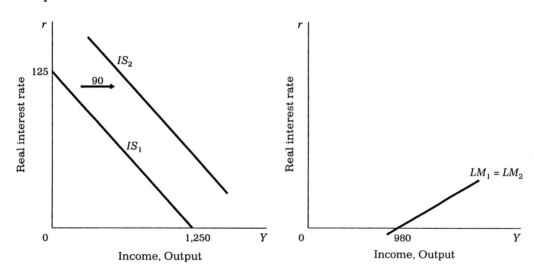

      slope of *IS* curve = $-1/10$; slope of *LM* curve = $1/8$

   d. $r = 15$ (percent); $Y = 1,100$; $I = 40$; $C = 710$

   e. -150

   f. The *LM* equation remains unchanged. The new *IS* equation is $Y = 1,340 - 10r$.

   g. The shift in the *IS* curve is equal to 90. The *LM* curve does not shift.

   h. $Y = 1,140$; $r = 20$; $I = 20$; $C = 734$

    i.   54

    j.   Government purchases are higher in Part h. Since taxes and output are the same as Parts h and i, consumption is also the same. Since the interest rate is lower in Part i, investment is higher. Advocates of expansionary fiscal policy may argue that the United States is badly in need of public spending in areas like education, defense, and infrastructure. Advocates of expansionary monetary policy, on the other hand, would tout its effect on investment, which might spur economic growth as the capital stock grows.

2. **a.**   The IS curve would shift left to IS_2. Both Y and r would fall.

    Graph for Problem 2a

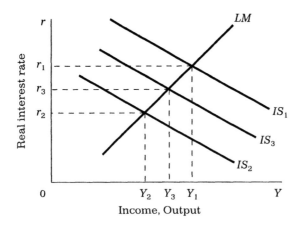

    b.   Since part of transfers are saved, the reduction in G would dominate. The IS curve would shift left (to IS_3) by a smaller amount than in Part a. Both Y and r would fall.

    c.   The reductions in Y and r would be smaller in Part b than in Part a.

    d.   If the money supply does not change, the results would be almost identical to those in Part a. The reductions in Y and r may not be as great if these countries spent some of their grants to increase their imports from the United States.

3. **a.**   By reducing household wealth, the stock market decline would shift both the consumption and total planned expenditure curves downward.

    b.   Consequently, the IS curve would shift to the left, and both Y and r would fall.

    Graph for Problem 3b

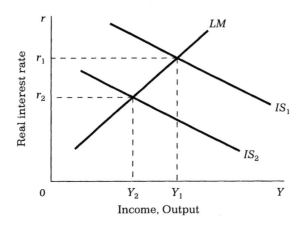

5. a. When the *MPC* is large, *ceteris paribus*, the slope of the planned expenditure curve will be large, and the multiplier will be large, resulting in a flatter *IS* curve in Country A. Intuitively, as r falls, investment rises and GNP increases via the direct effect on investment and multiplier effects on consumption. The latter will be larger when *MPC* is bigger, since people will then consume a greater fraction of the increase in disposable income in each successive round. The shape of the *LM* curve is unaffected by the *MPC*. Graph for Problem 5a

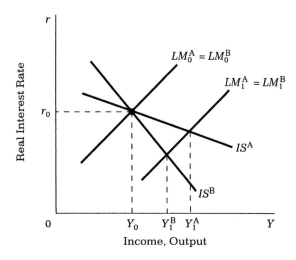

b. Monetary policy will be more effective in changing Y in Country A, where the *IS* curve is flatter.

6. a. The *LM* curve would remain stationary. The economy would move along a stationary *LM* curve in response to shifts in the *IS* curve. GDP would rise when private spending increases and would fall when private spending decreases. Graph for Problem 6a

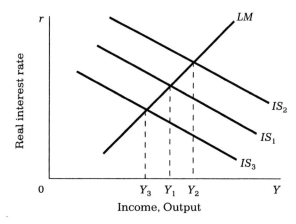

b. As Y increases in response to a shift in the IS curve to the right, the money demand curve would shift to the right. To keep the interest rate constant, the money supply would have to rise, shifting the LM curve downward (to the right).

Graphs for Problem 6b

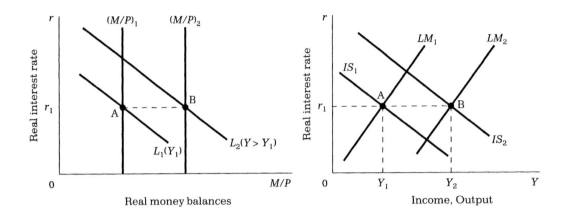

c. As Y decreases in response to a shift in the IS curve to the left, the money demand curve would shift to the left. To keep the interest rate constant, the money supply would have to fall, shifting the LM curve upward (to the left).

d. In Parts b and c, the Federal Reserve's policy exacerbates the fluctuations in Y following shifts in the IS curve. Consequently, a stable money supply would better stabilize the economy if the disturbances stem primarily from shifts in the IS curve.

7. **a.** A decrease in taxes shifts the *IS* and *AD* curves to the right. The *SRAS* and *LM* curves do not shift in the short run.

Graphs for Problem 7a

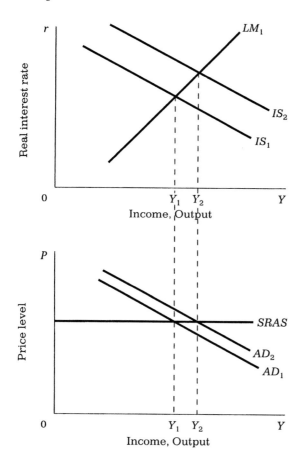

The equilibrium levels of Y, r, and C all rise. The equilibrium level of I falls, and G and P do not change in the short run (given the horizontal *SRAS* curve of Chapter 9).

b. The Federal Reserve increased the money supply at the same time as taxes fell. Consequently, both the *IS* and *LM* curves shifted to the right. This shifted the *AD* curve even farther to the right.

Graphs for Problem 7b

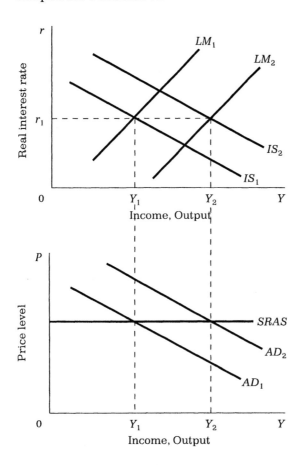

The levels of Y and C rise by more in Part b than in Part a. The remaining variables, r, I, G, and P remain constant.

8. The Federal Reserve should increase the money supply (which would shift the LM curve down, or to the right), and the government should simultaneously reduce G and/or increase T (which would shift the IS curve left). Real GDP could remain unchanged, but the reduction in the real interest rate would increase investment.

9. **a.** If consumption rises as the interest rate falls, the IS curve would be flatter because now both consumption and investment would increase when r falls. The LM curve is unaffected.

   b. A flat IS curve will enhance the short-run effectiveness of monetary policy.

   c. A flat IS curve will flatten the slope of the AD curve.

10. a. Graphs for Problem 10a

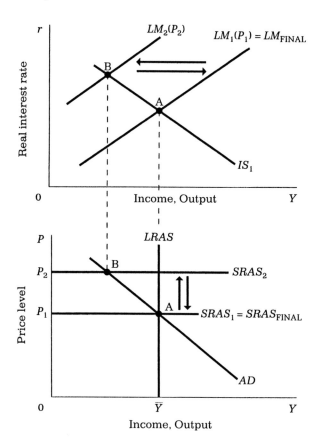

b. In the short run, the *SRAS* curve shifts upward. This increases *P* and thereby shifts the *LM* curve upward (to the left). Since output falls below its natural rate, the *SRAS* curve will shift downward in subsequent periods. As it does, *P* will fall and the *LM* curve will shift back downward (to the right) until it reaches its initial position, at which point *Y* and *P* will also reach their initial levels. (This assumes that the natural rate of output is unaffected.)

11. At the initial equilibrium the nominal interest rate is almost zero. If the announced monetary expansion increases expected inflation, the real interest rate would fall by the full amount of the increase in expected inflation at each level of the nominal interest rate. Consequently, the *IS* curve would shift upward by the increase in expected inflation. As the Japanese central bank increases the nominal money supply, the *LM* curve will also shift right. The equilibrium levels of *i* and *Y* would rise and the equilibrium level of *r* would fall.

Graph for Problem 11

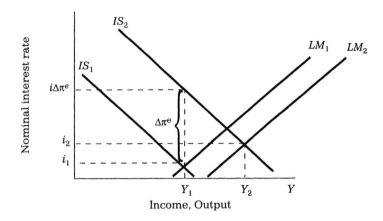

12. The sharp increase in stock prices during the 1990s increased household wealth and thereby increased consumption, shifting the *IS* curve to the right. The optimistic perceptions of the profitability of new technologies increased investment, shifting the *IS* curve further to the right. As a result, *Y* would increase substantially, as it did during the 1990s.
Graph for Problem 12.

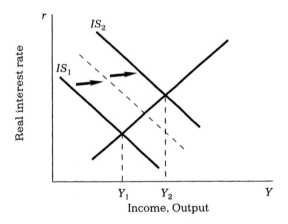

CHAPTER 12

Fill-in Questions

1. floating exchange rates
2. fixed exchange rates
3. fixed exchange rates; floating exchange rates
4. devaluation; revaluation
5. Mundell-Fleming model; devaluation; revaluation
6. fixed exchange rates

Multiple-Choice Questions

1.	c	2.	d	3.	c	4.	c	5.	a	6.	b	7.	a
8.	b	9.	d	10.	c	11.	b	12.	d	13.	d	14.	a
15.	b	16.	c	17.	d	18.	c	19.	b	20.	d	21.	b
22.	d												

Exercises

1. **b.** 2; 50; 400; 0.75; 10
   c. 40; 0.025
   Graph 12-1

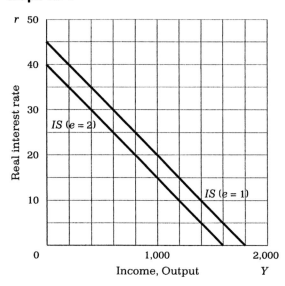

   d. depreciation; rise; 1; 100; 45; 0.025
   e. depreciation; increase; upward; right; 50; upward; 50; right; 50; 4; 200; appreciation; decrease; downward; left

2. **a.** 50; 1,200
   Graph 12-2

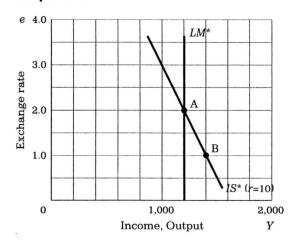

   b. 1,400; rise; upward; increases
   d. 2; 1,200; A

3. a. 2; 1,200

Graph 12-3

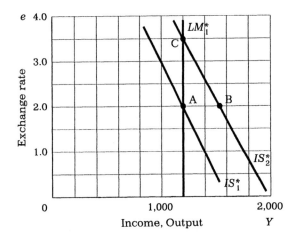

b. increasing; decreasing; increase; right

c. greater than; decreases; increase; rises; decrease; increase; rises above; increases

d. has no effect on; increases; fall; has no effect on; decreases

e. right (downward); rise; right

Graph 12-4

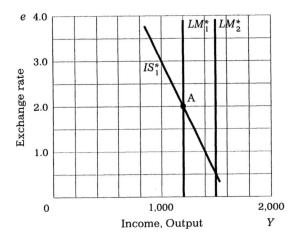

increases; decreases; rise

f. increase; the interest rate; out of; depreciate; increases

4. a. 2

Graph 12-5

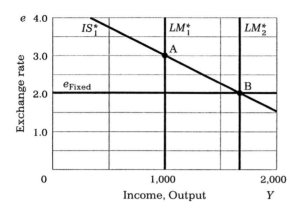

b. greater than; 3; 3; 3; 1.50

c. increases; right; increase; right

d. less than; 1; 1; 2

Graph 12-6

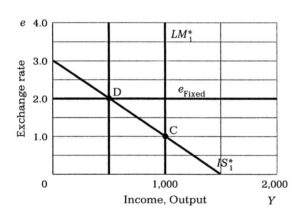

e. decreases; left; decrease; left

5. a. **Graph 12-7**

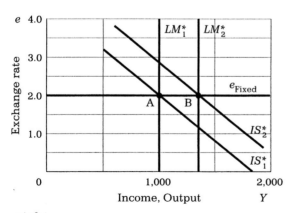

right

b. have no effect on; increase; increase; right; 2; increase; have no effect on

c. right

Graph 12-8

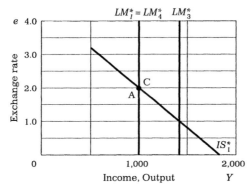

increase; decrease; falls below; selling; buying; decrease; left; 2; have no effect on; have no effect on; equal to; remain constant

d. buying; selling; increase; right; increase; left; decrease

6. a. higher

b. rises; decrease; left

c. decrease; right

d. depreciation; increase

e. increases; LM*; left; decrease; LM*; left; LM* left

Graph 12-9

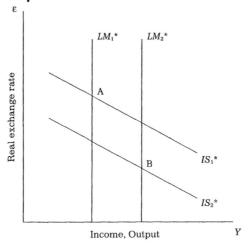

7. a. less than; remain constant

b. downward; fall; rise

Graph 12-10

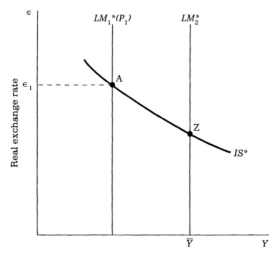

Graph 12-11

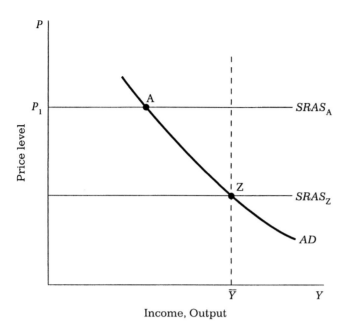

Income, Output

c.   increase; supply; LM^*; right; fall; rise; rises; rise; remains the same; remains the same

8. a.   increases; increases
    b.   rises; rises; increase; increase; depreciation
    c.   increase; increase; more; flatter

Graph 12-12

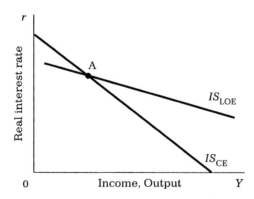

d.   more; less

Problems

1. As the money supply begins to contract, the domestic interest rate will begin to rise above the world interest rate. Capital flows into the domestic economy as both foreigners and domestic investors wish to buy additional U.S. bonds and assets. This will push the foreign exchange rate above the initial fixed exchange rate. Arbitragers will then sell foreign currency to (and buy domestic currency

from) the central bank. As a result, the domestic money supply will rise until the foreign exchange rate and the domestic interest rate fall back to their initial levels, at which point the money supply and real income will be equal to their initial levels.

2. The main advantage to leaving the EMS was that Britain regained control over the use of monetary policy for stabilization purposes. Specifically, Britain wanted to pursue policies to end a severe recession. The main disadvantage was increased uncertainty regarding future exchange-rate movements among European Economic Community (EEC) members, which may impede trade. Other critics believe that Britain's departure removed a mechanism that provided useful discipline to British monetary authorities.

3. **a.** Participating countries would lose the limited ability they currently have to conduct independent monetary policies, but much of this has already been lost. Future monetary stabilization policies would have to be coordinated. The effects of fiscal policies would increase slightly.

   b. Nonparticipating countries currently have considerable ability to conduct countercyclical monetary policies, but these policies would have to be coordinated in the future. Fiscal policies would become more powerful because under their current floating exchange rates, fiscal policy does not affect output.

4. During a recession, actual output is presumably less than the natural rate of output. Consequently, over time the domestic price level will fall. This will increase the real money supply and shift the *LM** curve to the right. As a result, the real exchange rate will fall, and the trade balance will rise along with national income.

5. The export restrictions will shift the *NX* curve to the left. Consequently, the *IS** curve will shift to the left.

   a. If the country has a flexible exchange rate, the *LM** curve is vertical. Consequently, the exchange rate will fall, but real GDP will remain unchanged.
   Graph for Problem 5a

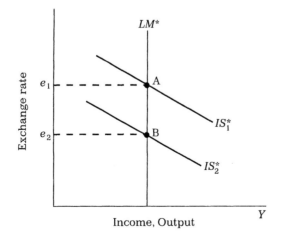

b. If the country has a fixed exchange rate, the LM^* curve will also shift to the left to keep the exchange rate constant. Consequently, real GDP will fall. Graph for Problem 5b

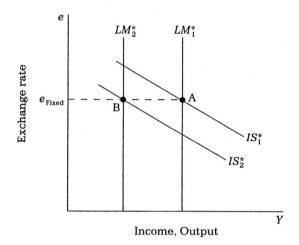

6. A crisis in confidence will raise a country's risk premium. Consequently, the domestic interest rate will rise. This will shift the IS^* curve to the left and the LM^* curve to the right. If, however, the country has a fixed exchange rate, it will be compelled to sell foreign currency and shift its LM^* curve to the left of its original position. This will reduce real GDP.
Graph for Problem 6

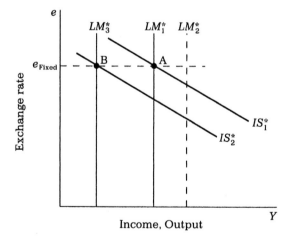

7. Renewed stability would reduce these countries' risk premiums. Consequently, their domestic interest rates would fall. This would shift the IS^* curve to the right and the LM^* curve to the left. Under a regime of flexible exchange rates, the countries' exchange rates would rise while real GDP would fall. (In reality, other developments have helped these countries increase their real GDP.)

Graph for Problem 7

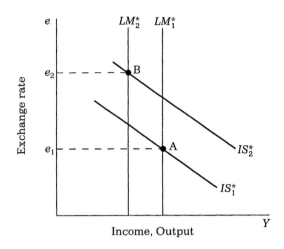

8. **a.** The shift in Argentina's net export curve would also shift its *IS** curve to the left. If Argentina kept the initial dollar-peso exchange rate of 1:1, it would have to buy up pesos, thereby shifting its *LM** curve to the left. Consequently, its real GDP would fall. Since Argentina is being treated as a small open economy, its interest rate would remain at the world interest rate:

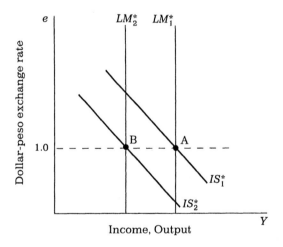

b. Once again, the shift in the net export curve would shift the *IS** curve to the left. If Argentina abandoned its fixed dollar-peso exchange rate, however, it would have fallen (i.e., the peso would have depreciated) to point B and there would have been no effect on real GDP:

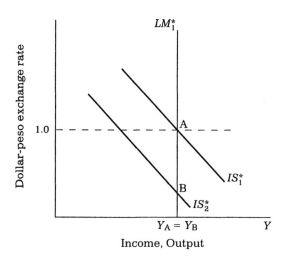

9. The reduction in consumer confidence will shift the *IS* curve to the left.
Consequently, the domestic real interest rate will fall. As a result, net capital
outflow will increase along with net exports. The foreign exchange rate will
decline and net exports will rise, cushioning the decline in GDP.

Graphs for Problem 9

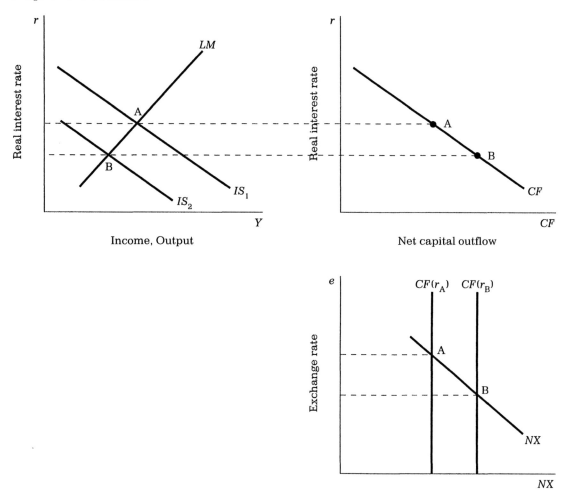

10. a. The net capital outflow curve will shift right as foreigners wish to buy fewer U.S. assets and lend less to U.S. borrowers at any given interest rate.
Graphs for Problem 10

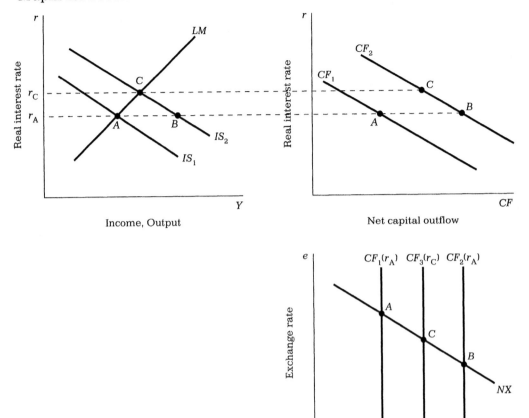

b. At the original real interest rate, the U.S. trade balance will increase (to Point B in the graph) and the foreign exchange rate will fall.

c. Since the decline in the exchange rate (and increase in net exports) occurred at the original interest rate, the *IS* curve will shift right to Point B. The *LM* curve will not shift.

d. The domestic real interest rate rises to Point C.

e. As the real interest rate rises, we move along CF_2 to Point C. Comparing Points A and C, the levels of net capital outflow and net exports have increased.

f. U.S. national income and output have risen (although other factors may affect them adversely).

11. To keep the real exchange rate constant, *CF* must not change, which will occur only if the real interest rate does not change. To increase *Y* without changing *r*, the Fed must increase the money supply while the government simultaneously pursues expansionary fiscal policy by increasing *G* or cutting *T*. This will shift both the *IS* and *LM* curves to the right.

Graphs for Problem 11

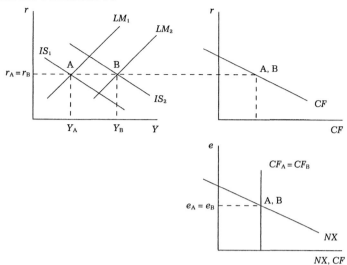

CHAPTER 13

Fill-in Questions

1. sticky-wage model
2. imperfect-information model
3. sticky-price model
4. Phillips curve
5. NAIRU
6. demand-pull inflation
7. cost-push inflation
8. adaptive expectations
9. rational expectations
10. sacrifice ratio; rational expectations; adaptive expectations
11. natural-rate hypothesis
12. Hysteresis

Multiple-Choice Questions

1. c	2. b	3. b	4. c	5. a	6. c	7. c
8. b	9. d	10. d	11. a	12. a	13. c	14. d
15. a						

Exercises

1. **a.** equal to; greater than

   b. Graph 13-1

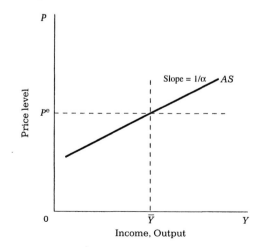

slope = $1/\alpha$

    c. upward (to the left); downward (to the right); increase

2. **a.** 4; 56; 5; 60; marginal product of labor

    b. equal to

    c. 16

Graph 13-2

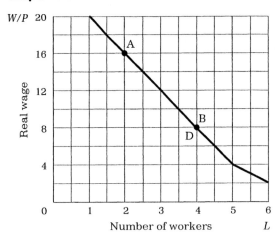

Graph 13-3

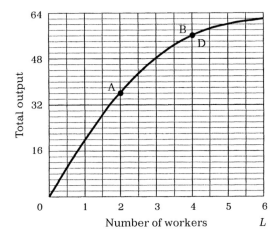

d. 16; 36

Graph 13-4

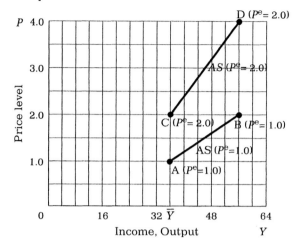

e. 16; 16; falls; 16; 8; rise; 4; rise; 56

f. fall below; increase; above

g. 32; 2; 2

h. 32; 32; 8; 4; 56

i. increase; upward; decrease; downward

3. b. $1; 1; 1; 100

Graph 13-5

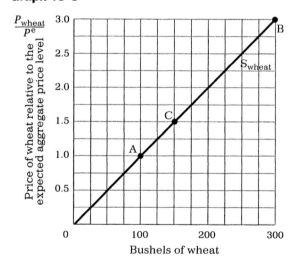

c. $3; 1; 3; rise; 300

d. $1; 1; 1; 100

e.   200; 200; 100; 2; 2; 1.5; 150

Graph 13-6

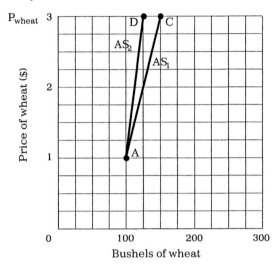

f.   1; greater; less

g.   200; 200; 140; 2.4; 2.4; 1.25; 125; steeper; steep; 1; 100; vertical

4. b.   rise; raise; increase; increase

c.   0; equal to; greater than; decreases; increases; decreases; decreases; flatter; horizontal; 1; all

5. a.   increase; *LM*; downward (to the right); increases; rises above; flexible; equal to

b.   equal to; 1

c.   increase; decrease; increase; 1; 1,400; 1.4

d.   greater than; increase

e.   1.4; 1.4; upward; 1.4

Graph 13-7

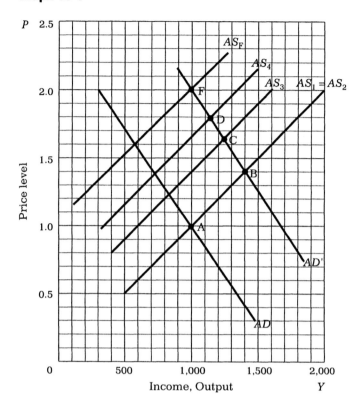

f.   approximately 1,220; approximately 1.65; fallen; risen
g.   greater than; increase; 1.65; 1.65; upward; 1.65
h.   greater than; increase; upward; greater than; 1,000; 2; 2
i.   no change; an increase
j.   more; more

6. a.   positive; less
    b.   10; 0.4;

Graph 13-8

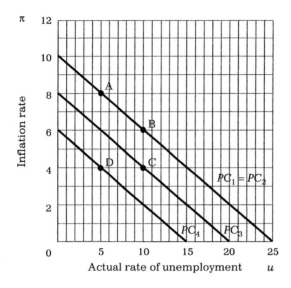

equal to

c. decreasing; increasing; decreasing; 8; right

d. 10; 6

e. less than; fall; downward

f. 6; 6; 6; 8; 0.4

g. 10; 4

h. less than; fall; downward; 4; 4; 4; 6; 0.4

i. 5; 4; equal to; stay the same; remain stationary

j. 4; 5; 5; 10; 4; 4; 2.5; 5; sacrifice

k. more; more; lower

l. 5; 8; 15; 4; 4; 4; 6; 0.4;

Graph 13-9

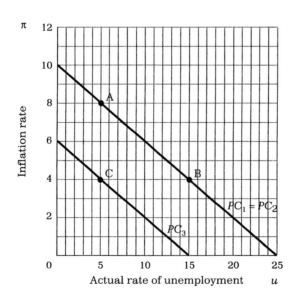

5; 4; equal to; 10; 4; equal to

m. shift upward

Problems

1. a. $L = 100/(W/P)^2$

b. $Y = 200/(W/P)$

c. $Y = \overline{Y} = 50$

d. $Y = 50P$

e. $P = Y/50$

Graph for Problem 1e

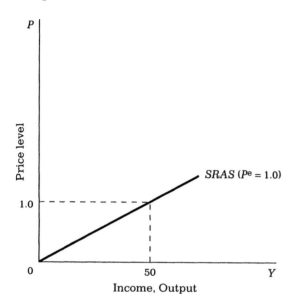

3. If real GDP falls (or unemployment rises) along with an increase in inflation, this probably represents a supply shock or an upward shift of the Phillips curve. Since the economy began at the natural rate of output, there is no reason for expected inflation or the expected price level to rise suddenly. Consequently, we could characterize the inflation as cost-push. If real GDP rises (or unemployment falls) along with the increase in inflation, this probably results from a shift in aggregate demand or a movement along a Phillips curve. Consequently, we could characterize the inflation as demand-pull.

4. a. If the variation in output is due primarily to shifts in the aggregate demand curve, then the aggregate supply curve is relatively stationary. According to the sticky-wage model, nominal wages are sticky and firms will hire more workers and increase output as higher prices reduce real wages. This is contrary to the empirical evidence.

b. If the variation in output is due primarily to aggregate supply shocks, the aggregate supply curve is shifting. In the case of an oil price shock, the increase in oil prices will shift the aggregate supply curve upward, raise the price level, and reduce real GDP. If nominal wages are sticky, real wages will fall along with output, resulting in a procyclical movement of real wages.

5. **a.** Workers would probably choose to index wages to the consumer price index because this would keep the purchasing power of their wages constant.

   b. Firms would probably choose to index wages to the price of the product they produce because this would stabilize the real cost of their labor input relative to their output. More generally, they would choose the producer price index or the GDP deflator.

7. **a.** In December 2001, the actual unemployment rate in the United States was 5.8 percent, the actual rate of inflation was about 1.5 percent, and the expected rate of inflation according to many surveys was about 2.5 percent. Most economists believe that the natural rate of unemployment lies between 4.5 and 6 percent. Suppose the natural rate of unemployment is equal to 5.5 percent:

   Graph for Problem 7a

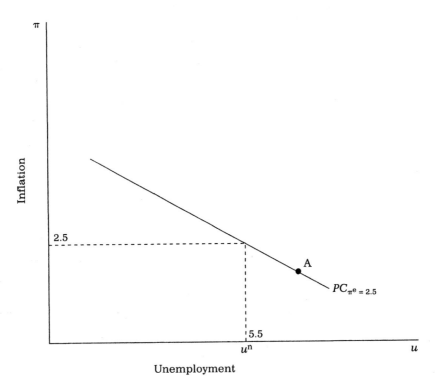

   b. Since the actual unemployment rate is greater than the natural rate of unemployment, over time inflationary expectations will fall. This will shift the Phillips curve down and unemployment will move toward the natural rate.

8. According to the hysteresis theory, the natural rate of unemployment may rise during a recession, leading to a reduction in the natural rate of output. This would shift the long-run aggregate supply curve to the left.

CHAPTER 14

Fill-in Questions

1. inside lag
2. outside lag
3. inside lag; outside lag
4. Automatic stabilizers
5. index of leading indicators
6. Lucas critique
7. political business cycle
8. time inconsistency
9. Monetarists
10. Automatic stabilizers

Multiple-Choice Questions

| 1. b | 2. d | 3. c | 4. b | 5. b | 6. c | 7. d |
| 8. c | 9. d | 10. a | 11. c | 12. d | 13. b | 14. c |

Exercises

1. **a.**   less than; less than
    b.   fall; downward; equal to

Graph 14-1

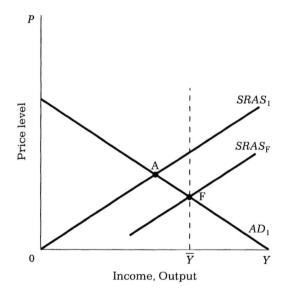

rise; fall

c. increase; increase; decrease; right

Graph 14-2

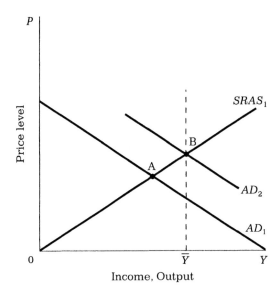

rise; rise

d. greater than; shorter
e. more; more; less
f. inside; outside

2. a. 6; 0.2; below
   b. 0; 5; 0; 5; −5; 0; 7; 6
   c. 0; 5; 0; 5
   d. 5; 5; 6; equal to
   e. quickly

3. a. 0; 3; 0; 3
   b. 3; 3; increased; 4; decreased; 2
   c. decrease; increase

Problems

1. a. If the unemployment rate were 6.1 percent (which is close to our estimate of the natural rate), it is probably better not to change either fiscal or monetary policy. The economy will soon correct itself, and the considerable lags in policy mean that they might take effect after the economy reaches the natural rate of unemployment, which will cause further fluctuations in output and unemployment.

   b. If the unemployment rate were 10.1 percent, it is probably better to pursue expansionary monetary and/or fiscal policy. In the absence of any policy changes, the unemployment rate would eventually return to its natural rate, but it might take a long time. Although economic forecasts are unreliable and policy lags exist, it is probable that the economy will still be far from its natural rate when the policies do take effect.

2. The acceptance of rational expectations may reduce the need for policy activism because it tends to shorten the amount of time it takes for the economy to return to the natural rate of output. If wages and/or prices are sticky, however, the economy will not immediately move back to the natural rate of output, and policy activism may be desirable.

3. **a.** Democratic administrations must be pursuing more expansionary monetary and/or fiscal policies during their first or second years. These policies will shift the aggregate demand curve to the right.

   b. If people have rational expectations and the imperfect information model of the economy is correct, wages and prices are flexible, and output would be affected by changes in fiscal policy and by unexpected changes in monetary policy. If Democrats persistently pursued more expansionary monetary policies, workers and firms would soon expect this behavior and it would not affect GDP. Consequently, the observed patterns could occur in the long run only if there were systematic differences in fiscal policy.

4. According to the Phillips curve, in the long run the economy will be at its natural rate regardless of the rate of inflation. Therefore, while more independent central banks may choose lower inflation rates, they will have no effect on the long-run level of unemployment.

5. **a.** According to the best measures of GDP available in each time period.

   b. According to the measure of GDP that is available for both time periods.

   c. It is generally acknowledged that macroeconomic stabilization measures have become more widely used since World War II. If the economy has also become more stable, this would support the continued use of these policies. If the economy has not become more stable, the effectiveness of these policies would be questionable.

7. **a.** 2%

   b. 1%

8. **a.** −0.25%

   b. 4.5%

   c. The Fed was worried the recession would worsen.

9. **a.** Optimal $\pi = 0$.

   b. In the long run, unemployment will be at its natural rate since $\pi = \pi^e$.

CHAPTER 15

Fill-in Questions

1. government debt
2. government debt
3. capital budgeting
4. cyclically adjusted budget deficit
5. Generational accounts
6. traditional view of government debt
7. Ricardian equivalence

Multiple-Choice Questions

1. c	**2.** d	**3.** a	**4.** a	**5.** c	**6.** b	**7.** a
8. d	**9.** b	**10.** c	**11.** d	**12.** c	**13.** b	**14.** d
15. a	**16.** a	**17.** b	**18.** d	**19.** d	**20.** b	**21.** c

Exercises

1. **a.** 60; 0.13; 260
    b. 0; 200; 0.13; 260; 200
    c. 0; 2,000; 2,000; 200; 2,200
    d. 1; 1.1; 2,000; 1; 2,000; 2,200; 1.1; 2,000; equal to; 0; overstate
    e. 0.03; 3; 0.03; 60; 60; 200; 60; 260; 0
2. **a.** IS; right; increase; increase; increase; fall; investsment
    b. remain constant; appreciation, remain constant; increase; net exports; increase; increase; increase
    c. an increase; an increase; flatter; smaller
    d. decrease; increase
    e. decrease; decrease; fall
3. **a.** increasing
    b. 1,100; 1,100; 1,100; equally well off; have no effect; remain constant
    c. have no effect on; remain constant
4. **a.** decrease; decrease; increase; left
    b. deficits; surpluses
    c. would not; would not

Problems

1. According to the traditional view, households' current and expected future disposable incomes would fall and current consumption would fall. According to the Ricardian view, the current tax increase would be offset by an expected future reduction in taxes, resulting in no change in consumption.
2. **a.** Current consumption would remain unchanged because people would expect future taxes to rise.
    b. Current private saving would rise by $100 billion because current disposable income rises by $100 billion and consumption remains unchanged.

c.   Current national saving remains unchanged. Private saving rises by $100 billion, but public saving falls by the $100 billion tax cut.

3. For the prospective emigrant, a tax reduction in the current year represents an increase in income because the expected future tax increase will not have to be paid by either the emigrant or her descendants. Thus, the current consumption of the prospective emigrant will increase. In the whole economy, however, a tax reduction represents no change in the sum of current and expected future income, and current aggregate consumption is unaffected.

6. a.   According to the simple Keynesian consumption function, current consumption is a function of current disposable income. Therefore, consumption will begin to be affected by the tax cut only when it takes effect, four years from now. Yet the plan still provides for an eventual reduction in the deficit.

   b.   According to the forward-looking view of consumption (which will be called the permanent-income hypothesis or the life-cycle hypothesis in the next chapter), current consumption depends on the sum of current and expected future income. Since the future tax increase will decrease future income, it will also decrease *current* consumption, along with the eventual budget deficit.

   c.   According to the theory of Ricardian equivalence, the future tax increase will affect the official deficit when it takes effect, but it will not affect consumption. According to the government budget constraint, people will merely expect a tax decrease sometime in the future (after four years), and they will dissave in order to maintain their levels of consumption.

   d.   If people have liquidity constraints, the future tax increase will still reduce consumption when it takes effect even if Ricardian equivalence is valid. The tax increase will reduce disposable income when it becomes effective. Although people may wish to dissave and maintain consumption, they may not be able to do so if they do not have the resources (liquidity) and cannot borrow.

7. If Brazil does not default on its debt, the U.S. guarantee will probably have no effect on the U.S. budget deficit. One might, however, argue that the U.S. guarantee increases the riskiness of U.S. government debt. As a result, U.S. government borrowing costs and U.S. government budget deficits might both rise.

8. a.   Increases in government purchases will shift both the *IS* and *AD* curves to the right in the short run. Although the increase in real GDP will also increase tax revenues, the budget deficit will increase along with r, Y, and P. Thus, higher deficits will be associated with higher prices and higher interest rates. (Although the increase in P will also shift the *LM* curve upward a bit, both Y and r will still rise.)

Graphs for Problem 8a

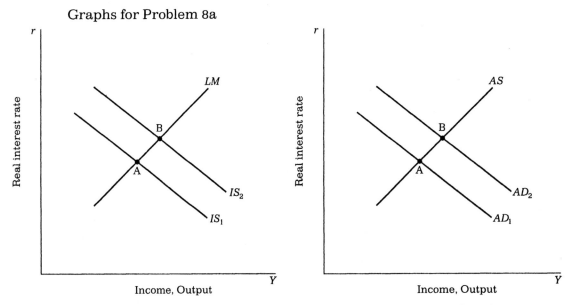

b. Declines in consumer or business confidence will shift the *IS* and *AD* curves to the left, reducing *r*, *Y*, and *P*. As *Y* falls, income tax revenues fall, and the budget deficit will increase. In this case higher deficits will be accompanied by *lower* prices and lower interest rates. (Although the decrease in *P* will also shift the *LM* curve downward a bit, both *Y* and *r* will still fall.)

Graphs for Problem 8b

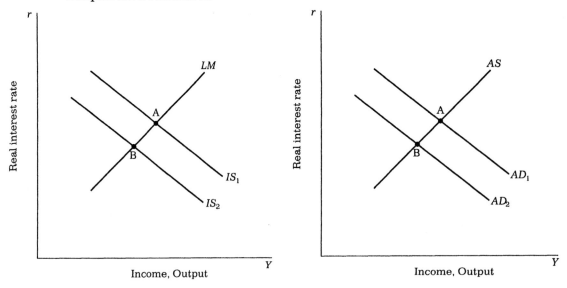

CHAPTER 16

Fill-in Questions

1. marginal propensity to consume
2. average propensity to consume; average propensity to consume; life-cycle hypothesis (or permanent-income hypothesis); permanent-income hypothesis (or life-cycle hypothesis)
3. budget constraint
4. intertemporal budget constraint
5. discounting
6. indifference curve
7. marginal rate of substitution
8. normal good
9. income effect; substitution effect
10. income effect; substitution effect
11. borrowing constraint
12. life-cycle hypothesis; precautionary saving
13. permanent-income hypothesis; Permanent income; transitory income
14. random walk; random walk

Multiple-Choice Questions

1. b	2. d	3. b	4. a	5. c	6. c	7. b
8. b	9. c	10. b	11. b	12. d	13. d	14. d
15. c	16. d	17. d	18. a	19. a	20. c	

Exercises

1. a. **Graph 16-1**

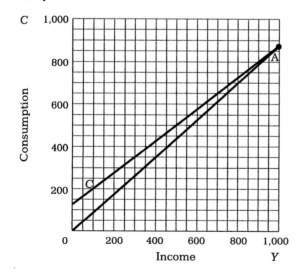

 b. the fraction of each additional dollar of disposable income that households spend on consumption; 0.75; remains constant; 0; 1

 c. 0.75; 125; 0.75; 125; 1.25; 0.75; 125; 1; 0.75; 125; 0.875; decreases

 d. 875; 875; 1,000; 0.875; *APC*; *APC*; decreases

2. **a.** 0; 1; decreases

  b. decrease; remain constant

  c. 0; 1; decreases; remain constant; 0

  Graph 16-2

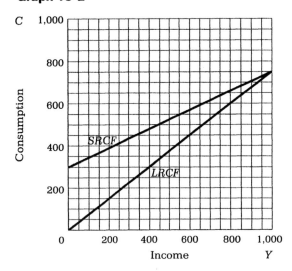

3. **a.** 105

  b. 105; 100

  c. 110.25

  d. 110.25; 100

  e. $FV_T = \$100 \, (1 + i)^T$; $PV = FV_T/(1 + i)^T$

4. **a.** 12; 12; 12; 0.50; 12; 30; 1.5

Graph 16-3

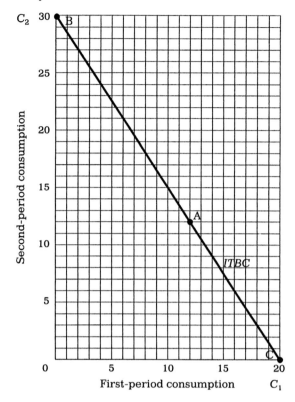

b.   0.50; 1.5; 1.5; 50

c.   12; 0; 12; 0; 12; 12; 12; 0.50; 12; 30; 0; 12; 12; 1.5; 20

5.   **a.**   **Table 16-1**

(1)	(2)	(3)	(4)	(5)	(6)	(7)	(8)
C_1	8.0	9.0	10.0	11.00	12.0	14.0	16.0
C_2	18.0	16.0	14.4	13.09	12.0	10.3	9.0
$U = C_1 C_2$	144.0	144.0	144.0	144.00	144.0	144.0	144.0

b. **Graph 16-4**

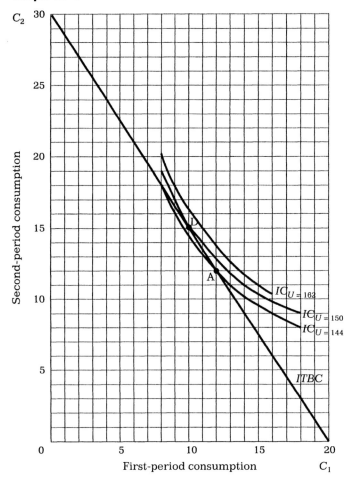

144

c. **Table 16-2**

(1)	(2)	(3)	(4)	(5)	(6)	(7)	(8)
C_1	8.00	9.00	10.0	11.00	12.0	14.0	16.00
C_2	18.75	16.67	15.0	13.64	12.5	10.7	9.38
$U = C_1 C_2$	150.00	150.00	150.0	150.00	150.0	150.0	150.00

d. **Table 16-3**

(1)	(2)	(3)	(4)	(5)	(6)	(7)	(8)
C_1	8.00	9.0	10.0	11.00	12.0	14.0	16.0
C_2	20.25	18.0	16.2	14.73	13.5	11.6	10.1
$U = C_1 C_2$	162.00	162.0	162.0	162.00	162.0	162.0	162.0

e. right (upward); increase; marginal rate of substitution

g. 12; 12; $IC_{U=144}$; 144

h. $IC_{U=150}$; 150; 2; 3; 12; 3; 15; 10; 15; 150; right (above)

6. **a.** 31.17; 1.5

Graph 16-5

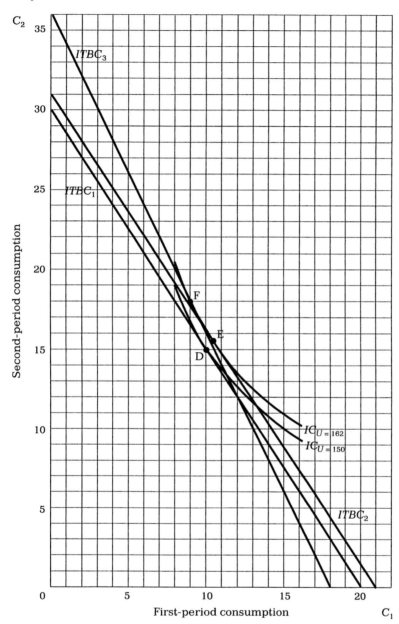

equal to

b. 162; 162; 15.59; increased

c. 12; 12; 12; 36; 2; 162; 162; 18

d. income; substitution; decreasing; increasing

e. increases; increases; decreases; increases; increase; decreases

7. **a.** R; T

b. 60; 45; 15; 40,000; 45; 60; 30,000; 30,000; 3; 4; 10,000; 1; 4; 0.75; 75

c. 40,000; 45; 1,800,000; 1,800,000; equal to

Graph 16-6

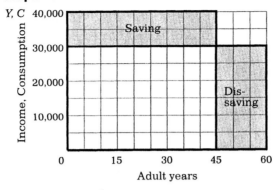

d. R; T; T; 60; 45; 0.75; 0.0167; 1.67

Graph 16-7

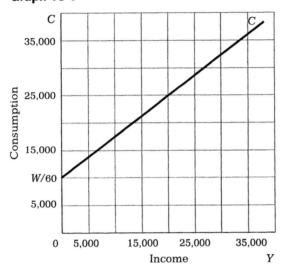

0.0167; 0.75

e. 0.75; 0.0167; 0.75; 0.0167; $120,000; $40,000; 0.80; 0.75; 0.0167; $120,000; $80,000; 0.775; falls; 0.85

f. 0.80

8. a. 75

b. Table 16-4

(1)	(2) Y^P	(3) $C = 0.75Y^P$	(4) Y	(5) $APC = C/Y$	(6) Y^T
College professor	$80,000	$60,000	$80,000	0.75	$0
Artist in a good year	$80,000	$60,000	$100,000	0.60	$20,000
Artist in a bad year	$80,000	$60,000	$60,000	1.00	–$20,000

c. not change; not change; decrease; not change; increase

d. decrease; decrease

e. increase; decrease

f. decrease; saved; permanent; consumed

g. remain constant

Problems

1. **a.** $MPC = 0.8$; $APC = (100/Y) + 0.8$

b. If $Y = 100$, $MPC = 0.8$ and $APC = 1.8$

If $Y = 200$, $MPC = 0.8$ and $APC = 1.3$

As Y rises, the MPC remains constant and the APC decreases.

2. $1136.16; $885.84; bond present values and prevailing interest rates move in opposite directions.

3. **a.** Graph for Problem 3a

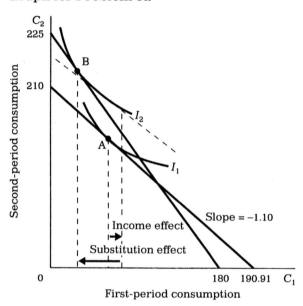

Note: We have assumed that the substitution effect is larger than the income effect.

e. if the income effect is bigger than the substitution effect

5. **a.** $MPC = b$; $APC = (a/Y) + b$

b. $d(MPC)/dY = 0$; $d(APC)/dY = -a/Y^2 < 0$

7. The life-cycle and permanent-income models of consumption imply that consumption is relatively stable from one year to the next. Consumption is not as volatile as current income because people do not respond very much to temporary changes in income. Consequently, private spending will be relatively stable (since consumption is by far its largest component), and policy activism will usually be unnecessary.

8. **a.** $C = (1/25)W + (2/5)Y$

b. $C = \$30,000$

9. A reduction in tax rates has two effects on current saving. The substitution effect reduces current consumption and increases current saving. The income effect, on the other hand, increases consumption in each period and, hence, reduces current saving. Consequently, the net effect of a reduction in tax rates on interest and dividends is ambiguous and depends on the relative sizes of the income and substitution effects.

11. **a.** According to the Keynsian consumption function, the tax cuts had their biggest effects on future rather than current disposable income. Consequently, they would change both disposable income and consumption by relatively small amounts in 2001–2002.

b. According to the permanent income hypothesis, current consumption depends on permanent disposable income, which was substantially increased by the tax cuts when they were passed by Congress. Consequently, consumption in 2001–2002 would also rise substantially. The 5–10 year deferral would reduce the effects on permanent income, but by a much smaller amount.

c. Even if one accepts the permanent income hypothesis and people wanted to increase current consumption in response to these large increases in permanent income, those who were subject to borrowing constraints would not be able to borrow to do so, and they might not be able to increase their consumption in 2001–2002.

d. According to adherents of the Ricardian equivalence proposition, the tax cuts would not affect consumption at all, regardless of their timing, as long as they did not change people's expectations of future government spending. People would assume that at some point in the future, taxes would have to be raised by an amount equivalent to the Bush tax cuts.

12. **a.** According to the Keynesian consumption function, an acceleration of the tax cuts would increase current disposable income and thereby have a large effect on consumption in 2002.

b. According to the permanent income hypothesis permanent income would be only slightly affected by the acceleration of the tax cuts because people already expected their taxes to be cut within the next few years. Consequently, the main effects of the acceleration would be to increase transitory income, and the effects on consumption in 2002 would be small.

CHAPTER 17

Fill-in Questions

1. Residential investment; business fixed investment; inventory investment
2. neoclassical model of investment
3. depreciation
4. real cost of capital
5. net investment; depreciation
6. neoclassical model of investment; real cost of capital
7. corporate income tax
8. corporate income tax
9. investment tax credit
10. Tobin's q
11. stock market; Tobin's q
12. financing constraints
13. production smoothing; inventories as a factor of production; stock-out avoidance; work in process
14. accelerator model

Multiple-Choice Questions

1. a	2. b	3. d	4. b	5. c	6. a	7. b
8. b	9. a	10. c	11. b	12. b	13. d	14. b
15. c						

Exercises

1. **a.**   20; 15; 10; 5; 20

Graph 17-1

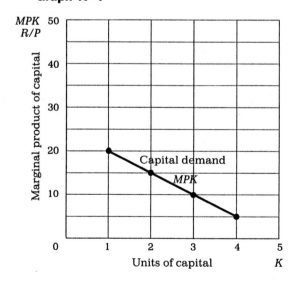

b. 2; 4; more

c. **Graph 17-2**

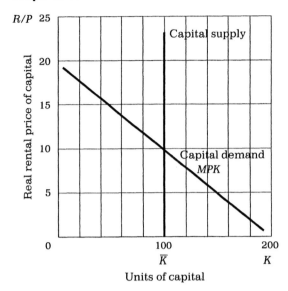

10

d. right; fall; higher; right; increasing; right; increasing

2. **a.** 0.03; $10; $15; $12; $22; $44

b. increase; decrease; increase; quickly; shorter

c. 0; 5

d. increase; increase

3. **a.** equal to; r; δ; r; δ; add to; positive; subtract from; negative

b. equal to; zero; decrease; increase; decrease; increase; add to; increase; rises; similar to; fall

c. have no immediate effect on; increase; add to; increase; added; fall

d. increase; decrease; increase

4. **a.** zero

b. right

Graph 17-3

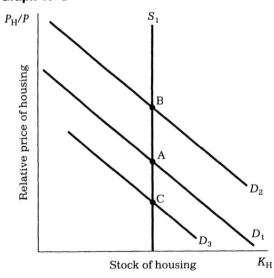

increase; increase; increase; right; fall

c. left; decrease; decrease

5. a. **Table 17-3**

(1) Period	(2) Output Y	(3) Change in Y	(4) % Change in Y	(5) $I = 0.2(\Delta Y)$ $= 0.2(Y - Y_{-1})$	(6) % Change in I
0	1,000				
		100	10.00		
1	1,100			20	
		100	9.09		0
2	1,200			20	
		100	8.33		0
3	1,300			20	
		50	3.85		−50
4	1,350			10	
		0	0.00		−100
5	1,350			0	

b. much larger; unstable

Problems

1. a. Graph for Problem 1a

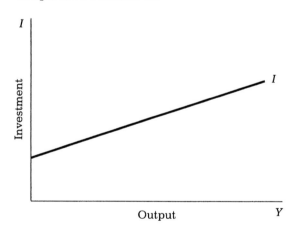

b. Investment might rise as real output rises either because of an accelerator effect or because investment may be linked to sales or sales expectations that rise with Y.

c. i. The slope of the planned expenditure curve would become steeper. Now when Y increases, both consumption and investment will increase.

   ii. The government-purchases multiplier will increase. When government purchases increase by $1, there will now be multiplier effects on both consumption and investment. Increases in government purchases will consequently lead to additional spending (and output) in each round.

  iii. The *IS* curve will become flatter; the slope of the *LM* curve is unaffected.

  iv. The *AD* curve will become flatter; the slope of the *SRAS* curve is unaffected.

2. a. $2,300

 b. $4,100

3. The (nominal) cost of capital $= P_K[i - \Delta P_K/P_K + \delta]$, where the second term $\Delta P_K/P_K$ represents the rate at which capital prices are changing. If capital prices are rising at the same rate as the aggregate price level, $\Delta P_K/P_K = \pi$, and the cost of capital becomes $P_K[i - \pi + \delta] = P_K[r + \delta]$. If $\pi > \Delta P_K/P_K$, $(i - \pi) < (i - \Delta P_K/P_K)$ and the use of the real interest rate will underestimate the true cost of capital.

4. a. $MPK = 64(K)^{-2/3}$

 b. 64; 16; 7.11; 4

  Graph for Problem 4b

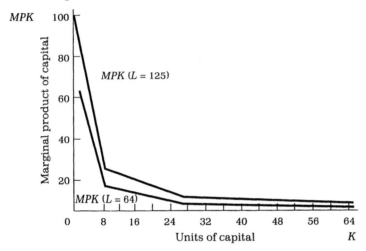

 c. $MPK = 4(L/K)^{2/3} = 100(K)^{-2/3}$; $MPK = 100$; 25; 11.11; 6.25

5. The *IS* curve would shift to the right, increasing both the equilibrium levels of output and the interest rate.

 a. The increase in the interest rate would increase the cost of capital, reduce the profit rate from owning capital, and thereby decrease investment according to the neoclassical (cost-of-capital) theory of investment.

 b. The increase in *Y*, however, would increase investment (via an increase in inventories) according to the accelerator theory.

6. The baby-bust generation shifted the housing demand curve to the left. The relative price of housing would fall, along with new investment in housing.

7. The demand for housing would shift to the left, reducing the relative price of housing and investment in housing. The profits of home builders would fall in the short run.

CHAPTER 18

Fill-in Questions

1. balance sheet
2. reserves; 100-percent-reserve banking
3. fractional-reserve banking
4. reserve-deposit ratio; currency-deposit ratio
5. financial intermediation
6. monetary base; high-powered money
7. money multiplier; currency-deposit ratio; currency-deposit ratio; reserve-deposit ratio
8. open-market operation; reserve requirements; discount rate
9. excess reserves
10. portfolio theories; dominated asset
11. Transactions theories; Baumol-Tobin model
12. Baumol-Tobin model
13. near money
14. federal funds rate

Multiple-Choice Questions

1. b	2. d	3. a	4. b	5. d	6. d	7. c
8. b	9. d	10. a	11. c	12. d	13. b	14. b
15. c	16. b	17. d	18. a	19. c	20. c	21. d

Exercises

1. a. 1,000; 3,000; 25; reserve requirements
    b. 10; Reserves = $260 million; Deposits = $1,010 million; Loans = $750 million
    c. 25; 25; 10; 7.5; Reserves = $252.5 million; Deposits = $1,010 million; Loans = $757.5 million
    d. 7.5; 7.5; Reserves = $257.5 million; Deposits = $1,007.5 million; Loans = $750 million
    e. 25; 25; 7.5; 5.625; Reserves = $251.875 million; Deposits = $1,007.5 million; Loans = $755.625 million
    f. 5.625; 5.625; Reserves = $255.625 million; Deposits = $1,005.625 million; Loans = $750 million
    g. 3,023.125; 1,000; 3,000; 23.125
    h. 0.25; 40
    i. 10; exactly; more than
2. a. deposits; reserves
    b. 3; 2; 1.6; 1; 1; 5
    c. decrease; decrease; 1.0; equal to; 1/*rr*; deposits

3. a.   purchase; increase; greater than; increases; greater than; fall
    b.   increase; increase; decrease
    c.   more; rise; increase; increase

Problems

1. $10,000; In this model, $cr = 0$. Thus, the money multiplier $= 1/rr = 10$.
2. a. $m = 2$
    b. $m = 1$; There is the case of a 100-percent-reserve banking system, in which there are no loans. Any increase in the monetary base leads to an equal increase in the money supply, either in the form of currency held by the public or deposits.
3. a. $dm/d(rr) = -(cr + 1)/(cr + rr)^2 < 0$
    b. $dm/d(cr) = (rr - 1)/(cr + rr)^2 < 0$, unless $rr = 1.0$
4. a. $dC/dN = F - iY/2N^2$
    b.   At the optimum, $dC/dN = 0$. This implies that $N^* = \sqrt{iY/2F}$.
    c. $d^2C/dN^2 = iY/N^3 > 0$. This second-order condition confirms that the total cost of holding money reaches a local minimum at N^*.
5. a. $N^* = 12$
    b.   monthly; $6,000
    c. $3,000
7. $\left| (dM/di) \right| \times (i/M) = (1/2)(YF/2i)^{-1/2}(YF/2i^2) \times i(YF/2i)^{-1/2} =$
    $(1/2)(2i/YF)(YF/2i) = 1/2$
    $(dM/dY) \times (Y/M) = (1/2)(YF/2i)^{-1/2}(F/2i) \times Y(YF/2i)^{-1/2} =$
    $(1/2)(2i/YF)(F/2i)Y = 1/2$

CHAPTER 19

Fill-in Questions

1. real-business-cycle theory
2. intertemporal substitution of labor
3. Solow residual
4. Labor hoarding
5. new Keynesian economics
6. menu costs
7. aggregate demand externality
8. coordination failure

Multiple-Choice Questions

1. b	2. b	3. a	4. b	5. c	6. b	7. d
8. d	9. d	10. d	11. a	12. c	13. c	14. b
15. c	16. d	17. b	18. c	19. b		

Exercises

1. **a.** **Graph 19-1**

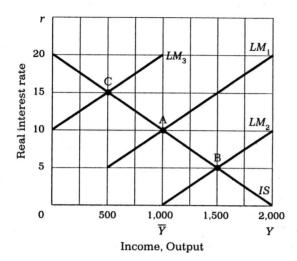

   equal to; remain constant; remain constant
   b. greater than; rises; left (upward); equal to; A
   c. less than; falls; right (downward); equal to; A
   d. equal to; vertical

2. **a.** 20,000; 20,000; 22,000
   b. 22,000; equal to; 0.1; $10; $11; 1
   c. 30,000; next; this
   d. 30,000; 33,000; 22,000; this; next
   e. 20,000; 24,000; 22,000; this; next
   f. more; increase; increase; less; more; decrease; decrease
   g. more; increase; increase

Problems

1. **a.** As r rises, people want to work more in the current period and less in future periods because of intertemporal labor substitution.
   b. $L = 400$; $Y = 1,800$
   c. $L = 625$; $Y = 2,250$
   d. $L = 400$; $Y = 2,160$

2. First graph for Problem 2

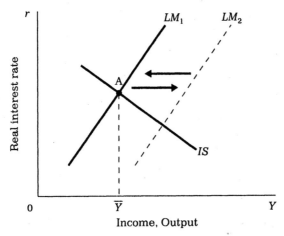

According to real-business-cycle theory, the economy is always at its natural rate of output $\overline{Y}$, that is, at Point A above. Expansionary monetary policy normally shifts the LM curve to the right (downward), from LM_1 to LM_2. Since this pushes actual output Y above its natural rate $\overline{Y}$, the aggregate price level P rises. As P rises, the real money supply falls back to its original level and the LM curve shifts back to LM_1.

Second graph for Problem 2

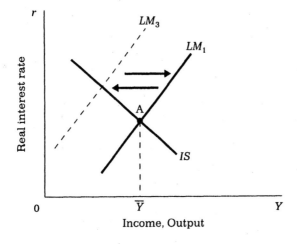

Contractionary monetary policy normally shifts the LM curve to the left (upward), from LM_1 to LM_3. Since this pushes Y below $\overline{Y}$, P falls, increasing the real money supply to its original level, and the LM curve shifts back to LM_1.

3. Solow residual = 1/3 percent.

4. Staggering of wage contracts, as in the United States, makes the overall level of wages and prices adjust more slowly. In countries in which labor contracts are synchronized, on the other hand, wages and prices should adjust more quickly, thereby moving the economy toward the natural rate of output more quickly and shortening recessions.

5. a.   If both sides are worse off in the event of a war than they would have been if they had both compromised, the war would be the result of a coordination failure.

   b.   If one side is better off with the war than it would have been even if both sides had compromised, the war is not the result of a coordination failure.